SACRED GEOGRAPHY OF THE ANCIENT GREEKS

SUNY Series in Western Esoteric Traditions
David Appelbaum, editor

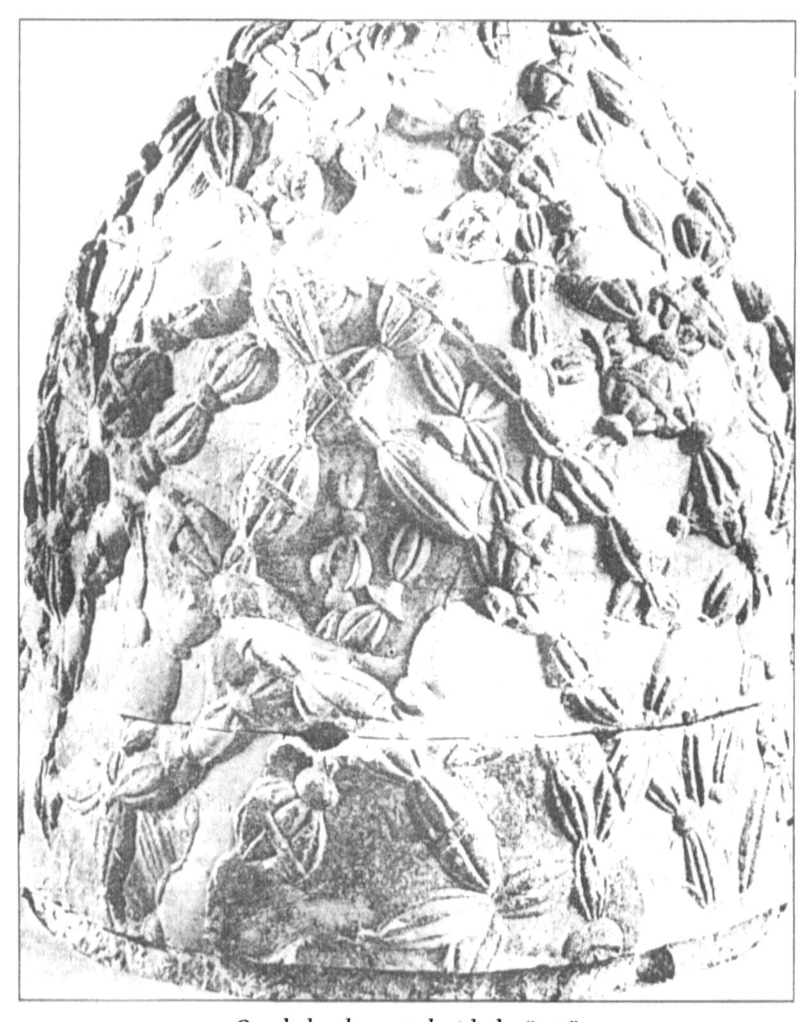

Omphalos decorated with the "net."
(Copy from the Roman period, Museum of Delphi.)

Sacred Geography of the Ancient Greeks

Astrological Symbolism in Art, Architecture, and Landscape

Jean Richer

Translated by Christine Rhone

STATE UNIVERSITY OF NEW YORK PRESS

Published by
State University of New York Press, Albany

For information, address State University of New York
Press, State University Plaza, Albany, N.Y., 12246

Library of Congress Cataloging-in-Publication Data
Richer, Jean, 1915–
[Géographie sacrée du monde grec. English]
Sacred geography of the ancient Greeks : astrological symbolism in art, architecture, and landscape / Jean Richer ; translated by Christine Rhone.
p. cm. — (SUNY series in Western esoteric traditions)
Includes bibliographical references and index.
ISBN: 9780791420249 (pbk.)
1. Astrology/Greek. 2. Sacred space—Greece. 3. Shrines—Greece. 4. Art and religion—Greece. 5. Greece—Religion.
I. Title. II. Series.
BF1674.R513 1994
133.5'0938—dc20 94-11960
CIP

10 9 8 7 6 5 4 3 2 1

Contents

Maps

The translator would like to thank David Fideler, Lanier Graham, Ayeshah Haleem, and John Michell for their warm and generous support of her work.

—Christine Rhone, 1994

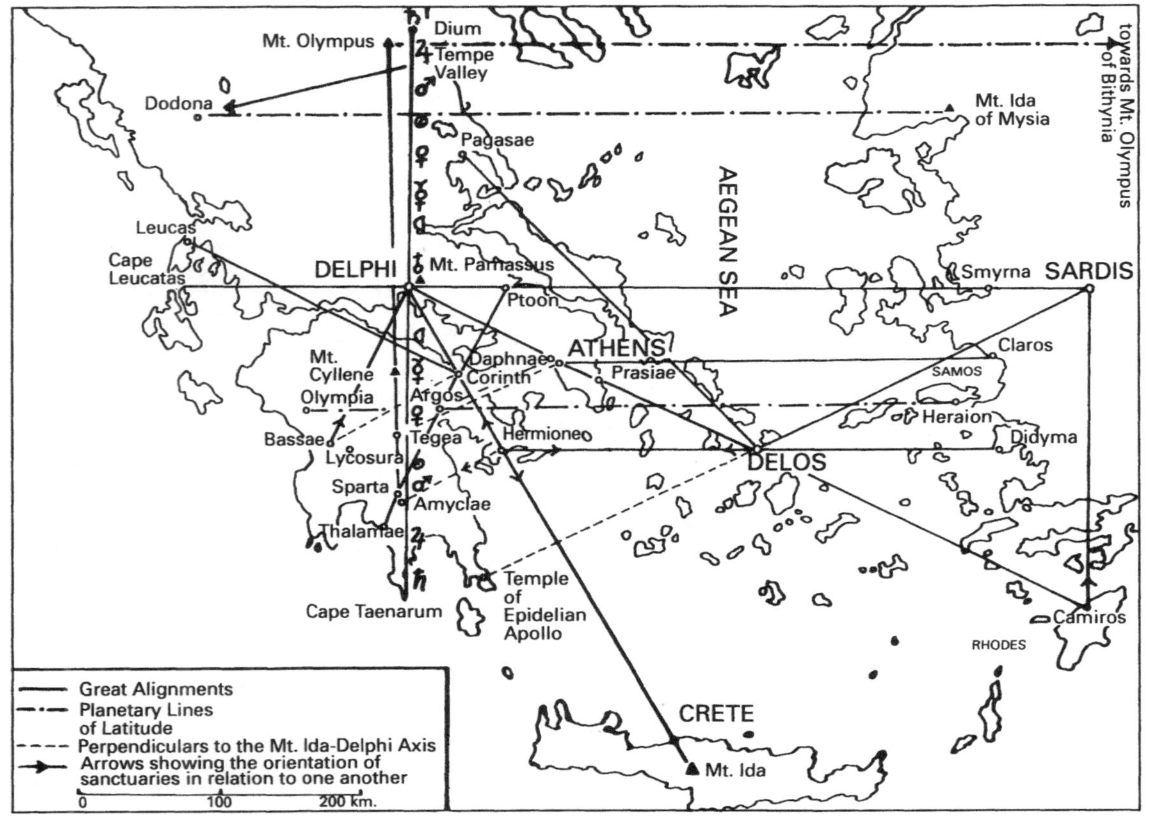

Map 1. *The Great Alignments.*

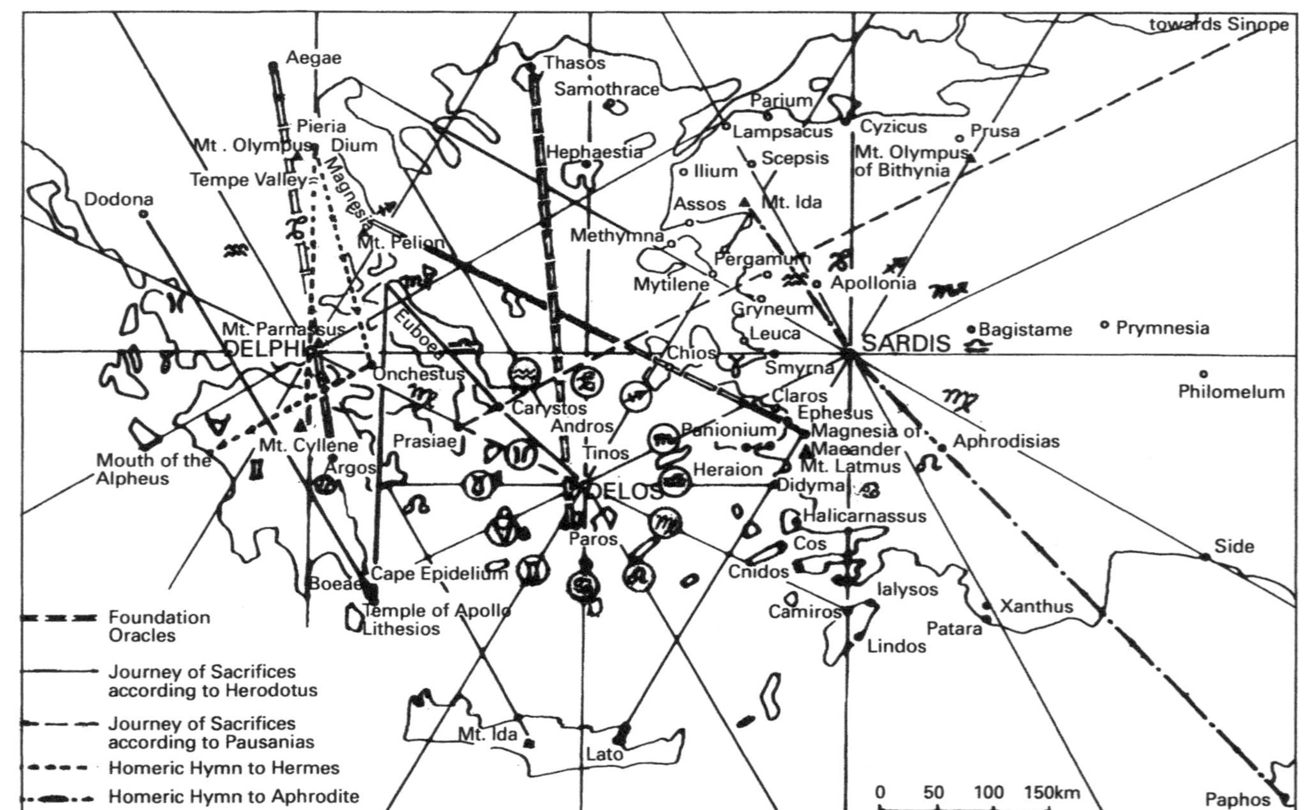

Map 2. *Foundation Oracles. Journeys of Sacrifice. Homeric Hymns.*

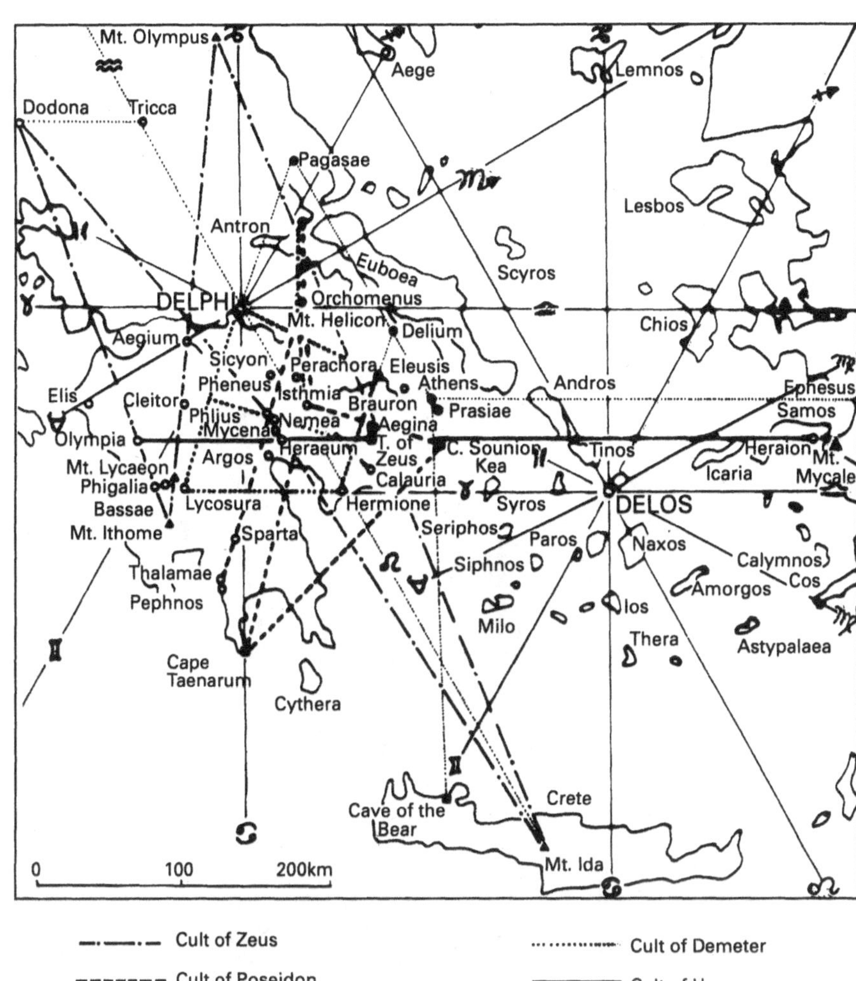

Map 3. *Divine Cults.*

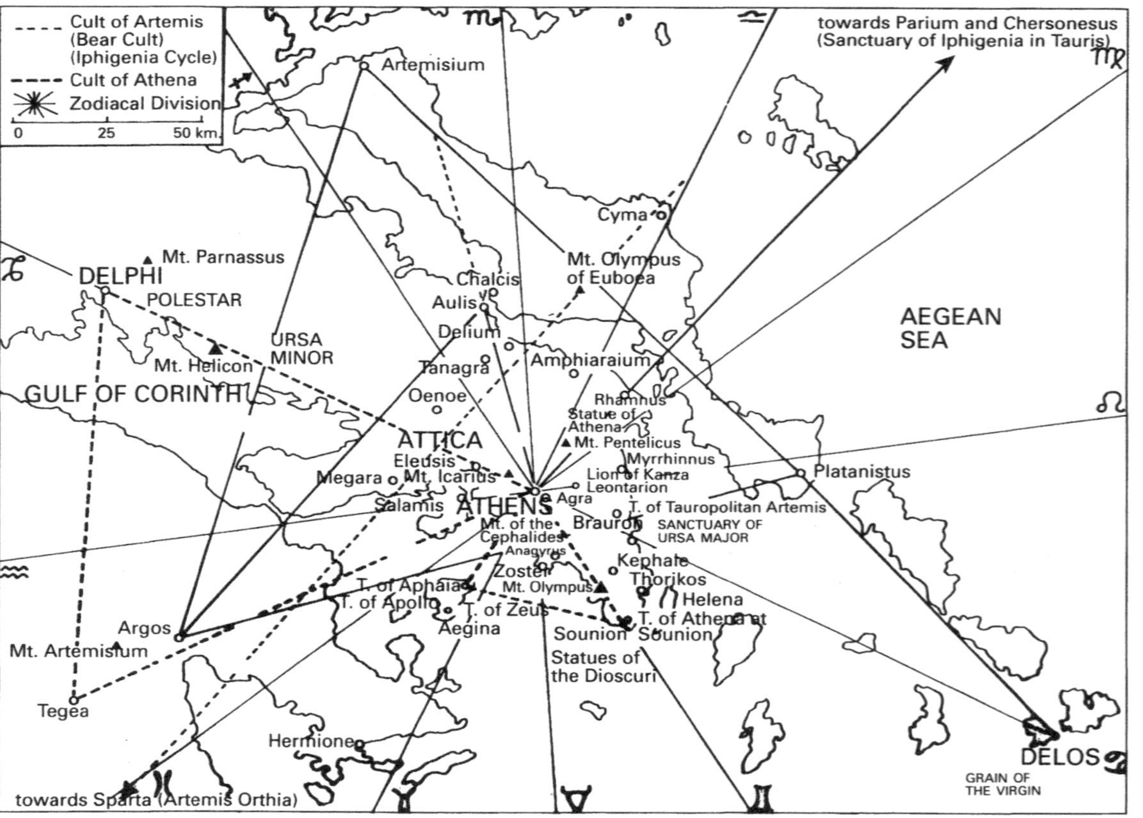

Map 4. *The Zodiacal Division of Attica. The Iphigenia Cycle and the Cult of Artemis.*

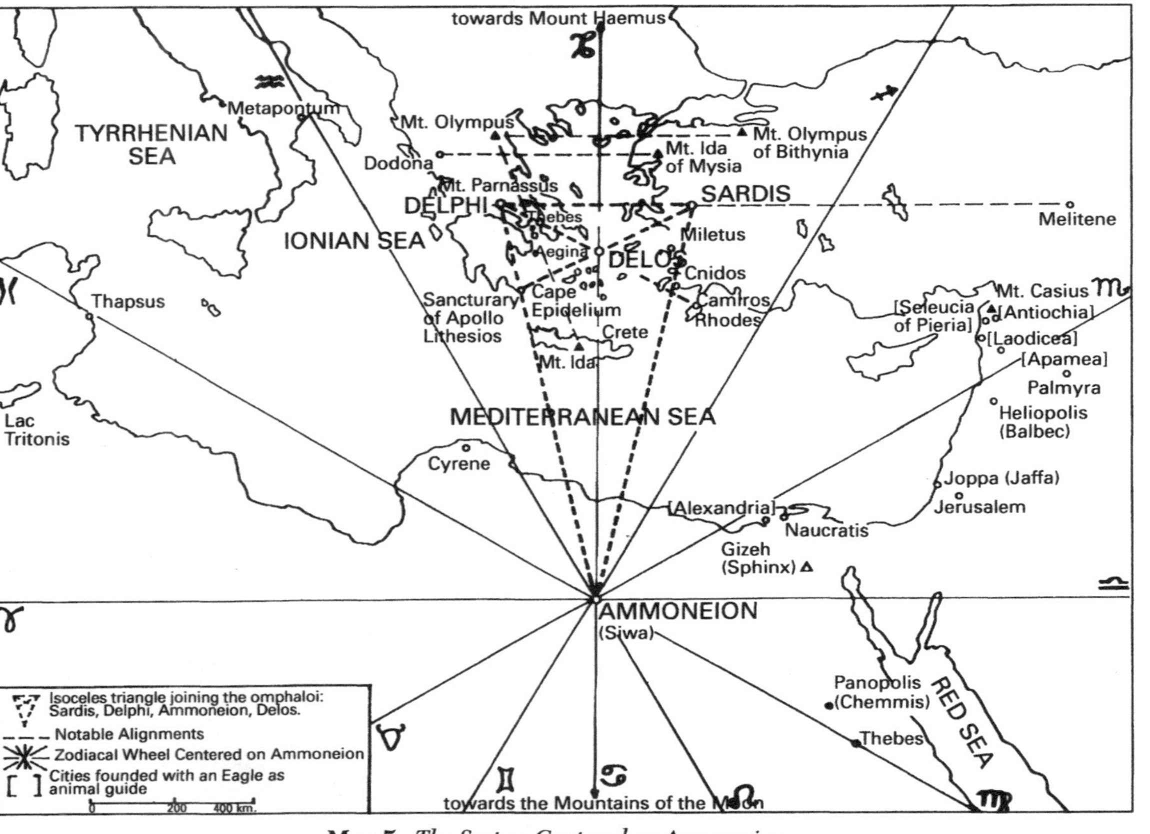

Map 5. *The System Centered on Ammoneion.*

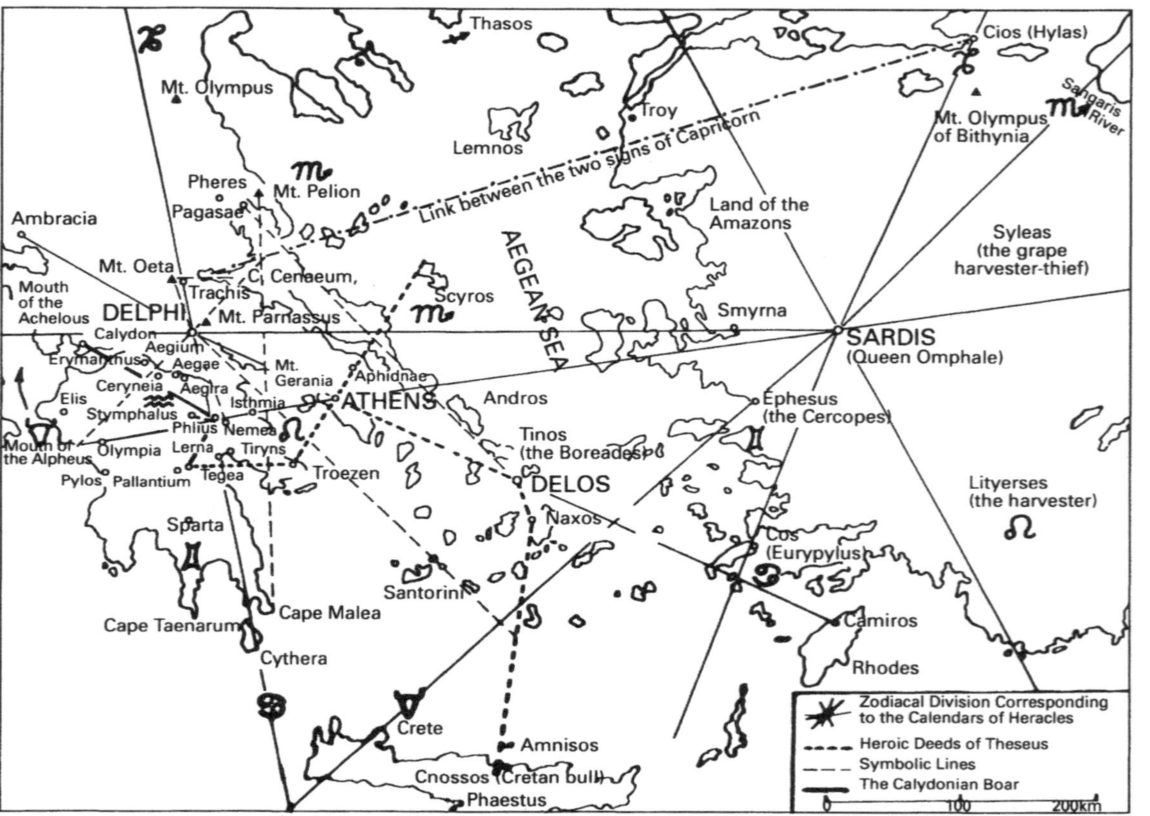

Map 6. *The Calendars of Heracles and the Heroic Deeds of Theseus.*

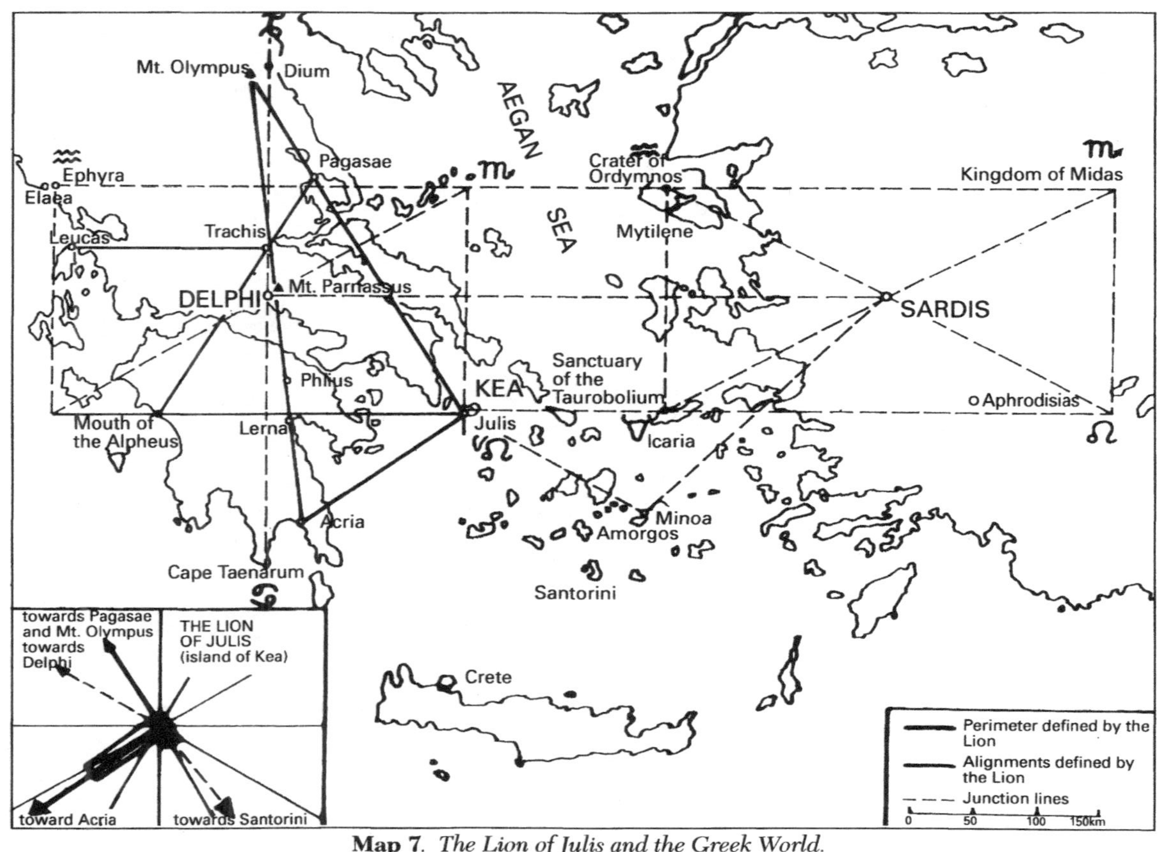

Map 7. *The Lion of Julis and the Greek World.*

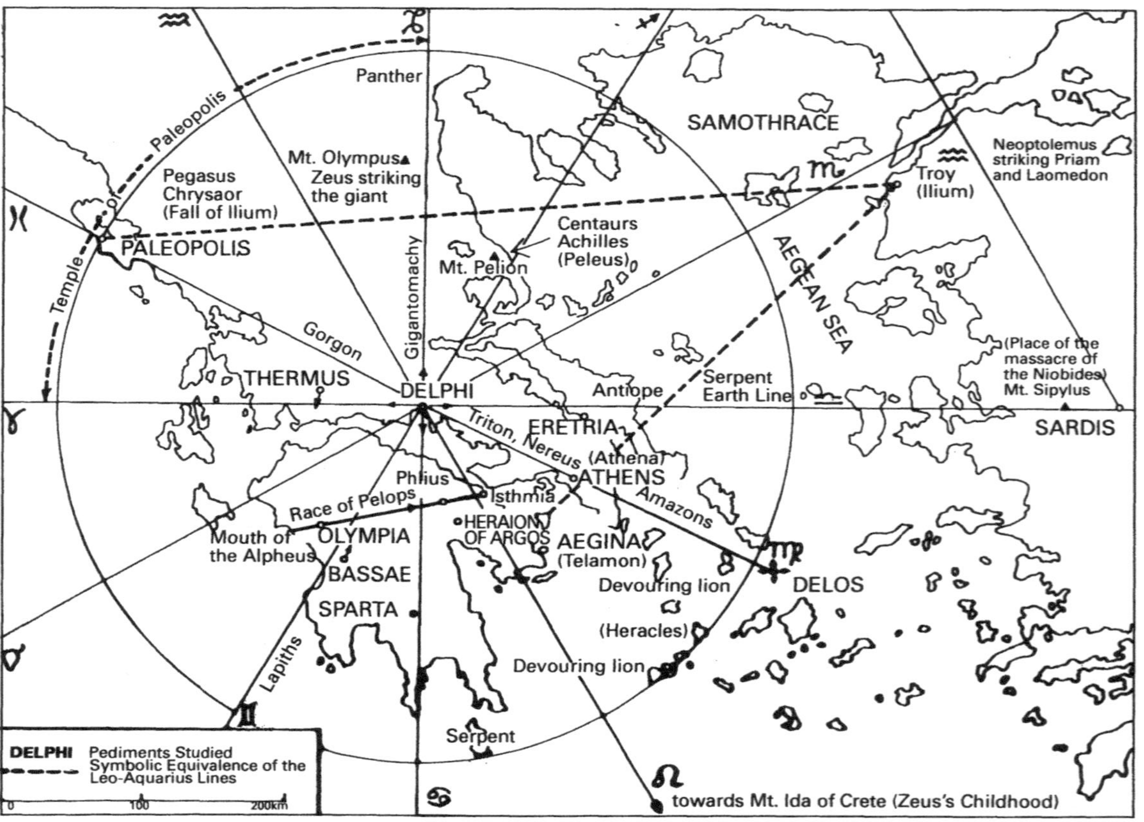

Map 8. *Sculpted Pediments and Zodiacal Geography.*

Foreword

χαῖρε, Θεῶν, μήτηρ, ἄλοχ', Οὐρανοῦ ἀστερόεντος!
(Hail, mother of Gods, thou wife of starry Heaven!)
—*Homeric Hymn to the Earth*, 17.

This book is the gift of a springtime at Delphi.

It is above all a long meditation on the forms of religion and art of Greek antiquity.

To the sound of the right invocation, the gods of ancient Greece come back to life over the distance of centuries. Born of the earth, of space, of the sea, and of the starry sky, they are still here among us, still alive. Among the inspiring ruins of the great temples, the sleeping gods are always ready to be revived.

Nobly they advance, dance, engage in combat, or take their ease, sculpted on pediments and metopes, painted on vases and shields, stamped on fine coins that are as beautiful as medals. If one looks closely, one may see their movements. In lending an ear, one may hear their words. All of them, heroes and gods by their forms, ornaments, and gestures, express their place in the orderly world that the Greeks called *cosmos*.

I hesitated for quite some time over the best form to give this study. I decided on that of an authentic narrative, stating the facts and discoveries mainly in the order in which they occurred. However, by its very nature, my account must also analyze and dissect what may have been universally perceived by the eye of the spirit.

The ideas, figures, and documents here assembled describe the mystical or sacred geography of Greece. The work was born from long contact with the Hellenic earth. A series of intuitive perceptions, which first came to me as beautiful mental images, has been confirmed in a surprising manner by the evidence I describe and by the irrefutable testimony of monuments. The transition from poetic reverie to scientific theory was made progressively—over days, weeks, and years. The subject I am grappling with is immense; to my knowledge it has never been seen as a whole. An ample harvest of documentary proofs has nevertheless already been made. I believe that these should be the subjects of wider research which, because of the many fields touched upon, would require the cooperation of specialists from various disciplines.[1]

It has long been my firm conviction that all the religious and poetic experience of peoples and individuals of the past is, at certain special moments, available to whoever can recapture it.[2]

Although I have learned a great deal in preparing this work, I nevertheless do not expect any great "profit" from its publication.

My task has been mainly to order and to make as clear as possible my many observations and deductions. The principles are very simple. To follow, one needs no more than the rudiments of astrological vocabulary. Sometimes the structure of the material becomes rather complex, at least in appearance.

When the number of "coincidences" between what one is seeking and what one finds exceeds a certain proportion (and is even close to 100 percent), and when one finds hundreds of converging facts that all fit into an consistent explanation, it is perhaps permissible to speak of a demonstration. When a theory may be used predictively and invariably leads to objectively verifiable facts, it is scientifically valid.

Aware of the magnitude of my undertaking, I have attempted to give clear maps and diagrams and the best selection of supporting texts and documents.

I will only slightly excuse myself for not being a professional Hellenist. To gather the relevant facts and then demonstrate what had originally seemed true, a certain habit and enjoyment of research was necessary. My linguistic knowledge, despite its great gaps, was adequate for collecting the documents, facts, and texts. As a professional archeologist or Hellenist, I might not have been able to overcome the inhibitions due to educational and other prevailing biases.

What is more, I must confess that, being busy with other things, I allowed two years to elapse between my original intuitive insight and the beginning of serious work.

I began with a very general inquiry into the selection of temple sites and the supposedly "abnormal" orientations of certain sanctuaries. The foundation and starting point of my work was the theory of alignments.[3]

At the beginning of the historical period, the religious beliefs of all the inhabitants of what is now Europe and Asia Minor seem to have shared many common elements, in particular the cult of a great solar god.

The origin of this cult is indistinguishable from the awakening of human consciousness. Almost everywhere the most highly evolved and complex forms of worship must have been superimposed on the subsisting remnants of prehistoric lunar/solar cults. The most important thing was the persistence of an astral religion in certain locations: this is well documented and proved. The sites of the most ancient temples of Greece had probably been selected by priests, the great initiates of a heliacal religion. The same beliefs and values that resulted in the erection of the megalithic alignments and groupings that still exist in many parts of Europe may have dictated the choice of the great temple sites.

At a first stage in my research, archaic Greek coins were of great help and provided a decisive series of confirmations.[4]

After having discovered the existence of the three great zodiacal wheels of the Aegean, centered on Delphi, Sardis, and Delos, it became apparent that Attica, a favored province, had been a world on its own in the eyes of the ancient Greeks and should be studied separately.

I was able to rediscover that lines of latitude had been marked, in addition to the zodiacal wheels. My diagrams soon suggested new interpretations of certain mysterious texts, such as "the journey of sacrifices" of the *Homeric Hymns* to Hermes and to Aphrodite. Various passages of *The Iliad* and the works of Plato also took on new meaning. My diagrams shed light on the nature of certain heroes and gods. Poseidon, Athena, Hephaestus, Heracles and Theseus maintained specific relationships with sacred geography and with the calendar. What is more, many myths set up symbolic relationships between identical points in different zodiacal wheels. And finally, they provided a key to deciphering the surviving texts of the Delphic oracles.

By the converse procedure of analyzing mythical stories, I discovered a system centered on the oasis of Ammon. The Lion of Julis, an intriguing monument on the island of Ceos, seems to have acted as a guardian of the calendar in the distant past, revealing the existence of another ancient system.

A study of the shield devices that were painted on many vases showed that all the astrological symbols I was investigating on coins have the same meaning on shields, and that most of these images had either planetary or zodiacal significance. In a great many cases, for example, a pair of fighters stood for a "pair of forces" that were either antagonistic or complementary. Such symbols took on a double meaning when the signs simultaneously referred to the place of origin of the bearer of the shield. It thus became clear that the symbols on coins and in ancient blazons had a common astrological origin.

At first I thought that one volume would be sufficient to communicate my main discoveries. But it soon became clear that I would have to establish both a grammar and a vocabulary of symbolism to be able to interpret the multiple zodiacal images on vases and bronzes. Several chapters are devoted to this essential work. Once the principal astrological symbols were established, I was able to show that the armlets of shields indicated, among other things, the home province of the bearer of the shield. Zodiacal diagrams could be given for hundreds of vases, but for the time being only a few characteristic examples will be discussed.

From my point of view, the reward for this lengthy research is the chapter on the tympanal decoration of temples and the zodiacal structure of sanctuaries. Placed at the end of the volume, it was in fact written last during 1964. There I was finally able to give satisfactory answers to several questions I had asked myself six years earlier. The first cycle was complete, and my trip to Samothrace closed the circle on what I had learned at Delphi.

I have set aside for a second book the study of zodiacal geography extended to the whole Mediterranean world, some general questions on Greece (a brief concluding summary is given here), and an examination of the many monuments of the Roman era. In the present work I will broach the problems concerning Greek calendars and the important role of astrology in funerary symbolism. On the latter point, my research adjoins and furthers the works of F. Cumont.

♦

Better than long descriptions, two anecdotes on various stages of my research will explain my method, which always combines intuition with deductive reasoning.[5]

Having determined the existence of the omphalos of Sardis, by means of the simple geometry described in chapter 4, I decided first to construct a zodiac with Sardis as the center and then to try and predict the symbols that should appear on the most ancient coins of the Greek cities of Anatolia by referring to the symbols of the Delphi zodiac.

Already knowing that the most significant points on the lines were where they intersected the coasts, I posited the following:

♦

1. Leo: Patara, Xanthus. Probable symbols: lion, chimaera
2. Virgo: Side. Probable symbol: Athena
3. Aquarius: Lampsacus. Probable symbol: winged horse (Pegasus).

I *then* checked the catalogue of the coins in the British Museum.

1. Coins from Lycia were stamped with a complete array of symbols of Leo. Some of these even bore a lion on one side and a winged horse on the other (Leo-Aquarius axis) (map 11, fig. 30).
2. The Great Goddess of Side was Athena, who had an important sanctuary in that city and whose image naturally appeared on its coins (map 11, fig. 31).
3. All the ancient coins from Lampsacus of the fifth century showed a winged horse (or a hippalectryon) (map 11, fig. 36).

I had assumed that latitudes had been marked out from the existence of the earth line (Delphi-Sardis), the line of Hera temples, the solar line (Hermione-Delos-Didyma), and the line of the Olympuses, and I had drawn all the latitudes on a map of Greece according to the Pythagorean diagram.

At a point on the Peloponnese, exactly where the south-north axis intersects the hypothetical "line of Hermes," I had inscribed the sign of Hermes:☿.

One and a half years later, when I had begun a systematic reading of the *Homeric Hymns*, I noticed that the point I had marked was the summit of Mount Cyllene, birthplace of the god.

♦

This book may be controversial. My greatest hope is that a few educated and competent individuals, including archeologists and historians of religion, would be willing to attentively and impartially examine these theories.

To observe the significance of the sun, moon, and stars in the genesis of myths certainly does not mean a return to the errors of the old "Naturism." And hasn't enough nonsense already been written claiming that religious facts can be explained purely from a historical and sociological standpoint?[6]

Others may say that on some issues my work agrees with the hypothesis of pan-Babylonianism. In reality it presupposes an even greater cultural unity of the ancient world. Cylinders of cuneiform writing have recently been uncovered in the excavations of the palace of Cadmus at Thebes, and Cyrus H. Gordon has just shown the common roots of Greek and Hebrew civilization,[7] so this is not a time when the hypothesis of oriental influence on the culture and the calendar of the Greeks may be judged excessive or hazardous. These influences are almost self-evident in the artistic sphere.

The evidence of the monuments shows in an undeniable way, but not yet clearly perceived, that during more than two thousand years, the Phoenicians, the Hittites, the ancient Greeks, and then the Etruscans, the Carthaginians, and the Romans, had patiently woven a fabric of correspondences between the sky, especially the apparent course of the sun through the zodiac, the inhabited earth, and the cities built by humanity.

If these conclusions are accepted, we have the beginnings of a meta-archeology. In fact, by simple geometry and starting from known sites, it becomes possible to locate certain points in Greece and Anatolia where methodically conducted excavations should give interesting results. These are, for example, where some of the lines intersect the coasts: Prasiae in Attica, Hermione in Argolis, Delium, the cave just south of the modern mouth of the Alpheus, Patara. A team of experts, including astronomers, geographers, archeologists, and historians, could take full advantage of the concepts I am proposing. This would revive an important aspect of the Greek past, the common heritage of the West.[8]

I ask of the sceptical and those who would remain insensitive to the poetic beauty of what I describe to withhold judgment and to read this book bearing in mind the words of Descartes: "The assent of many voices is not a valid proof for truths which are rather difficult to discover, because they are much more likely to be found by one single man than by a whole people."[9]

Translator's Preface

I first found this book in a dusty bookshop in the old alchemical quarter of Paris at the end of a long summer afternoon. I was not smoking a Gauloise, but the man in the bookshop did happen to look like a miniature Jean-Paul Sartre, very alert and owl-like. Hearing that I had been researching a French author who had spent his life in obscurity writing on sacred sites and significant alignments, he said, "Oh, don't bother with him! If you want to see some serious work on the subject, you must look at the work of Jean Richer." The next day, I had this book and articles by Richer's brother, Lucien, in my hands. And thus began the odyssey of this translation.

A year later, I visited Jean Richer and his wife at their home in the south of France. At one end of the house, in a high niche overlooking the hills of Provence, was a statuette of an owl. I asked Richer whether the statue was symbolic. "Yes", he said, "it is a reference to the sign of Virgo and the Virgo-Pisces axis". To my question whether there was a Piscean symbol at the other end of the house, he replied, "No. The Pisces reference is by implication."

Like symbols themselves, like prophetic dreams, Richer's work on sacred geography can be approached from many levels. He extends the range of astrological symbols from the familiar ones—the fish for Pisces, the bull for Aries, and so on—to encompass Olympian and pre-Olympian deities, circumzodiacal constellations, figures of myth and legend, revealing the stratum of stellar beliefs that underlay ancient Greek religion. This expanded range of astrological symbols becomes a key to interpreting the motifs of architecture, sculpture, vase painting and other artefacts. These motifs were not chosen merely for aesthetic reasons, as compositional devices or pictorial narrative, but were chosen to express a specific temporal and spatial meaning of the artwork in relation to a sacred center. This was most often an oracle site, a timeless place between the realms of Earth and the god-like stars. Every object of sacred art, great or small, was thus a point in a single web of meaning that imbued it with a talismanic power.

What emerges from Richer's research matches Plato's description in *The Republic* and *The Laws* of the ideal state, whose inhabitants and land were to be divided into twelve parts, each one named after and ruled by a zodiacal deity. Seen from an aerial perspective, this geographical layout would look something like a twelve spoked wheel or a clockface with each section representing a month of the solar year. The arrangement was an imitation of the pattern of the heavens, inscribed onto the earth through temple placement, and observed through the annual round of religious and musical ritual. It was an act of honoring the Twelve Gods and harmonizing the movements of daily life with the grand order of the universe.

Plato's description is said to be a codification of what had been a very ancient practice. Evidence that variations of this practice were widespread among early societies in different parts of the world is examined in my *Twelve Tribe Nations*, co-authored with John Michell and approached from a Platonist perspective.

Richer, however, did not begin with Plato's writings, but came upon the supporting texts some time after his research on Greece was under way. Born in Paris in 1915, the son of a watercolor artist, he earned a doctorate in literature and, during the course of his career, held teaching positions in Paris, Athens, Algiers, and Nice. He made his reputation as an author in the early post-war period with monographs on Gérard de Nerval, on whom he came to be considered a major authority. These were followed by publications on Musset, Lamartine, Gautier, Verlaine, Cazotte, Nodier, and Shakespeare.

Richer's studies of Nerval are characterized by sustained analysis of the poet's use of symbolism, a fertile ground for such work. Nerval was a visionary obsessed with Pythagorean correspondences, archetypes, and states of consciousness, all the elements of the imaginal world. Convinced that sleep put one in communication with the world of spirits, he made no distinction between the dreaming and the waking states, but lived his life as a waking dream, punctuated with bouts of madness. *Aurélia*, a capstone work symbolizing Nerval's whole spiritual quest, begins with the words, "Our dreams are a second life."

In the late 1950's, Jean Richer and his wife, Renée, moved to Athens, where they lived for several years, traveling as much as they could around the countryside to see the antiquities. Richer's curiosity was aroused by the placement of certain temples of Apollo, such as Bassae, situated high in the mountains, apparently in the middle of nowhere, and Tegea, in a vast, featureless plain of Arcadia. He became convinced that the selection of these temple sites could not be arbitrary. One night, while sleeping in a room on the slopes of Mount Lycabettos, a monolithic hill in Athens sacred to Gaia, Richer was given the clue to the mystery in the form of a dream.

He saw Apollo, figured as a *kouros* statue, facing away from him, and in very slow motion, pivoting clockwise 180 degrees. When the statue faced him full on, Richer awoke, and, still under the spell of the dream, he grabbed the first map of Greece he could find and penciled in a straight line joining Delos, Athens, and Delphi. The first piece of the puzzle was in place. Sometime later, as his research continued, Richer saw that this line stood for the Virgo-Pisces direction in the zodiacal system centered on Delphi.

The present volume of Richer's studies on sacred geography and astrological symbolism is a break-through work, both highly intuitive and analytical. It is the first part of a triptych. The second volume extends the studies of the tradition to the Mediterranean regions of the Roman Empire, and the third, *Iconologie et Tradition,* traces it through Christian art from the fourth to the eighteenth centuries. Both the first and the third volumes earned Richer awards from the Académie Française. It would appear that the tradition, issued from ancient Egypt and Mesopotamia and relayed through Asia Minor, Phoenicia, Greece, and Rome, survived in fragments for several millenia.

This English edition corresponds to the third French edition, with some minor cuts and variations in sequence. I had originally intended to work closely with Richer on this translation, but his death in 1992 prevented me from doing so. I have made every effort to ensure accuracy and clarity in the text and to update the footnotes. In addition to those mentioned on my dedication page, I would like to thank William D. Eastman, Dr. David Appelbaum, Cathleen Collins and the production staff at SUNY Press, and Joscelyn Godwin of Colgate University.

Christine Rhone 1994

Preface

Guy Trédaniel has kindly suggested a new edition of *Sacred Geography of the Ancient Greeks*, first published in 1967. I thought I would take this opportunity to add some new information, together with more documentary photographs.

A fresh attempt will be made to place the facts in context of world history and of the zodiac and to propose a chronology.

The monuments in chapter 14 alone show clearly that the knowledge of the precession of the equinoxes goes back much further than is generally recognized.

Hipparchus (between 158 and 126 B.C.) really did no more than "rediscover" what had been known in far earlier times.

What is more, the use over the centuries of calendars based on the heliacal risings of the stars requires observation of the phenomenon. This type of observation was made first in Egypt and then in Greece; it is proved by known calendar tables. A fourth-century calendar table found at Miletus gives the important risings and settings of the stars for eighteen out of thirty days of Aquarius (the other days, when there was nothing special to observe, were marked by plain holes).[1]

Before the invention of the zodiac, which goes back to the eighth century B.C. in a form similar to that of today, ancient astronomers had observed the distances between the fixed stars of first magnitude, which were their main celestial markers. One may wonder whether Taurus might not originally have stood for Aldebaran, Leo for Regulus, Virgo for Spica, and so on. Even after the general adoption of the zodiac and the division of the annual path of the sun into twelve sectors of thirty degrees, it is probable that the heliacal risings of the great reference stars that marked the course of the year remained very important. Cyril Fagan has already established[2] that the ancients used a fixed sidereal zodiac in which the Pleiades were at 5 degrees Taurus, Aldebaran 15 degrees in the same sign, Regulus 5 degrees Leo, Spica 29 degrees Virgo, and Antares at 15 degrees Scorpio.

This is why one may assume that the relationship between a given area of the Greek territory and a given part of the zodiac was permanently fixed: Olympia was associated with Aldebaran, Sparta with Gemini, Delos with the Virgoan Ear of Grain, Hephaestia of Lemnos with Antares, Aegae with Vega. Leros was in relation to Arneb (Alpha Leporis). At the inauguration of the great sanctuaries, "stretching the cord" must have occurred at the heliacal rising of the star that was in relationship with the site.

From the Sumero-Babylonian period onward, the bull symbolized both earth and spring; the lion, fire and summer; the deer, air and autumn. Hence the groups of fighting animals taken from Mesopotamian art, described as "dynamic symbols of seasonal variations" in chapter 14. The constant overlapping of symbols for the equinoxes and solstices of two consecutive ages is enough to show that the phenomenon of the precession was known, even if not measured exactly. Every age was associated with the sign for the beginning of spring and its opposite (the autumnal equinox), as well as the signs for the summer and winter solstices. One must therefore always consider not just a single sign, but two zodiacal axes that intersect at right angles. In brief, these represented magnetic fields that balanced and compensated for one another in pairs or by fours. Solar calendars, such as the Egyptian, the Athenian, and others, began at the summer solstice.

It follows from this that the most important symbols were those for signs of the zodiac in a squared or an opposing position. In any age the two most prominent signs were always those of the spring equinox and the summer solstice.

Each great age also appears to have corresponded to a different pole. And in this way one arrives at the following key for interpreting the symbolism:

1. Age of Taurus	Equinoxes: Taurus, Scorpio Solstices: Leo, Aquarius
2. Age of Aries	Equinoxes: Aries, Libra Solstices: Cancer, Capricorn
3. Age of Pisces	Equinoxes: Pisces, Virgo Solstices: Gemini, Sagittarius
4. Age of Aquarius	Equinoxes: Aquarius, Leo Solstices: Taurus, Scorpio

Each city and every region of Greece had its own calendar. In Egyptian astronomical tradition there was another type of calendar where the beginning of the year was related to the heliacal rising of Spica. This harked back to a more ancient age, the Age of Gemini:

Age of Gemini	Equinoxes:	Gemini, Sagittarius (Swan)
	Solstices:	Virgo, Pisces

The remarkable eighth-century "oriental style" amphora found in Boeotia and in the collection of the National Museum of Athens (fig. 1) must be studied in light of a calendar in which the year began at the summer solstice marked by the heliacal rising of Spica at 29 degrees Virgo. In my opinion, the central figure represents a 29-degree Virgo/29-degree Pisces axis. The hair and the triangular head of the goddess stand for Spica. The whole of the drawing on the main face of the vase may be read in this manner:

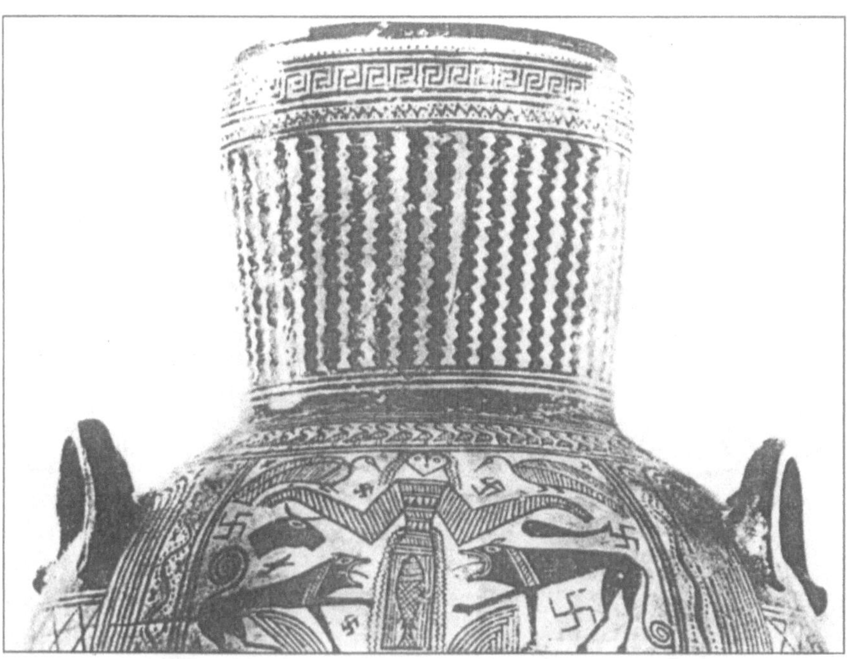

Figure 1. *Theban amphora (National Museum, Athens).*

Central goddess: Virgo-Pisces

Guinea-fowl or peacock: Aries	Guinea-fowl or peacock: Libra
Bull: Taurus	Arm of Ophiuchus: Scorpio
Lion: Leo	Lioness: Aquarius

The frieze of swans on the border repeats the symbolism of the Gemini-Sagittarius axis. The swastikas are solar symbols. The drawing on the other side of the vase is here reproduced (fig. 2).

These images essentially describe the Hare-Eagle (or Hare-Swan) axis, in other words, the opposition of the stars Arneb-Altaïr or Arneb-Deneb. One must bear in mind that in Arabic, *Arneb* means hare, *teïr* or *taïr* is bird, and *Deneb* means Eagle's tail (*Aetos*).

The interpretation for the vase as a whole may be diagrammed (fig. 3).

One is here dealing with the end of the Age of Gemini. What is striking is the absence of the sign for Gemini proper (no doubt reserved for Sparta), but there are about sixty swans! In eighth-century work one often sees images of a great winged goddess who sometimes looks like the Gorgon holding swans in her hands; this specifically refers to the Virgo-Sagittarius square or summer (fig. 4).

A comparative study of the pediments of the temple at Corcyra and the Hecatompedon of Athens (pp. 198–203) added weight to the importance of the

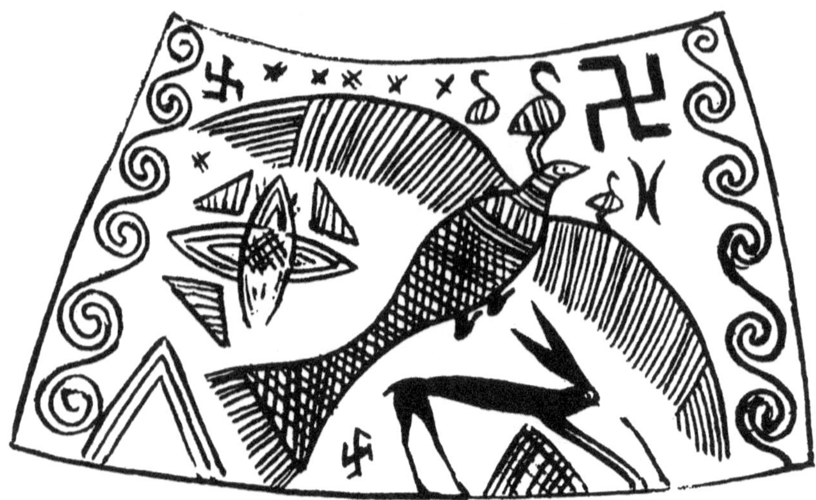

Figure 2. *The other side of the Theban amphora.*

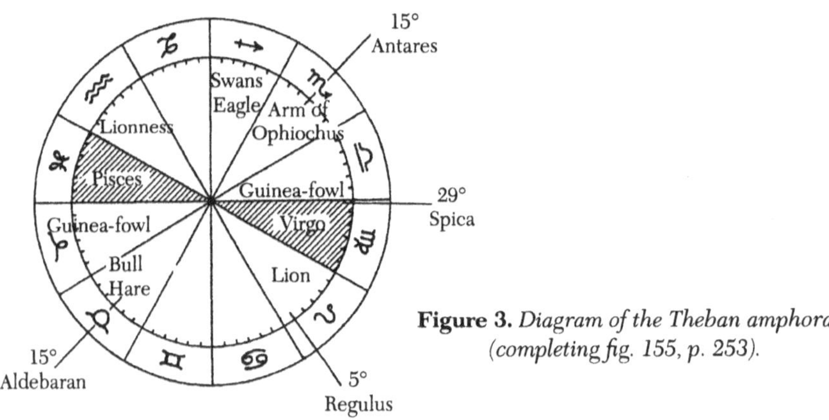

Figure 3. *Diagram of the Theban amphora (completing fig. 155, p. 253).*

Virgo-Pisces axis. An examination of the decor of the temple of Athena in the Troad gave further proof. And surely it is not a coincidence that the first line that I drew on the map of Greece was the Delphi-Daphnae-Athens-Prasiae-Delos line.

The American work *Hamlet's Mill* of 1969 is a great compilation in the manner of Frazer's *Golden Bough*,[3] based mainly on a thesis developed earlier by Mr. Jean-Charles Pichon[4] that the phenomenon of the precession has been known from earliest antiquity. For the "historical" (or prehistorical?) period, the authors state[5] that in the "Golden Age," that is, towards 6500 B.C., Gemini and Sagittarius marked the equinoxes, whose path was visibly marked in the sky as the Milky Way. During this age the solstitial axis was Virgo-Pisces.

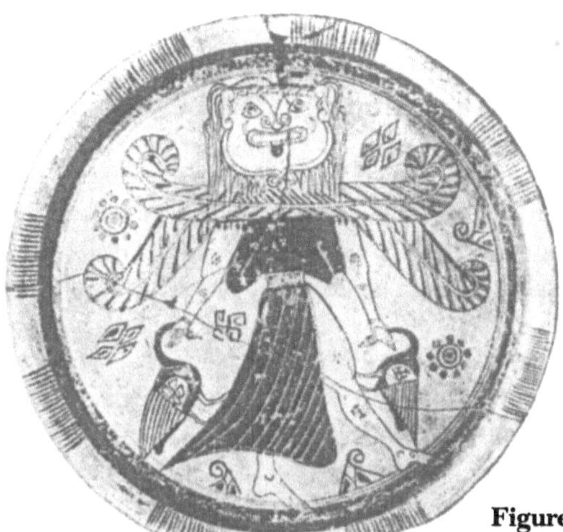

Figure 4. *Rhodian plate from Camiros (British Museum).*

A look at the myth of Leda brings grist to this mill. The myth, as I have shown (cf. "The Loves of Zeus," p. 144), refers to the Gemini-Sagittarius axis. But even Robert Graves, who says that Leda and Latona[6] have the same name, did not see that the myth of Leda really duplicates that of Latona. The Anatolian goddess (the "lady" or "sovereign") gave her name to both Latona and Leda. The swan's feathers scattered in the sky may symbolize the Milky Way. From the union of Zeus and Leda were born two sets of twins (who echo the twins Apollo and Artemis). From one egg were born Castor and Pollux, who in later speculation represented the summer and winter sun, and from the other egg came Helene/Selene and Clytemnestra. The latter remained associated with the zodiac but was transferred to Mycenae in the solar region of Leo; Helene became an image of the moon. It is now more understandable why in *Astronomica* Manilius associates Apollo with Gemini and Artemis-Diana with Sagittarius (while the sun is generally associated with Leo and the moon with Cancer). This was an attempt to put the history of the zodiac in harmony with the precession of the equinoxes. Historians of religion now generally accept the idea that Latona, Apollo, and Dionysus are deities who originated in Anatolia. At the latitude of Delos (the same as Didyma's), the sun rises at an angle of 30 degrees above the horizon at the time of the summer solstice.

The very first coins were struck in Lycia in the seventh century, and these were already stamped with zodiacal symbols. I have been able to show that all coins, up to and including those of the fifth century, bear symbols either of deities or of the zodiac. And from these coins I have reconstituted the ancient Greek zodiac, which is a composite, including symbols of Egyptian origin. Others come from Babylonia (via Phoenicia, as we will see). Some recall the Celtic zodiac.

To get an overall view of the multiplicity of symbols of equivalent meaning, the reader may refer to the tables on pages 100, 101 and 159–160. A guiding summary is given here. Circumzodiacal constellations are often taken to represent the zodiacal sign in which they are located. It is as though any constellation within a celestial sector of thirty degrees could stand for the sign.

This table may be used to interpret thousands of monuments from the Middle East and the Mediterranean area and objects in every museum in the world—what is utterly astonishing is that since 1967, when this book was first published, archeologists have been incapable of using it! This speaks volumes about the rigidified state of some minds and the negative effects of a certain kind of "ultra-rationalistic" education. I have already given some examples of interpreting the monuments in *Delphes, Délos et Cumes*. In this book I give yet another in the detailed study of the temple of Athena in the Troad, which stands as an anthology of the symbols studied. The table is as follows:

Ordinary Name of the Sign	Current Symbol	Other Symbols	Heroes Characters, Objects
ARIES	Ram	Sphinx, Monkey	PHORCYS
TAURUS	Bull	Hare	ZEUS IN BULL-SHAPE GERYON
GEMINI	Dioscuri	Horsemen, Horse	THAUMAS
CANCER	Crab	Octopus, Spiral	SHIP ARGO, HYDRA, TYPHON, CERBERUS
LEO	Lion	Dog (Sirius)	CHIMAERA
VIRGO	Virgin	Ear of Grain, Gorgon	THESEUS
LIBRA	Balance	Sphinx	THEMIS OR DIKE
SCORPIO	Scorpion	Eagle (Rooster)	ECHIDNA, OPHIUCHUS, ALTAR
SAGITTARIUS	Centaur	Arrow, Swan	CHIRON, ACHILLES
CAPRICORN	Sea-goat	Lyre, Dolphin	GRIFFINS

Ordinary Name of the Sign	Current Symbol	Other Symbols	Heroes Characters, Objects
AQUARIUS	Water-bearer, Amphora, Cantharus	Horse/Winged Horse (Pegasus)	SIRENS, DIONYSUS, PANTHER, IVY
PISCES	Fish	Boar	CETO, TRITON, NEREUS

Some symbols may raise many questions. This is true of the boar, for example, which is discussed on pages 69–71. One cannot help noticing the constant mythological association of Artemis with the boar and the bear. An ancient polar goddess, Artemis is the immutable center, the law of the cosmos. And since the law of humanity is death, she was to be identified in turn with the terrible white goddess Gort, Gorgopa, or Gorgona. She is also Circe, the goddess of the circle or of destiny.[7] But when the gods succeeded the goddesses, some of the attributes of the Great Goddess were transferred to Kronos, a supreme god, and then to Apollo Karnaios. Both were gods of the *Karn*, meaning a high place or a tumulus (cairn), a pile of stones. The root KRN, which expresses ideas of power and height, is found not only in these divine names but also in many Greek place-names. For example, Corinth comes from kar, "head" or "summit,"[8] which refers to the heights of the Acrocorinth.

Strabo tells us (X, 452) that the heroic founder of Ambracia and Leucas, the son of Cypselus, king of Corinth, was called Gorgos. He thus bore the name that rules Virgo, the sign opposing Pisces, where Ambracia was located in the Delphic system. There are also the Apollo of Kyrtones in Boeotia, the Asclepieion of Gortynia in Arcadia, and the various Gortyns (in Phoenician, *'Qortan* means "walled city".)

The close analogy between the Hittite myth of Kumarbis and that of Kronos has long been recognized.[9] In both cases one finds a castration rite and the substitution of a stone for a child. The stone swallowed by Kronos and regurgitated at Delphi becomes the omphalos. Thus the baetyl is a sacred stone that has fallen from the sky, heaven-sent, and physically marks the union of heaven and earth, a process by which celestial divinity enters the universe. This is why a distinction between the gods of fertility and of the heavens is illusory: the great gods are both at once from the very beginning.

At Delphi the year was divided between Apollo and Dionysus. However, other gods partly kept their character of guardians of the zodiacal signs. Hera is associated with Taurus; Poseidon is the ancient guardian of Gemini; Athena rules Virgo; Hephaestus, Scorpio. As for Dionysus, he remains a cantharus-god, associated with Aquarius and winter.

As already mentioned, an oriental and mainly Sumero-Babylonian origin of the Greek zodiac seems highly probable. However, the migration of symbols remained problematic, despite the remarkable line of latitude defined by Tushpa-Melitene-Sardis-Delphi, which seems to indicate that the Hittite kingdoms acted as relays. What is more, it appears that the arrival of several waves of Phoenicians into Greece may have been influential. These migrations have left various traces in toponymy and mythology that serve as chronological references.

Even before the discovery of oriental seals in the Cadmean palace, the oriental origin of Thebes, founded by Cadmus (whose very name means "the Oriental"),[10] perhaps towards 1400 B.C., was generally accepted. I plan to show that the city was built around the "tomb of Amphion," which must have been in reality a ziggurat. A city in the form of a lyre was erected to complete the monument. The city walls were connected to the tower and had seven doors that corresponded symbolically to the seven strings of the instrument and the seven planets.[11] I neverthless consider that the system studied here must have been introduced into Greece at a later period, quite likely at the same time as the Phoenician alphabet.

In this respect an important reference point is the introduction of the goddess Aphrodite into the Greek pantheon. Jean-Edmond Dugand has established that the goddess's name derives from Astarte. He also confirms that it was indeed the Phoenicians who introduced the cult of Aphrodite, which, according to Herodotus, came from Ascalon, first into Cyprus and then into Cythera.[12] I here quote a few essential lines from the work of my colleague:

> We must believe Herodotus (I, 105) when he says that the Phoenicians founded a famous sanctuary of Aphrodite Urania in the island modeled on her temple at Ašqelon (Ascalon). . . .
>
> On Cythera in 1849, a cuneiform dedication of Narān-Sin, son of Ibiq-Adad, king of Ešuna, was found . . . which refers to the last quarter of the nineteenth century B.C.
>
> Thucydides (IV, 5) names the three main centers of Cythera: Scandia and two places called Cythera, like the island . . . (Scandia) was the port. Hesychius explains in a verse that Σχάνδεια was "a sort of headgear."
>
> If one interprets Κύθηρὰ in Canaanitish, whence the Hebrew *Kĕtĕr, kōtĕrĕt,* which means "crown, tiara," we obtain one of those doublets that are the joy of the toponymist. (*Chypre et Canaan*, pp. 246 and 247)

Crown and headgear refer to the head. Whose head is it in this case?

If one assumes that the Phoenicians also brought with them a system of symbolic correspondences that put the Greek territory as a whole into relationship with the heavens, or appropriated such a system, it immediately becomes clear that it is the head of the Hydra. This constellation stretches across a quarter of the zodiac. In relation to Delphi, if the head of the fabulous animal is at Cythera in the region of Cancer, part of its body is at the island of Hydra in the region of Leo.

The main advantage in encountering this is to confirm the depth of oriental influence in the spread of astral beliefs throughout Greece. I must also add that the Delphi-Cythera axis corresponds to the direction of Canopus (Alpha Carenae).

It also provides a means of dating that should not be underestimated. In 2000 B.C. the spring equinox was at 0 degrees 30 minutes Taurus and in 1900 B.C. at 29 degrees 08 minutes Aries. This time span would account for the superimposition of the two systems of coordinates for the equinoxes and solstices mentioned earlier (A, Taurus-Eagle and Leo-Aquarius; B, Aries-Libra and Cancer-Capricorn).

It would therefore have been towards the time when the spring equinox was changing signs that the correspondences between the regions of Greece and the zodiacal constellations were adopted (while bearing in mind Fagan's reservation that the ancients would always have used a fixed sidereal zodiac).

To return to the constellation of Hydra, I spoke in the first edition of the origins of Aphrodite and indicated that the female Hydra corresponds to the island of Hydra in the system centered on Delphi. I wonder whether the hydra, a whitish, transparent sea monster, might not have been identified with the sea-foam, whence was born the goddess Aphrodite, through a para-etymology.

According to the current state of my knowledge and deductions, the Lion of Kea, discussed in detail in chapter 12 with its associated system, would appear to be the main monument relating to the period between 2050 and 1800 B.C. A subsequent study of Hesiod's *Shield* may well shed more light on this.

♦

As has just been seen for a more recent period, the identification of Cythera with the head of the Hydra through Phoenician etymology was remarkable in itself.

But this could take on its full scope of meaning only if other Greek place-names of Phoenician origin were significant in terms of sacred geography. Obviously, it would be impossible to base the argument on a single example. This is why I have had recourse to linguistics and to the cooperation of my colleague J.-E. Dugand, who has kindly given me a list of place-names of Phoenician origin that he has drawn up for the whole of the eastern Mediterranean. According to his deductions, these names correspond to a period of Phoenician influence in the entire Aegean area and all around Greece between about 1100 and 800 B.C. Some of the etymologies come from *Hellenosemitica* by M. C. Astour published in 1965.

Cos and the Owl: One outstanding etymology immediately appeared on this list; it derives the name of the island of Cos from *Kos/Keso:* "night bird, owl." An extension of that important line, the very first that I drew, joining Delphi to Delos, intersects the island in such a way that it is put intô symbolic relationship with the sign of Virgo, which the owl symbolizes, in both the Delphic and the Delian systems.

Asopus and the Harvest God: The name of the river Asopus, generally taken as the boundary between Attica and Boeotia, derives from the word *'Asaph-'Asoph*, "to amass, to harvest." This is the name of a "harvest god," according to Astour. Now, the source of this river is also on the 0 degree Virgo line, which was in symbolic relationship with Spica, the Ear of Grain (this image appeared on the coins of Metapontum). I have mentioned the supposedly agrarian deities of the windswept island of Delos on p. 18. These are harvests of the spirit, rather than harvests of grain.

Taenarum or the Oven: The name of Cape Taenarum derives from *tannūr* (oven), in Assyrian *tinûru*. This identifies the site as the entrance to the furnace of Hades.

Dirke: Various Boeotian place-names refer to Canaanitish deities. This is true of the name of the fountain Dirce near Thebes, to be compared with Derceto and *'Anat ba'alat darkât* ("Anat, lady of justice"), which is also related to the Theban Onca and the sign of Libra.

Ithaca, Island of the Middle: The name Ithaca is comparable to the Hebrew *tōk* ("in the middle of") and *tāwik* ("the middle"). The island is in the middle of the Ionian islands. Also, the north of the island is at the latitude of Delphi, so the name indicates the middle latitude in relation to the center.

The Phoenician etymologies of some other place-names either confirm my previous deductions or agree with generally accepted etymolgies. Euboea means "rich in cattle"; the northern part of the island is cut by the Taurus-Scorpio line. In speaking of Cephallenia, Hesychius glossed *"Krana"* as *"Kephale."* And the name Delos (also known as Ortygia, or "quail") seems related to the Phoenician *dālwion*, "quail."

So besides the sign of Cancer encountered in relation to Hydra, a constellation that extends over the whole southeast quarter, these place-names implied the signs of Virgo (Cos and Asopus) and Libra (Dirce). The names Taenarum and Ithaca also contributed important symbolic references. I am not going to discuss the various names that refer to light, whiteness, fire, or air, because these should be studied separately. One rather gets the impression that the whole system of Greek islands was seen as the equivalent of the starry skies. I did not hope to find an example for every sign of the zodiac, but the relationships that have just been mentioned are already far too numerous to be mere coincidence; they suggest a coherent system.

♦

It was essentially starting from seventh and sixth century coins from mainland Greece, the islands, and Anatolia that I began to reconstruct my system of zodiacal coordinates with certainty. At that time I was working with generally accepted analogies. And the vital influence of Lycia (from the Hittite *Lukka*) must be emphasized; the very name means "light," and both the god Apollo/

Aplunia and coins of the zodiacal type originated there. Lycian coins display an extraordinary range of symbols of Leo (p. 272, n. 21).

I repeat that, contrary to general opinion, the problem of latitudes was resolved in antiquity, probably by means of bearings made on the stars. How can the fact that the three major Hera temples at Olympia, Argos, and Samos are at exactly the same latitude be otherwise explained? This line of Hera temples raises an interesting question, by the way. In looking at the map of Greece (map 1, p. xiii), one should find at that latitude a line of Aphrodite. One may deduce from its absence that the system antedates the inclusion of Aphrodite in the Greek pantheon. The date suggested by J.-E. Dugand for the transition of Astarte to Aphrodite is "between 1200 B.C. and 900 B.C." I believe one may say 900 to 850 B.C. While for the system described on map 7, p. xix, I can confirm a date of 2050 to 1800 B.C., for the second period, that of the full development of the system of zodiacal coordinates, I arrive at this series of related references.

Invention of coins in Lycia	CIRCA 700–680 B.C.
Aphrodite integrated in the Greek pantheon	CIRCA 900–850 B.C.
Adoption of Phoenician writing in Greece and of the system of zodiacal coordinates	CIRCA 1000–850 B.C.

My thesis is, in brief, that a system of coordinates based essentially on the four seasons and the four cardinal points would have been superseded, towards 800 B.C. at the latest, by a system of zodiacal projection, partly of Phoenician origin. The series of latitudes symbolizing the planets would be associated with the more ancient system.

In closing, an important point about cartography must be made: the lines that I am suggesting must be drawn on Mercator projection maps. On these, parallels and meridians intersect at right angles, and straight lines drawn will represent rhumb lines that define a constant angle to the north.[13]

—Jean Richer 1983

Chapter 1

Theory of Alignments

The god, whose oracle is at Delphi, does not speak, does not hide: he shows by signs.

—Heraclitus (Fragment 93)

1. Delphi: Apollo and Athena

It all began during a first visit to Delphi in the spring of 1957. How could anyone not be filled with inspiration by the majesty of this site and its evocative combination of Greek deities? In the temple of Apollo, the god of celestial fire is associated with Gaia, the earth, and with Dionysus. Next to the sanctuary of Apollo stands that of Athena.[1] The form of Delphi itself suggests a sacred marriage. As Mircea Eliade has said: "Delphi, most famous of the clefts of ancient Greece, owed its name to this mythical image; 'delphi' signifies in fact the female generative organ."[2] The union of heaven and earth is implicit in the view of the gorge of the Phaedriades and the sacred mountain of Parnassus, stairway to the heavens.

The very shape of the sanctuaries unites the image of the earth with the projection of the heavens. The omphalos, the navel of the earth, lay in the most sacred part of the temple of Apollo. Nearby was the seat of the Pythia, who drank from the Castalian spring before giving prophecy.

I was intrigued by a certain detail of the cult at Delphi: the sacred drama of the battle of Apollo with the serpent Python was enacted there about every eight years. Now, the serpent not only is a symbol of the earth but also represents the path of the sun through the zodiac. One quarter of the thirty-three year cycle of the "mean sun" is just over eight years.

It has long been known that the development of peoples and civilizations is influenced by the great rhythms of the earth and of the celestial bodies. The Greeks, like all ancient peoples, were aware of this and wished to put their cities and temples under the protection of forces that ruled particular places and times, mountains, springs, and rivers. But the connection between Delphi, site of Apollo's main sanctuary, and Delos, his traditional birthplace, remained a mystery. I also wondered about the relationship of Apollo and Athena.

After a second trip to Greece in the spring of 1958 my original intuitive insight came to me. On the map of Greece I sketched a line joining Delphi to Athens and, to my surprise and great satisfaction, I saw that an extension of that line went to Delos. A spatial relationship between the three sacred sites was thus revealed. It was already more understandable why at Delphi there was a sanctuary of Athena Pronaia by the modern road coming from Athens. Before the entrance of the temple of Apollo used to stand another statue of Athena.

The movement from Delos to Delphi can be interpreted as a symbol of the daily path of the sun, as Creuzer has already observed.[3]

From the time when I first began to draw my lines, I wondered what the ancient Greeks knew of the shape of their country. Surviving maps or those composed according to ancient geographical texts are almost useless.[4] My later observations were to show that, although there were errors in the calculation of distances, especially in mountainous country, on the whole the ancients were well aware of the positions of sites in relation to one another, and especially of significant alignments. This makes good sense for a people of shepherds and navigators who were used to taking bearings on the stars. Many texts, such as the beginning of Aeschylus's *Agamemnon*, indicate that news was communicated by means of fire signals on high places. Aeschylus's text mentions a series of relays between Troy and Argos, which is an excellent way of determining certain alignments.

2. The Meridian of Delphi: Tempe–Delphi–Sparta–Cape Taenarum

By simple deduction I was led to consider the geometric figures that could connect Delphi with other parts of Greece. (For everything that follows see map 1.) It was naturally appropriate to pay most attention to the sites of the principal temples and religious traditions. Several geometrical constructions were possible: lines, triangles, arcs of circle, or even spirals. But because the overall shape that the Greeks ascribed to their country isn't known, the complex triangulations I first thought of were impossible. It soon became obvious that I would have to restrict my study to major alignments in relation to legends about the origin or the transfer of oracles.

Two legends, seemingly contradictory, but really complementary, establish the connection between Delphi and an Apollo who is both Cretan and Hyperborean, and the link between Delphi and Tempe.

The most ancient sanctuary of Greece, and for a long time the only one, was that of Zeus at Dodona, the "Druidic" oracle of a woodland people. During the period in the development of Hellenic religion when Apollo was becoming the dominant Greek god and was acquiring, by more or less explicit delegation, some of the attributes of a supreme deity, merging at times with Helios and Dionysus, the Tempe valley became quite prominent and it was from there, it would appear, that the cult of Apollo spread throughout Greece. According to the tradition told by Pausanias (IX, 30), it was from Tempe that the cult of Apollo was brought to Delphi. There is also the legend of Zeus releasing eagles or swans from the ends of the earth and the two birds crossing at Delphi. Of particular interest in this tradition is that it seems to be an allegorical description of a geometrical figure. This could be, for example, the intersection of two arcs of circle. An arc can be drawn on the map of Greece with the probable site of Tempe as the center of a Dodona-Delphi curve, because the distances from Tempe to Dodona and Tempe to Delphi are equal. This distance is also equal to that between Delphi and Prasiae. This port, the modern Porto Rafti, is located where the Delos-Athens-Delphi line cuts the coast of Attica.[5] And it was from that very place that the sacred Theores set sail for Delos. In determining the site of Delphi, it is as though the legendary birds had been simultaneously released and had flown towards one another at a presumably uniform rate, one of them leaving from Tempe, and the other from Prasiae (and hence the direction of Delos).

The line joining Dium-Tempe-Delphi-Taenarum is identical to the meridian of Delphi. A line drawn very close to it, slightly deviating to the northwest, joins Amyclae, Sparta, Tegea, and the summit of Olympus.

The noteworthy position of Sparta foreshadows the city's prominent role in the history of the Delphic oracle. I believe that the evolution of this oracle, according to Pausanias's description of its successive temples, must essentially be seen as an allegory.[6]

3. Bassae, Tegea, Corinth

In my further travels in Greece, I was struck by the unusual and apparently arbitrary placement of certain great sanctuaries of the Peloponnese. Why was the temple of Tegea on an otherwise featureless point of the immense plateau of Arcadia? Why was the temple of Apollo at Bassae high in the mountains at an altitude of more than a thousand meters? Could anything but predetermination have dictated the choice of such sites? From the work of Mircea Eliade already mentioned two relevant comments were to guide my research. One had to do with the meaning and function of the omphalos: "It is from a 'center' (navel) that the creation of the world starts and, in solemnly imitating this primary model, every 'construction,' every 'fabrication' must operate from a starting 'center.' "[7] The other concerned the fundamental meaning of the triangle for the Greeks, which symbolized fertility, the source, the matrix, the universal principle of generation.[8]

My attempts with triangulation were not always successful. I will mention only what is of interest to introduce some simple alignments.

An almost equilateral triangle joins three important sanctuaries of Athena at Delphi, Athens, and Tegea (as the Protectress). One may therefore assume that a triangulation, with Athens and Delos as two of the points, had in all likelihood governed the choice of the site of Tegea.

The height of this triangle passes very near Corinth. The unique position of this city, key to the isthmus, where there was also a great sanctuary of Apollo, suggested that it had to some degree acted as a center.[9]

The selection of the site of Apollo's temple at Corinth seems to have been as much for geographical considerations as for geometrical and astronomical reasons. The imposing mass of the Acrocorinth acts as a gigantic gnomon in relation to the temple. From the summit of the Acrocorinth and the northwest corner of the temple of the Syrian Goddess (the celestial Astarte) on the upper terrace, the eye follows the slope of the mountain to the exact southwest corner of the temple of Apollo, as any visitor to the Acrocorinth can see. And directly opposite, on the other side of the gulf, rise Mount Helicon and Parnassus, whose steep slopes overhang Delphi to the northeast.

4. From Crete to Hyperborea

The Homeric Hymn to Apollo indicates that there were ancient relations between the sanctuaries of Knossos and Pytho and that the temple of Apollo was originally served by Cretan priests.

The Delphi-Corinth line (i.e., Mount Parnassus–Acrocorinth) defines a direction parallel to the mountain range of Pindus and to the line between Patrae and Cape Malea. But the original generating center really seems to have been the summit of Mount Ida in Crete, reputed cradle of the supreme god of Hellenic mythology.

Since the other gods are no more than emanations of Zeus, unique aspects of his power, this has bearing on the legend of the Cretan origins of the Delphic Apollo, whose name is associated with the dolphin. The legend seems to contradict those suggesting a Hyperborean origin of the cult of Apollo. On the line in question, the Castalian spring at Delphi may represent the female element in counterpoise to the male element of Parnassus. This symbolism also applies to the Acrocorinth at Corinth, a name meaning "city of the summit," and its springs of upper and lower Pirene (it is known that the priestesses of the Syrian Goddess practiced sacred prostitution).

The Mount Ida–Corinth–Delphi direction symbolizes the vital spirit of the country of Greece. This line intersects parallels of latitude at a 60-degree angle and may be considered as the projection over part of the earth's surface, taken as flat, of the Leo-Aquarius cosmic axis, which defines the same angle in relation to the line of the equinoxes.

This axis is the cosmic signature of Greece and makes it a mirror of the celestial harmony of the zodiac and the planets of the solar system.

If the other end of the cosmic axis is taken as the origin, Apollo, instead of coming from Crete, is coming or returning from the "Hyperboreans" of Scotland or even of Iceland.

Incidentally, the equivalence of Hyperborea and Egypt is easily explained if one accepts the existence of a primordial tradition, probably of "Hyperborean" (or Borean) origin, from which Egyptian civilization and religious practices would also have derived.

These thoughts adjoin Charles Picard's comment: "Who knows whether the Delphians had not worshipped both a Creto-Anatolian Apollo who had come to Delphi by sea, with its priests of Knossos, and another god by the same name, believed to be 'Hyperborean' or 'Lycian'; this would explain the variety of his divine epithets."[10]

At almost a right angle to the Delphi–Mount Ida axis lies Delos, and at the point where this line cuts the coast of Ionia stood the other great oracle of Apollo at Claros. Extended southeast, it ends at Cape Epidelium, site of the ruins of a temple of Apollo Delios (map 1). It is parallel to the Corinth-Bassae line.

My brother, Lucien Richer, has shown that an extension of the Delos-Athens-Delphi axis through Europe coincides with an alignment of sites dedicated to Saint Michael. This line goes through Monte Sant' Angelo, Sacra di san Michele, Mont-Saint-Michel, Saint Michael's Mount, and Skellig Michael. It would seem that Saint Michael was the true successor of the Apollo associated with this axis (see *Atlantis*, May–June 1977).

5. Leucas

My reconstruction of the system of references would have remained incomplete if, at this stage in my research, I had been unable to find the site on the Greek coast that was for the ancients the allegorical place of the daily death of the sun god Apollo-Helios. An extension of the Delos-Athens-Delphi line passes near Arta, the ancient Ambracia, a Corinthian stronghold in enemy territory, which was long in conflict with Corfu, also on this line. But this wasn't what I was looking for.

The sanctuary at Leucas with its tradition of a ritual dive seemed to be the place I was seeking. Carcopino has described it:

> There was a succession of priests of Apollo on the island from at least the seventh century B.C. to the time of the Roman empire. To my knowledge there were two temples to the solar deity of the golden arrows at Leucas: one on the fatal cliff at the southern end in the western part of the island, the other in the northeast, near the city with which Thucydides associates it. . . . Of the second nothing remains but a memory. Of the first, a few debris of indistinct age may still be seen near the lighthouse. There is nothing to show that the sanctuary on the isthmus was built earlier than the neighboring city, founded by Corinthian colonists toward 635 B.C., to which it was subordinate, and the sanctuary on the Rock must be considered as an annex of the other and subsequent to it. . . .
>
> [According to Aelian,] the ritual dive sacred to the priests of Apollo took place at the end of a processional festival, and was followed by the sacrifice of an ox or bullock for the purpose of getting rid of the flies, which, after gorging themselves on the sacrificial blood, did not take long to die.

In describing the evolution of the rite, Carcopino has said that by Strabo's time the ordeal was no longer practiced more than once a year. He also noted:

> To avoid defections from among the faithful, threatened by losses in population and resources, the priests of Leucas decided to substitute for the defectors. They practiced the sport of the sacred dive, which they performed both in the name of the city and, by substitution, in the name and at the expense of individuals.[11]

By a procedure opposite that of the eminent scholar, who was researching the moral and spiritual meaning of the rite for the Pythagoreans, I was able to define a working hypothesis on the origin of the dive from the White Rock.

Now, since the sanctuaries of Apollo at Leucas were founded by Corinth, this city once again could have acted as a generating center. If one draws from Corinth a parallel to the Delos-Delphi line, one will arrive at the island of Leucas. A right angle (which can be interpreted as the image of a fall) ends at Cape Leucatas.

I suggest the following hypothesis. Every evening, the sun appears to die in the west. In the history of religions, especially that of Mexico, the purpose of human sacrifice was to give the day star the strength necessary to traverse the darkness and to be reborn. Couldn't one suppose that at Leucas there may originally have been a daily human sacrifice, which gradually became weekly, then monthly, and finally annual, with the substitution of animal for human victims in the process? Certain rites of Leucas and Patrae hint at such a transition.

Strabo[12] says that in his time on Apollo's feast day every year a criminal victim was thrown from the cliff of Leucas. Feathers were glued to his body and live birds were even tied onto him to slow his fall. The victim was spared if he came out of the water alive, so fishing boats were waiting at the foot of the cliff for his rescue.

In Pierre Chantraine's *Dictionnaire étymologique de la langue française*, the article on ΛεΥχός indicates that the word is "part of a great family of words meaning 'light': Latin, *lux*; Greek, λέυσσω, λύχνος; Indo-European **leuq*/**louq*, etc." The symbolic importance of places bearing a name derived from this root, which are generally associated with the sunrise or the sunset, may be deduced from this.

6. The Four Temples of Hermione

I was especially interested in the point where the Mount Ida–Delphi line cuts the coast of Argolis. On the map I pinpointed Hermione.

The site seemed noteworthy. It was at the latitude of Delos, and a right angle struck from the Mount Ida–Delphi line at Hermione intersected Amyclae. Also, Hermione occupied a position that is almost symmetrical to that of Delphi in relationship to Corinth.

These purely topographical indications, giving a quadruple spatial definition, led me to believe that Hermione must have been an important site in the cult of Apollo. I researched the existence of any texts to support this. A page of Pausanias then provided a series of suggestive relationships, which were enough to show the nonarbitrary nature of my constructions and to encourage me to pursue my research. Pausanias wrote on Hermione:

> Of Apollo there are three temples and three images. One has no surname; the second they call Pythaeus, and the third Horius (of the Borders). The name Pythaeus they have learned from the Argives, for Telesilla tells us that they were the first Greeks to whose country came Pythaeus, who was a son of Apollo. I cannot say for certain why they call the third Horius, but I conjecture that they won a victory, either in war or by arbitration, in a dispute concerning the borders (*horoi*) of their land, and for this reason paid honors to Apollo Horius.[13]

More interesting than the traveler's cumbrous and spurious explanations are the names he mentions, because the name Pythaeus suggests Pytho, the ancient name for Delphi. Should one assume some connection between the cult at Hermione and that of Apollo Lykeios at Argos?

What is more, Hermione is on the Mount Ida–Delphi line, a line whose more distant origin is in Egypt. Hermione marks the extreme frontier of this line in the Poloponnese. Did Pausanias believe in his own explanation? Or did he wish to avoid overtly mentioning the cult of Horapollo, derived from the cult of the Egyptian solar god Horus? This name inevitably springs to mind when one thinks of this passage of Plutarch in *Isis and Osiris:* "It is said that Typhon took Nephthys to wife, and that Isis and Osiris, being in love with each other even before they were born, were united in the darkness of the womb. Some say that Aroueris, whom the Egyptians call Horus the Old and the Greeks Apollo, was born of this union."[14]

There was rather widespread conviction in antiquity that Hellenic religion was at least partly of Egyptian origin. Horodotus also confirms this. In regard to the sanctuary without a special name, Pausanias says that at Hermione, on the feast of Demeter-Chthonia, children wreathed with hyacinths took part in the procession. So it could be that this sanctuary was sacred to Apollo as the slayer of Hyacinthus, which relates to the esoteric side of a cosmic religion in which astral influences were predominant.

A look at map I will show that one may assume the presence of four temples of Apollo at Hermione:

1. Apollo-Horus (southeast)
2. Pythian Apollo (northwest)
3. Apollo, slayer of Hyacinthus, worshipped at Amyclae (southwest)
4. Delian Apollo (east).

The more ancient fourth sanctuary is described by Pausanias (XI, 34, 10) as being sacred to Helios and must be related to Delos.

I then traveled to Hermione, and this visit revealed the outstanding nature of the site, finally convincing me of its relevance.

The modern village, which occupies a part of the ancient city, is situated on a narrow spit of land orientated almost exactly east-west. It lies under the lee of the island of Dokos farther south, which has the same orientation as the peninsula.

The temples of Hermione have not been thoroughly researched and excavated. Greek researchers have brought to light some mosaics of Byzantine basilicas in the village. What might still lie underneath them?

At the eastern end of the peninsula, facing south, there is a slope, as a villager showed me, that has patches of vegetation with peculiar circular irregularities. The slope makes a hollow sound when it is struck and may well hide cupola tombs.

7. The Oracle of Ptoon

The remarkable case of Hermione, coming after my preceding observations on Delphi, Delos, Corinth, and Leucas, suggested a sort of preestablished agreement on the geographical position of the sites, their structure, and their cult significance. Another interesting example of this harmony appeared on the map of Greece. The cities of Corinth, Argos, and Sparta lay on a straight line and at a right angle to the Delphi-Delos axis. Extended northeast, this line intersects the latitude of Delphi at a point corresponding to the sanctuary of Ptoon.

A visit to Ptoon therefore seemed useful. I made the journey there in the spring of 1960 (the later construction of the northern highway has made it more easily accessible.)

How could anyone miss the obvious similarities between this site and that of Delphi? In both, the temple was in the heart of the mountains in a gorge with a gushing spring that promised continuity of the oracle. Like at Delphi, Apollo is associated with the earth. On the southern slope of the valley, near the temple of Apollo, stands a sanctuary attributed to Demeter.

Upon leaving this inspiring place at sunset, I took a few photographs of the temple terrace and the general view with Mount Ptoon in the background. Examining them several days later, I saw that Mount Ptoon has the clear outline of a human profile. There are certainly many rocks and mountains in Greece in whose shape the human eye may discern a face, with the aid of some imagination. Among the best known is the "head of Zeus" formed by Mount Jouctas, behind the Heracleion of Crete and Knossos. But Mount Ptoon is a case that deserves special mention because it may have been a factor in the placement of the sanctuary. Oddly enough, Vincent Scully, who attributes such importance to these simulacra in his book *The Earth, the Temple and the Gods* (1962), missed this head, although it is quite clear on photographs of the site (figs. 5 and 6).

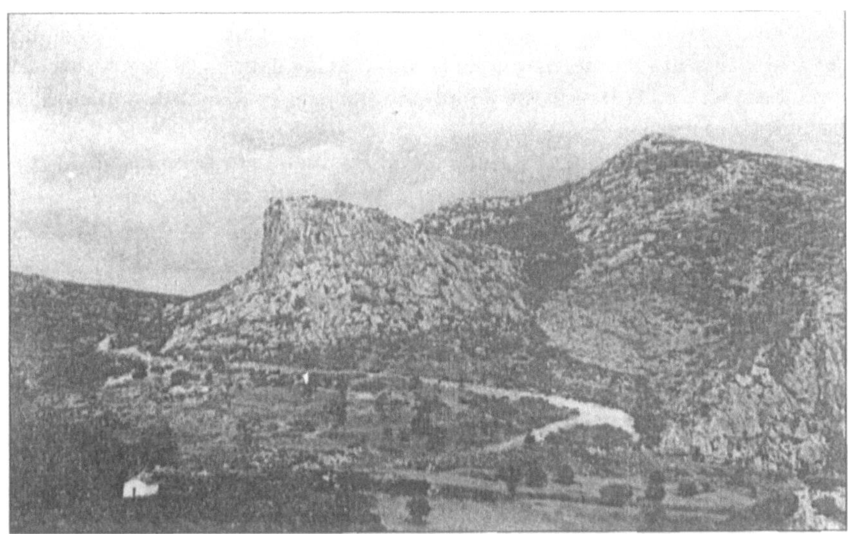

Figure 5. *Mount Ptoon and the sanctuary of Apollo.*

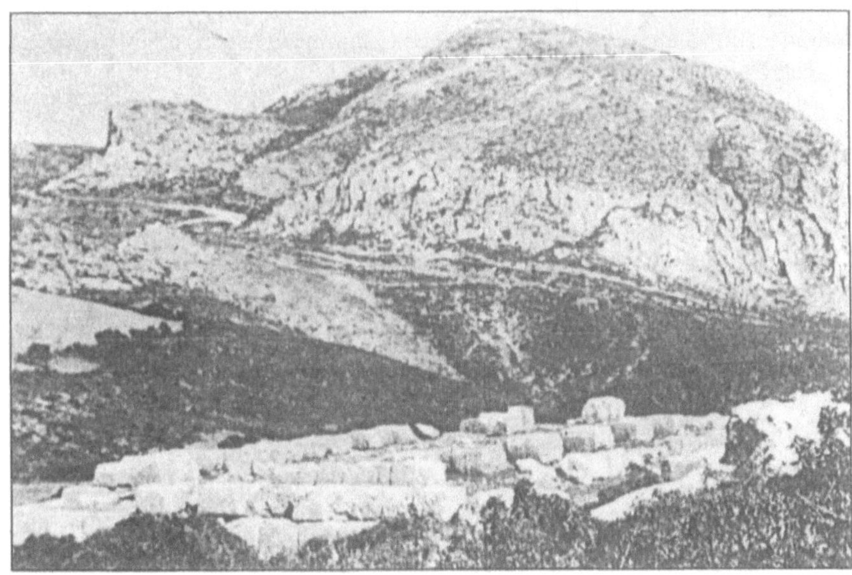

Figure 6. *Mount Ptoon seen from the sanctuary of Demeter. (Photos J.R.)*

8. The Apparently "Abnormal" Orientations of Temples: Bassae, Delos

Archeologists generally seemed to agree that the "normal" orientation of a sanctuary and especially of a *naos* of Apollo was east-west with the entrance to the east. Any other orientation was said to be "abnormal," and attempts were made to take into account local customs, the requirements of the terrain, etc.

Now, some of the most famous and greatest sanctuaries of Apollo, notably those of Delos and Bassae, have orientations that are at first glance unusual and even inexplicable. At Bassae the temple's entrance is to the north-northeast; at Delos it faces west.

For Bassae it is ordinarily claimed that the limited dimensions of the terrace forced the builders to orientate the temple to the north, that is, towards the mountain. One only need examine and measure the site even cursorily to be convinced that a rather minimal embankment, executed in twenty other places in a spectacular way (for example, the five foundations of the temple of Hera at Perachora, the nine foundations of the temple of Aphaia at Aegina, and the mound of Calydon), would have allowed the temple to be orientated east-west without changing its dimensions. A door in the east wall at Bassae brought the rays of sunrise to the statue of the god and, according to Corbett, as transmitted by Scully, it also gave a view of Mount Lycaeon, a major site in the cult of Zeus. However, has anyone realized that, orientated as it is to the north, the temple's entrance faces the direction of Delphi? In addition, the plan of the sanctuary of Apollo at Bassae is identical to that of the temple at Delphi.

At Delos there is nothing obvious to justify the orientation of the temple to the west. But so placed the entrance faces Hermione, which is on the same latitude, and where the cult of Helios-Apollo may have begun somewhat earlier than at Delos.

Another "abnormal" orientation long eluded me: that of the most ancient temple of Apollo in Rhodes, situated at Camiros and facing north. The solution to this enigma was to put me on the track of other discoveries (see chapter 4). In my opinion, these so-called "abnormal" orientations will be seen to obey certain definite rules if, instead of studying each temple separately, one is willing to consider the network of the great Apollonian sanctuaries as a whole. I will be giving many examples of this. Such observations can also be used to confirm what is known from other sources of the probable dates of the temples' construction.[15]

Chapter 2

Interpretation of the Alignments The Zodiacal Wheel Centered on Delphi A Text of Plato's

For about a year I did no more than observe these significant alignments. In my first notes, nevertheless, I had already written:

"The Mount Ida–Delphi direction symbolizes the vital spirit of the country of Greece. This line intersects parallels of latitude at a 60-degree angle and may be considered as the projection over part of the earth's surface, taken as flat, of the Leo-Aquarius cosmic axis, which defines the same angle in relation to the line of the equinoxes.

This axis is the cosmic signature of Greece and makes it a mirror of the celestial harmony of the zodiac and the planets of the solar system." (p. 4).

Periodical trips back to France, especially to Brittany, opened my eyes to a deep analogy between what I was observing in Greece and the almost unknown civilization that erected the megaliths.

The great solstitial alignments of Stonehenge, Carnac, Lagadjar, and the solar ritual of death and resurrection suggested by the drawings in the amazing tumulus of Gavrinis could help to reveal what may have been one of the secrets of Delphi. These solar temples were aligned according to a law.

From then on everything seemed to fall into place and it quickly became clear that the Greeks, like the ancient Mesopotamians and the Egyptians, had wanted to make their country a living image of the heavens.

A whole system of symbolic correspondences began to emerge, a system still somewhat fragmentary but already rather impressive. It suggested many relationships that were confirmed by certain divine or geographical names, by many coins and vases, and by poorly understood details of Greek religious history.

Texts, few in number but important in content, to which others may later be added, came to support my observations. Others required a fresh reading and reinterpretation.

Before beginning this second chapter of my narrative and analysis, I will give a table of the important alignments discussed so far (map 1).

Lines through Delphi:

Delos-Athens-Delphi line.
Mount Ida–Hermione–Delphi line.
Dium-Tempe-Delphi-Taenarum line (meridian of Delphi).

Parallels of latitude:

Hermione-Delos-Didyma parallel.
Athens-Claros parallel.
Delphi–Mount Ptoon parallel.

Other lines:

Mount Olympus–Tegea–Sparta–Amyclae–Taenarum.
Claros–Delos–Cape Epidelium.
Mount Ptoon–Corinth–Argos–Sparta–Thalamae.
Pagasae-Delos.
Corinth-Leucas.

If a zodiacal division of twelve signs is hypothetically placed over these lines, taking Delphi as the center, each line going through Delphi should mark the beginning of a sign, which would then give (map 2):

Hermione: 0 degree Leo
Delos and Athens: 0 degree Virgo
Tempe: 0 degree Capricorn
Sparta: end of Gemini, beginning of Cancer.

By drawing twelve thirty-degree angles touching these four points, I was able to establish a complete system of references.

The beginning of the cycle, which symbolizes spring and corresponds to the spring equinox, was in the Ionian sea before the cliff of Leucas. So for convenience in the later reading of the figure, a circle was drawn with the radius the distance from Delphi to Leucas, and Leucas became the first point of the division of the circle into twelve.

1. Cephallenia or Aries

The beginning of the sign of Aries is therefore theoretically in front of the White Rock. This may explain the ram's heads on certain coins from Delphi[1] appearing with the dolphins that relate to the city's name and the legend of the arrival of Apollo (map 9, fig. 1).

The great island of Cephallenia is entirely in the sign of Aries. Its very name means "head," which is usually taken to mean the shape of the island. But

Cephallenia doesn't look much like a head. By tradition, however, the sign of Aries corresponds to the human head.[2] Both legend and numismatics are here in curious agreement.

Cephallenia, center of Ulysses' "island kingdom," was a flourishing center of pre-Mycenaean civilization. The names of heroes associated with the history of the island are Helios and Cephalus.

Finally, all the ancient coins from Cranii[3] have a ram's head on the front and on the obverse a ram's hoofprint (map 9, fig. 2).

2. "Cow-eyed" Hera. Olympia

In the zodiacal wheel the beginning of the sign of Taurus is situated towards the coastal town of Cyllini, which is west of Elis (the excavations and research now underway at Cyllini and Elis may reveal the existence of a cult of an auxiliary Apollo in conjunction with a taurine Hera).

The worldwide spread of the bull cult is associated with a certain stage in the social evolution of pastoral peoples, and the bull, so often offered in sacrifice, appears on a great many Greek coins without there necessarily being a direct relationship among the cities having used this symbol at one time or another and the zodiacal sign of Taurus. In the Greek world the bull cult was of Cretan and Phoenician origin, as is shown, for example, by the story of Zeus and Europa.

To return more directly to my line of reasoning, the sign of Taurus is said to be one of the houses of the planet Venus. In this sign the goddess takes on a maternal and authoritarian aspect, which allows her to be identified with the Greek Hera.

Now, the great sanctuary of Olympia is located in Taurus, and there, it is said, the cult of Hera antedated that of Zeus. Some coins from Olympia[4] are stamped with a profile of Hera facing to the right (fig. 38, p. 51).

I will simply mention here and discuss in detail later that there was an alignment of Hera sanctuaries: the three great Greek temples of Hera at Olympia, Argos, and Samos are on exactly the same parallel of latitude.

3. Gemini and Sparta

"Castor and Pollux, you who live in divine Lacedaemon, by the lovely flowing stream Eurotas," wrote Theognis.[5]

The Twins were the sons of Tyndareus, king of Sparta. According to Pausanias,[6] they were born at Pephnos on the southern coast of the Peloponnese on the borders of Laconia and Massenia.

The tomb of Castor was shown to visitors at Sparta.

The great Lacedaemonian oracle of Thalamae was in immediate proximity to Pephnos. These two places are at the end of the Ptoon-Corinth-Argos-Sparta line.

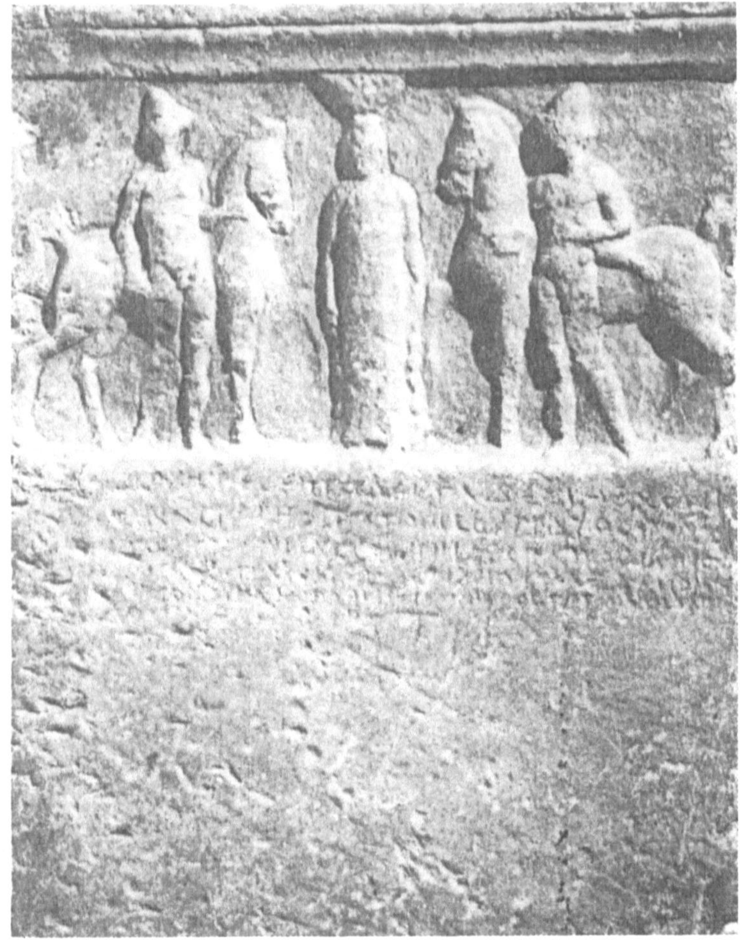

Figure 7. *Helen and the Dioscuri (Museum of Sparta).*

Texts, coins, and a great many stele (map 9, figs. 3 and 4) confirm the prominence of the cult of the Dioscuri at Sparta. A stele from the second century B.C. (fig. 7) in the collection of the Museum of Sparta, shows Helen with the Dioscuri. Their cult spread from Sparta through the ancient world, especially to Taranto and Rome. Double kingship, at Sparta as at Rome, was related to the cult of the Dioscuri.

By tradition the mentor of the two brothers was the centaur Chiron. As I will soon show, he represents the opposite zodiacal sign.

These are really two complementary aspects of the symbol of the horse.[7] The Dioscuri, who are very similar to the Hindu Açvins, are usually depicted as two young horsemen. And just as the Sanskrit verb *açwasimi*, related to their name, means "to breathe," the third zodiacal sign in western tradition is associated with the chest and the breath of life.[2]

It is also highly probable that the black mare-headed Demeter worshipped at Phigalia, whose wooden statue was consumed by fire and then restored by decree of the Delphic oracle, according to Pausanias (VIII, 42), relates to one of the meanings of this zodiacal sign.

The expedition of the Twins against Athens, where they freed their sister Helen (inhabitant of the neighboring sign of Cancer), who had been abducted by Theseus, describes the rivalry between the two Mercurial signs of Gemini and Virgo. They went on to occupy the deme of Aphidnae, a name meaning "country of the dead." According to tradition, the spouses of the Dioscuri were Hilaeria and Phoebe, two luminous daughters of Apollo[8] and two phases of the moon.

In a general way the historic rivalry of Sparta and Athens is curiously marked by the astrological meanings of their signs: the fraternal and egalitarian organization of Sparta is countered by Athenian intellectualism, more abstract and detached.

4. Cancer and the Moon

The zodiacal sign that comes next is Cancer, traditionally attributed to the moon. On the coast of Laconia were two neighboring cities, Helos ("the humid": Cancer is a water sign) and Acria. In the latter Pausanias was shown the temple and marble image of the Mother of the Gods. The Acrians believed that it was the most ancient sanctuary of this goddess in the Peloponnese.[9]

The island of Cythera is also in Cancer. Venus Cytheraea very probably began as a lunar goddess. A latecomer to Olympus, she was at first the voluptuous inhabitant of a southern isle. Moon or planet, she seems to have been born of the sea, but this is not necessarily true of all images of her. One example is a vase kept in Genoa where Eros is welcoming a goddess who is rising above a line that could be any horizon line.[10]

Helen sailed away from the port of Gytheum; according to the Pythagoreans, she was Helene-Selene, a symbol of the moon.[11]

It is known that both Pythian Apollo and Apollo Lykeios were worshipped at Argos (map 9, fig. 5 and fig. 38, p. 51). A characteristic coin shows a wolf between dolphins.[12]

This appears to be one example of a recurring phenomenon. This part of Greece adopted, for the sake of balance, or perhaps to avoid or compensate for certain malefic influences, a zodiacal symbolism belonging to the opposite sign. Argos is in fact situated in Cancer, opposite Capricorn, which is also known as the Wolf.[13]

In some Egyptian zodiacs, between the sun and Sothis, there was the sign Knem, symbolized by two tortoises.[14] The tortoise could therefore be the symbolic ancestor of Cancer, situated between Cancer and Leo. This zodiacal position in the diagram is that of the island of Aegina, whose symbol was the tortoise.

The tortoise appears again on coins from Lycia, which is located in a homologous position in the system centered on Sardis.

5. Leo, the Solar Sign

As mentioned before, the Leo-Aquarius axis, coinciding with the Mount Ida–Parnassus line, symbolizes the vital spirit of the Greek country as a whole and emphasizes the unity of the Creto-Mycenaean tradition. Leo is the supreme solar sign. The presence of three temples of Apollo and one of Helios at Hermione is rather significant in itself. I have already suggested that these temples should probably be seen in relation to the other great sanctuaries of Apollo. In the system now being looked at, Hermione would have acted as a secondary center.

Apollo Lykeios. L. de Ronchaud has written: "We cannot fail to recognize the god of light (λύχη) in Apollo Lykeios (Λὺχιος), whose cult was established on part of the coast of Asia Minor from very ancient times." According to a tradition similar to that of the Hyperboreans, the sanctuaries of Lycia, and principally the one at Patara, were the abode of the god for six months of the year:[15] "The cult of Apollo Lykeios probably came from Asia to Athens, Argos, Sicyon, Troezen, and all the way to Lycorea near Delphi. In these places the same ideas, through a sort of derivation, became the origin of fables in which the wolf (λύχος) symbolized winter being chased away by the sun."

The Wolf, as I have already said, is one of the names of the wintry sign of Capricorn.

The particular shape of the Peloponnese suggests that all of Argolis was considered to be associated with the sign of Leo, while under the protection of Hera.

If one assumes that the Leo sector really begins at the line from the sanctuary of Apollo Lithesios to Delphi, then Argos, Sicyon, and Troezen are well within that sign. This apparent anomaly may go back to a division of the zodiac into ten signs. The sign of Leo then began 15 degrees farther west.

De Ronchaud says further: "In some fables, the wolf seems to play in Greece the role of the lion in the Orient; in the legend of Danaus, we see it fighting the bull, a struggle which gave rise to the founding of the temple of Apollo Lykeios. Coins from Argos and Argolis bear from the beginning the image of a wolf whose head is sometimes surrounded by rays."

Lycia was also ruled by Leo, as will later be seen.

The Great Goddess of Troezen was an Artemis Protectress of Wild Animals, and the temple of Pythian Apollo in the island of Sikinos is related to this sign.

The result of all this seems to be that the ancients considered the solar influence of Leo to be blended with the lunar influence of Cancer in the eastern part of the island of Pelops.

The phenomenon of the precession of the equinoxes explains that, during successive periods, an area was first considered to be ruled by one zodiacal sign and later ruled by the following one.

The Lion and the Dog-days. Several coins from Ceos, the modern island of Kea, discovered at Julis and Carthaea, bear the head of Aristaeus on one side. He was, we are told, an agrarian god who introduced agriculture and bee-keeping to the islanders. On the reverse side is a leaping dog, representing Sirius and the dog-days (map 9, fig. 6). This, explains A. B. Brett, is because the deified hero had "stopped an epidemic that occurred under the influence of the constellation of the Dog."[16]

In reality the dog-days corresponded to the time when the risings and settings of Sirius coincided with those of the sun, which at that time was when the sun was in Leo.[17] In this system, Ceos is in that sign. The presence of the bee, a solar insect, on the same coins also relates to Leo, which is the house of the sun.

But here is something even plainer: at Ceos, one kilometer northeast of the capital, also called Ceos and which was the ancient Julis, there is an ancient colossal stone sculpture of a lion six meters long.[18] It seems highly probable that in antiquity there must have been a certain number of colossal statues meant to put a province or a region under the special protection of a zodiacal deity. Let me immediately cite the great Dioscuri of Cape Sounion. A systematic study of the writings of the ancient geographers from this point of view should yield other examples.

Certain cult statues, such as those of Athena in the Parthenon and on the summit of Mount Pentelicus, the Artemis of Ephesus, etc., also had zodiacal significance and will be discussed later from that angle. I will also delve into the lion of Ceos and even devote a whole chapter to it (chap. 12).

Before going on to the next sign, let me mention that the island of Hydra is situated in the place belonging to Hydra in a terrestrial projection of the constellations with Delphi as the pole.

6. Athens, Delos and the Sign of Virgo

It is for this sign that the most striking and impressive system of correspondences can be established.

For one thing, this is because the goddess Artemis, born at Delos, was Apollo's sister and also because the cults of Athena and Apollo were connected. The relationship between Athena and Virgo is already sufficiently eloquent (map 9, fig. 7). Delos is no doubt related to the star Spica, whose name means "Ear of Grain," in the constellation Virgo. This would explain one of the original names of the island: Asteria.[19] The Delphi-Athens-Delos line, extended southeast, intersects the island of Rhodes at Camiros, site of the island's most ancient sanctuary of Apollo.

Both at Athens and Delos one finds a trio of goddesses associated with the three decans of the sign of Virgo. This division into three exists for virtually all the signs of the zodiac. It is very obvious in the case of Virgo because the sign is so important. Some authors like Wilamowitz are surprised to see "agrarian" deities in a sterile and windswept island like Delos,[20] but this becomes understandable when they are envisioned as astral deities. The very nature of Delos as sacred earth and the prohibition of giving birth or dying there are also characteristic of the sign of Virgo.

At Athens the three virgins were named Aglauros, Herse, and Pandrosos. They were three from the beginning, I believe, not a pair who gave birth to a third, contrary to what is sometimes claimed.[21]

A rather late coin from Athens shows a particularly enlightening array of symbols (map 9, fig. 8). Next to Athena's owl stands a nude male figure, seen from the front, believed in all probability to be the cult statue of Delian Apollo. In his right hand, he is holding a *kalathos* (fruit or bread basket) containing statuettes of the three Charites and, in his left hand, a bow. Two little winged griffins are standing on either side. The "Hyperborean" griffins were sacred to Apollo and guarded his treasures.[22]

This coin in fact seems to be a picture of the colossal statue of Apollo at Delos, created by Tectaeus and Angelion, two sculptors of the Cretan school. The Charites were shown holding musical instruments.[23]

As already mentioned, Prasiae was the little port on the coast of Attica whence the sacred ship Theoris sailed for Delos every year. I wonder whether at least one of the colossal statues of Porto Rafti might not have been an Athena (see note 5 of chap. 1).

7. Libra, Harmonia, and Thebes

The sanctuary of Libra is Mount Ptoon in Boeotia. It is on the latitude of Delphi and has affinities and similarities with it. In some traditions Ursa Major and Ursa Minor were compared with the two plates of a Balance, suggesting another analogy between the pole and the sign of Libra proper.[24]

Libra is a "Venusian" sign. The prominent role played by a heifer in the legend of Thebes associates the two Venusian signs of Taurus and Libra, which was fulfilled in the marriage of Cadmus and Harmonia. The Athenians had Athena, so their Theban rivals adopted Harmonia, said to be the daughter or spouse of Cadmus, and they stamped their coins with her image[25] (map 9, fig. 9). At the time of the Theban hegemony, their coins showed an owl with open wings in imitation of Athens. The Theban Aphrodite should probably be identified with Harmonia to some degree. Pausanias saw three wooden images of her which were said to have been carved from the figureheads of Cadmus's ships.[26]

The rivalry between Attica and Boeotia can be seen as a conflict between the Mercurial sign of Virgo and the Venusian sign of Libra, more sensual, more material, but very balanced.

In astrological terms Harmonia also represents the result of the coupling of forces from the opposition of Ares and Aphrodite (Aries-Libra). "The Pythagoreans," writes J. Carcopino, "were to legitimize . . . the adultery of Ares and Aphrodite, as told by Homer, by the birth of the daughter of the guilty couple, Harmonia."[27]

The sphinx was the ancient guardian of the sign of Libra. Its presence on coins from Chios (map 9, fig. 10) is explainable when one considers that in the Delphic system the northern part of the island is in Libra, since the Delphi-Ptoon-Sardis parallel intersects the island. One would rather expect this island to be part of the system centered on Delos, whose existence will soon be revealed. The presence of the sphinx on its money must also indicate a colonization of the island by the Boeotians. This historical point is confirmed by much supportive evidence studied by M. Sakellariou in *La Migration grecque en Ionie*. By virtue of the association of Ptoon and Thebes with Libra and the autumnal equinox, a mountain near Thebes bears the name Mount Sphinx.

A Historical Confirmation: Daphnae. It is known that the Delphic oracle commanded that a temple of Apollo be built on Mount Aegaleos in Attica;[28] this is the site of Daphnae.

Had this temple not fit into my proposed diagrams, the whole exercise would have, from my point of view, become questionable. But it is easy to see that Daphnae is a secondary point, in the sign of Virgo, that completes the studied alignments.

The site of Daphnae is determined by a right angle to the Delos-Athens-Delphi line struck from Hermione.

The sanctuary is placed at one of the angles of a rectangle of which two other angles are at Hermione and Argos, respectively, while the Argos-Ptoon line forms the northwest side of the rectangle.

An extension of the Hermione-Argos-Cleitor line goes to Leucas, the vernal point, and the Cleitor-Delphi line, parallel to the Hermione-Athens line, also forms a rectangle with the aforementioned lines.

8. Scorpio or the Eagle

For astrological, historical, and geographical reasons, the signs of Libra and Scorpio first appear as a unit. I have already said that opposing signs were really pairs of forces, simultaneously antagonistic and complementary, and for the astronomical reason mentioned earlier (note 13), there may be interesting exchanges of symbols between them. I have just mentioned something of this nature in speaking of the birth of Harmonia and the role played by the sign of Taurus in the origin of Thebes.

In Greek, Scorpio was called the Claws of the Scorpion, but the earlier symbol for this sign was the Eagle.[29] Since the north of the island of Euboea was in this sign, the city of Chalcis adopted the symbol of an eagle snatching away a serpent, which often appears on its coins (map 9, fig. 11). The same symbol appears on coins from Olympia, located in the opposing sign of Taurus[30] (map 9, fig. 12). The zodiacal eagle then became identified with the eagle of Zeus.

9. The Land of the Centaurs: Chiron the Sagittarian

In antiquity Mount Pelion was called the land of the centaurs. Near the summit of the mountain a cave known as "the lair of Chiron" may still be visited.

Nordic father of the arts and sciences, the good centaur had been the student of Apollo and Artemis. Among his disciples were not only Castor and Pollux, but also Cephalus and Asclepius. The sanctuary of Pagasae probably represents the sign of Sagittarius. The coins of Thessaly were often stamped with horses, which refer both to the famous local breed of horses and to the lingering memory of the centaurs. Many of the coins show scenes of bullfighting. This word seems to be the origin of the name centaur, which may derive from *centein tauros*, "to stab the bull."[31]

When the Magnesians began minting coins, these portrayed the centaur Chiron holding a branch.[32]

The general symbolism of this sign associates it with the period preceeding the winter solstice.[33]

The sign of Sagittarius is "Jupiterian." The ship of the Argonauts, the Argo, and the legend of Jason were symbolically associated with this part of Greece. Like for the sign of Taurus, it would appear that the "Jupiterian" signs were also under the influence of Hera, since Thessaly was attributed to her.

10. Capricorn and Hyperborea

This "Saturnine" sign seems to be associated with the origin of several important features of Greek religion. Mount Olympus, domain of the gods, and the woodland sanctuary of Tempe, whence Delphi originated, were in Capricorn.

According to Eratosthenes, "Capricorn resembles Aegipan, his father; he has the legs of a goat and horns.

He was given this honor because he had been suckled with Jupiter, according to Epimenides in his *History of Crete,* and he was with Jupiter on Mount Ida when the latter left to wage war against the Titans." The theater of this battle was Olympus. The text I have just quoted is a clear reference to the Mount Ida–Hyperborea line and also establishes a symbolic equivalence between Mount Ida and Olympus.

So far as the origins of the Delphic oracle are concerned, several texts must be interpreted allegorically. First is a passage from Diodorus of Sicily:

> In ancient times, the oracle was discovered by goats, which is why the Delphians still prefer to sacrifice goats before a consultation. The discovery, it is said, happened like this:
>
> There was a cleft in the earth, where the *adyton* of the sanctuary is now located. Goats were grazing around it, Delphi not yet being inhabited. Every time a goat came close to the edge and peered down, it began to leap in a curious manner and to bleat in a strange voice.

> Surprised at the wonder, the curious goatherd approached the cleft, and the same thing happened to him. The goats were in fact behaving like humans who fall prey to the phenomenon of 'enthusiasm," and the goatherd began to predict the future."

It seems highly probable that this very unlikely story really refers to northern Greece and especially to Tempe, ruled by the sign of Capricorn, whence came the oracular tradition.

Celestially, the constellation of the Arrow, of which Eratosthenes also speaks, is located in Capricorn.

"Apollo made it to avenge Asclepius against the Cyclops, who had forged lighting for Zeus. They then hid the arrow in the land of the Hyperboreans, where the temple of feathers is also located." That the part of Greece attributed to Capricorn was associated with the legends of Apollo's stay in Hyperborea is to be expected because of its geographical position. As for the temple of feathers that so strongly fascinates the Hellenists,[34] might it not be the celestial temple where the "language of the birds" was spoken, another name for the "phonetic cabala" so dear to Plato?

In chapter 18 I will look at the foundation oracle of Aegae (Edessa), whose coins are stamped with a goat (map 9, fig. 13). The city is situated in Capricorn in relation to Delphi.

11. Aquarius

"Some think he is Ganymede," said Eratosthenes. For Aquarius we are in the presence of a religious tradition more ancient than Delphi, probably part of an earlier cycle but making the transition with the historical era, which is better attested. Instead of a great sanctuary of Apollo, one finds the sanctuary of Zeus at Dodona, which probably succeeded an oracle of Saturn. The sign of Aquarius is "Saturnian." The great oracle of the dead recently discovered at Thesprotia above Lake Arethusa, not far from the mouth of the Acheron, is also in this sign and significantly placed. All the known coins of Epirus have been assembled in a recent study.[35] It is interesting that most of them bear images either of Zeus and Dione or the attributes of a supreme deity. What is more, the coins of Elaea (map 9, fig. 14), a city not far from the mouth of the Acheron, bear Pegasus on one side and Poseidon's trident on the other, an intriguing combination of a symbol that represents Aquarius and the cult of the horse god.

Pegasus, Bellerophon and the Leo-Aquarius axis. It is well known that Pegasus is the symbol of the city of Corinth. A winged horse, the "colt," appears on almost all of the city's coins as well as on those of its colonies of Ambracia, Leucas, and Anactoria (map 9, fig. 15). This is a very beautiful hieroglyph for the sign of Aquarius. Pegasus was said to have been born in the far west, which corresponds to the position of the constellation Pegasus in relation to the zodiac. The very name derives from πήγη, spring, and the celestial animal is associated with wells and fountains. Both the spring of Hippocrene on Mount Helicon and one near Troezen gushed forth from beneath his hoof. The meeting place of Pegasus and Bellerophon, a solar hero, was none other than the spring of Pirene in Corinth.

Now, Corinth is situated on the Leo-Aquarius axis, and the two other springs mentioned are in the sign of Leo. Ambracia, which had also adopted the symbol of Pegasus, is in Aquarius. This is a significant example of the play of opposing and complementary signs.

According to Strabo (*Geog*. 7.7.60), Ambracia was founded by Gorgos, son of Cypselus, tyrant of Corinth.

Contrary to what the name may suggest, Aquarius is an air sign, which is manifest in Pegasus's wings.

I also believe that the association of Dodona with the sign of Aquarius may help explain the epithet *Naios* given to Zeus on almost all the inscriptions found at Dodona.[36] This would be the same association as in the name *Selloi,* which would derive from a poetic word, *Helos,* meaning water.

The sacred oak of Dodona may symbolize the world tree and the time when the solstitial axis coincided with the Leo-Aquarius direction.

But words like *Naios* and *Helos* must be understood in the purely symbolic sense, since Aquarius is really an air sign: this sheds some light on the type of divination by the sound of the cauldron (solar symbol) or by the voice of the Pleiades.[37]

A passage of Pliny describes an intriguing fountain at Dodona. It gave an "icy water" which, among other miraculous properties, could rekindle extinguished torches when they were dipped into it.[38] Could this be a simple riddle: the fluid that can rekindle fire is fresh air!

What is more, the legends transmitted by Herodotus about the Egyptian origin of the oracle at Dodona must be understood in connection with those of the origins of Delphi. A line from Thebes of Egypt to Dodona would be almost parallel to the Mount Ida–Parnassus line.

The island of Corfu (Corcyra) is almost entirely in the sign of Aquarius.

Some coins from Corfu bear an amphora, others a cow suckling a calf (map 9, fig. 16). I see this as an excellent expression of the spiritual meaning of Aquarius, which dispenses and broadcasts knowledge.[39] It is well known that there were close connections between the people of Corfu and the oracle of Dodona.

12. Pisces. Cassiopeia

Since Leucas was sacred to Aries and most of Corfu was in Aquarius, only a very small section of the Greek territory could belong to Pisces. One may therefore assume that in antiquity Dodona combined the functions of both signs, which is easily justified, since the sign of Pisces is "Jupiterian."

This small Piscean area was nevertheless significantly known as Cassopaea, and it included the city of Cassiope, from the name Cassiopeia, the constellation situated before Pisces in relation to the pole.

♦

Having thus divided the Greek territory into twelve parts with Delphi as the center and having studied them in detail, I realized that I was in the presence of a consistent and coherent system of references, each area of ancient Greece having been sacred to a sign of the zodiac.

I then had to consider how far such a system could have extended, and if possible to research its origin and fields of application. The scope of my research was to progressively widen and cover many aspects of Greek life and art.

13. A TEXT OF PLATO'S

The division of historical Greece into the twelve signs of the zodiac, which had thus been clearly revealed, had quite probably left traces in certain texts.

The work of P. Saintyves, *Deux Mythes évangéliques: les douze apôtres et les soixante-douze disciples* (1938), contributed some important information.On the question in general, he wrote:

> The influence of the stars in the sky, and especially of the twelve signs that mark the path of the moon and the sun, could be enhanced and made entirely benevolent if the earth itself was arranged as a reflection of the heavens. The division of a state, population and territory, into twelve sectors was an expression of reverence for the gods of the zodiac, the twelve great celestial deities, and it would surely attract their blessings. That this was true in Chaldea, at least towards the year 2000 B.C., can hardly be doubted.[40]

All the peoples who either adopted the Chaldaean zodiac or established a set of twelve signs by imitation divided their countries into twelve sectors, which were governed by twelve chieftains.

With regard to Greece, an especially important text for my purpose is *The Laws* of Plato (Book V). Here is the essential passage:

> Next, the founder must see that his city is placed as nearly as possible in the center of the territory, after selecting a site possessed of the other favorable conditions for his purpose; (it will not be difficult to discover or to state them). Then he must divide his city into twelve parts; but first he should establish and enclose a sanctuary of Hestia, Zeus, and Athena—which he will call the citadel—from which he will draw his twelve divisions of the city and its whole territory. Equality of

> the twelve regions should be secured by making those of good soil small and those of worse soil larger. He should then make a division into five thousand and forty allotments. Each of these, again, should be bisected and two half-sections, a nearer and a remoter paired together to form an allotment, one which is contiguous to the city with one on the border. . . . Of course, the legislator must also divide the population into twelve sections, constructing these sections so as to be as nearly as possible on an equality in respect of their other property, of the whole of which he will have made a careful record. Next he will be at pains to assign the twelve divisions to twelve gods, naming each section after the god to whom it has been alloted and consecrated, and calling it a tribe. Further, the twelve segments of the city must be made on the same lines as the division of the territory in general, and each citizen must have two houses, one nearer the center of the state and the other nearer the border. . . .
>
> Our immediate concern, now that we have resolved on the division into twelve parts, must be precisely to see in what conspicuous fashion these twelve parts, admitting, as they do, such a multitude of further divisions, with the subsequent groups which arise from them, down to the five thousand and forty individuals—this will give us our brotherhoods, wards, and parishes, as well as our divisions of battle and columns of route, not to mention our currency and measures of capacity, dry and liquid, and of weight—to see, I say, how all these details must be legally determined so as to fit in and harmonize with each other.[41]

The number 5040, which is so important in Plato's system of divisions, is the product of the first seven numbers: "The whole integer series, of course, admits division by any number and with any quotient, while our 5040 can be divided . . . into fifty-nine quotients and no more, ten of them, from unity upwards, being successive."[42] And further on (*The Laws*, VI) the philosopher goes on to say that although 5040 is indivisible by 11, 5038 is divisible by 11 and by 458. In terms of the relationships of 5040 with astrology, it has the advantages of being divisible by 7 (the seven planets), by 12 (the twelve signs), by 36 (the thirty-six decans), by 72 (the 72 spirits), and by 360 (the degrees of the zodiac).[43]

Plato writes in *The Laws*, Book V:

> Whether a new foundation is to be created from the outset or an old one restored, in the matter of gods and their sanctuaries—what temples must be founded in a given community, and to what gods or spirits they should be dedicated—no man of sense will presume to disturb convictions inspired from Delphi, Dodona, the oracle of Ammon, or by old traditions of any kind of divine appearances or reported divine revelations.[44]

In *The Laws* and in *The Republic,* Plato refers to the authority of Delphi and does so repeatedly. It is therefore highly probable that his plan of the ideal society was in many ways a later codification of what had been an ancient practice.[45] I believe this to be especially true of the division of the country into twelve sectors that corresponded to the gods of the zodiac.

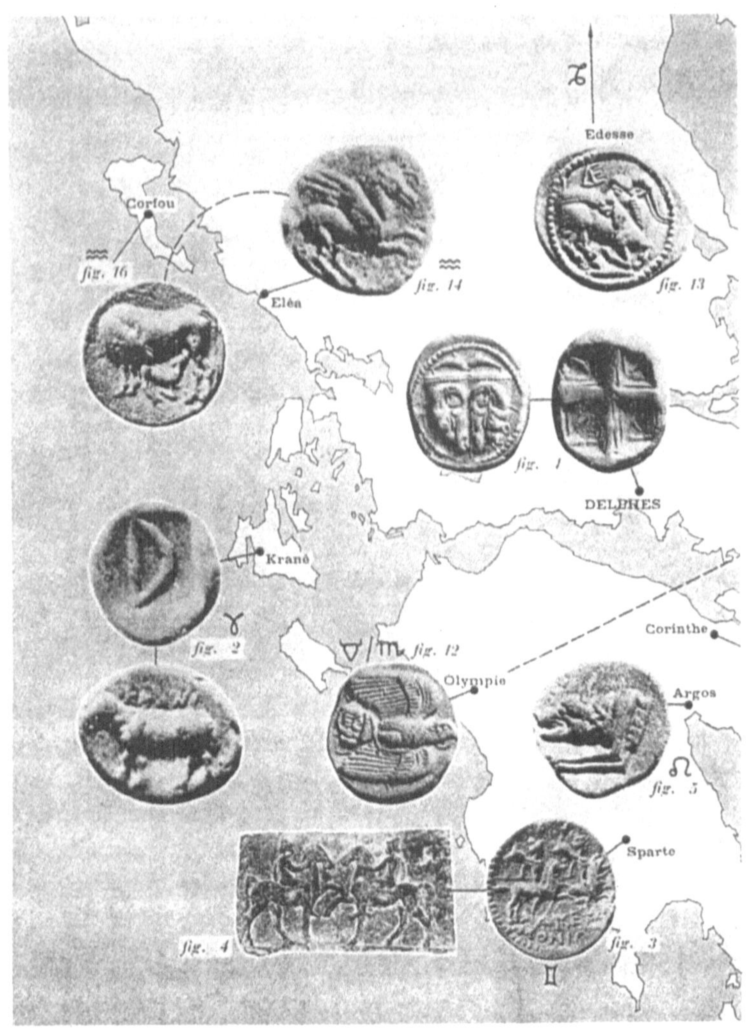

Map 9. *The Zodiacal Wheel Centered on Delphi.*
Figure 1. *Coin from Delphi: dolphins and heads of rams.*
Figure 2. *Coin from Cranii (Cephallenia): ram and ram hoof.*
Figure 3. *Coin from Sparta: the Dioscuri on horseback.*
Figure 4. *Stele of the Dioscuri (Museum of Sparta).*
Figure 5. *Coin from Argos: wolf.*
Figure 12. *Coin from Olympia: eagle and serpent.*
Figure 13. *Coin from Edessa (Aegae): goat.*
Figure 14. *Coin from Elaea: Pegasus.*
Figure 16. *Coin from Corfu: milking cow.*

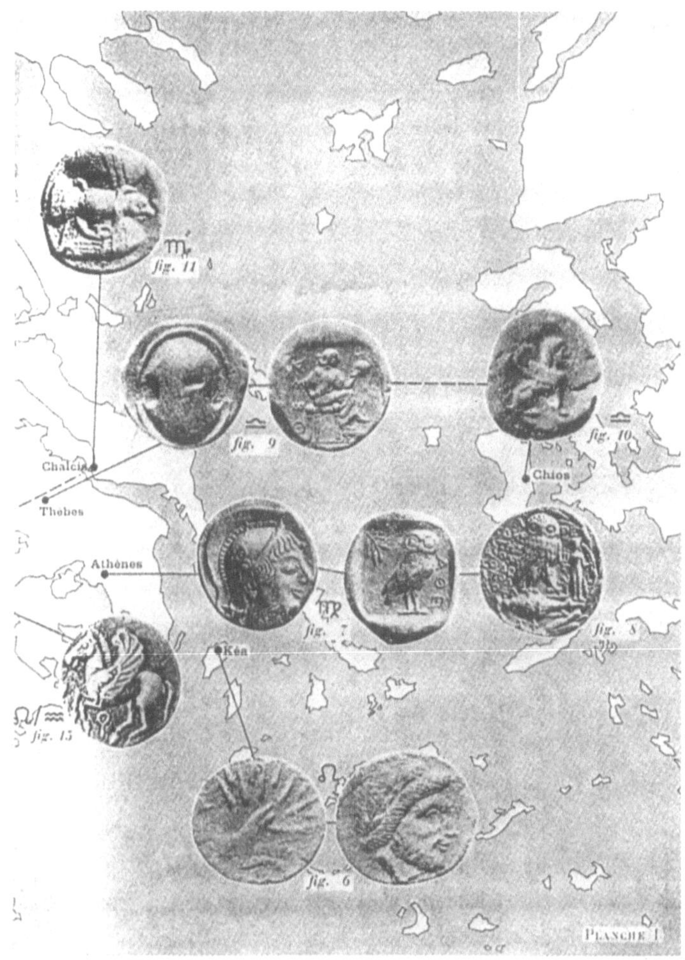

Map 9 (continued). ***The Zodiacal Wheel Centered on Delphi.***
Figure 6. *Coin from Ceos: dog barking to Sirius and head of Aristaeus.*
Figure 7. *Coin from Athens: head of Athena and owl.*
Figure 8. *Coin from Athens: owl and statue of Delian Apollo holding the three Virgins of Delos.*
Figure 9. *Coin from Thebes: Harmonia and the shield of Ares.*
Figure 10. *Coin from Chios: sphinx.*
Figure 11. *Coin from Chalcis: eagle and serpent.*
Figure 15. *Coin from Corinth: Pegasus.*

Chapter 3

The System Centered on Delos

Asteria, perfumed with incense, around you the islands have formed a circle like a chorus of dancers.

—Callimachus, *Hymn to Delos*

1. The Zodiacal Division

As has just been seen, Plato attributed equal authority to the oracles of Delphi and Ammon. Now, Delos and the oracle of Ammon in the oasis of Siwa are on the same meridian, which forms a north-south axis. This axis seems to have played the same role in the Aegean islands as that of Cape Taenarum–Delphi–Olympus in continental Greece. That is, it represented the world axis in this part of the ancient world during a certain period.

This obviously implies that the problem of longitudes had been resolved far earlier than is generally believed, in an empirical manner. A series of proofs, which I will merely observe, will be given to support this statement.[1]

Let me immediately say that the temple of Apollo Lithesios on the southern coast of Cape Malea lies exactly on the Delphi-Ammoneion line, as though its primary meaning were to indicate the southeast direction.

Delos itself was conceived as the island of the rising sun, hence its symbolic association with gold, emphasized by the *Hymn* of Callimachus. Its coins show the Apollo line and a delta (map 10, fig. 17).

A system of division into twelve zodiacal signs with the center at Delos is described in the following table (map 2):

1. Aries: Hermione (ancient temple of Helios described by Pausanias). Syros: Delion to the north of Hermopolis.
2. Taurus: Cape Epidelium (sanctuary of Apollo).
3. Gemini: Dictynnaion of Crete (there was probably a temple of Apollo in close proximity).
4. Cancer: Temple of Delian Apollo at Paros; Delion of Naxos.
5. Leo: Delion of Minoa (island of Amorgos).
6. Virgo: Delion of Nisyros (on the Delphi-Delos-Camiros line): Delion of Cos. Delion of Halicarnassus.
7. Libra: Cult of Delian Apollo at Ortygia near Ephesus.

8. Scorpio: Temple of Apollo at Claros.
9. Sagittarius: Temple of Delian Apollo at Phanaeus in Chios. Probable temple at Lesbos. Clazomenae, on the coast of Anatolia, whose coins were stamped with a swan.
10. Capricorn: Temple of Hephaestia at Lemnos. (Perhaps another unknown sanctuary on the south coast?)
11. Aquarius: Cult of Delian Apollo at Marathon; Delion near Euripus opposite Eretria; Delion of Eretria; Island of Andros ("Man").
12. Pisces: Temple of Apollo at Prasiae; Delion of Phaleron.

In considering these main sanctuaries, one finds in nine cases out of twelve Delia whose exact locations are either known or which are documented by texts or inscriptions. These may be subdivided into three groups:

A. The sanctuary of Cape Epidelium (2), the Delion of Euripus (11) and Prasiae (12) are in continental Greece or in the Peloponnese. (To these may be added, secondarily, Marathon, Phaleron, Hermione, as well as Tegyra of Boeotia, associated with a Mount Delos at Lake Copais.)
B. Two sanctuaries are on the Ionian coast: Ortygia near Ephesus 7 and Claros. (8)
C. Seven Delia (1, 3–6, 9, 10) are located on islands of the Aegean.

2. The Signs

a) Ram-Whale Sector: Seriphos. The staters of Seriphos (circa 550–420 B.C.) (fig. 8) that depict a frog probably had an astral significance. I think that this frog stands either for a star in the constellation of the Whale or Marine Monster (Cetus), or else for the whole constellation in miniature. An Arab name for Beta Ceti is *Al Difdi' al Thānī* or *Difta*, translated into Latin as *Rana Secunda* (Formalhaut of southern Pisces being the "first frog"). The "marine monster" would have become a simple frog, which is not without irony; however, in Greek the word βάτραχος also designates the frog-fish, an ugly fish with a gigantic head.

b) Taurus: the Sanctuary of Cape Epidelium, Boeae. Pausanias says that the wooden image of Apollo he saw in this sanctuary had formerly been at Delos. It was supposed to have miraculously been washed there on the waves of the sea, into which it had been cast by a barbarian during the sack of the island by Menophanes, an officer of Mithridates.[2]

This is very probably a pious legend concocted to establish some connection between Delos and this sanctuary.

A hare (the constellation of the Hare is in Taurus) was associated with the foundation legend of Boeae, a city whose name means "bull", which exactly marks the 0 degree Taurus axis in the system centered on Delos.

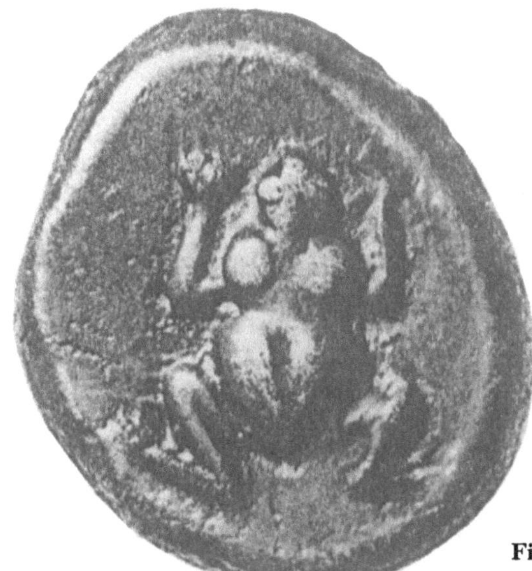

Figure 8. *Stater of Seriphos (circa 550–420 B.C.).*

c) Siphnos and the Eagle. Coins and local legends here again bring confirmations. It is interesting to see the process of opposition coming systematically into play, which consisted in adopting the symbol of the opposing sign. This may have been a form of conjuring magic meant to attenuate the malefic aspect of influence of a zodiacal sign by countering it with the influence of its opposite. Certain rivalries between the inhabitants of the islands may also have played a role in the choice of symbols. Thus the island of Siphnos, which was situated in Taurus, adopted the eagle of the opposing sign, as did Olympia[3] (map 10, fig. 18).

d) The Dictynnaion. Dicte was a Cretan nymph, a follower of Artemis, similar to Britomartis. As the "Artemis of the Net," she was also identified with Artemis herself.

The legend of Britomartis, who, pursued by Minos, threw herself into the sea at Cape Psacum and was caught in fishermen's nets, to which she owed her name Dictynna, may recall an ancient ritual dive, humanized like at Leucas. Britomartis had a sanctuary at Sparta under the name Artemis Issoria (the Lady of the Lake).[4] At Aegina she was identified with the goddess Aphaia.[5] Britomartis was the descendant of Carmanor by Eubulus, and her parents were Carme and Zeus. Carmanor, a Cretan priest, had received Apollo and Artemis after the slaying of the Python and had purified them, which indicates that Artemis was substituted for an ancient Mother Goddess. Now, the known documents show that such a Cretan goddess was already known as Britomartis.[6] Therefore, it would have been she who, from a Mother Goddess, was transformed into an eternal virgin, a moon goddess identifiable with Artemis. Since the western part of Crete is in Cancer in the Delphic system, it is understandable that such a goddess could also have reigned at Cythera and in the southwestern part of the Peloponnese before being in her turn supplanted by Aphrodite[7] (see p. 15).

What is more, there was a sanctuary of Britomartis at Delos.[8] The sacred island is the point where the "Mistress of Beasts" of Anatolia and the Britomartis of Crete merged into a single deity. This figure was to become the Greek Artemis, who thus was truly born at Delos.[9]

These thoughts suggest that there probably also was a sanctuary of Apollo near the Dictynnaion. The temple site, on a high peninsula of difficult access, is probably holding some surprises in store for us.

e) Cancer: Paros and the Goat. On some coins from Paros appears a kneeling goat. This may indicate mastery over Capricorn, the sign opposing Cancer, where Paros is located.[10]

From my point of view, the very frequent images of the octopus and the spiral (single or double) in Cretan art are connected with the fact that most of the island was in Cancer in the Delian system.

THE CASE OF SANTORINI. Herodotus (IV, 147–48) repeats three times in a row that the earlier name for the island of Thera (Santorini) was Callista. This must indicate that the island was in symbolic relationship with Ursa Major (Callisto). This only has meaning in relation to the Delphic system, where the island is located in the sign of Virgo. In addition, there is a remarkable right triangle defined by Brauron-Cave of the Bear-Thera (Callista).

The name Thera harks back to θερία, "summer," a word found in Pindar and Herodotus which also means the heat of summer. This corresponds well with the position of the island in the Delian system, just south of Delos in Cancer, a sign of the summer solstice, and with the volcanic nature of the island.

This is fresh confirmation of the greater age of the Delphic system in relation to the Delian.

There is no reason to dwell on the name of a supposed eponymous hero, who was obviously a later invention.

LATONA. Latona and her sanctuary of Lato in eastern Crete seem associated with Cancer. The quadrilateral between Prasiae-Lato-Xanthus-Apollonia (map 2) joins two sanctuaries of Apollo and two sites sacred to his mother. According to legend, after being transformed into a she-wolf, Latona spent some time in Lycia, which is a possible origin of the province's name.[11]

All the places mentioned in the *Homeric Hymn to Apollo* (vv. 30 ff.) having to do with Latona's quest to find a place to give birth to Apollo and Artemis are located around the perimeter of the Aegean Sea and are part of the zodiacal wheel centered on Delos. That no site in the Peloponnese is mentioned in the hymn has often been commented on. The cycle of Delos is also the cycle of Latona.

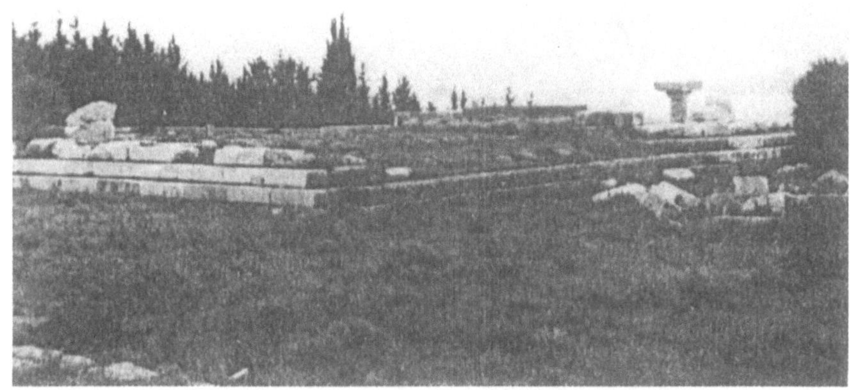

Figure 9. *The terrace of the sanctuary of Delian Apollo at the Asclepeion of Cos. (Photo J.R.)*

f) Sign of Virgo. Besides the Delia of Nisyros and Cos (fig. 9), the sanctuary of Athena at Lindos must be associated with Virgo in the Delian system.

g) The Stag and the Autumnal Equinox. The word for deer (*elaphe*) was at first a doublet of the word for bull, from *aleph*, which meant the beginning of the year. Pausanias (VI, 20) says that at the spring equinox, in the month of Elaphios, the Elaeans made sacrifice to Kronos on the summit of a mountain whose name meant "time."[12]

But it seems probable that, because of a symbolic equivalence of the equinoxes, the deer became the hieroglyph for the autumnal equinox in calendars beginning at that time of year. I believe that this would explain the presence of the deer on the coins of Miletus or Ephesus (map 10, fig. 19), where in fact it would be equivalent to the sign of Libra. To my knowledge no one has yet made this deduction. (It is also true that no one had seen that Pegasus represented Aquarius!) The deer will be seen again in studying the symbols of the directions of space and the seasonal variations.

The Theban sphinx, another symbol of the equinox, appears on the coins of Chios[13] (map 9, fig. 10).

h) The Taurus-Scorpio Axis: Orion. The myth of Orion, associated with the Delian system, is studied further on, so to avoid unnecessary repetition, I will simply refer the reader to chapter 11, section 5.

i) Sagittarius. Centaurs appear on coins from Chios[14] and Thracian cities[15] (map 10, fig. 20).

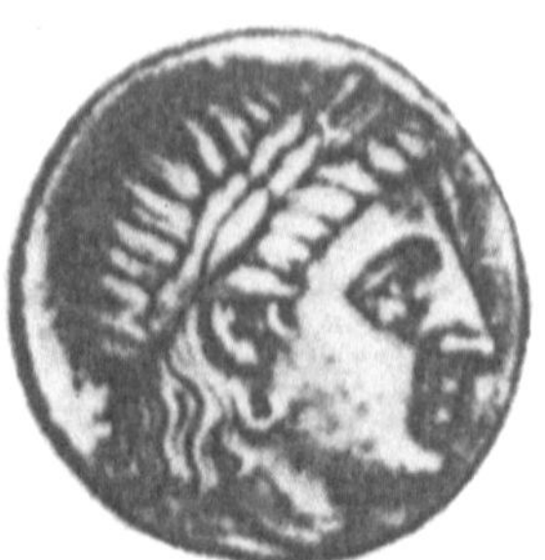

Figure 10.
Hemidrachma of Mitylene.

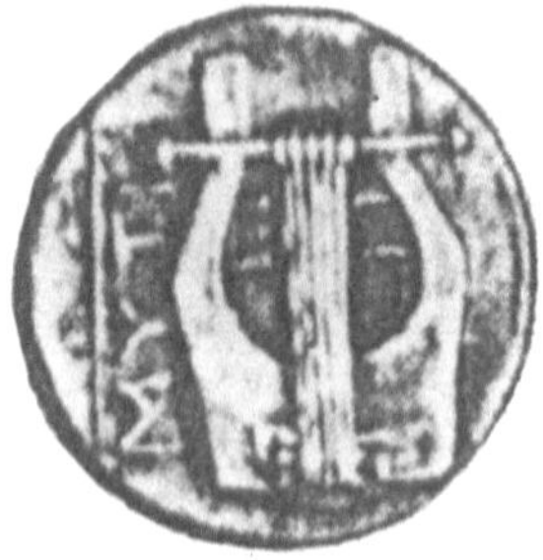

The coins of Lesbos were stamped with a lyre by reference, it is sometimes said, to the myth of Orpheus, but it also corresponds to this part of the zodiac in the Delian system. The head of Apollo wreathed in laurels appears on the hemidrachma here reproduced (fig. 10).

j) Capricorn: Scyros and Lemnos. The designs of the few remaining coins of Scyros (the island, under the political domination of Athens, does not seem to have had an independent mint) suggest its geographical position in the Delian system.[16] Appearing on them (map 10, fig. 21) two goats, back to back, the heads turned toward the center, represent the zodiacal sign of Capricorn. Between them is a five-lobed fig leaf; below, a horizontal line represents the earth. On the reverse side, a star symbol emphasizes the astrocosmic significance of the coins' symbolism.

In the Delian system, Scyros is situated in Capricorn. The fig leaf stands for the mystical tree and suggests the south-north axis of Ammoneion-Delos-Lemnos that unites the three worlds. This axis passes to the east of the island, however, so the leaf could have been placed to the right of the goats. The designer may have put it in the center for aesthetic reasons. Finally, the earth line corresponds to the latitude of Delphi, which passes south of the island. The symbolism as a whole indeed describes the position of the island of Scyros.

The authenticity of these coins has sometimes been questioned. According to Babelon,[17] the larger pieces may not be genuine and were struck in imitation of the smaller. Whatever the case, the important thing here is that the type in itself is certainly authentic, because it is highly unlikely that a forger could have combined the symbols in such a significant way by chance.

It has also been suggested that the coins be attributed to Camiros because of the presence of the fig leaf. This suggestion is interesting, since Camiros is on another north-south axis which will be described later on. But the presence of the earth line only has meaning if the coins come from an island north of the latitude of Delphi. These coins, however, would describe the position of Lemnos even better, since that island is bisected by the south-north axis, which fits the design more closely. I therefore conclude that these curious coins come from either Scyros or Lemnos.

The symbolic association of Lemnos with Capricorn and the winter solstice explains an enigmatic verse of the *Iliad* (XIV, 230), where it is said that Hypnos (sleep), the brother of death, lived at Lemnos. People, whose lives are ruled by the sun, sleep the longest during the period of the winter solstice. This time is also associated with the gateway of the gods and an honorable death. The griffins on the coins of Abdera[18] are associated with the north. These are the fabulous animals of Apollo, guardians of the country of the Arimaspi, beyond which lies Hyperborea.

k) Sign of Aquarius. Two cities near the Aquarius direction in relation to Delos stamped their coins with a cow suckling a calf similar to the image on some coins of Corfu: Olynthos in Chalcidice[19] (map 10, fig. 22) and Carystos in the south of Euboea.[20] Therma (the modern Thessalonica) was situated on the Leo-Aquarius axis.

I was able to verify on site that the altar of Apollo at Pagasae is orientated to the southeast. The angle of its axis in relation to north is 145 degrees. It is therefore turned towards Delos. This is also the place where the events of Hesiod's *Shield* occurred.

The myth of Aristaeus[21] establishes many relationships among an ancient eight-part division centered on Delos, the twelve-part zodiacal division at Delos, and the system centered on Delphi.

Of the division into eight there visibly remains the line joining Pagasae, Delos, and Minoa of Amorgos (where there was a sanctuary of Pythian Apollo).

The very name of the island of Andros means "man," which symbolizes Aquarius. This correspondence is confirmed by staters from the island, dating from the seventh and sixth centuries, where an amphora appears (fig. 11). In Barclay V. Head's *Historia Numorum* (p. 482), one sees that in the fourth century the coins of Andros bore images of either Dionysus himself or his symbols, thyrsos, cantharus, panther, and thus once again Aquarius in the system of Delos.

There is some question as to whether the most ancient coins decorated with an amphora should be attributed to Andros or to Kea (Ceos). The attribution to Andros is much more probable because, as will be seen (p. 129), the coins of Kea have symbols rather of Leo, which mark the attachment to Delphi.

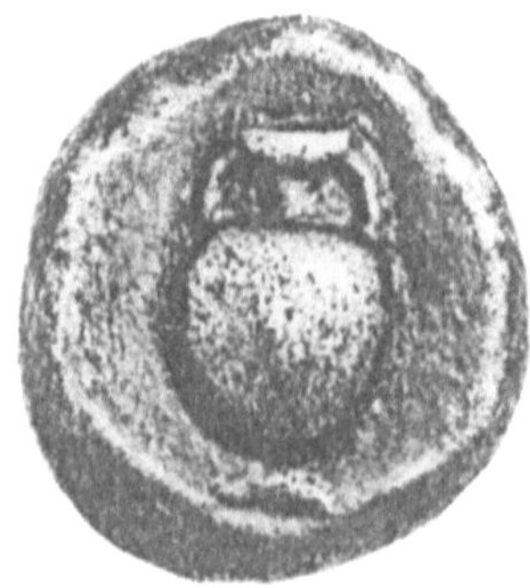

Figure 11. *Stater of Andros (seventh century).*

3. Delphi and Delos

I conclude from all these observations that there was an Ammoneion-Delos axis as well as a system whose omphalos was the island of Apollo. This system, perhaps slightly more ancient than that of Delphi, is closely connected with it. The relay between the two centers is created by means of the Camiros-Delos-Delphi line. The latitude of the Hermione-Delos-Didyma solar line also establishes communication between the two zodiacal wheels.

What is more, the Prasiae-Pagasae line cuts the north coast of Boeotia at Delium and the Pagasae-Delphi-Prasiae triangle is a right triangle. The Hermione-Eleusis line, parallel to the Delphi-Pagasae line, also finishes at Delium.

This place therefore seems to have acted, together with Prasiae, the port of departure of the Delian Theores, as a relay point between Delphi and Delos. Strabo says that a sanctuary of Apollo was located there, which duplicated the one at Delos.[22]

4. Delphi and Sardis

Camiros of Rhodes, Claros, and Ortygia were the probable relay points between the zodiacal wheel of Delos and that of Sardis, which will be studied in the next chapter.

The Corridor of Latona. The places where Latona was held in highest veneration define what may be called the corridor of Latona, marked in the northwest by Eretria and Delium, and in the southeast by Halicarnassus and Cos. The corridor follows a direction parallel to the beginning of Virgo in both the Delian and Delphic systems and finishes at Xanthus and Patara. This may be compared with what is known of the Lycian origin of the goddess. The Lato direction from Crete to Ephesus defines a right angle to this corridor.[23]

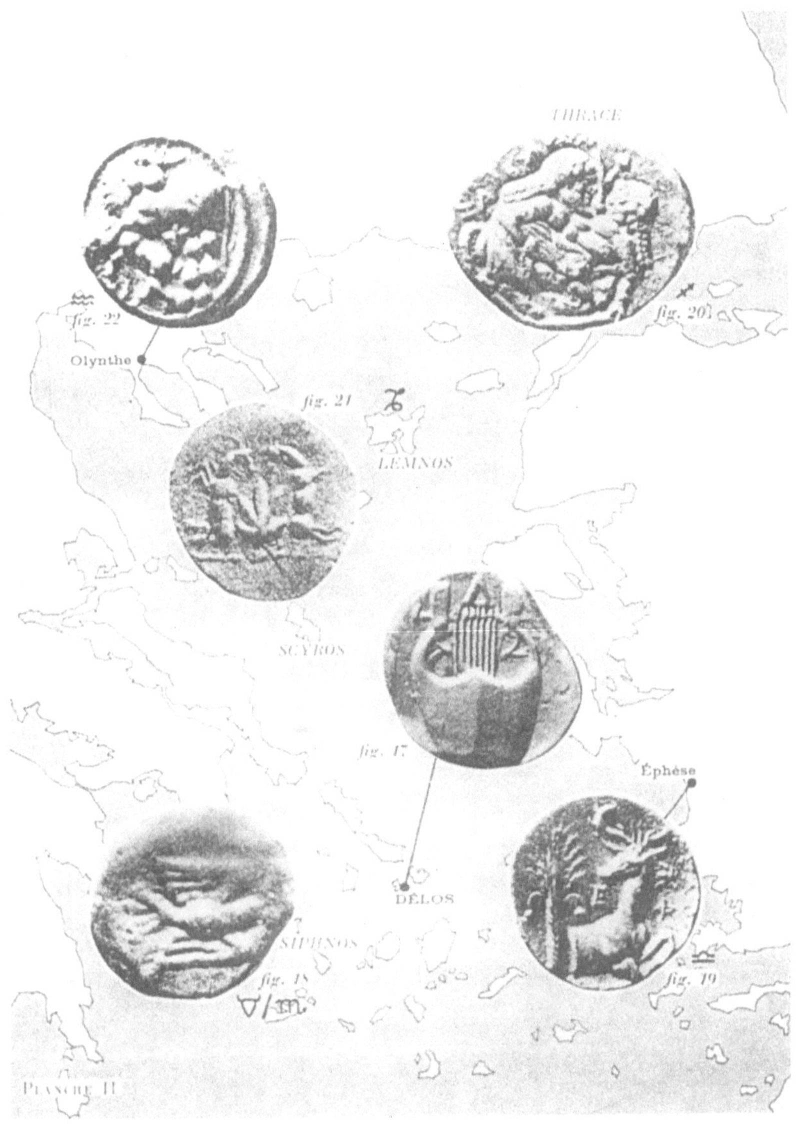

Map. 10. *The Zodiacal Wheel Centered on Delos.*
Figure 17. *Lyre and delta.*
Figure 18. *Coin from Siphnos: eagle.*
Figure 19. *Coin from Ephesus: doe and palm tree (Libra).*
Figure 20. *Coin from Thrace: centaur and nymph (Sagittarius).*
Figure 21. *Coin from Scyros or Lemnos: goat (Capricorn), axial symbol, earth line.*
Figure 22. *Coin from Olynthos: milking cow.*

Chapter 4

An Anatolian System Centered on Sardis

"Neither the earth nor the sea had a center or navel; if ever they had one, the gods, and not mortals, know where it would be."

—The Oracle of Delphi[1]

Certain questions remained unanswered. During a visit to Rhodes I had gone to Camiros. I believed that there I would find a temple of Apollo orientated to the northwest, since Camiros is on the extension of the Delphi-Athens-Delos line. Now Camiros, the most ancient sanctuary of Apollo on the island of Rhodes, is orientated north-south with the entrance to the north. This was an example of an "abnormal orientation" whose significance at first eluded me.

Aside from this, the very name of the ancient sanctuary of Didyma indicated that it had belonged to the sign of Gemini. Ionia, according to Marie Delcourt, was equated with the diaphragm of the world.[2] And the part of the human body from the bronchia to the diaphragm corresponds to the sign of Gemini.

This agrees with the opinion of Lucian of Samosata: "At Delphi, the virgin prophetess is a symbol of the celestial virgin; the dragon under the tripod is endowed with voice only because there is a dragon shining among the stars, and the oracle of Apollo at Didyma is so named, I believe, by allusion to the heavenly Gemini" (*On Astrology*, 23).

Starting with these comments, I drew two straight lines on the map. The south-north line struck from Camiros passed through Sardis, and a line from Sardis at a 30-degree angle to the first, corresponding to the angular distance between Cancer and Gemini, intersected Didyma (map 2). It thus appeared that Sardis, the ancient capital of the kingdom of Lydia, where Cybele and Artemis were held in high veneration, was located on the earth line at the exact latitude of Delphi.

1. The Omphalos of Sardis

A certain group of legends related to Lydia have meaning only if the capital of this kingdom had at one time acted as a generating center.

According to various ancient authors, Herodotus in particular,[3] the kings of Lydia belonged to the dynasty of the Heraclides, the first of whom was named Manes (that is, he represented the avatar of a cycle).[4]

As Marie Delcourt has said:

> The relationship of the words demands, after having spoken of the omphalos, that something be said about this Omphale who made Heracles dress as a woman and spin at her feet. Omphale's name means umbilical cord, which is every man's destiny. The rite of transvestitism occurs in the initiations, and bisexuality is often associated with a process of immortalization. Between the old Delphic stone and the queen of Lydia, there is surely more than a mere assonance.

The name of this legendary queen of Lydia brings one back to astral rites and to Sardis. That authentic monarchs of this kingdom had borne names of abstractions, of demigods or of gods[5] is, by the way, not out of the question. But this would then mean that they were identified with the principle they were named after: a dynasty of Heraclides and a Queen Omphale express an association with the zodiac. To these may be added Attis, son of Manes, in whose reign the great Lydian migration to the west would have taken place. The name of this son of the "great legislator" clearly denotes a servant of Cybele. What is more, Strabo presents him as a descendant of Heracles and Omphale.[6]

Very little attention has been paid to the fact that certain coins from Delphi and Sardis are strikingly similar. Despite their late date, they provide a useful comparison, worthy in the sense that they must have expressed a still living tradition.

A coin from Delphi dating from Hadrian's time (map 11, fig. 23) shows a rock supporting the omphalos around which a serpent is entwined.[7]

Coins from Sardis show the serpent around a basket-omphalos (map 11, fig. 24). This *cista mystica*[8] generally contains a drawn bow (map 11, fig. 25). This means that the serpent represents an attribute both of the earth and of Apollo, which establishes a symbolic identity of the two centers, Delphi and Sardis.[9]

It seems worth recalling that the minting of coins was a Lydian invention.[10] The Lydians, who taught the Greeks this skill, may also have transmitted the custom of stamping their coins with zodiacal symbols. The most ancient known coins of the kings of Lydia show the lion and the bull, solar symbols (map 11, fig. 26). The same animals reappear on many pieces from Anatolia and Ionia in association with other symbols. They most often have a very general meaning.

2. The Zodiacal Wheel Centered on Sardis: the Signs

a) Aries. On the coast of Anatolia at the latitude of Sardis is a place named Leuca, like the Leucas corresponding to the spring equinox in continental Greece. Was some rite enacted there similar to the one documented at Leucas?

Clazomenae may have been the site of the sanctuary that represented Aries. Many coins from that city, dating from the fourth century B.C., are stamped with the head of a ram .[11]

This symbol is found on coins from Samos, perhaps because of its close proximity.[12]

b) Taurus: the Triple Hera of Samos. The protome of a bull is the characteristic emblem on many coins from Samos, from 700 B.C. onward. The bull is shown in the sacrificial position, the head lowered and the front legs bent, which duplicates the image of Taurus in the Greek zodiac[13] (map 11, fig. 27).

Geographical names are once again repeated in places that have the same symbolic meaning in the zodiacal wheels. Samos corresponds to Samos of Triphylia on the west coast of the Peloponnese, mentioned by Strabo (VIII, III, 19).

A bronze in the Samos museum, published by Ernst Buschor, adds a valuable confirmation to my proposals. This is a triangular ornament which, by comparison with other objects of the same form and dimensions, is believed to be a frontal ornament for a horse. It was found on the site of the temple of Hera at Samos, which suggests that it was used during ceremonies or processions that took place there (fig. 28, p. 51).

Now, this bronze represents a nude goddess bearing three other similar goddesses on her head and shoulders. In the upper corners are two kneeling bulls facing away from each other (in the sacrificial position, but whole).

The very shape of the object is significant: it is the truncated section of a disc. If the sides are extended and measured, the angle from the center is 30 degrees. This means that it represented a zodiacal sign, which is obviously the sign of Taurus. The goddess is both single and triple because there are three decans in the sign.[14]

In the Sardis system Samos is in Taurus, and the temple of Hera is on the Hera line. It is therefore easy to deduce that the bronze in question is an image of the triple Taurean Hera of Samos, analogous to the triple Virgin of Delos.

Certain statues of Hera of Samos found on the site of the Heraion show the goddess holding a young hare, a common symbol for Taurus (fig. 12). On the island of Icaria to the west of Samos stood the sanctuary of the Taurobolium, which will be mentioned again.

Southwest of Samos lies the island of Arke, whose name is related to αρχή, which means "origin, beginning." This must refer to the fact that the island is situated, like Samos, in the sign of Taurus in the Sardis system, which formerly marked the spring equinox and the beginning of the year. The root *archis*, associated with light, is discussed in note 32, p. 278.

The sanctuary of Claros was probably connected with this sign in both the Sardis and Delos systems.

On some coins from Leros one finds Scorpio, symbol of the opposing sign.[15] Hyginus associates the constellation of the Hare (which is in the zodiacal sign of Taurus) with the island of Leros.[16]

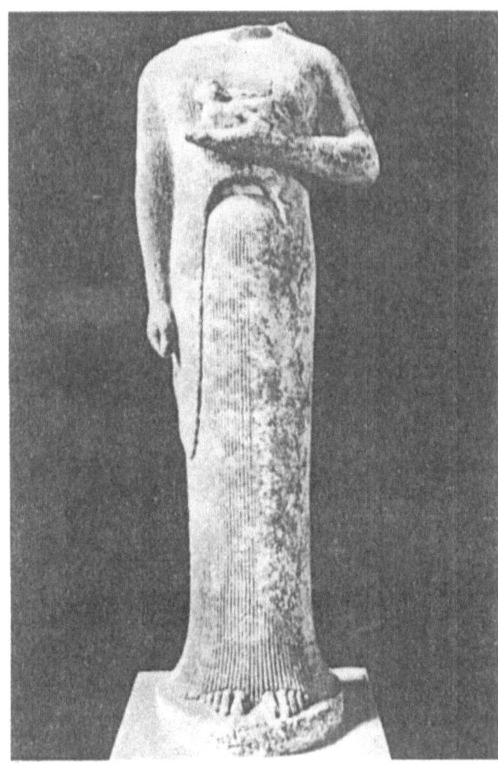

Figure 12. *Statue of Hera of Samos offering a young hare, second quarter of the sixth century (Staatlichen Museum, Berlin).*

c) Ephesus and Scorpio. On a statue of the Great Artemis recently found at Ephesus, the goddess is wearing a necklace of the signs of the zodiac pictured in the order that they occupy in the sky and not in the order of their terrestrial projection.

What is more, the signs are shown in such a way that Scorpio is prominently displayed on the front of the breast, emphasizing its importance. The site where the statue was erected must therefore be related to the sign of Scorpio. This symbol also gives the goddess an "infernal" character because of Scorpio's affinities with Hephaestus and Hades.

I have already given quite a few examples of these inversions of signs. This statue explains them: the ancients simultaneously considered two complementary systems, that of the zodiac projected on the surface of the earth, and the reverse, which is the real order of the signs in the sky.

Thus Boeotia, which is in Scorpio in the Delphic system, was at the same time considered to be influenced by Taurus. And in the Sardis system, the region of the gulf of Cayster, located in Taurus, was also under the influence of the opposing sign of Scorpio.

The statue of Ephesus will be studied in detail in another volume where the statues of Artemis from the Roman era will be examined.[17]

d) Gemini. The very name of the sanctuary of Didyma pertains to this sign and was a reference in reconstructing the Sardis system.

It interesting to see how Didyma and the sign of Gemini are connected. The Dioscuri Tyndaridae are essentially heroes of Laconia, and all attempts at finding a relationship between their legend and the region of Miletus are fruitless.

The symbolic correspondence is established in another way: Branchos was the son of Smicros, a hero from Delphi who had settled at Miletus, where his father Democlos had "forgotten" him. Before he was born, his mother had a vision of the sun descending into her mouth, going though her whole body, and coming out of her belly.

This is why the son to whom she gave birth was called Branchos, which means "bronchia," and it was he who founded the oracle of Didyma.[18] The bronchia, as already mentioned, are symbolically related to the sign of Gemini.

The Apollo Philesios sculpted in bronze by Canachus of Sicyon for the temple of the Branchidae, of which various reproductions survive, was holding up a fawn in his right hand. Apollo and Artemis were twins; the fawn probably symbolized the goddess, beloved and protected by her brother.[19]

e) Cancer. The crab often appears on coins from Cos (map 11, fig. 29) and from Cnidos.[20] Its presence slightly west of the south-north axis is explained by the particular orientation of the solstitial line (cf. p. 67). There was also an important sanctuary of Apollo at Triopion, where the assembly of the Cnidian hexapolis had its seat.

f) Leo: Bellerophon, Apollo "Lykeios." The famous sanctuary of Xanthus in Lydia was, it is believed, situated on the coast at the site of the modern Patara (it has not yet been definitively located, and certainly not excavated), and it corresponded to the sign of Leo. According to tradition, Patara was the abode of the god for six months of the year. In *The Aeneid* Virgil says: "When Apollo leaves the Lycian winter and the shores of Xanthus, when he returns to his native Delos to renew the choruses . . . "[21]

Herodotus compares the cults at Patara and Babylon in Book I (181–182) of *The Histories.* On the summit of the topmost tower of the ziggurat of Zeus-Belus at Babylon, there is "a great temple with a fine large couch in it, richly covered, and a golden table beside it. The shrine contains no image and no one spends the night there except (if we may believe the Chaldaeans who are the priests of Bel) one Assyrian woman, all alone, whoever it may be that the god has chosen." Herodotus goes on to say that the god was thought to come personally into his temple and rest on this bed, as he does in Thebes in Egypt. Herodotus adds that he doesn't believe a word of this and then mentions "yet another instance in the Lycian town of Patara, where the priestess who delivers the oracles when required (for there is not always an oracle there) is shut up in the temple during the night."[22]

The winter residence of the solar god was situated in the Sardis system precisely in the sign of Leo, the solar sign, which was in reality his place of origin. Clement of Alexandria (*Hortatory Address*, IV, 47) mentions as works of either Phidias or Bryaxis the statues of Zeus and Apollo at Patara, and the sculpture of lions lying near them.

The legend of Bellerophon partly unfolded in Lycia. It was in this country that the hero fought the chimaera (a monster often identified with a jet of blazing natural gas), associated with the sign of Leo. Bellerophon was honored as a hero both at Corinth and in Lycia. Coins from Lycia associate this province with the Leo-Aquarius axis with certainty. This is exemplified by the superb coins of the Lycian dynasts dating from about 450 B.C., where we see a seated lion on one side and on the other Pegasus facing to the right[23] (map 11, fig. 30).

Similarly, Apollo "Lykeios," who was very probably the patron of Xanthus, was honored at Argos, Sicyon, and Troezen, cities situated in Leo or to be considered as such in the zodiacal wheel of Delphi.[24] On the coast of modern Albania, in the Aquarius sector of the Delphic wheel, the presence of the place-name Chimaera establishes a relationship with the region of Patara in the Sardis system.

Thus the areas of Greece and Anatolia governed by Leo and occupying similar points on the map are found related in legend and cult in two different ways (see chap. 11, section 8).

g) Virgo. The beginning of this sign corresponds to Side, where the line cuts the coast. Athena was the Great Goddess of Side. She is pictured on most of the coins of this city[25] (map 11, fig. 31).

The city's most famous sanctuary was the temple of Athena, which has been excavated. From the third century B.C., games were organized at Side in honor of Athena and Apollo.

h) Libra. To the best of my knowledge, the only coin from Asia Minor where a Balance appears comes from Prymnesia, a city situated a little to the north of the latitude of Sardis, toward the east.[26]

Other coins from the cities in the region east of Sardis, in particular from Bagistame[27] and Philomelum[28] (map 11, fig. 32), show a bust of Mên with the lunar crescent behind his shoulders. He is a Lydian deity, called Lunus by the Latins, also identified with the goddess Mena whose name, like Selene, means "brilliant."[29] A rather late but very significant relief associates the god Mên with the sign of Libra with absolute certainty.[30]

i) Scorpio. Scorpio was also symbolized by the eagle. In this sign lay Amisos and Sinope, whose coins were stamped with a marine eagle on a dolphin[31] (map 11, fig. 33). Another aspect of the sign of Scorpio in relation to Sinope will be given in chapter 8, section 4.

j) Sagittarius. Coins of Bithynia from the reign of Prusias II (180-149) display an imagery that establishes a symbolic correspondence between Mount Pelion and Olympus of Bithynia. Appearing on them, like on some Magnesian coins, is the centaur Chiron playing a lyre[32] (map 11, fig. 34).

The medal of Nicaea showing "the human–legged horse of the Nicaeans," struck in the third century A.D. in honor of the emperor Gordianus the Pious, described by G. Dumézil,[33] is therefore not a unique phenomenon, since Nicaea is also in Sagittarius in the Sardis system.

k) The Winged Boar. Because of the slight displacement of the solstitial line in relation to the south-north axis, the sign of Capricorn does not seem, in this system, to be represented in the ordinary way.

Cyzicus is situated exactly north of Sardis. Quite unusually, this city has a great variety of coins with many different zodiacal signs, as though it summarized the whole zodiac in itself. Very often the dolphin appears, which is a symbol of the pole and probably of Sagittarius. Particularly significant from my point of view are the coins from Cyzicus showing a winged boar[34] (map 11, fig. 35). I will return to this image in relation to the Leo-Boar solstitial axis. It is, I believe, a substitute for the sign of Capricorn. The peninsula of Cyzicus was also known as Arcton.

l) Aquarius. The line corresponding to the beginning of the sign cuts the coast at Lampsacus. Many coins of this city dating from about 500 B.C. (map 11, fig. 36) bear the protome of a winged horse, that is, Pegasus, which is a symbol of Aquarius.[35] Coins from Scepsis (map 11, fig. 37) are also stamped with a winged horse.

The place of the abduction of Ganymede, a character related to this sign, was traditionally Mount Ida of the Troad. This legend admirably sums up the spiritual meaning of Aquarius:

> Physical union does not exist for God. Here is the meaning of the Cretan myth: a certain Ganymede rose so high towards the gods that, it is said, he became their guest and their cupbearer, that is, his soul was freed from the fetters of matter and, with divine wisdom, became its master.[36]

In Quintus of Smyrna's *Posthomerica*, VIII, 429–43, Ganymede intercedes in favor of Troy; in chant XIV, 325, there is mention of a sanctuary of Ganymede at Troy.

One of the acroteria at Cassiope, now in the Museum of Joannina, represents the abduction of Ganymede (fig. 13). The name Cassiope probably refers to Cassiopeia, who is associated with the myth of Perseus. The Perseus-Cassiopeia axis is close to the Leo-Aquarius axis, and the homeland of Perseus is Midea in Argolis.

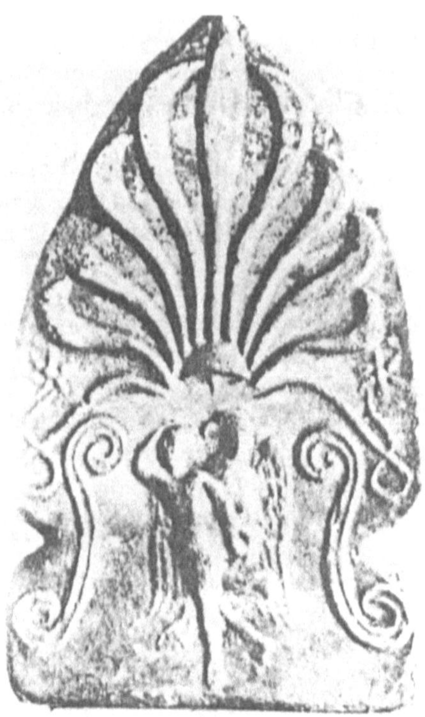

Figure 13. *The abduction of Ganymede, acroterium from Cassiope (Museum of Joannina).*

m) Pisces. Perhaps because of the inherent softness of Pisces, the inhabitants of Aeolis preferred to adopt Athena as a patronness, associated with the opposing sign of Virgo, who became the Great Goddess of Pergamum.

This region is the land of the Amazons who, according to Diodorus of Sicily,[37] fought under the command of Athena; Myrina was founded by an Amazon by that name. The sanctuary of Apollo at Gryneum was related to the sign of Virgo.

It seems very probable that the zodiacal wheels centered on Delos and Delphi were conceived in imitation of the Sardis zodiac (which therefore would be the most ancient).

This confirms the Anatolian origin of Apollo, whose prototype is probably the Hittite god Appalunia or Apalunas, who played the same role of "guardian of the gates" (Agyieus) (really "guardian of the ways"), an expression which must be understood in the sense of guardian of the gates and ways of the solstices[38] (see chap. 6, pp. 64–65).

A Babylonian origin has already been attributed to Apollo by P. Nilsson. It has also been proposed that Leto be identified with the Lycian goddess Lada, herself probably a form of the Semitic Alilat.

Although beginning at Delphi in Greece, Apollo most often appears as an usurper, dethroning more ancient deities, the antiquity of the great sanctuaries of Asia Minor that play an important role in the zodiacal wheel is well documented. The sanctuaries of Patara (Xanthus), Didyma, Claros, and Gryneum existed long before the Greek colonization of Asia Minor.[39] Pausanias affirms this in speaking of Didyma and Claros.[40]

3. The Three Zodiacal Wheels of the Aegean

Map 2 is a composite of the three zodiacal wheels that have been examined in turn. The longest zodiacal lines are:

1. Two Leo-Aquarius axes:

Mount Ida of Crete–Hermione–Delphi–Tricca.
Xanthus-Sardis-Lampsacus.

2. Two Scorpio-Taurus axes parallel to one another and at right angles to the Leo-Aquarius axes:

Lampsacus–southeast tip of Lemnos–Delphi–mouth of the Alpheus.
Amisos–Claros–Delos–Cape Epidelium.

3. Two Virgo-Pisces axes:

Camiros-Delos-Athens-Delphi-Corcyra.
Side-Sardis-Gryneum-Therma (Thessalonica).

I have shown that the existence of the three geographical groupings establishes three series of symbolic correspondences of multiple significance.

This sheds light on various aspects of Greek mythology, especially parallel legends about characters such as Heracles, Orion, Perseus, and Bellerophon, who in a certain sense represent the conflict between human action and celestial forces. Their legends have double and triple layers of equivalent meanings, which will be studied more deeply in chapter 11.

Map 11. *The Zodiacal Wheel Centered on Sardis.*
Figure 23. *Coin from Delphi: omphalos and serpent.*
Figure 24A. *Coin from Sardis: basket-omphalos, serpent, and Apollo's bow.*
Figure 24B. *Coin from Sardis: basket and serpent.*
Figure 25. *Coin from Sardis: basket and serpent.*
Figure 26. *Coin of the Lydian kings: lion and Sirius.*
Figure 27. *Coin from Samos: bull.*
Figure 28. *The triple Hera of Samos (frontal ornament for a horse, probably used in processions): the Triple Goddess and the sign of Taurus.*
Figure 29. *Coin from Cos: Cancer.*
Figure 30. *Coin from Lycia: winged horse and lion.*
Figure 31. *Coin from Side: Athena.*
Figure 32. *Coin from Philomelum: the god Lunus or Mên (associated with the sign of Libra).*
Figure 33. *Coin from Sinope: eagle and dolphin.*
Figure 34. *Coin from Bithynia: centaur.*
Figure 35. *Coins from Cyzicus: boars.*
Figure 36. *Coin from Lampsacus: Pegasus or hippalectryon.*
Figure 37. *Coin from Scepsis: Pegasus.*
Figure 38. *The Hera line represented by coins: from left to right, coin from Olympia (head of Hera); coin from Argos (head of Hera, wolf and dolphins); coin from Samos (head of Hera).*
Figure 39. *Coin from Camiros: five-lobed leaf, symbol of the world tree.*
Figure 40. *Coin from Smyrna: turreted head of Cybele.*

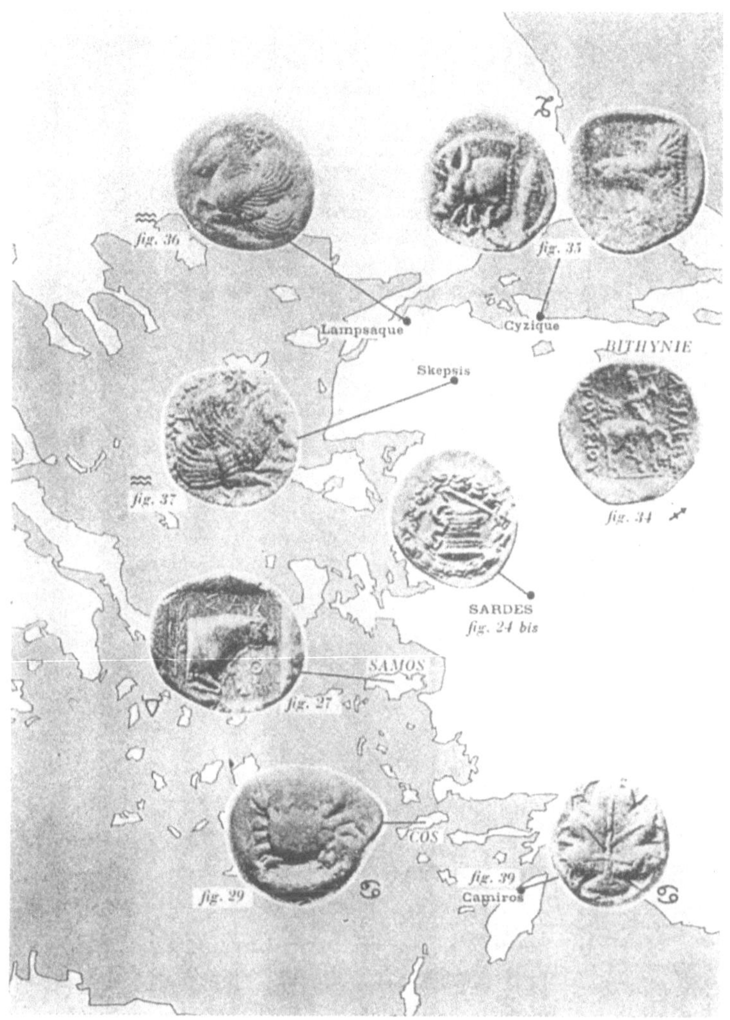

Map 11. ***The Zodiacal Wheel Centered on Sardis.***

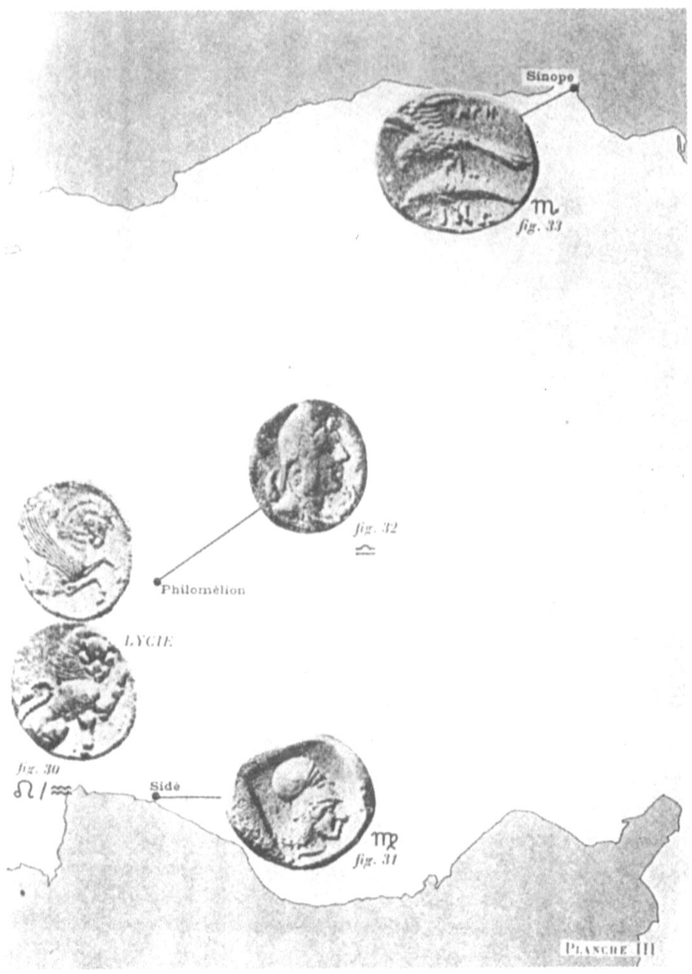

Map 11 (continued). ***The Zodiacal Wheel Centered on Sardis.***

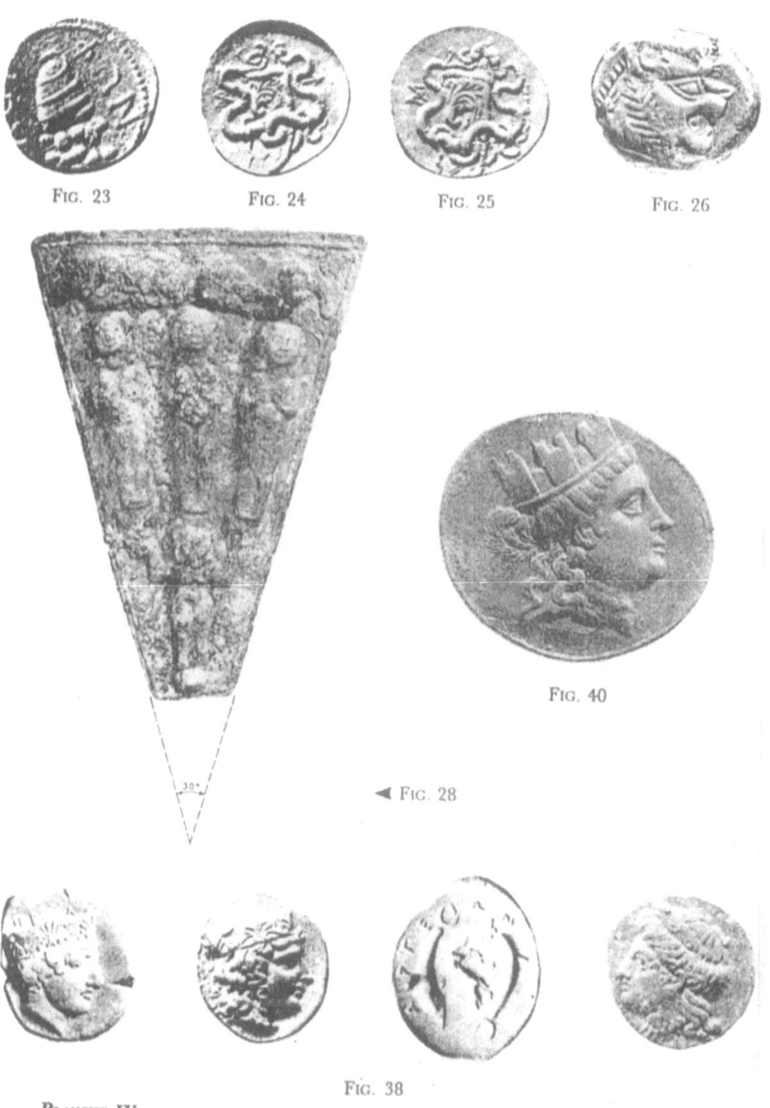

Map 11 (continued). *The Zodiacal Wheel Centered on Sardis.*

Chapter 5

The Constellations, Return to Delphi Demeter, Artemis, and Athena

1. Ursa Major: Artemis, Brauron

The east coast of Attica seemed to have played quite a prominent role in the zodiacal systems that have been discussed in the preceding chapters.

After examining the map, and knowing nothing of the excavations at Brauron, I made my first visit there on 5 October 1958, and arrived when Greek archeologists had just pulled from the mud a beautiful metope of Zeus, Latona, Apollo, and Artemis, a work now in the collection of the National Museum of Athens (fig. 14).

It immediately seemed to me that the cult of Iphigenia, who is identified with Artemis, the sister of Apollo, should be integrated with the zodiacal system.

Now, it has long been known that the curious rite of ἄρχτεΥσις or ἀρχτεία was celebrated at Brauron as well as at Athens. Every five years on the festival of the Brauronia, little girls, or rather certain little girls wearing saffron-colored robes (χροχωτός), were brought to the goddess and consecrated to Artemis for a period of five years and were then known as the "she-bears" (ἄρχτος).[1]

The later discoveries at Brauron, especially the charming statues of the little "she-bears," are evidence of this (fig. 15). A fine museum at Brauron now houses almost all the sculptures that have been found on the site. Many vases and small objects are also on view, among which are some charming sculpted plaques in terra-cotta from the sixth century, of which one represents Artemis Cithaerea.

The very position of Brauron between the Polestar (Delphi) and Spica of Virgo (Delos) indicated that Brauron was the sanctuary of the constellation of the Great Bear.

The origin of the name Artemis may be traced as being composed of *Arth*,[4] for ἄρχτος and of θέμις, which is the personification of a great power, "the order established by the Gods" (a word related to the Sanskrit *dharma*).[2] Artemis is thus the ruler of the law of the Bear, which is the very order of the heavens.

Since the Polestar is symbolically situated at Delphi, one can see why Diodorus of Sicily wrote on the Pythia of Delphi: "It is said that in ancient times the oracles were given by virgins because of their physical purity and their kinship with Artemis."[3]

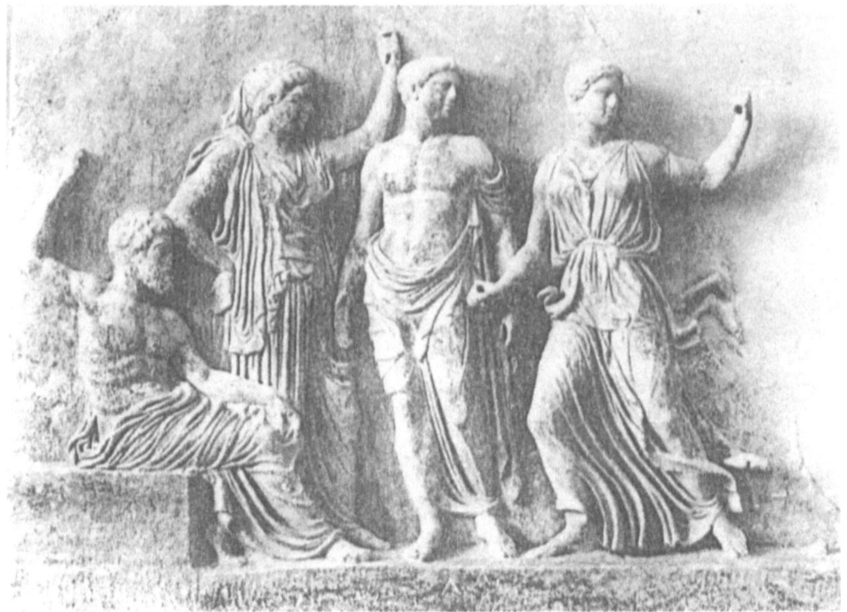

Figure 14. *A beautiful metope representing Zeus, Latona, Apollo, and Artemis (fourth century).*

Through a deviation of meaning that is easily understood, Artemis was partly identified with another goddess, perhaps an Anatolian "Mistress of Beasts," or else was later given this attribution (see also chap. 20).

At Brauron, Artemis was identified with Iphigenia; "The name Iphigenia, meaning 'born of the power' or 'who gives birth to power,' shows that she was a fertility goddess. As a chthonian force that is both benign and terrifying, she was the giver of strong children and,—like Artemis—she sometimes took the life of women in labor.[1] I wonder whether she might not be seen as a goddess of causality in the most general sense of the word.

Interesting and enlightening geometrical relationships connect the main places associated with the legend of Iphigenia on the one hand, and the sanctuaries of Euboea on the other (see map 4).

The distances Argos-Cape Artemisium and Argos-Platanistus are equal, and nearly equal to the distance Cape Artemisium–Platanistus, so that these three points form an isoceles triangle that is almost equilateral. The height of this triangle struck from Argos passes very near Aulis; a line parallel to the height struck from Sparta passes through Eretria and Cyma. Also, the Argos-Platanistus line intersects Brauron.

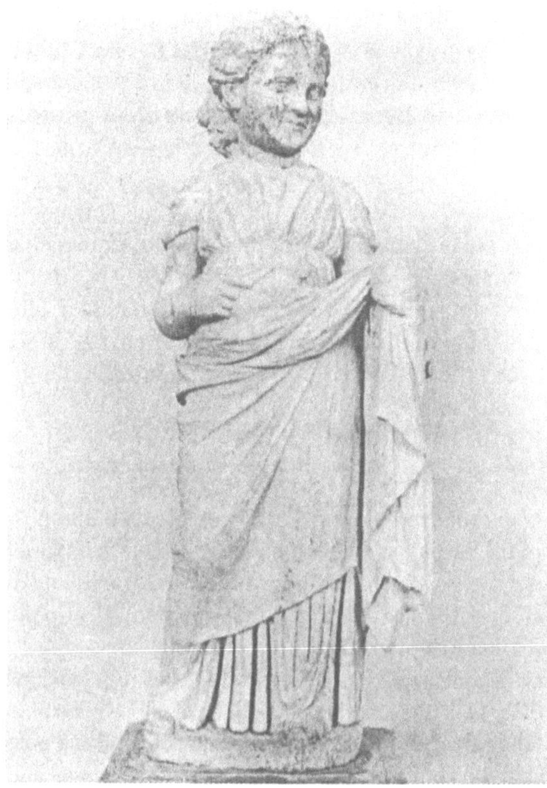

Figure 15. *"Little she-bear," offering the hare of the spring equinox, symbol of the beginning of the year (fourth century).*

A temenos of Artemis Brauronia stood on the acropolis of Athens. The angle between Brauron-Athens-Aulis is 120 degrees. The bisectrix of this angle cuts the coast of Attica at Rhamnus, where the foundations of a temple of Nemesis and a temple of Themis are still visible. If this line is extended on the map, it passes through Parium on the coast of Propontis, where there was an important sanctuary of Artemis, and it ends at the Chersonesus at the site of the temple of Iphigenia Taurica.

An extension of the Brauron-Argos line goes through Arcadia, whose name is related to Arcas-Arcturus, and ends at the "tomb of Callisto" at Crunos (Pausanias, VIII, 3, 6 ff.).

What has been said of the origin of the name Artemis helps in understanding the connection between Artemis-Iphigenia and Themis. The geometrical relationships have a demonstrative value in themselves. The cycle begun at Aulis closes at Brauron, and the balance beam of the scales of justice is at Rhamnus. The primary role of Euboea seems to have been to facilitate certain alignments because the essence of the legend is inscribed in the Argos-Aulis-Brauron triangle, curiously superimposed over the cult of the bear. Although no legend has Iphigenia transformed into a she-bear instead of a hind, there is the story of the nymph Callisto, who was part of Artemis's retinue. The beloved of Jupiter, she became "the constellation of the Great Bear." She probably really represents one of the seven stars of the constellation, her guardian Arcas being Arcturus the Herdsman.[4]

Artemis is constantly associated with the boar and the bear. This could represent the transition from a polar symbolism (the bear) to an equinoctial symbolism (the boar of the winter solstice).

The transfer of the Balance, which was first a symbol of the Great Bear, into the zodiac, already mentioned in the preceding chapter, is apparent in the direct etymological relationship between the names Artemis and Harmonia, unintentionally revealed by F. Vian.[5]

2. Ursa Minor

Coming from Attica and going in the direction of Delphi, one meets the imposing mass of Mount Helicon before Parnassus. Its name Helice indicates its function according to Eratosthenes:[6] the sky seems to spin round it, at least theoretically, in this system. If Delphi and Parnassus stand for the hypothetical pole, Helicon is the constellation of Ursa Minor.

The constellations of Ursa Major and Ursa Minor define the relationships between the zodiac and the other stars. The characteristic square of the constellation Pegasus is found by extending the $\beta\alpha$ line from Ursa Major beyond the pole and Cassiopeia. This was enough to establish a connection between Pegasus and Ursa Minor, starting from between Pegasus and Mount Helicon. Pegasus is also related to the Leo-Aquarius cosmic axis, the ancient line of the solstices.

Similarly, the link between the cult of Apollo-Helios and that of the other Parnassian deities is made through the cult of the Muses.[7] Now, the Muses are the daughters of Harmonia, who specifically governed Thebes and Boeotia. Their number, which is sometimes seven, sometimes nine, may be related to the number of northern stars. Here again is the Harmonia-Artemis equivalence.

These observations also raise the question of the change of the Polestar in the evolution of the system of references.[8] Several instances of the symbol of the lizard will later be found, which stands for the constellation Draco, where the Polestar was formerly located.

3. Return to Delphi: the *Agrenon*

In October 1960, I returned to Delphi, preoccupied with my research. It then occurred to me that there was an unresolved mystery about the omphalos, having to do with the lines that I have just described. The various extant images of the "navel" of the earth and notably the most ancient one of all, discovered in a wall of the temple's terrace,[9] are covered with a tangled network that is believed to represent bands or threads of wool. This is generally called an *agrenon* or "net."[10]

Marie Delcourt has written on this subject:

> The old fetish, which was said to be the stone regurgitated by Kronos, was anointed with oil every day and entwined with raw wool on festivals. One might be tempted to see in the *agrenon* no more than a type of decoration, but then it would be difficult to explain why this network appears, sculpted in high relief, on the marble omphalos meant to represent the primary principal of devotion for the faithful, and that it is reproduced on almost all the images of the sacred stone.

In some representations the *agrenon* becomes a more prominent feature: this is true of a painted amphora from Naples, reproduced by Jane Harrison, where Apollo is sitting on the omphalos garnished with the net.[11]

On the shape of the omphalos itself Marie Delcourt has made these perceptive comments:

> No one, I believe, is surprised to hear the Greeks call a conical protrusion on a plane surface the omphalos, although the navel of the human adult is a concave scar. A convex omphalos has bearing on two concrete realities: the navel of a pregnant woman at the end of her term and that of a newborn baby, which doesn't flatten for several days. Symbolism of fertility, of birth.[12]

And that it is indeed: the omphalos represents the navel of a pregnant woman whose name is Ge.

The meaning of the omphalos is the same as that of the egg, which in turn is symbolically related to the heart. This is what René Guénon has effectively shown:

> The similarity in shape between the heart and the egg . . . can have real meaning only if they share deeper relationships; now the fact that the omphalos and the baetyl, which are undeniably symbols of the center, are often ovoid, like the omphalos of Delphi, shows that this must have been the case. . . .
>
> The world egg is the image, not of the cosmos in its state of full manifestation, but of that from which its development will unfold; and, if this development is represented as an expansion taking place in every direction from its starting point, it is evident that this starting point will necessarily coincide with the center itself.[13]

In my opinion, the *agrenon* is a graphic image of this expansion taking place in all directions.

The sculpted network on various images of the omphalos at Delphi is quite similar to the grids that I have drawn on the map of Greece. It could therefore have a direct bearing on the role of Delphi as a generating center, and especially on the association of the cults of the earth and of Apollo. The angles between the lines of the network correspond to those determined by the Mount Ida–Hermione–Delphi axis and its Cape Epidelium–Delos–Claros perpendicular.

A stone omphalos has also been found at Claros, but it is plain, without a net. This, from my point of view, is understandable since Claros is only one point on the network, not the center.

In the eyes of certain archeologists, an almost insurmountable difficulty lies in the fact that in our modern concept of the social order, the creation of such an organized system would require a central authority and, in the present state of our knowledge of Delphi, there doesn't ever seem to have been an amphictyony that was capable of imposing its authority over the whole of Greece. I think that this way of approaching the problem leads nowhere.

There could very well have been a tacit agreement between the various peoples of Greece based on an identity of fundamental beliefs. In this way a genuine distribution of functions (in every sense of the word) would have been made among the different regions. People for whom the order of the world is essentially identical with the order of the heavens, and all sharing the same astral beliefs, are perfectly capable of achieving such a system of temples and sanctuaries over the course of several centuries, simply by conforming to a religious tradition that was secularized and undisputed.

It seems highly unlikely that the knowledge of the zodiac, discovered by the Chaldaeans, could really have been "lost" and then later rediscovered by the Greeks as has sometimes been claimed. But it could, during a certain period, have been forgotten by the majority of people and been the subject of a secret religious teaching. It is even rather probable that what I am attempting to explain here was one of the great secrets of Delphi.

The text of Plato quoted in chapter 2, which is of vital importance for my thesis, would indeed appear to be a later codification of an ancient practice.

4. Demeter-Gemeter

It is historically documented[14] that the oracle at Delphi, site of the earth-sky hierogamy and the supplanting of Ge by Apollo, was directly responsible for the founding of the temple of the Eleusinian Demeter at Pheneus in Arcadia.

Beginning with this undisputed fact, I will research the geographical connections between Delphi and the great sanctuaries of Demeter in Greece. Let me first mention the existence of the Lycosura-Hermione and Delphi-Ptoon parallels. These are places where there was a special cult of the earth. It is known that there was a sanctuary of Demeter at Hermione,[15] and where the sanctuaries of the triple goddess at Lycosura[16] and of Demeter near Ptoon were located (map 1).

At both Delphi and Ptoon one encounters the juxtaposition of the cults of the earth and of Apollo. At Ptoon the two sanctuaries are situated on either side of a valley at a short distance from one another. Many terra cottas of female figures dating from the sixth and fifth centuries have been excavated from the sanctuary of Demeter.

The great sanctuary of Demeter of Thermopylae at Anthela (site not definitively identified) may well have been located where an extension of the Lycosura-Delphi line cuts the coast, that is, towards Nicaea. If one draws the Lycosura-Delphi and Hermione-Eleusis lines (the importance of the cult of Demeter at Eleusis hardly needs emphasizing), one will obtain a geometrical figure that is an exact parallelogram. Now squares and regular quadrilaterals in general have a symbolic relationship with the earth.[17] The fourth point of the figure is none other than Mount Olympus of Euboea, situated on the earth line.

The Lycosura-Eleusis line is parallel to the line from Delphi that corresponds to the symbolic 0 degree Taurus direction (an earth sign formerly related to the spring equinox). The Hermione-Delphi line (cosmic axis) is naturally perpendicular to both of these.

If, through the point of intersection of the Lycosura-Eleusis and Delphi-Hermione lines, one draws the perpendicular to the Lycosura-Delphi and Hermione-Eleusis lines, one will obtain a point on the Lycosura-Delphi line: this is the site of Pheneus. The line in question is the height of the regular trapezius Delphi-Eleusis-Hermione-Lycosura.

This simple construction interrelates the sanctuaries of Apollo and those of Demeter or the earth grouped at Mount Ptoon, Delphi, Hermione, and Lycosura.

The first seat of the Delphic amphictyony was the sanctuary of Demeter at Anthela near Thermopylae,[18] a site that should, as I have said, be sought near Nicaea. Therefore, a Thermopylae-Delphi line drawn towards Pheneus and Lycosura must be the true origin of the figure that I have reconstructed.

While Apollo supplanted Gaia at Delphi, at Mount Ptoon, Hermione, and Lycosura the cults of Apollo and Demeter continued to coexist.

The ancestry of Artemis and Athena has been established by Parke in this manner:

$$\text{Ge} \longrightarrow \text{Themis} \begin{array}{l} \longrightarrow \text{Artemis} \\ \longrightarrow \text{Athena} \end{array}$$

The historian makes this statement: "The original identity of the snake and the earth goddess was forgotten or mostly ignored, and what had probably been the site of the earth goddess's shrine was dedicated instead to Athena Pronaia, a harmless ally of Apollo."[19]

Pausanias[20] mentions the cult of Artemis-Iphigenia side by side with the cult of Demeter at Hermione, and according to Strabo, near Hermione there was a "shortcut" down to Hades.[21]

What is more, the very origin of the name Artemis (see p. 53) shows the filiation Themis (another name for earth)—Artemis. These various relationships account for the association of the god of Delphi with Athena, the serpent goddess, and Artemis, ruler of Ursa Major.

5. Artemis

It would thus appear that the goddesses Demeter, Artemis, and Athena derived from a Great Mother Goddess who was both earth and moon. This impression will be confirmed by a study of the distribution of the sanctuaries of Artemis and Athena.

I have composed a map of the cult of Artemis based on the list of her great sanctuaries in the index of Strabo's *Geography*[22] and her cult places or sacred sites named in Callimachus's *Hymn.*[23] The legend of Artemis of the Net (Dictynna) and the Artemis-Iphigenia cycle have also been taken into account.

From the curious map thus obtained, which unfortunately cannot be reproduced here, it would seem that Artemis is a complex deity, resulting from the fusion into a single figure of at least three goddesses of different origins:

1. An Anatolian and "Ephesian" Artemis, Mistress of Beasts and of the moon.
2. A Great Goddess of Crete and the Cyclades.
3. A goddess native to Peloponnese, associated with Laconia, Taygetus, and Arcadia (cf. Callimachus).

The cult of the Cretan Artemis could have arrived in Peloponnese via Cythera. In this scheme, Delos can be considered as the symbolic island where the fusion of the three goddesses into one took place, but the birthplace of Artemis was also given as Ephesus.[24]

Artemis always kept something of her complex origin. That is why she was to be identified with the triple Hecate, who is simultaneously infernal, terrestrial, and celestial.

1. As an infernal goddess, she has affinities with the sign of Scorpio, which governs Ephesus. Her weapons were, incidentally, forged by Hephaestus.
2. As a terrestrial deity, she is Artemis Taurica:
   - as a virgin goddess, she rules in the corresponding sign at Brauron;
   - as the goddess of wild beasts, she is at home in the sign of Leo;
   - as a huntress, she suggests Sagittarius.
3. Celestially, she is the moon and governs the sign of Cancer, next to Leo, where her brother Apollo is master.

The sign of Cancer was to be most particularly attributed to her. However, in its capricious course the moon also travels throughout the sky, which is why the whole zodiac is its domain, as it is Apollo's. Callimachus (*Hymn*, 53) speaks of thirteen cities sacred to Artemis, but unfortunately does not name them. And there are thirteen lunations in a solar year. Therefore, Artemis, like Apollo, possesses her own sign but is at home everywhere.

6. Brauron, Ephesus, and the Cave of the Bear

Until now I have emphasized the role played by Brauron in the system centered on Delphi, while observing the significant relationships of this sanctuary with various places in the cycle of Iphigenia.

This is the time to bring up two rather fascinating facts:

1. Brauron is on the same latitude as Ephesus, another high place of Artemis, which claimed the honor of being the birthplace of the goddess.
2. In Crete, in the Akrotiri, not far from the monastery of Gouverneto, is the cave of the bear, the cave of Cydonia, where natural concretions have been carved into a statue of a she-bear. The modern name is σπηλιά τῆσ παναγìας[25] (which is well in keeping with the transmission of cults and beliefs, even of paganism to Christianity).

Now, this cave is situated very precisely on the meridian of Brauron[26] (see map 3). Perhaps one should look for a sanctuary of Artemis at Carpathus that would complete a rectangle?

7. Athena

In Greek mythology the sign of Virgo plays a starring role. Some believe the name Athene to come from the name of the rock of the Acropolis.[27] But the presence of the form *a-ta-na po-ti-ni-ja* for "Athena mistress"[28] on Cretan tablets makes me wonder whether the name of the goddess couldn't simply mean "the immortal" (ἀθανάτη). According to Strabo,[29] her birthplace was Alalcomenae in Boeotia, and therefore in the sign of Virgo in the Delphic system. The cult of Athena was very prominent all over this part of Boeotia: at Haliartus, Thesprotia, and at Coronea. The temple of Athena Itonia was situated on the banks of the river Couralium, whose name seems to come from *Kora* or *Koura*, meaning "Virgin." Pausanias indicates that this temple was the seat of a Theban amphictyony.[30]

Athena is a flagrant example of a zodiacal deity promoted to the rank of Great Goddess. Sprung from the forehead of Zeus, she is a marvelous incarnation of an intellectual and Mercurial sign. According to Eratosthenes, she also represents Dike (Justice), daughter of Zeus and Themis; she is also Ceres, Isis, Fortuna, etc.

Because of the importance of Athens in Greek history, the very sign of Virgo acted as a generating center. Thus an extension of the Tegea-Athens line goes to

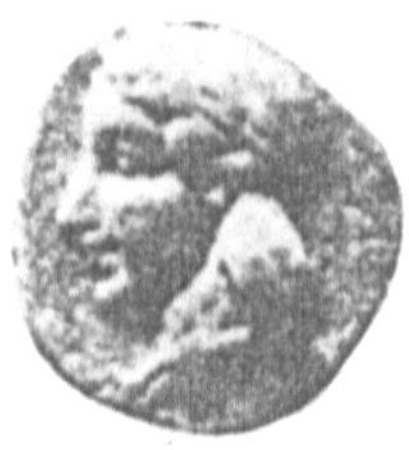
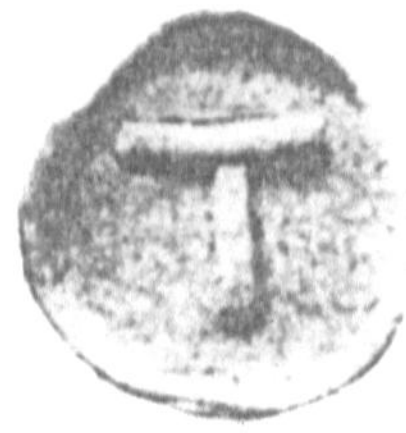

Figure 16. *Coin from Tegea.*

Pergamum, where the Great Goddess of the city was Athena. Again the coins of the three cities are eloquent, showing the profile of the gray-eyed goddess.[31] Figure 16 shows a coin from Tegea with the image of Pallas.[32]

In the Virgo sector of Greece, it is well known that the distance from the Parthenon to the temple of Athena at Cape Sounion is almost equal to the distance between Cape Sounion and the temple of Aphaia at Aegina, so that the three sanctuaries define a triangle that is almost isoceles[33] (map 4).

An examination of the distribution of the great sanctuaries of Athena reveals a rather impressive overlapping of three triangles: Delphi-Athens-Tegea (almost equilateral), Athens-Tegea-Sounion, and Athens-Sounion-Temple of Aphaia at Aegina (isoceles, see map 4).

The community of origin of Athena and Artemis seems symbolized by the isoceles triangle: Dictynnaion of Crete-Delos-Temple of Aegina. The Dictynnaion of Crete is one of the points in the Delian system. At Delos there was a sanctuary of Artemis of the Net, and at Aegina she was identified with Aphaia.

The Cretan Britomartis seems to be an ancestral form of the Great Goddess from whom both Artemis and Athena descended.

What is more, the three triangles of Athena just described overlap the Hera line, another aspect of the Great Goddess, and this line intersects Cape Sounion.

It is highly probable that the essential purpose of these geometrical figures was to create unity and solidity in a cosmos that was conceived as the harmonious equilibrium of the three planes of the underworld, the earth, and the celestial spheres. And my next subject will be the symbolic axis that joins the three worlds with the circles of the planets.

Chapter 6

The World Axis and the Planetary Lines Symbols of the Pole

What is the oracle at Delphi?
The Tetraktys, the very thing which is the Harmony of the Sirens.
—Pythagorean maxim

The following alignments in latitude have been considered thus far: (1) The sanctuaries of Apollo at Lycosura, Hermione, Delos, and Didyma; (2) the sanctuaries of Hera at Olympia, Argos, and Samos; (3) the line of Apollo and the earth: Leucas-Delphi-Ptoon.

1. The Gateways of the Solstices

The lines just mentioned are perpendicular to the meridian of Delphi, which corresponds to the Cape Taenarum–Delphi–Mount Olympus line from south to north. I will now show that this line really has a double meaning: it is both polar and zodiacal, and it represents the projection of the cosmic axis on the zodiacal plane.

Without stating it directly, Marie Delcourt anticipated that the symbolism of the omphalos implied more than one plane and wrote, "To the genital meaning of the navel is added a symbolism related to its position at the intersection of the two axes of the human body, a vertical median line and a horizontal along the diaphragm."[1] This image takes on all its meaning if one visualizes a man who is standing at Delphi and observing the movement of the sun in the sky.

The words of René Guénon further this idea:

> The vertical axis, in so far as it unites the two poles, is evidently a north-south axis. In the transition from a polar to a solar symbolism, this axis will have to be, as it were, projected onto the zodiacal plane, but in such a way as to keep a certain correspondence, one could even say an equivalence, that would be as exact as possible with the original polar axis. Now, in the annual cycle, the winter and summer solstices are the two points that correspond respectively to the north and to the south

> in the order of space, just as the spring and autumn equinoxes similarly correspond to east and west. The axis that will fulfill the desired condition is thus the one that joins the two solstitial points; and it can be said that this solstitial axis will then act as a relatively vertical axis, which it effectively is in relation to the axis of the equinoxes. . . .
>
> The cosmic cavern could have two opposed "zodiacal" gateways, in accordance with the axis that has just been envisaged, which would correspond respectively to the two solstitial points, one being the entrance and the other the exit. The notion of these two "solstitial gateways" is explicit in most of the traditions, and is generally given great symbolic importance. The entrance is sometimes called the "gateway of humanity," who in this case could be initiates to the "lesser mysteries" and the profane, because they have yet to transcend the human state. The exit is then by contrast known as the "gateway of the gods," through which pass only those who have access to supra-individual states.[2]

On this point, as on many others, the Pythagoreans were transmitting an ancient tradition which is also clearly expressed in the *Bhagavad Gita*.[3] The best-known Greek texts in this respect are Proclus's summary of Numenius in his commentary on Plato's *Republic*, and Porphyry in *De Antro Nympharum*, chapters 21 and 22.[4]

According to these authors, the descent of souls along the Cancer-Capricorn axis occurred in the following order: spheres of (1) Kronos, (2) Zeus, (3) Ares, (4) Apollo, (5) Aphrodite, (6) Hermes, (7) Selene.

The ascent of souls took place in the reverse order, starting from the center of the earth.

If this scheme is transposed to the zodiacal diagram for Greece (map 1), one sees that the Taenarum (the modern Cape Matapan)–Delphi–Mount Olympus line represents the cosmic axis joining the three worlds, which is identical to the Cancer-Capricorn solstitial axis.

If one assumes that latitudes were marked at theoretically equal intervals, one will obtain a certain number of striking correspondences with the planetary spheres. Aphrodite, a goddess of recent invention, will have to be replaced by Hera in two instances. The most striking associations can be made for the first part of the journey associated with the incarnation of souls. Where the lines cannot be drawn with certainty, given the current state of excavations in Greece, the significant latitudes will simply be pointed out (map 1).

2. The Descent of Souls: from Taenarum to Delphi

a) Taenarum was considered a very important "entrance to the underworld" and is no doubt related to Hades and Kronos. According to legend, Heracles had brought Cerberus to Cape Taenarum.[5] (See also p. 68.)

b) Sparta is presumably related to Ares.

c) The Lycosura-Hermione-Delos-Didyma line is a solar line. This suggests why the coins of Miletus were often stamped with a lion, the supreme solar animal, and with Sirius in Leo, which pertains to the summer solstice. Miletus also laid claim to being a center.[6] This same line also passes through Syros, an island long sacred to the sun.[7]

d) The Olympia-Argos-Samos line is the Hera line. At Samos Hera seems to have had the same taurine nature as at Olympia. The goddess was born at Argos or, according to some mythographers, at Samos. It seems to me that the substitution of Hera by Aphrodite in the Pythagorean sequence must be interpreted to mean that the spouse of Zeus was originally and primarily conceived as a goddess of femininity. Mount Latmus in Anatolia, place of the ritual love of Selene-Hera and Endymion, is also on the Hera parallel.[8] (Fig. 38, p. 51 represents the Hera line by means of coins of Olympia, Argos, and Samos.)

e) Mount Cyllene, situated on the solstitial axis and birthplace of Hermes, is related to a line of Hermes that passes through Sicyon, Megara, Athens, and Ephesus. I will later comment on the *Homeric Hymn to Hermes*, an outstanding astrological text.

f) A lunar line must pass through Rhamnus, site of the love of Leda and the swan.

g) Delphi: The Leucas-Delphi-Ptoon parallel represents the earth line in the planetary symbolism. In the proposed layout the Polestar is above Delphi on the "upper" part of the world axis. Delphi communicates with the center of the earth. It is the site of the hierogamy, whence the superimposition and the implicit equivalence of the oracles of the earth and of Apollo. This was the meaning of the canal that pierced the stone omphalos. It was an image of the cosmic axis and the interpenetration of the earth and the heavens.[9]

Apollo Aygieus. A cult of Apollo as the guardian of doors and gateways is well documented. Pausanias mentions it at Acharnae near Athens, at Argos, and at Megalopolis, but it seems to have been most prominent at Tegea. There he was represented four times, according to Pausanias, each Tegean tribe having erected a statue of him.[10] Now, Tegea is situated on the solstitial line, and Apollo Aygieus is the guardian of the gateways and doors of the solstices, so the four statues seen by the traveler referred, I believe, to a division according to the four cardinal points.

An antique idol of Lacedaemonia portrayed Apollo with four arms and four ears, which has the same symbolism. Pausanias (III, 20, 9) also saw seven columns at Sparta representing the seven planets.

3. The Ascent of Souls: from Delphi to Olympus

On the second half of the axis, which corresponds to the ascent of souls towards the heavens, a few markers can be placed. Hera was the patroness of Thessaly, whose latitudes encompass the sanctuary of Pagasae.

The Dodona-Tricca latitude is heliacal. A line of Ares would intersect Lemnos, site of the loves of Ares and Aphrodite. The place of the ascent of souls towards the heavens indeed seems to be the sanctuary of the gods on the summit of Olympus; it is the "gateway of the gods." Many legends, even modern ones, perpetuate the tradition of the mysterious nature of the upper plateau. According to Lucian, who was probably well aware of what he was saying, the assembly of the gods took place on the heights of Olympus at the time of the winter solstice.[11]

Besides the sanctuaries on Olympus, there was another great temple of the master of the gods at Dium on the northern slope of the mountain. And finally, Olympus of Bithynia below Prusa is situated at the same latitude as Olympus of Thessaly.

All this probably represents an attempt to distribute the planetary lines over exactly four of our modern degrees of latitude. The interval between Cape Taenarum and the Lycosura-Hermione-Delos solar line is exactly one degree of latitude. The distance between this line and the Delphi-Ptoon earth line is a little more than one degree, but equal to the interval between the the earth line and the other Dodona-Tricca solar line.

One must bear in mind how difficult it must have been to strictly coordinate geo-astronomic determinations in a country having such irregular surface features and ragged coastlines, and probably by very simple means of taking bearings on the stars.

The system of cosmic references is thus complete: Taenarum is the nadir, Delphi the center, and Olympus the zenith. The six directions of space and the center are present;[12] the remnants of the planetary lines give the zodiacal diagram greater vitality and meaning. The mystical significance of the Cancer-Capricorn axis is confirmed by the Pythagorean texts that have been mentioned. And the maxim quoted at the beginning of this chapter seems to admirably summarize the concept of the unity of the zodiacal diagram (the tetraktys, which relates to the four directions of space and the 360 days of the year) and the planetary alignments (the "sirens"). The existence of Delphi and the alignments of sanctuaries is, however, much earlier than Pythgoreanism, which only took up and revealed far more ancient doctrines.

4. World Axes and Planetary Lines in the Systems of Delos and Sardis

A) Delian system. The Ammoneion-Delos axis finishes at the highest point of the Balkan Mountains, the antique Haemus, homeland of Boreas. This is the modern Jumruktchal, which at 2,380 meters is somewhat lower than Olympus of Thessaly (2,911 m), but higher than Olympus of Bithynia, the modern Uludag[13] (2,327 m). I unhesitatingly see this as the "gateway of the gods" of this system, which is all the more evident since the cult of Boreas at Delos is so well documented.[14]

The cults of Delos, such as they have been studied by H. Gallet de Santerre, show the juxtaposition of the symbols of the world axis and those of the south-north axis in this island.

1. THE WORLD AXIS. This is clearly symbolized by the palm tree in whose shadow Latona gave birth to the divine twins, according to myth.

2. THE CULT OF CAPRICORN. It was on Mount Cynthus that Artemis hunted the wild goats with whose horns her brother built the *Keratinos Bomos* ("Altar of Horns"),[15] an allusion to the Cancer-Capricorn axis. The presence at Delos of the sacred tree and the altar of horns visibly supports my concepts in every way. The association of the primitive Apollo with the lion[16] relates to the ancient Leo-Aquarius solstitial axis.

B) Sardis System. The south-north axis of this system is the Camiros-Sardis line. Coins from Camiros bear a five-lobed fig leaf (map 11, fig. 39), which represented the world tree. What is more, Plutarch in his treatise *On the E of Delphi* says that the number five was sacred to Apollo.[17] And in his *Isis and Osiris* (#56), he indicates the para-etymology that associates πέντε, five, with πάντα, the universe, the whole.

Here it seems that the solstitial axis is represented by the Miletus–Sardis–Olympia of Bithynia line. The purpose of its slight deviation from the south-north direction is to put the "gateway of the gods" into relationship with a high mountain peak.

A coin from Scepsis (fig. 17)[18] depicts a palm tree, which alludes to the former Leo-Aquarius solstitial line taken as the world axis.

There is a striking equivalence between the bear cult such as it was practiced at Munychia, next to Miletus, and the cult at Brauron; its rite is as characteristic as that of the ἀρχτεία.[19] Now, if one is willing to accept that the solstitial axis is the one I have indicated, one will obtain a zodiacal scheme that is strikingly similar to that of Attica (see chap. 7 and map 4).

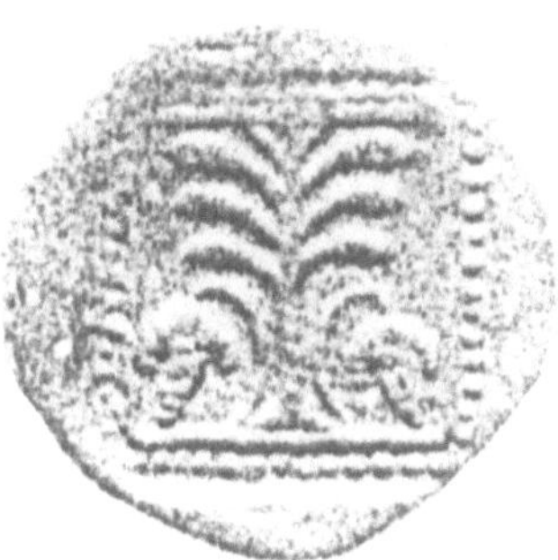

Figure 17. *Coin from Scepsis.*

C) The Planetary Lines of Latitude. These can be partially rediscovered:

a) The temple of Apollo Lithesios, whose name refers to the stone regurgitated by Kronos which became the omphalos, and the temple at Camiros, a very ancient sanctuary in Rhodes, seem to indicate a line of Kronos.

b) A connection between the Sardis and Delphi systems is made by the Lycosura-Hermione-Delos-Miletus solar line. Miletus was a city whose remarkable destiny was closely connected with that of the oracle of the Branchidae. The presence on coins from Miletus of solar animals in pairs, such as two masks of lions and two confronted roosters,[20] suggests both the sign of Gemini and the solar line. The lion, the supreme solar animal, frequently appears with Sirius.[21]

c) One better understands the legends of a supposed Athenian origin of Ephesus[22] when one sees that the city is on a line of Mercury going through Athens.

d) Mount Latmus marks the Hera line extended past the Heraion at Samos, one of the birthplaces of the goddess. The mountain was the traditional site where Hera, assimilated to the moon, celebrated her ritual marriage with Endymion.

e) Ancient Smyrna, where the earth was venerated as Cybele and Nemesis, is on the Delphi-Sardis earth line. Here again the evidence of the coins is eloquent[23] (map 11, fig. 40). On the slopes of Mount Sipylus stands one of the most ancient statues of the Mother of the Gods, whose origin was attributed to Broteas, son of Tantalus, himself the son of Omphale.[24] As is also true of the Delphic system, it is more difficult to reconstitute the latitudes north of the earth line. It is nevertheless striking that:

f) Olympus of Bithynia, the "gateway of the gods" of the system, is on the same latitude as Olympus of Thessaly.

The design of the three zodiacal wheels of the Aegean (map 2) clearly brings out the great alignments of latitude, especially the Didyma-Delos-Hermione-Lycosura heliacal line, and the axis of the Olympuses, which in modern latitude is forty degrees north. The axis of the planetary modulations is the Melitene (Malatya)–Sardis–ancient Smyrna–Ptoon–Delphi parallel (map 1).

Faced with such astonishing systems of correspondences, one is almost forced to postulate the existence of "great teachers," who at a rather remote date, situated at the very latest at the time of the "return of the Heraclides" (that is, about 1000 B.C.) showed the inhabitants of the Greek world where to build their temples and the general principles for selecting the site of a sanctuary. Religious conservatism was such that these sites were maintained even after the real reasons for their choice had been forgotten or lost from sight. One may assume that knowledge of astronomy, particularly of the zodiac, found refuge at Delphi. The fact that one can, in an incomplete but nevertheless very striking way, reconstitute the system of references, and the presence of certain names of constellations in toponymy (e.g., Helicon and Cassiope) show that one is dealing with an important and hitherto neglected aspect of Greek culture. This gives

Greece its place among the great traditional cultures, next to those of India, Chaldea, Egypt, and Etruria.

5. The Nonzodiacal Constellations and Symbols of the Pole

If one examines the plates in G. Thiele's work *Antike Himmelsbilder*[25] that reproduce manuscripts, very late from my point of view, but which nevertheless contribute a valuable documentation on Greek astrological tradition, one will notice the importance attributed by the ancients to constellations which, without being exactly situated in the zodiacal band, are in immediate proximity to it. The constellation of the Charioteer is located between Taurus and Gemini. This corresponds well with an identification of the celestial Auriga with Myrtilus, son of Hermes and the charioteer of Oenomaus, king of Elis. The entire story of the race of Pelops has the characteristics of a solar myth.[26]

The group of constellations situated in the direction of Capricorn, starting from the Polestar, includes a set of symbolic figures that are particularly associated with the pole and Hyperborean Apollo: the Swan, the Dolphin, the Arrow, and the Lyre.[27] The star γ of Delphinus is very close to the solstitial axis. One may well wonder whether the image of the dolphin didn't acquire a polar and astral meaning from the time when the solstitial axis came to be associated with the Cancer-Capricorn direction. This would shed new light on the association of the dolphin with Delphi, coinciding with the *delphis*-Delphi phonetic relationship, and Apollo Delphinios would become identical with the guardian of the solstitial axis. Many coins stamped with a dolphin allude to a Delphic and Hyperborean Apollo. This is the case in particular of the Argive coin where one sees a swan between two dolphins.[28]

6. The Boar, Symbol of the Pole; the Oath on the Boar

The boar seems to be a doublet of the bear, and whenever it appears on coins, winged or wingless, its significance is either polar or associated with the winter solstice. Thus a winged boar appears on coins from Clazomenae[29] (fig. 18), a city turned towards the north, and from Ialysos, situated in the north of the island of Rhodes.[30] A boar is shown on certain coins from Methymna[31] (fig. 19), a city at the northern tip of the island of Mytilene. On coins of Lycia where the tortoise and the boar are figured, they symbolize this kingdom's claim to comprise a world in itself and refer to the Cancer and the Aquarius-Pisces regions, thus, once again, the solstitial axis (fig. 20).

Perhaps the bear-boar equivalence is based on a pun ἄγριος = ὗς = ἄρχτος In other Indo-European languages the linguistic kinship is more obvious (Latin, *ursus-us*). In English, the same word (bear-boar) designates the two animals.[32]

In both the legends of Adonis and of Meleager, it is the Hyperborean Artemis, guardian of the pole, who sends the killer boar. At Patrae bear cubs and boars with other wild animals were sacrificed to Artemis.[33] There is also Pausanias's

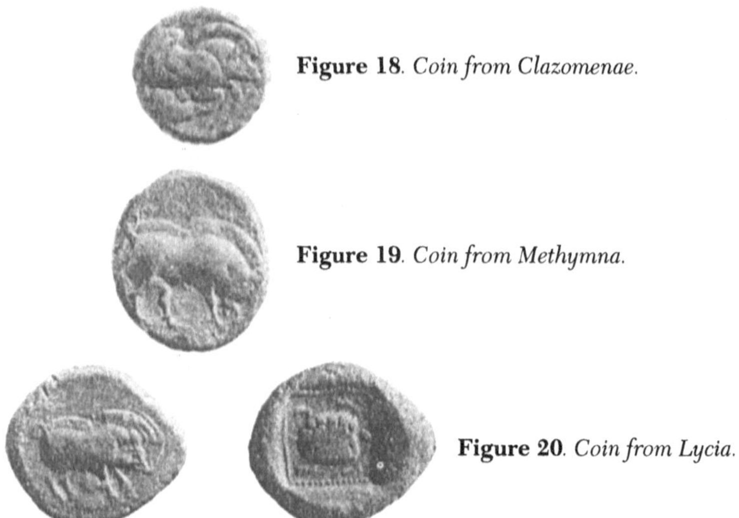

Figure 18. *Coin from Clazomenae.*

Figure 19. *Coin from Methymna.*

Figure 20. *Coin from Lycia.*

description of the throne of Apollo at the tomb of Hyacinthus at Amyclae. (Hyacinthus, an ancient agrarian deity who was supplanted by Apollo, was portrayed, not as a young man, but as an old man with a beard). The decor of the throne as a whole featured myths associated with the zodiac. The lower part of the throne described the hunting of the Calydonian boar and Heracles slaying the children of Actor.[34] This also relates to a sign of the Boar in an ancient zodiac which I will later try to reconstitute and to the solstitial meaning of the boar (winter solstice).

Starting from the study of Greek coins alone, I had already established the symbolic and linguistic equivalence of the boar and the bear, when I came upon René Guénon's fascinating study on "The Boar and the Bear."[35] There one reads, "The boar formerly represented the constellation which later became the Great Bear. This substitution of names is a manifestation of what the Celts symbolized by the conflict of the boar and the bear, that is, the revolt of the representatives of temporal power against the supremacy of spiritual authority." The author goes on to say that for the Greeks the revolt of the Kshatriyas was symbolized by the hunting of the Calydonian boar.[36] The first blow was struck by Atalanta, who had been suckled by a bear. The name Atalanta could indicate that the revolt began either in Atlantis itself or among the heirs to its tradition. R. Guénon also compares the golden apples in the legend of Atalanta with those of the Garden of the Hesperides, the daughters of the West, of Atlas, like the Pleiades.[37]

The polar significance of the boar elucidates the meaning of oaths taken on the boar, which to the best of my knowledge has never been shown. If the boar is, as I believe, a polar symbol, it is the very image of stability and the immutable center. It is now understandable why, according to Pausanias,[38] Heracles exchanged oaths with the sons of Neleus on the remains of a boar in a place known as the tomb of the boar in Stenyclerus in Messenia. It also explains the sacrifice of a boar, which was then cast into the sea to "feed the fish," when Agamemnon swore that he had never offended the chastity of Briseis in *The Iliad,*[39] and similarly, the oaths of the Olympian athletes on "slices of boar meat."[40] This is a vestige of what was probably an ancient tradition; all these oaths are sworn by the pole that does not change.

Chapter 7

The Zodiacal Division of Attica and the Mysteries: Agrae and Eleusis

1. The Zodiacal Division

According to Pollux,[1] Cecrops divided the Athenians into four groups, each group into three tribes, and every tribe into thirty clans. The four groups, twelve tribes, and 360 clans were each under the invocation of a different hero or spirit of the constellations. This is understood in *The Suda* (*Genetai*), where it is said: "The distribution of the Athenians corresponded to the four seasons, the twelve months and the thirty days in every month."[2]

While it would seem rather difficult to reconstruct this system in its entirety, I shall nevertheless attempt to rediscover its main outlines in the light of my earlier observations. An important clue lies in the great statues of the Dioscuri that stood at Cape Sounion. One of them, which is almost intact, is in the National Museum of Athens (fig. 21). Of the other there remains only a foundation where the feet of another colossal statue are still visible. Now, if the Parthenon is taken as the hypothetical omphalos of Attica and the beginning of the sign of Gemini is at Sounion, the polar direction would be the direction of Delphi. This means that the Cancer-Capricorn axis would be identical to the Delos-Athens-Delphi line (map 4). It should be understood that here, as in other cases that will be looked at, "polar" direction does not necessarily mean north, but the direction of the spiritual focus of the community.

Various correspondences immediately spring to mind. The southeast part of Attica becomes something of an equivalent to the south coast of the Peloponnese. The temple of Poseidon at Cape Sounion echoes his temple at Taenarum. The very name of the island of Makronisi, which was called Helena in antiquity, shows that its role in relation to the coast of Attica was analogous to that of Cythera to the Peloponnese, as well as an association with the moon and the sign of Cancer.

Strabo (IX, I, 22) said that the island was called Cranae and took on the name Helena because it was the place of the union of Paris with his mistress. He refers to a passage in *The Iliad* (III, 443).

The legend told by Pausanias about the return of the descendants of Cephalus is probably an allusion to the zodiacal division of Attica. Their tenth generation was allowed to return to Attica after a long exile in Cephallenia to

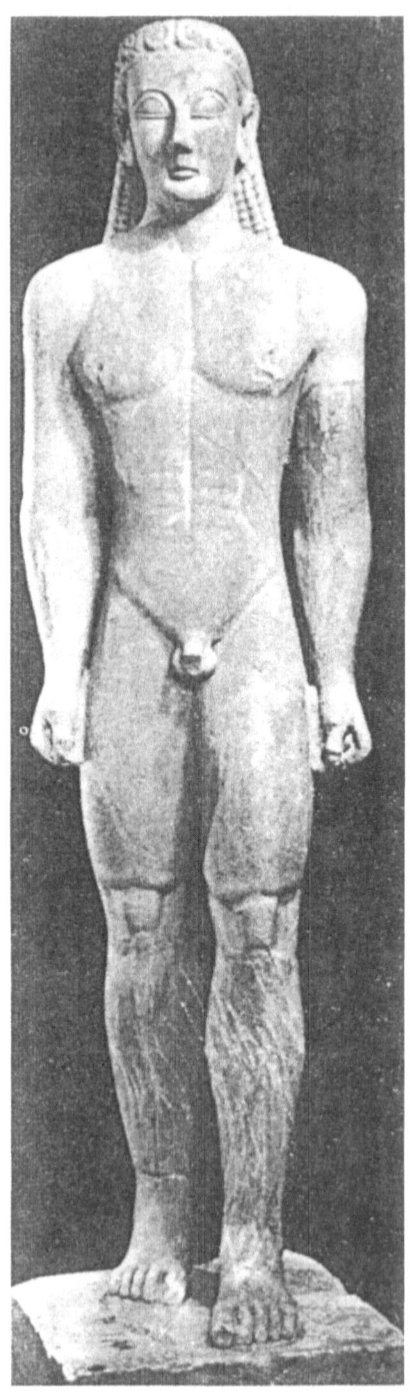

Figure 21. *Dioscurus of Sounion (Attica).*

expiate the murder of Procris.[3] They arrived on the coast of Attica at the closest landfall to Hymettus (the mountain of "many colors"), a point which corresponds precisely to Aries, represented by the Cephalidae (map 4).

In describing the sanctuaries of Attica, Pausanias mentions them in the exact order of the zodiacal signs. This is especially striking for the first four or five signs, which suggests that he knew of this division. First he names the sanctuary of Demeter "the lawgiver" at Alimus (sign of Aries), then the sanctuaries of Zoster and Anagyrus (sign of Taurus). He follows this by mentioning the cult of the Dioscuri at Kephale and even points out that, for the people of Kephale, the Dioscuri are the "Great Gods". The temple of Apollo at Prasiae represented the sign of Cancer for Attica. It also stood for Virgo and Attica itself in the Delphic system.

The rest of Pausanias's text is less precise because of an accumulation of details and anecdotes. One may nevertheless deduce from it that the main sanctuary of Apollo for the sign of Leo was at Myrrhinus. Also in this sign was the Lycaeum, named after Lycus, son of Pandion, founder of the cult of Apollo Lykeios in Attica. There is also a significant monument placed exactly on the line of the beginning of Leo in this system. This is the Lion of Kanza-Leontarion, at the foot of Hymettus about five hundred meters to the left of the Mesogeas road toward Koropi (fig. 22). This stone lion from the Hellenistic period (fourth or fifth century?) closely resembles the lion found at Izmir.[4] At present its head, turned to the left, seems to be looking towards the northwest (summer sunset). The lion is on a leveled terrace where a chapel of Saint Nicholas now stands. That the site has been occupied since antiquity is shown by the presence of a ringed enclosure in a nearby wood and many stones with traces of carving. And it is not impossible that a more ancient lion preceeded the present one.

The statue of Athena on the summit of the Pentelicus[5] and the sanctuary of Rhamnus were related to the sign of Virgo. (Every deme probably had its own sanctuary of Athena, the protectress of Attica.)

The legend of Icarius, who introduced the grape into Attica, and the story of the hanging of Erigone took place in the valley of Dionysus. The identification of Erigone with Virgo is to be expected, since this valley is on the northern slope of the Pentelicus in the sign of Virgo for Attica.[6]

The sanctuary of Amphiaraus, a hero of Theban origin, is associated with the sign of Libra, which characterizes Thebes.

The sign of Scorpio covers a sparsely populated region in the foothills of the Parnes, where there was a sanctuary of Pan. Sagittarius corresponds to the edge of the mountain closest to Eleusis. Apollodorus[7] relates that Poseidon, protector of horses, had brought the centaurs who had survived the massacre to Pholus and had hidden them in the mountain near Eleusis. This indeed corresponds to the sign of Sagittarius for Attica.

According to Diodorus of Sicily, Demeter specially founded the Lesser Mysteries in honor of Heracles to purify him of the murder of the centaurs.[8]

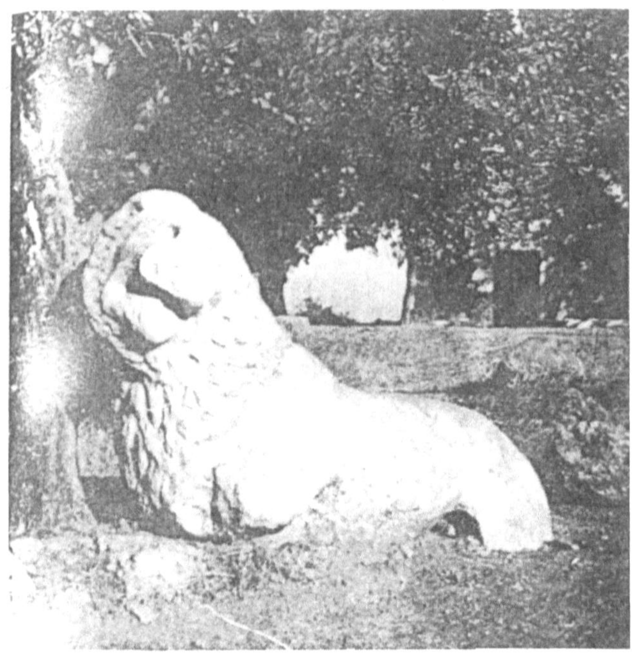

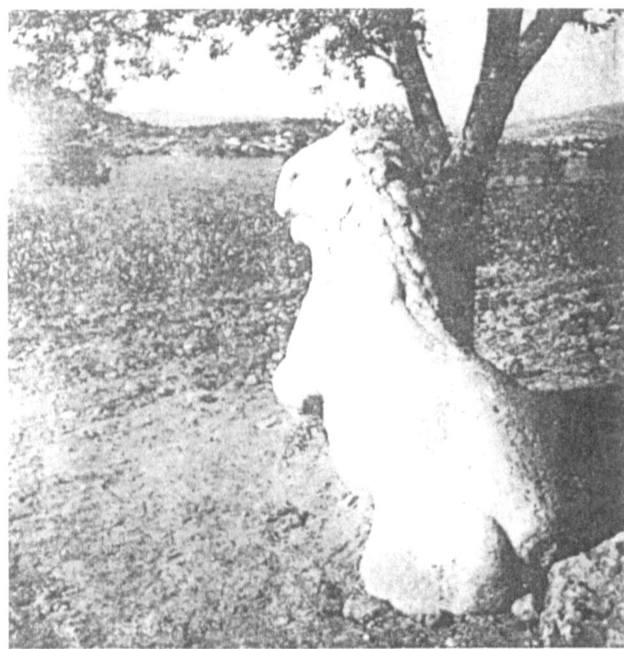

Figure 22A & B. *The Lion of Kanza (Leontarion, Attica).*

Since the murder took place in the heart of winter, I believe that Heracles had to wait until spring to be purified.[9]

2. The Mysteries: Agrae and Eleusis

It is interesting to see how the zodiacal wheel centered on Delphi is connected with the system proper to Attica. The "polar" direction for Attica is symbolically represented by 0 degree Virgo, since the province was placed under the special protection of Athena.

The Mysteries are associated with this Cancer-Capricorn direction of Attica.

Brauron, whose sanctuary of the Great Bear was part of the Delphic system, is associated with the polar direction and the sign of Cancer in Attica, the two solstitial directions being symbolically equivalent. Thus the young "bears" are associated with the idea of the incarnation of souls and the "gateway of humanity." Eleusis, in Capricorn, site of a much fuller initiation, corresponds to the "gateway of the gods."

One reads in Julian's *Orations*: "Thus the Athenians celebrate the Mysteries of Deo twice: the Lesser Mysteries when the sun is in Aries, and the Greater when it is in the Claws (Libra)."[10] In Greek the word for the sign of Libra is *zygos*, a word found in various forms in most Indo-European languages (in English, "yoke"), which is related to the Sanskrit *yoga*, meaning "union," especially the union of the soul with the divine.

The Lesser Mysteries thus took place towards the spring equinox, symbolized by the rock of Leucas at the beginning of the period of yearly increase, which reaches its maximum in June. The Greater Mysteries were celebrated during the autumnal equinox, at the beginning of the period of yearly decrease that lasts until the winter solstice (these are in relation to Delos).

Pausanias describes the location of the sanctuary of Agrae in this manner: "Across the Ilisus is a district called Agrae and a temple of Artemis Agrotera ("the Huntress"). They say that Artemis first hunted there when she came from Delos, and for this reason the statue carries a bow."[11]

The site of this sanctuary may be recognized southeast of the acropolis near the spring of Callirrhoe by the present church of Hagia Photini. This means that the sanctuary of Agrae was situated on the Delos-Prasiae-Acropolis-Eleusis-Delphi line and therefore on the suggested polar and solstitial axis. So the Greater and Lesser Mysteries took place on the solstitial axis of Attica, while their dates were those of the equinoxes. Thus the four essential times of the year were represented by a single axis. (See map 4.)

That the cult of Boreas is found on this polar and solstitial axis is not surprising. A well-known passage from Plato at the beginning of *Phaedrus* (III) tells us that the scene of Boreas's abduction of Oreithyia, the daughter of Erechtheus, took place on the banks of the Ilissus and that an altar to Boreas stood at the river crossing which led to the sanctuary of Agrae.

3. An Unusual Monument

I had already been aware for quite some time of an unusual monument which, according to the diagram, would correspond to the spring equinox for Attica.[12] Work on enlarging the Athens airport having required the removal of this monument some thousand meters further south, a Greek archeologist, M. Petracos, made a detailed study of it and excavated the site before the walls were transferred.[13] Against the longest wall was what may have been the pedestal of a statue. The remains of sculptures found near this pedestal, which Petracos kindly showed me, include the lower part of a small Gorgon's head and the debris of several animal statues among which are what appear to be the statue of a lion (thigh and tail).

Bearing in mind the text from Pausanias that has been quoted, I believe that these must be the remains of a symbolic monument commemorating the return of the Cephalidae, perhaps even a supposed "tomb" of the Cephalidae, rather than the monument of a historically known family. The zodiacal nature of the remains of the statues is undeniable: the Gorgon indicates the sign of Virgo, which governs Attica, and the lion Leo. The lion may have been accompanied by the dog of the dog-days, which would then be the smaller lion that Petracos believes he has identified among the pieces collected.

Chapter 8

Zodiacal Wheels as Keys to Decoding The Gods and the Zodiac

The zodiac and the gods of the zodiac seem more ancient than the gods of the planets. Zodiacal diagrams will act as keys to decoding or deciphering the hidden meaning of certain ancient texts, which have never before been interpreted from this point of view. They will also reveal the primordial significance of many gods of the Greek pantheon.

1. The Homeric Hymn to Hermes

According to the *Homeric Hymn to Hermes*,[1] believed to have been composed in the last third of the sixth century, Maia gave birth to the child of her secret love with Zeus on Mount Cyllene, where Pausanias was later to see the ruins of a sanctuary of Hermes.[2] It was quite rightly that pseudo-Hyginus associated Hermes with the constellation of the Charioteer, which is not far from Cyllene in the zodiacal projection. The cult of Hermes seems to have been derived from the religion of the sons of Arcas and the "Pelasgians."[3]

The main mass of Cyllene is on the south-north axis, and it corresponds in latitude to a line associated with the orbit of Mercury. It is to this, in fact, that the hymn is referring. Indeed, the first act of the newly born god was to make the seven-stringed lyre, called a phormix or cithara in the text, which is an image of the harmony of the planets (vv. 24 to 67). For this Hermes used the shell of a tortoise, symbol of the earth and the world.[4] After removing the tortoise, he stretched an oxhide around the shell and added "seven harmonious strings made of sheep-gut." Apollodorus, in a rationalistic vein that goes against the very spirit of the myth, puts the making of the lyre after the sacrifice of the cattle to "explain" the origin of the skin.[5] However, it is clear from Hesiod's *Theogony* that Hermes was the last-born of the seven great planetary gods. His birth is the fulfillment of the marriage of heaven and earth. Thus his most urgent task is to create the symbolical lyre, on which he first celebrates his birth and his parents Zeus and Maia (vv. 52 ff.).

The movements described later in the hymn take place along the south-north axis. The precocious infant travels from Mount Cyllene to Pieria, just north of Olympus in the region of the winter solstice, to steal the fifty cattle of the sun.

The cattle, says Apollo (vv. 193–95), were grazing under the watchful eye of a black bull (night?) and four vigilant dogs (the cardinal points, in my opinion).

In Chant XII of the *Odyssey*, Circe describes the island of Thrinacie, "where the Sun-god pastures his large herds and well-fed sheep. There are seven herds of cattle and as many flocks of beautiful sheep, with fifty head in each."[6] The number seems to represent a period of two years, each equal to about 350 days, but of different qualities (cows and sheep). This may mark the change of the beginning of the year from the bull to the ram and thus be related to a reform of the calendar. The year, however, has never been divided into seven. This number stands for the seven planets and the seven days of the lunar week. The number 7 × 50 could be interpreted as a way of adjusting different ways of measuring the lunar-solar year. Similarly, in the *Hymn to Hermes*, the number forty-eight (50 – 2), which could also be a number of weeks, represents both the four seasons and the twelve signs of the zodiac.

In the hymn, it is at first surprising to see Hermes driving cattle backwards, passing by Onchestus in Boeotia and arriving at the Alpheus. Hermes is traveling against the course of the zodiacal year (see map 2) along a path almost parallel to the Leo-Aquarius axis. At Onchestus (the future site of an amphictyony) he makes a ninety-degree turn and follows the Scorpio-Taurus axis to the mouth of the Alpheus. He herds the solar cattle to a short distance north of ancient Pylos, where he hides the animals in a cave after sacrificing two of them, thus reducing their number to 48 (4 × 12).[7] This journey of initiation suggests a reform of the calendar and a renewal of the year, as a result of the completion of the harmony of the planets. Norman O. Brown[8] quite rightly underscored the "magical" aspect of the theft of Apollo's cattle by Hermes. It is highly probable that towards 2000 or 2200 B.C. the mouth of the Alpheus was in symbolic relation to spring, then situated at 0 degree Taurus. This also gives the approximate date of the birth of the god. So one may assume that the author of the hymn either knew of the precession of the equinoxes or was echoing a tradition that took it into account.[9]

The letter *alpha*, associated with spring, is related to the name Alpheus, and *aleph* in Phoenician meant "ox" or "cow." It is said that Cadmus changed the order of the alphabet but left *alpha* in first place because Boeotia is the country of cattle.[10] (see p. 18).

Historians of religion agree that Hermes was an ancient god of cairns, milestones, and boundaries. To put him into relationship with the beginning of the zodiacal year is to assign him the same role in the zodiac. The young god sacrifices two cattle, bringing their number to a multiple of twelve, and divides them into twelve parts (vv. 127 ff.), corresponding to the twelve months and the Twelve Gods. He himself is one of the twelve and abstains from eating the flesh of the sacrificed animals, despite his hunger[11] (vv. 130 ff.).

As Norman O. Brown has said, the cult of the Twelve Gods is documented earliest at Olympia and Athens[12] (about 580 at Olympia, towards 511 at Athens) and seems associated with the cults of Hermes and Hestia, a goddess who represents the omphalos and the whole divine assembly. Hermes, last-born of the seven planetary deities (even if he succeeded a more archaic bearded god) was the last to arrive among the Twelve Great Gods; Dionysus, when he was later added, took the place of Hestia. Thus it is natural to see him fulfill the planetary harmony and to found the cult of the Twelve Gods.

He then returns to his cradle on Mount Cyllene; Apollo comes to fetch him to present him to Zeus: this corresponds to another movement along the south-north axis. Together Apollo and Hermes were to return for the cattle hidden in the cave of the Alpheus. Hermes, however, enchants Apollo by playing his lyre. The leader of the choir being present, the chant takes on great intensity: "And next the goodly son of Zeus hymned the rest of the immortals according to their order in age, and told how each was born, mentioning all in order as he struck the lyre upon his arm" (vv. 429 ff.).

Hermes also invents the syrinx (pipes of Pan) (vv. 511–12), whose symbolism is similar to that of the lyre. Apollo has no plan to reestablish the former order of things. He makes an alliance and exchanges attributes with Hermes. But the cattle, bulls, or rams that Hermes was to herd are related to the beginning of the zodiac.[13] In exchange for the cithara, Apollo gives Hermes the geomantic oracle of Thriae on the slopes of Parnassus.[14] That is, he associates it with the very functioning of the center. The three old soothsayers, made forever young, were to become the Charites.

An astrological interpretation based on the zodiacal diagram illuminates an important detail of the beginning of the hymn, which tells us that the queenly Maia gave birth to him at dawn on the fourth day of the month (v. 19). It is easy to calculate that, if the sun was at the beginning of Taurus, on the fourth day of the lunation, the moon was in Gemini, a "Mercurial" sign corresponding to the site of Mount Cyllene. Thus the hymn is giving us an actual horoscope for the birth of Hermes. The sun was at the beginning of Taurus; the moon and the ascendant (he was born in the morning) were in the sign of Gemini: he was to be a clever god endowed with a gift for practicality. As R. Paingeard[15] has anticipated, the origin of the concepts which were to make of Hermes a demiurge are very ancient. To the best of my knowledge, however, no one has pointed out that they were already the very substance of the *Homeric Hymn*.

2. Hermes and Athens: the Charites; Cephalus

Various myths with which Hermes is associated must be integrated with the diagrams. I will first look at the connections of the god with the daughters of Cecrops, bearing in mind that the "Mercurial" line of latitude joins Mount Cyllene and Athens (map 1).

At Athens, the three Charites seem to have succeeded a mother-daughter pair (Auxo-Hegemone); there were also originally two Charites at Orchomenus.[16]

It must have been during the time when the zodiacal scheme was being adopted that the Graces became three young women, three sisters, at both Athens and Delos. Each one then symbolized a decan of the sign of Virgo (they also succeeded the "Thriae," which I believe can be identified with the Triple Gorgon). The daughters of Cecrops were called Aglauros, Herse, and Pandrosos. Also, certain traditions maintained that Pan, son of Penelope and Hermes, was born in Mantinea. The bas-reliefs showing Hermes with the Charites and in Pan's lair have a definite astrological meaning: the three decans of Virgo and their ruler, Hermes, are transferred to the other "Mercurial" sign of Gemini, birthplace of Pan and Hermes.[17] Hermes is again connected with Attica through the fact that he is given as the father of the hero Eleusis. And the son of Hermes and Herse is none other than Cephalus, whose association with spring is already known. So this is, once again, a very coherent system in which even apparent contradictions may be understood through the variety of viewpoints and the evolution of beliefs.

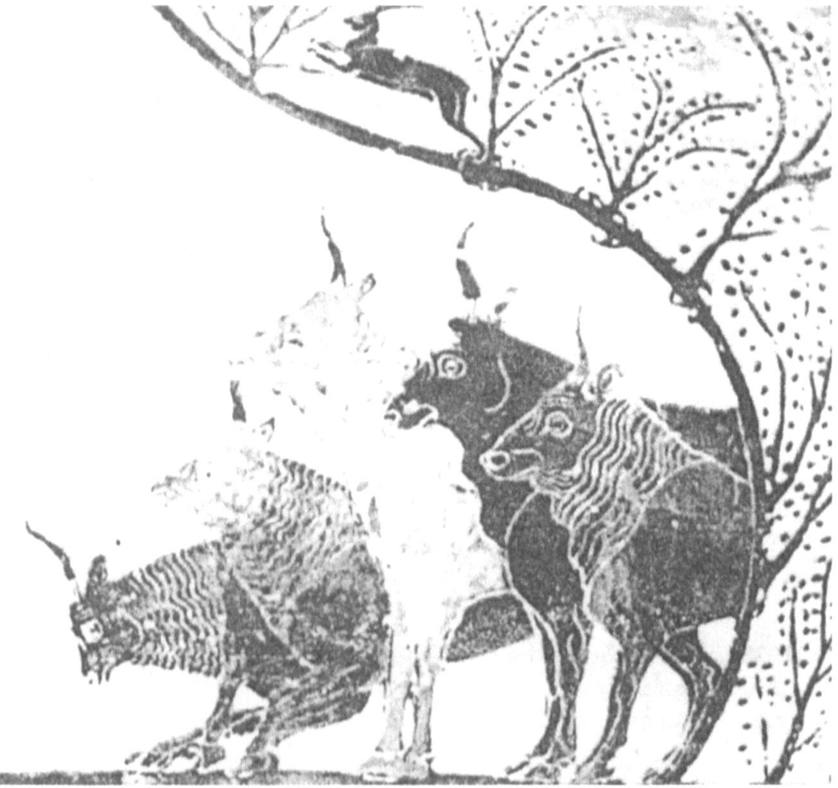

Figure 23. *The vase of the spring equinox: Apollo's cattle stolen by Hermes and the hare of of Taurus perched in a tree.*

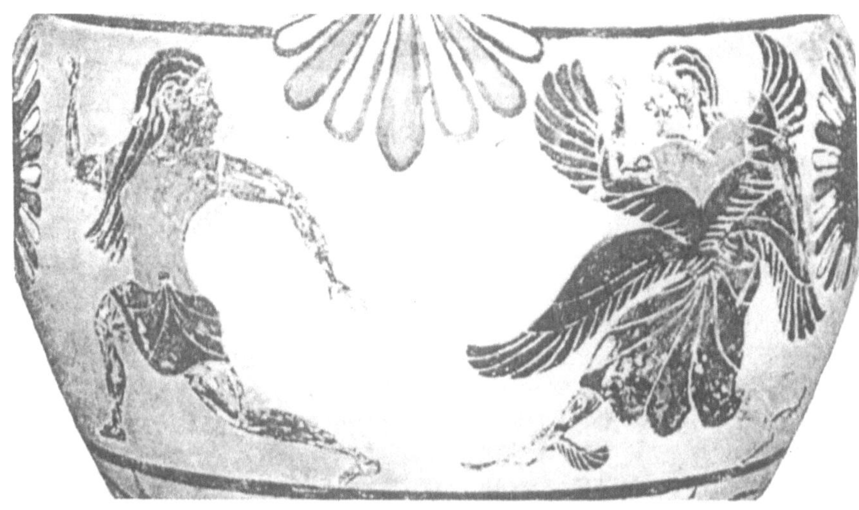

Figure 24. *Eos pursuing Cephalus.*

An Ionian vase in the Louvre (fig. 23) corroborates my interpretation of the *Hymn to Hermes*, of which it is an illustration. Above Apollo's cattle there is a little hare perched in a tree. Could this be a charming artistic fantasy? Who on earth has ever seen hares climbing in trees? This image takes on its full meaning when one remembers that the constellation of the Hare is in the zodiacal sign of Taurus and that it indeed belongs in the sky.

On the other side of the vase, Eos is in pursuit of Cephalus (fig. 24). This vase could in fact be named "vase of the spring equinox," since both sides evoke Greek myths related to the area from the mouth of the Alpheus to Cape Leucatas and to the change of the spring equinox during the historical period.

3. The Homeric Hymn to Aphrodite

This hymn, like the one to Hermes, probably dates from the sixth century. The zodiacal diagrams give greater understanding of certain facets of the text. First of all, the journey of Aphrodite, in whose heart Zeus had awakened an incoercible passion for Anchises, takes place along the Paphos–Mount Ida (or Paphos-Scepsis) direction, that is, along the Leo-Aquarius axis in the Sardis system (map 2).

Cyprus is geographically located in the sign of Leo, while representing the moon for Anatolia. Now, in the hymn, Aphrodite becomes a doublet of Artemis, a "Mistress of Beasts." She hurries toward Ida with a procession of wild animals in rut: "gray wolves, fawning on her, and grim-eyed lions, and bears, and fleet leopards, ravenous for deer."[18] The goddess of Paphos embodies the two aspects of the Chaldaean Ishtar.[19] As the goddess or star of morning she is the patroness of action and combat; as the goddess or star of evening she presides over love.

After her union with Anchises, the goddess tells him of the attraction of the gods to the mortals and describes the abduction on Mount Ida of Ganymede, who is a symbol of Aquarius. In the original form of the legend, the young man was swept away in a storm, by a whirlwind, and not snatched up by an eagle: "Verily wise Zeus carried off golden-haired Ganymede because of his beauty, to be amongst the Deathless Ones and pour drink for the gods in the house of Zeus—a wonder to see—honored by all the immortals as he draws the red nectar from the golden bowl."[20] Coins from Scepsis, the city where Anchises reigned, bear the image of Pegasus characteristic of the sign of Aquarius[21] (map 11, fig. 37). Hence, there seems to be a direct and narrow relationship between the zodiacal diagram and the text of the *Homeric Hymn to Aphrodite*.

4. Hephaestus. Scorpio. The Journey of Sacrifices. The Sacrifices. Sexual Magic

Light may be shed on the nature of the god Hephaestus by comparing two rather strange texts, one by Herodotus, the other by Pausanias, which are often quoted but have never been given a satisfactory interpretation. These parallel texts, which are really complementary, describe the journey of sacrifices.

First is the passage from Herodotus:

> But the people who tell us by far the most about them are the Delians; for, according to them, certain sacred offerings wrapped up in wheat straw come from the Hyperboreans into Scythia, whence they are taken over by the neighboring peoples in succession until they get as far west as the Adriatic; from there they are sent south, and the first Greeks to receive them are the Dodonaeans. Then, continuing southward, they reach the Malian gulf, cross to Euboea, and are passed on from town to town as far as Carystus. Then they skip Andros, the Carystians take them to Tenos, and the Tenians to Delos.[22]

If this journey is examined in relation to the zodiacal wheels on the map of Greece, one will see that the Dodona–Cape Malea line is an exact parallel to the Aquarius-Leo cosmic axis, and that the Cape Malea–Euboea–Andros–Delos itinerary connects this axis to a Scorpio-Virgo line (map 2).

Scorpio is traditionally the sign of sacrifice, especially, being ruled by Mars, of the blood or death sacrifice, while Virgo is the sign of the bloodless sacrifice.

This is the same journey as the one indicated by Callimachus in his Hymn IV, *To Delos*, (vv. 282–91). The sacrifices arrive from Dodona and go to "the holy city and the mountains of Malea," then to the plains of Boeotia and Euboea, and thence to Delos. The omission of Andros and Tenos is easily explained by the fact that the direct line from Euboea to Delos necessarily goes through these two islands (map 2).

The "holy city" of Cape Malea can only be Boeae (Boae) whose very name means "cattle." A hare is similarly associated with the foundation legend of the neighboring city of Sidace (Pausanias III, 22, 12). The temple of Apollo at Cape Epidelium, as well as that of Apollo Lithesios, belonged to the territory of the Boeaens.

Here then is the text of Pausanias:

> At Prasiae is a temple of Apollo. Hither they say are sent the first fruits of the Hyperboreans, and the Hyperboreans are said to hand them over to the Arimaspi, the Arimaspi to the Issedones, from these the Scythians bring them to Sinope, thence they are carried by Greeks to Prasiae, and the Athenians take them to Delos. The first fruits are hidden in wheat straw, and they are known of none.[23]

The Arismapi and the Issedones were, like the Scythians, people "of the north" who lived in the regions that correspond to modern Rumania and southern Russia. The beginning of the text therefore has the same meaning as the first part of the passage in Herodotus and has to do with a "Hyperborean" or "Borean" origin in relation to the Leo-Aquarius axis. If the Sinope-Prasiae line is drawn on the map, while taking the zodiacal wheels into account, this line, in its turn, creates a relationship between the sign of Scorpio in the Anatolian system and the sign of Virgo in continental Greece. Also, this line is perpendicular to the two Leo-Aquarius axes (Xanthus-Lampsacus and Hermione-Corinth-Delphi) and to the Dodona–Cape Malea line. What is appearing here is the astrological aspect of squaring. The two journeys have the same symbolic significance and put the spiritual sign of Aquarius, the former sign of the winter solstice, into relationship with two kinds of sacrifice, connected by geographic locations.

Some of the sacrifices are associated with the Martian sign of Scorpio, others with the Mercurial sign of Virgo, and the transition is made, as one might expect, from the blood sacrifice to the bloodless.

Arrived at this point in my deductions and observations, I must question some of their implications. There is a strange god in the Greek pantheon by the name of Hephaestus. This god is very prominent at Lemnos, where he was said to have been hurled by Zeus, and at Athens, where he was was specially venerated in association with Athena. Now, according to the diagrams, the island of Lemnos and in particular the site of the temple of Hephaestus are in the sign of Scorpio in the Delphic system.

So is Samothrace, the island of the Cabiri, secondary divinities with whom Hephaestus has more than one affinity. The sanctuary of the Cabiri at Lemnos is situated just opposite the temple of Hephaestus and the city of Hephaestia, to the north of the bay of Ekatokephales, a winding break in the Gulf of Purnia. Below the sanctuary of the Cabiri lies the cave "of Philoctetes."

What is more, a text of Plutarch (*Isis and Osiris*, 28 ff.) reveals the existence of a strange colossus in the city of Sinope: "Ptolemy Soter dreamt that he saw the colossus of Pluto at Sinope, and since he didn't know that it existed and had never seen it, he had no idea of what it looked like."

The rest of the text tells us that this statue, which was the origin of the cult of Sarapis, was thought to be a statue of Pluto (Hades), because it had Cerberus and the dragon as emblems. It could also validly be considered to represent Hephaestus. Of greatest importance from my point of view is his "infernal" nature, clearly characteristic of Scorpio, the sign in which Sinope was located in the Sardis system.[24]

Having taken these spatial locations into account, my considered opinion is that the god Hephaestus was originally a guardian of the zodiacal sign of Scorpio.

A linguistic confirmation that is not to be disregarded is offered by A. de Paniagua, who writes:

> In Sanskrit, *pha* designates a ceremony in honor of the Kinnaras, during the course of which a great sacrifice was made. Now, "sacrifice" is *isti*. By joining the two words and adding an expletive prefix, in this case *e*, we obtain the composed word *e-phai-isti* with regard to 'Ηφαιστος. This example of a god taking on the name of a sacrifice is not unique. . . . He was definitely a sacrifice become a god.[25]

Hephaestus, god of sacrifices, is also a sacrificed god. He is especially associated with the magical and constricting nature of sacrifice. This is why the other gods ridiculed him.

His association with Athena and Athens is therefore more understandable. The two zodiacal deities share common characteristics and form a dyad. Hephaestus is born from Hera alone, as Athena is from Zeus. They are two aspects of the same divinity, which is also demonstrated by the similarity of the zodiacal glyphs for Virgo ♍ and Scorpio ♏ . These hark back to a distant past, earlier than the introduction of the sign of Libra into the zodiac, when the two signs were one.

The god Hephaestus and his relationship with Lemnos have been studied in detail by Marie Delcourt.[26] Her work contributes much supportive evidence. From my point of view, the main result of her work is that Hephaestus is primarily related to the sign of Scorpio and secondarily to the Leo-Aquarius axis, through the astrological aspect of squaring.[27]

Hera, bound or immobilized by Hephaestus, gives an image of the Taurus-Scorpio opposition. Similarly, when Ares and Aphrodite are freed from the fetters of Hephaestus, Ares hurries towards Thrace (Aquarius direction in the Sardis system) and Aphrodite towards Paphos (direction of Leo in the same system).[28]

Everything about the simultaneously sexual and infernal nature of the magician Hephaestus reinforces his connections with the sign of Scorpio and emphasizes his analogy with Athena. He is indeed her male counterpart: to the power of virginity corresponds the controlled sexuality of the magician. These are two analogous and equivalent aspects of sacrifice. Hephaestus bears a *pilos* in the shape of a phallus and has the crooked feet of a sorcerer. He represents the acquisition of magical powers through the sacrifice of sexuality, the transformation and transposition of sexual energy.

God of sexual magic, Hephaestus is also particularly associated with miraculous births. His desire was naturally to be directed towards Athena. From their unsuccessful union was born the serpent Erichthonius. This is because Hephaestus was preceeded in the sign of Scorpio by an ancient serpent-god, Ophion (who will be discussed again). His master is Cedalion, who prefigures him and is almost identical with him. Hephaestus is associated with fire, especially the volcanic fire of Lemnos.

The great legends of Lemnos are colored by the characteristics of the sign of Scorpio. An unpleasant loss of the sense of smell plays an important role in the legend of the Lemnians. Similarly, in the legend of Philoctetes, a character associated with fire like Hephaestus, famous for having lit the funeral pyre of Heracles and who was to arson Troy, a serpent (or some venomous creature) appears, sent by the angry Hera, and bites him on the foot. The stench given off by his wound is so unbearable that the Greeks, who are bound for Troy, abandon him at Lemnos.

In my opinion, the rite which consisted in going to fetch the new fire at Delos represents a change in the axis of reference. This is the transition from volcanic fire to solar fire, from Scorpio to the solstitial axes, from the system centered on Delphi to that of Delos. The freedom from servitude (and bad odors) associated with Scorpio would have gone hand in hand with a renunciation of magical powers. Marie Delcourt has perceived that this was related to a solar cycle.[29] The exact date of the ceremony of the new fire is unknown. I think that its most probable date would have been very close to the summer solstice.[30] The change in the axis of reference can also be interpreted as describing the adoption of a new calendar. In my second volume, I shall examine various symbols and monuments that describe the history of the calendar in allegorical terms, which specifically commemorate the transition from the Taurus-Scorpio axis (year beginning at the equinox) to the solstitial axis, and vice versa.

The three examples of the *Hymn to Hermes*, the *Hymn to Aphrodite*, and the texts of the journey of sacrifices demonstrate how the zodiacal wheels can illuminate certain previously unfathomable texts of Greek antiquity. Note that most of the journeys take place along directions identical to the lines of the solstices (Aquarius-Leo or Capricorn-Cancer) or those of the equinoxes (especially Taurus-Scorpio). Sometimes the symbolic journeys occur in directions parallel to the great zodiacal axes.

This key to decoding may well be of future use in interpreting other texts. My present vision of archaic Greek civilization is that every aspect of it was completely imbued with astral and astrological beliefs. In an article entitled "Errances and passions divines,"[31] Jacqueline Duchemin mentions several journeys of enigmatic meaning. In my opinion, all of them should be interpreted in terms of sacred geography.

5. Poseidon, the Horse-god, and the Sign of Gemini

It is rather generally accepted that Poseidon was a god associated with the earth, the deputy of Demeter (πόσις Δᾶς). In a horse's shape, he coupled with the mare Demeter. He was associated with horses at Haliartus in Boeotia and Telphusa in Arcadia. A wooden statue of Demeter with a mare's head was venerated at Phigalia, which was restored by order of the Delphic oracle.[32]

Since Phlius was the omphalos of the Peloponnese,[33] a simple drawing shows that Mount Helicon must have been another site of Posedion's cult.[34] This is confirmed by the very text of the *Homeric Hymn to Poseidon*. The great Poseidon, we are told, is the shaker of the earth and the restless sea. As a marine god he possesses Helicon and the great realm of Aegeus (the Aegean Sea). The gods honored the Worldshaker with the attributes of being a tamer of horses and the savior of ships. As a horse-god, Poseidon is given as the father of Pegasus and the horse Arion. In parallel Indian myths, Vivasvat, changed into a horse, was united with the goddess Varanyu and she gave birth to the two Açvins, who correspond to Gemini. Now Castor and Pollux, as I have said, are also constantly associated with horses and portrayed on horseback. It would appear, by the way, that the sign of Gemini was preceded by an ancient sign of the horse.

Phigalia is on the line marking the beginning of Gemini, and there was a sanctuary of Poseidon Hippocurius at Sparta. At Cape Taenarum stood the colossal statue of Poseidon mentioned by Pausanias.[35] Taenarum is in the very heart of Dioscuric territory, since it was on the little island of Pephnos, said to be their birthplace, that Pausanias mentions seeing little statues of them.[36]

One encounters the same association of Poseidon with Gemini at Cape Sounion, site of the colossoi, of which one is still extant (see p. 73 and fig. 21). Conversely, Strabo tells us that the Dioscuri were known as the "Guardians of the Sea" and the "Saviors of Sailors."[37] This was one of the same functions of the two Cabiri of Samothrace, identified with the Dioscuri. It is therefore not surprising to see that one of the "palaces of Poseidon" was at Eges, at the foot of the heights of Samothrace.

If these deductions are correct, one should also find the cult of Poseidon at Miletus and at Didyma. And this is immediately confirmed: the mythical ancestor of the royal dynasty of Miletus was a Neleus, son of Poseidon, originally from Pylos in the Peloponnese (this is the Pylos of Nestor, the country of horses, in the sign of Gemini).

What is more, the cult of Poseidon Enipeus at Miletus establishes a connection between that city and a tributary of the Alpheus called the Enipeus.

The sanctuary of Didyma is very close to a Cape Poseidon.[38] Once again the latitude of Delos provides the link between the two systems of Greece proper and Anatolia. The fact that the cult of Poseidon is regularly associated with that of the Dioscuri leads me to believe that Poseidon is an ancient guardian of the zodiacal sign of Gemini who became a great god.

Other characteristics of the cult and legend of Poseidon seem to support this point of view. He never succeeded in reigning alone in any city. At Aegina he is supplanted by Zeus; at Naxos, Dionysus triumphs over him; at Troezen and Athens, Athena;[39] at Argos, he is supplanted by Hera. He surrenders all his rights to Delphi in exchange for Taenarum (which again draws attention to the great south-north axis). It may be surprising that he, and not Zeus, spoke on behalf of obtaining the freedom of Ares and Aphrodite, prisoners of the toils of Hephaestus. But isn't this because, like Aphrodite and Hephaestus, he is one of the zodiacal deities who became the great gods of Olympus?

A series of geometrical figures unites the great sanctuaries of Demeter and Poseidon, and makes the connection between Poseidon and Gemini. Readers may refer to the description of the rectangle defined by the great sanctuaries of Demeter (p. 59). Let me now add that the Pephnos-Phlius-Helicon and Cape Taenarum–Isthmia lines are parallel to the Lycosura-Pheneus-Delphi and Hermione-Eleusis lines.

Mount Helicon clearly appears as the place of the union of Poseidon and Demeter, the parents of Pegasus.

The sanctuaries of Poseidon at Taenarum, Isthmia, and Cape Sounion form a right triangle whose height passes at Calauria, seat of an important maritime amphictyony. I have seen on site at Calauria that the temple was orientated to a northeast-southwest direction, parallel to the Sounion-Taenarum line. According to Strabo,[40] Poseidon would have given Delos to Latona in exchange for Calauria. The author names the seven cities of the league: Hermione, Epidaurus, Aegina, Athens, Prasiae (on the coast of the Peloponnese), Nauplia, and Orchomenus. The presence on this list of Orchomenus, a Boeotian city located in the interior on the meridian of Isthmia, is a reference to the earthly origin of the god. This is why one often sees Poseidon or his trident on Boeotian coins.[41]

An Isthmia-Helicon-Orchomenus-Antron meridian marks the opposition-affinity of Poseidon and Demeter (map 3). Antron is the antique sanctuary mentioned at the end of the *Hymn to Demeter*.

All this makes me wonder whether the Demeter-Poseidon complementarity might not be a transposition of Gemini and Sagittarius, the two complementary and opposing signs of the horse.

Chapter 9

The Cult of Zeus Sardis, Delphi, and the Oasis of Siwa A System Centered on Ammoneion

1. Sites of the Cult of Zeus

The principal sanctuaries of Zeus are on high mountain peaks: Mount Ida and Mount Dicte in Greece, Mount Ida in Mysia, Olympus in Thessaly, Mount Lycaeon, Mount Ithome, etc. Mount Ida of Mysia and Mount Lycaeon were also known as Olympus. It is therefore not surprising to find Zeus associated with the great Leo-Aquarius axis.

The legends of his childhood among the Curetes and those concerning the Curetes and the Cabiri take place in sites that have been assigned to the signs of Leo and Aquarius. An important text in this regard is Strabo (X, 3, 1–6). This author discusses at length the location of a people called the Curetes in Aetolia or Acarnania (provinces attached to Aquarius or the ancient sign of the Boar in the Heraclean system centered on Phlius). He then compares Mount Ida of Crete with Mount Ida of the Troad, Lemnos with Samothrace, which are the regions of the Corybantes, Cabiri, Idaean Dactyls, Telchines, and Curetes. These areas correspond to the two great Leo-Aquarius cosmic axes in the zodiacal wheels of Delphi and Sardis (see pp. 4 and 45). According to legend, while Rhea was hiding the newborn Zeus, the role of the boisterous dancers was first to distract Kronos's attention, and then to cover up the sound of the babe's cries. So it was not without good reason that Strabo compared the role of the Curetes in Zeus's childhood to the cult of Dionysus.

Since the sign of Leo belongs primarily to the solar god Apollo, I am led to consider that the sign of Aquarius may be attributed to the master of the gods. This would correspond well with the location of the ancient sanctuary of Dodona (before the birth of the god Hermes, son of Zeus and Maia).

Simple geometrical relationships seem to unite the sanctuaries of Zeus, the places where the master of the gods was specially venerated, and sites dedicated to Hera. The throne of Zeus is on the summit of Olympus of Thessaly. Midway on the Mount Ida–Olympus line lies the island of Aegina. The great sanctuary of Panellenian Zeus occupied the highest hill of this island, which is the closest site on dry land to the middle of the considered line. The median of this line intersects Mount Ithome in Messenia, where there were human sacrifices to Zeus. Mount Lycaeon, a little to the north, was also sacred to a savage Zeus, the man-eating wolf.

The Mount Ithome–Mount Lycaeon direction goes to Olympus, and the Dodona–Mount Ithome line, almost parallel to Aegina-Olympus, passes near Olympia. The Mount Ida–Dodona line intersects Nemea, like the Stratos–Mount Thorax line. There were important sanctuaries of Zeus at Nemea and Stratos. In viewing this figure as a whole (map 3), one may well wonder whether the ancient Greeks didn't see a symbolic correspondence between Mount Ida of Crete and Olympus, on the one hand, and Dodona and the Dictynnaion of eastern Crete, on the other. Also, Dodona and Mount Ida of Mysia are appreciably at the same latitude (map 1).

2. The Sardis-Delphi-Ammoneion Triangle

I believe that I have succeeded in reconstituting the three zodiacal systems of the Aegean centered on Delphi, Delos, and Sardis, respectively, from studying the alignments of the great sanctuaries. The results of my deductions are confirmed in every case by an examination of the most ancient coins.

These zodiacal wheels have already shed light on the probable significance of certain enigmatic texts. As I have just briefly indicated, and as I will show in greater detail in the following chapters, they also illuminate certain myths and explain the variables in related stories and parallel myths that take place in different geographic locations but have identical meanings.

By taking a nearly opposite approach and studying the myths in which Libya, Egypt, and Palestine play a part, I have rediscovered, at least in general outline, a system centered on Ammoneion (modern oasis of Siwa) and its sanctuary of Zeus. The association of sanctuaries of Zeus with those of Apollo in symbolic geography should not be surprising. The great sanctuaries of Zeus, particularly Dodona, are associated with the Leo-Aquarius axes, and Mounts Ida of Crete and of Phrygia are equivalent. The oasis of Ammon is the origin of a third Leo-Aquarius cosmic axis, parallel to the two others, that goes toward Upper Egypt to the southeast, while it passes near Cyrene and then cuts southern Italy at Metapontum to the northwest.

Most striking are the geometric relationships uniting Ammoneion with Sardis, Delphi, and Delos. It is known that Plato attributed equal authority to the oracles of Dodona, Delphi, and Ammon when it was a question of founding a city (see p. 24). Now if on the map one joins Delphi, Sardis, and Ammoneion, one will obtain an interesting isoceles triangle whose height is double the length of the base.

The height of this triangle, struck from Ammoneion, intersects Delos. If it is extended northward, one finds in its proximity the peaks of the Balkan Mountains, ancient Haemus, the homeland of Boreas, the modern Jumruktchal. This peak seems to have played the same role on this south-north axis as Mount

Olympus to Delphi, as already mentioned. The sanctuary of Apollo Lithesios, whose name refers to the baetyl (sacred stone) of the omphalos, marks the Delphi-Ammoneion line (see p. 68).

The sanctuary of Apollo on the island Triopion at Cnidos, which was the seat of the Dorian hexarchy,[1] is on the Sardis-Ammoneion line. The geometrical figure obtained (map 5) graphically outlines the double origin of the system. This is, on the one hand, Babylonian (with relay via Sardis and Lycia) and, on the other, Phoenician and Egyptian, relayed by Libya and Crete. This strongly suggests that precise rules governed the generation of the great traditional centers in relation to one another.

Delphi and Sardis. Thus one better understands certain intriguing details of the history of the Delphic oracle that link Delphi with Lydia. In the treasury of the Corinthians at Delphi, Herodotus was shown Midas's chair, where the latter sat while administering justice, which had been donated by Gyges.[2]

On the well-known story of the accession of Gyges to the throne, related by the same historian,[3] H. W. Parke has written: "One cannot conceive that in Lydia by the early seventh century the Delphic oracle was already held in such veneration that a question of kingship could be asked of it by general agreement."[4] Now, this is not only conceivable, but quite natural, if, as my observations and deductions seem to indicate, the oracle of Delphi could at that time have been considered by the Lydians as the heir and legitimate successor to the oracle of Cybele at Sardis, as the same oracle which would merely have been displaced in longitude as a consequence of some ineluctable astronomical or historical phenomenon.

3. Myths and Monuments Confirming the Existence of This System

I am not able, at least for the moment, to describe the system centered on Ammoneion by finding detailed evidence for each zodiacal sign, as I was for the preceeding wheels. Myths and monuments nevertheless provide a series of cross-checks that are all consistent and allow me at least to define the six great zodiacal axes.

a) The Pisces-Virgo Axis. According to the legends of the Pelasgians, the goddess Athena was born near Lake Tritonis in Libya (the south of modern Tunisia). She was discovered there and brought up by three local nymphs who wore goatskins and became in her turn the teacher of Dionysus. Plato identified the patronness of Athens with the Libyan goddess Neith and the river Triton in Boeotia; near Lake Copais is the image of Lake Tritonis of Libya. The memory of a triple goddess still lingered there (Triton meaning the third), whose cult had been imported into Greece via Crete. Herodotus declares that the clothes and the aegis of Athena were inspired by the costume of Libyan women.[5] Lake Tritonis indeed corresponds to the Pisces direction in relation to Ammoneion.

Certain details of the legend of Perseus exactly describe this Pisces-Virgo axis: after beheading the Gorgon, Perseus casts the eye and the teeth of the Graeae into Lake Tritonis and then rests at Chemmis in Egypt.[6] Similarly, the myth of Belus, who was king of Chemmis, specially protected by Athena-Neith, and father of the twins Aegyptus and Danaus, seems to relate to a Libyan and Palestinian colonization of the Peloponnese via Rhodes. This has direct bearing on the system centered on the oasis of Ammon.[7] Belus's stay in Rhodes during his journey towards the Peloponnese establishes a connection with the sign of Virgo in the system centered on Delphi.

b) The Sphinx and Libra. An immense question that I do not claim to resolve, but which shows the great antiquity of this system, is raised by the fact that the Sphinx of Gizeh represents the guardian of the sign of Libra for Ammoneion. That is, it corresponds symbolically to Mount Sphinx and the sanctuary of Ptoon in Boeotia. The Sphinx of Gizeh is probably one of the most ancient monuments considered in this study. Its integration with the Libyan system seems to bear testimony to its extreme antiquity, probably associated with the discovery of the zodiac and the institution of the calendar.

c) The Sign of the Eagle (Scorpio). Heliopolis (Balbec), Palmyra, and Hierapolis are situated in the sign of the Eagle for Ammoneion. There are many documents on this point surviving from the Roman era.

d) Sagittarius. The name Chiron appears on archaic inscriptions at Thera (Santorini).[8] This does not necessarily indicate, as is generally believed, a cult "imported from Magnesia," but there is an analogous relationship between this island, situated in Sagittarius in relation to Ammoneion, and Magnesia, in the same sign in relation to Delphi. Let me add that Thera and Milo were part of the Dorian world, while the other Cyclades were Ionian.

e) The Solstitial Axis. As already noted in speaking of Ammoneion, the direction of north and Capricorn corresponds to Delos, and beyond to Mount Haemus, the legendary homeland of Boreas. Now, the cult of Boreas does seem to be of Libyan origin.[9] To the south are the "Mountains of the Moon," whose significant name relates to the sign of Cancer, the house of the moon.

It is rather remarkable that the signs of Sagittarius and Capricorn of the Ammoneion system define the Dorian world very precisely, whose eastern frontier was at Perga, while to the west it covered the southern part of the Peloponnese, including Rhodes, Cnidos, Halicarnassus, Cos, Crete, Carpathus, Astypalaea, Thera, Milo, and Cythera.

f) The Leo-Aquarius Axis. This axis connects the Upper Nile (Abu-Simbel area) with the direction of Cyrene. The Greco-Roman name for Edfu was Apollinopolis Magna. In studying the oracle of the founding of Cyrene by the people of Thera, I shall explain the probable role of astrological wheels in oracles of foundation and colonization. Thera was related to the sign of Leo in the Delphic system, while Cyrene was on the Leo-Aquarius axis in the system centered on Ammoneion.

4. The Legend of Ammon and the Ritual of the Oracle

Let us now scrutinize the legend of Ammon as transmitted by Diodorus of Sicily.[10] There it is said that Dionysus was the son of Ammon and Amaltheia, or Aries and the Goat (the spring equinox and the winter solstice); Dionysus was known as the "Kid" and was brought up by Aristaeus and Athena at Nyssa, on an island surrounded by the "River Triton" in Libya.

Ammon is a god more ancient than Kronos and Zeus. Fleeing the jealousy of his wife Rhea, Ammon sought refuge in Crete. This ram-headed deity seems to be the chief of the cohort of the "Ammonian gods," that is, the gods of the zodiac, of whom there were twelve, thirty-six, seventy-two, or three hundred and sixty. A statue of the god with four rams' heads, corresponding to the four directions of space, has been found at Ammoneion, and the god is commonly portrayed with two heads.

Lucian, or the unknown author of the treatise *On Astrology*, had no doubts on this and wrote: "The oracle of Ammon, established with the Lybians, is also associated with the heavens and with the wisdom that emanates from them; this is why Ammon is portrayed as a ram."[11]

The zodiacal nature of Ammon is confirmed by the presence of a sanctuary, on the way from Sardis to Delphi, dedicated to him at Thebes in Boeotia in the sign of Libra, opposed to Aries.[12]

The ram-god appeared on the sculpted frieze of the Siphnian Treasury, now in the Museum of Delphi, whose subject was a Gigantomachy (fig. 25). Other representations of Ammon have been studied in *Delphes, Délos et Cumes*, where this one was first mentioned.

Diodorus of Sicily described the procession of the oracle of Ammon in this manner:

> "Covered with emeralds and other ornaments, the idol of the god Ammon gives oracles in a very odd way. It is borne along in a long golden boat on the shoulders of eighty priests, who automatically go where the divine will pushes them. And following behind is a procession of young girls and women, chanting paeans and hymns all along the road.[13]

This procession, I believe, was an imitation of the circular movement of the stars, especially of the sun. The oracular interpretation of the direction taken by the solar boat was necessarily associated with the symbolism of the spatial directions and probably with the system of zodiacal domification. The number 80 should no doubt be interpreted as 12×6 (one priest per half a decan?) + 8, a possible reference to an ancient division of the zodiac into eight.

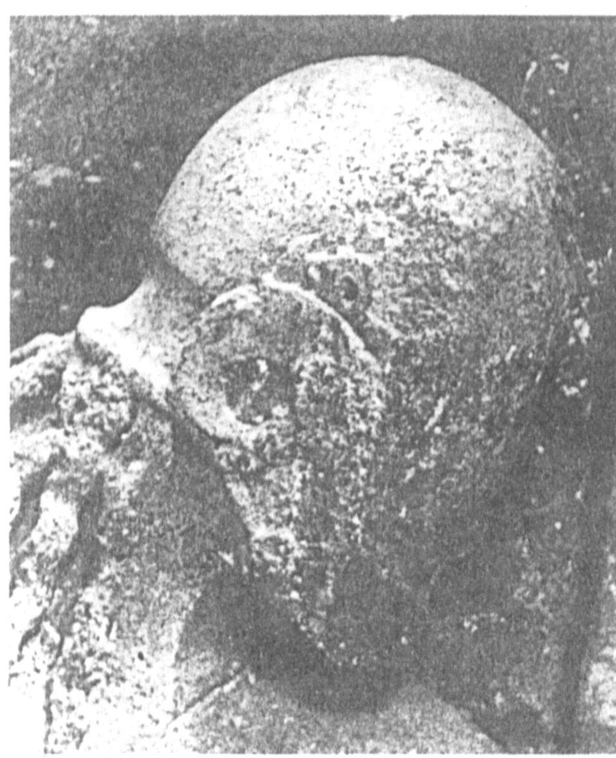

Figure 25. *Gigantomachy of the Siphnian Treasury: Ammon (Museum of Delphi).*

If one wishes to compare this to a mystical reality that is closer in time, one should look to the whirling dervishes, whose dance imitates the movement of the planets and the sun (and not to table-turning!). A comparison of this sort has been made by W. K. G. Guthrie on the Bacchanalia.[14] The procession of Ammon, the dances of the cult of Dionysus, and those of the mevlevis have similar meanings.

The sanctuary of Ammoneion, because of its position in the desert, seems to have simultaneously represented the omphalos of the system and the sign of Aries, the beginning and the totality of the annual cycle. A comparison of the statue of Ammon with a Sumerian image with the same meaning is, in this respect, extremely revealing. The four-faced Sumerian god represents the four seasons and the four spatial directions; under his foot is the ram of the New Year and the serpent he is holding represents the zodiac.[15]

At Gytheum, Pausanias[16] saw a sanctuary of Ammon whose significance as a marker was similar to that of the temple of Apollo Lithesios on the Delphi-Ammoneion line. We are, therefore, in the presence of a very vast cohesive unity.

Chapter 10

The Calendars of Heracles Guardians of the Signs

A statement repeated dozens of times, accepted as true since Hyginus and Eratosthenes, and included in many reference books is that the twelve labors of Heracles symbolize the twelve signs of the zodiac. But this statement, which is essentially superficial, is never followed by a table showing the correspondences between the labors and the signs, for the excellent reason that it cannot be done!

If one makes the attempt to unravel the problem, one will see that the Lion of Nemea does indeed stand for the sign of Leo, and the Hydra of Lerna, Cancer. The slaughter of the centaurs can also be related to Sagittarius. But here the difficulties begin already, because the destruction of the centaurs is not one of the twelve labors, and every effort to obtain a complete zodiac from the list of labors is in vain.

The problem must therefore be approached from another angle, and one soon realizes that the whole history of Heracles should be studied through the writings of an ancient geographer like Diodorus or a mythographer like Apollodorus. It is immediately obvious that one is dealing with a collection of traditions from successive stages in the history of a culture or civilization, which are sometimes quite difficult to coordinate. If, as is generally believed today, the heroes preceded the gods, the symbolism of the labors of Heracles must belong to a very ancient tradition. Diodorus of Sicily[1] said that there had been several Heracles, who themselves had been the heirs of a whole mythic history that included elements of diverse origins. The Hindu Hanuman, for example, is another hero like this, and the Babylonian Gilgamesh, whose history may have been transmitted to the Greeks by the Phoenicians, and again, the Phoenician Melqart.

The seeming complexity of the system that I am trying to reconstruct is, once again, associated with the precession of the equinoxes. In a distant past, toward the dawn of the historical era, when the first civilizations began a systematic observation of the sky, the spring equinox was in Taurus, the autumnal equinox was in Scorpio (the Eagle), and the summer and winter solstices in Leo and Aquarius (or the Boar), respectively.

These four cardinal signs always kept something of their original meaning even after the astronomical reality had changed. This was especially true of Taurus, which was long associated with the beginning of the year. However, from about 2000 B.C., the spring equinox actually occurred in the sign of Aries because of the displacement of the colure of the equinoxes. The autumnal equinox then corresponded to Libra, and the summer and winter solstices changed to Cancer and Capricorn, respectively. As far as the sacred geography of Greece was concerned, there obviously couldn't have been a sudden shift in the correspondences that had already been established between the different regions and the signs of the zodiac. Because of the change in the astronomic situation and before the new system had been accepted, there was a certain irresolution that resulted in superimpositions or double attributions, which are reflected in the legends and monuments. Examples of this have already been seen in the case of Argolis and Boeotia.

1. Heracles and the Peloponnese: the System Centered on Phlius

In looking at the Greek Heracles and the spatial correspondences concerning him, one must remember that he is associated above all with Argolis and the Peloponnese. The hero is constantly shown as trying to return to the country of his childhood. Alcides took on the name Heracles, "Hera's glory," because, born by chance at Thebes, he had been brought up at Tiryns, and Argolis is her domain. However, the deeper meaning of Heracles' name is "earth's glory."

One source that is crucial from my point of view is Pausanias's writings on Phlius, the omphalos of the Peloponnese. The association of cults at Phlius seems closely linked to the character of Heracles. On the acropolis of the city, an intriguing promontory that is orientated exactly east-west opens to a vast panorama, and a grove of cypresses described by the traveler sheltered a sanctuary of Ganymede-Hebe, Youth.[2]

Since Hesiod[3] said that Hebe was Heracles' spouse, and Phlius was the omphalos of the Peloponnese,[4] one should be justified in concluding that the site was, to some degree, the "home" of the hero. In this respect, the monetary symbolism (map 12, fig. 44) is equally revealing. Pausanias, in agreement with local tradition, associated with Phlius the legend of Heracles' slaying of Cyathus, the cupbearer of Oeneus, Heracles having been displeased with a drink that the young man had given him.[5] (This may mean that the Heracles-Hebe couple was preceded at Phlius by a Ganymede-Cyathus).

A final comment by Pausanias shows that we are indeed dealing with significant geographical relationships. In the market square at Phlius there was a bronze goat, partly made of gold, which I believe had more to do with a cult of Capricorn than the story about frozen vinyards that the villagers told the inquisitive tourist.[6] A Cancer-Capricorn line can be drawn which, deviating slightly from the south-north direction, intersects the following points: Cythera, Lerna, Phlius, Delphi, and Trachis (near Mount Oeta) (map 6). As might be expected, the Hydra of Lerna is assimilated to the sign of Cancer. A text of Apollodorus[7] has a crab coming to the aid of the Hydra and the crustacean then being promoted to the rank of a constellation by Hera. But this is, I think, a late interpretation, the symbolic meaning of the Hydra and the crab being the same. Celestially, the female Hydra is near Cancer.

In the Phlius system, the western part of Crete is in Cancer, as confirmed by a fine coin from Phaestus that shows Heracles killing the Lernaean Hydra of Lerna, while treading on a goat[8] (map 12, fig. 45).

To return to Capricorn, on the north coast of the Peloponnese appears a series of place-names that derive directly from the word for goat: Aigium, Aegae, Aegira. Trachis plays an important role in the legend of the death of Heracles; Apollodorus's story clearly reveals this.[9] Diodorus of Sicily says that the selection of the site of Oeta was by command of an oracle from Delphi. Suffering from the sorrows brought on by the tunic of Nessus, "He sent Licymnius and Iolaus to Delphi so that they could ask Apollo what they must do to be healed. . . . The god's reply was to bring Heracles and his weapons to Oeta and to build a great pyre next to him. He says that Zeus would take care of the rest."[10] The summit of Oeta, like Olympus, was sacred to the master of the gods.

It would seem that Heracles' funeral pyre corresponds to the "gateway of the gods" of a solstitial axis passing through Delphi and Phlius. Also, when Heracles receives the tunic sent by Deianira, he makes sacrifice to Zeus at Cape Cenaeum at the northwest end of Euboea, at the exact latitude of Oeta and in relation to a lunar line. The axis perpendicular to Delphi-Phlius, which corresponds, not to Aries-Libra, as one might think, but rather to Taurus-Scorpio, is the Olympia-Isthmia line. Thus one better understands why the great games of ancient Greece were held at Olympia, inasmuch as they were created in honor of Heracles.

The spring equinox of the system corresponds to the mouth of the Alpheus, a site of prime importance. The presence of the sign of the Boar in the Phlius zodiac suggests an ancient calendar of ten signs from which Aries and Libra were absent, and in which the year began at the summer solstice, then associated with Leo. So the axis of reference of this calendar may once have been the Nemea-Delphi-Mount Oeta direction. I thus arrive at the following system of correspondences (see table, p. 100).

In looking at the map, one sees that the directions of space are strictly respected and that the Peloponnese plays a role in seven different cases. By the way, oddly enough, for the three signs of the northeast quarter, the zodiac is completed by events that took place at some distance from the Peloponnese. The transition from the second to the third labor describes the Cancer-Capricorn axis. In the final analysis, this may be a division into eight or ten, in which the Aries-Libra axis is missing. The transition from the sixth to the seventh labor would describe a former equinoctial axis of Taurus-Eagle. In order to complete a ten-sign zodiac centered on Delphi instead of Phlius, the sign of the Boar must be replaced by Aquarius, symbolized by Nereus-Triton, the old man of the sea over whom Heracles triumphs.

A transition to the twelve-sign zodiac is impossible, because, in the heroic deeds of Heracles, the places related to the beginning of the year and to spring are represented by taurine creatures, such as the river Achelous, Deianira's suitor. Similarly, Perseus, a solar hero like Heracles, and as I will soon show, also associated with Leo, is substituted for him as the conqueror of the Gorgon, the ancient guardian of Virgo. So the sign of Aries is not really represented in the labors and deeds of Heracles, and Libra and Virgo are merged. Let me mention another interesting detail. According to one tradition, Chiron had a secret refuge in a cave at Cape Malea. And the Mount Pelion–Cape Malea line runs very nearly north to south, which demonstrates a rather good knowledge of the relative geographical positions of various sites on the Greek coast.

THE CALENDARS OF HERACLES

SIGNS	CORRESPONDING LABORS	COMMENTS
LION { I.—Leo	1st labor: Nemean Lion.	The queen has the characteristics of Virgo.
LION { II.—Virgo (and Libra)	9th labor: Girdle of Hippolyte, Queen of the Amazons.	The girdle corresponds to the hips and Libra.
EAGLE { III.—Scorpio	Admetus and Alcestis in the form of serpents. Resurrection of Alcestis. (Pherae in Thessaly).	On Scorpio, sign of Hephaestus, "infernal" sign (see pp. 85–87).
EAGLE { IV.—Sagittarius	7th labor: Horses of Diomedes. Slaughter of the Centaurs.	See the coins reproduced (map 12, fig. 46).[11]
V.—Capricorn	3rd labor: Hind of Ceryneia.	The hind here associated with the direction of north, the Hyperboreans, etc.
BOAR { VI.—Boar	4th labor: Boar of Erymanthus.	This sign here substitutes for Pisces.
BOAR { VII.—Aquarius	5th labor: Birds of Stymphalus.	These birds, having the characteristics of the sirens, were creatures of air (Aquarius is an air sign) living close to water (map 12, fig. 47).
VIII.—Aries-Taurus Region	6th labor: Stables of Augeas (king of Elis). Expedition against Pylos.	Augeas is "the brilliant," guardian of the solar oxen. Pylos is the "gateway" of the year.
IX.—Gemini	Expedition against Sparta.	
X.—Cancer	2nd labor: Hydra and the Lernaean Crab.	(See p. 98–99).

2. The Ancient Guardians of the Zodiac ("Hesiodic Guardians")

My observations establish that, in a certain number of labors, Heracles confronts monsters that characterize the signs of the zodiac. On this point as on several others, heroes like Theseus and Perseus were to imitate him but would become more specialized.

A list of pre-Olympian deities, principally established on the *Theogony* of Hesiod and *The Library* of Apollodorus[12] will be extremely useful for the subsequent research.

Aries: Phorcys
Taurus: Geryon
Gemini: Thaumas
Cancer: Hydra, Typhon, Cerberus
Leo: Chimaera (Orthus)
Virgo: Gorgon
Libra: Phix or Sphinx
Scorpio: Dracus, Ophion, Echidna
Sagittarius: Centaurs
Capricorn: Griffins
Aquarius: Sirens, Pegasus, Chrysaor
Pisces: Ceto, Triton-Nereus

3. Heracles and Omphale

According to Apollodorus,[13] the conflict between Heracles and Apollo over the Delphic tripod meant that Heracles wished to institute an oracle that would rival Delphi. Zeus (or in a more ancient tradition, Athena) then intervenes. Heracles, who had come to consult the Pythia about being purified of the murder of Iphitus, was then ordered by the oracle to be sold into slavery. And he served, for one year (or three), Queen Omphale at Sardis. This can only mean that Heracles went to renew himself with the power of the Delphic oracle, since, as I believe, the oracles of Delphi and Sardis were identical. Marie Delcourt, for one, was aware of this and wrote: "Between the old stone of Delphi and the Queen of Lydia there is surely more than a mere assonance."[14] In addition, a foundation oracle was to associate Delphi, Heracles, and Sardis. Wasn't Pelops himself the son of Tantalus who reigned at Smyrna, which is on the earth line joining Sardis and Delphi? The kings of Sardis were called the Heraclides, and Croesus was so eager to emulate Heracles that he wanted to die on a pyre like the demigod.

♦

I shall now attempt to reconstruct the cycle of Heracles of Sardis in general outline. This is a system of eight main directions, like that of Phlius, where eight of the traditional labors have been placed. Remaining are:

The Cretan Bull (eighth labor)
The struggle with triple Geryon (tenth labor)

The conquest of the golden apples of the Garden of the Hesperides (eleventh labor)
The descent to the underworld at Cape Taenarum (twelfth labor).

It is obvious that the Cretan Bull and triple Geryon both stand for the sign of Taurus. Since this sign is also already represented by Augeas and Elis, I am led to conclude that Taurus appears no less than three times in the traditional list of the twelve labors.

The Cretan Bull and triple Geryon must each represent a complete calendar in which the year began at the spring equinox. And one of these calendars is that of Sardis, in which the Cretan Bull symbolizes Taurus. So the eighth labor establishes the link between the systems of the Peloponnese and Sardis, a connection also represented by the Sardis-Phlius-mouth of the Alpheus line, which is identical with the Olympia-Isthmia line.

From the story of the adventures of Heracles in Anatolia, a zodiac can be reconstituted which, in its present bastardized form, is something of a parody of the other labors of Heracles. In order to arrive at an acceptable layout centered on Sardis, one is forced to eliminate Aries and shift the earlier system by one sign, putting Taurus first rather than Aries, then Gemini instead of Taurus and so on. In this way one arrives at a scheme that probably corresponds to a more ancient state of the sky than that of Phlius.

The symbolic "polar" axis was very probably the Cos–Mount Olympus of Bithynia direction.

Cancer. Significant in regard to Cancer is the sacrifice of the ram of the New Year at Cos in the house of Eurypylus. The character's name, which means "of the wide doors," refers to the solstitial gateways. The punishment of Hera and Hephaestus, who are associated with him, is an allusion to the equivalent axis in the Delian system.

At Cos, Heracles was honored as a god of marriage.[15] The rite of transvestism known to have been celebrated there must have been associated with the summer solstice and Cancer, the lunar sign. The change of season was interpreted as a change of sex; the decreasing days marked the beginning of the feminine half of the year.

Gemini. The brothers Cercopes, who are associated with the region of Ephesus, suggest a pleasant symbol of Gemini. The many images on vases and sculptures of Heracles holding them like pieces of wild game, their heads dangling, echo the hieroglyph for this sign.

Leo. Lityerses, the "accursed harvester," must undoubtedly be associated with Leo and harvesttime in Anatolia (Leo-Virgo sector).

Libra. Similarly, the thief Syleus appears primarily as a grape harvester. He probably represents the eastern part of Anatolia and the sign of Libra. He may even represent a Libra-Scorpio-Sagittarius sector, if one looks at other sites in the same episode: Aulis, Thermopylae, and Mount Pelion which, in the systems centered on Phlius or on Delphi, define a rather wide area that takes in the whole northeast quarter.

Scorpio. The Serpent of Sangaris corresponds to this sign, with which Hercules is usually associated in the character of the serpent-strangler.

Capricorn. The episode of Hylas is connected with Cios on the coast of Mysia and with Capricorn in the Sardis system. It was in this area, according to Strabo,[16] that some situated the myth of Typhon, another reference to the Cancer-Capricorn axis.

Aquarius. The expedition against Troy is associated with the sign of Aquarius (I will return to this).

Pisces. The marine monster Hesione (daughter of a king of Troy) represents the sign of Pisces.

In the system centered on Sardis, these zodiacal axes can therefore be found:

Cretan Bull: Serpent of Sangaris (Taurus-Scorpio)
Cercopes: Syleus (Gemini-Sagittarius)
Eurypylus: Hylas (Cancer-Capricorn)
Lityerses: Troy and the story of Hesione (Leo-Aquarius and Pisces), which corresponds to a division into eight.

Let me point out that, because of the degraded state in which these legends have come down to us, some correspondences are made by means of locations in space, while for others (Syleus, Lityerses) the connection is made through the calendar of field labors.

Furthermore, the Taurus-Scorpio and the Gemini-Sagittarius axes are merged, a tangible expression of the phenomenon of the precession of the equinoxes.

The connection between Hylas and Capricorn is not immediately obvious. But Cios was founded by the lapith Polyphemus, which sets up a relationship with Capricorn in the system centered on Delphi. Also, Apollonius of Rhodes tells us that the young people of Cios, who were sent as hostages to Heracles after the disappearance of Hylas, settled at Trachis under the guidance of the hero[17] who represents Capricorn in relation to Phlius. In this way subtle correspondences are interwoven between equivalent points in the different systems.

4. A More General System. The Directions of Space

A psychologist of the stature of Jung[18] saw the hero as an image of the "integrated man," who contains in himself the four elements and the four cardinal points. This concept doubtless corresponds to an aspect of the legend of Heracles.

But while it appears clearly that there was a system centered at Phlius and another at Delphi, it is impossible in the present state of our knowledge to fully reconstitute the one centered on Delos. There is, however, an important trace of such a system in the episode of the "Boreades," who were slain by Heracles at Tinos, an incident that would relate to the sign of Capricorn, the north-south axis, and the cult of Boreas, so characteristic of this system oriented to Mount Haemus.

In my subsequent study of the extension of the system of zodiacal correspondences over the whole Mediterranean basin, I shall have the opportunity to come back to certain features of the legend and travels of Heracles. But I can say right away that several very important episodes, particularly the tenth, eleventh, and twelfth labors, seem to designate both spatial directions and prominent sites in the systems centered at Delphi, Cumae, or Malta.

As already indicated, Geryon and his cattle stand for Taurus in a calendar of three seasons (see p. 118), and the story of the return of Heracles, driving the cattle before him, supports the hypothesis of a type of calendar that is valid for the whole Mediterranean basin.

Of such a system at least two axes can be found:

1. A Taurus-Eagle axis (island of Erythea–eagle of Prometheus).
2. A north-south or Cancer-Capricorn axis.

With to the north: Atlas or else the Ceryneian Hind in Istria.
And to the south: Antaeopolis in Lybia.

The pillars of Hercules, Hyperborea, and the Garden of the Hesperides stand for other directions in the same system, which I believe to be the southwest, the northwest, and the west, respectively.

5. Vestiges of an Earlier Zodiac in the Legend of Heracles; the Sign of the Boar

Only one symbol of the earlier zodiac has survived in the labors of Heracles: the Boar, which corresponds to the region later occupied by the signs of Aquarius and Pisces. The heroic deed of Heracles harnessing a lion and a boar to Admetus's nuptial chariot alludes to a sacred marriage that took place at the summer solstice, the Leo-Boar axis then functioning as the Leo-Aquarius cosmic axis. This has been partly perceived by Robert Graves.[19]

Certain incidents in the history of the hero immediately suggest the following zodiacal symbols:

The swan at Pagasae (Sagittarius sector).
The wolf and the seagull (Keix) at Trachis (Capricorn sector).

Two visits to Calydon in 1963 and 1964 revealed the role played by the ancient sign of the Boar in the system centered on Phlius. The very arrangement of the sanctuary at Calydon is in fact very telling. The sacred *theores* walked from the temple of Hera to the terrace of the temple of Apollo and Artemis, which opens to a good view of the Gulf of Patrae and the Erymanthus mountains. The mountains are invisible from the temple of Hera, being hidden by the high promontory of Varassova to the southeast. This clearly marked the symbolic equivalence of the boars of Erymanthus and Calydon.

The extensive embankment of a natural hill allowed the two temples of Apollo and Artemis to be oriented to a northwest southeast direction which defines an angle of 130 degrees to the north. If this angular value is transferred to the map of Greece, it becomes clear that the two temples were turned towards Phlius, omphalos of this system. I shall return to the question of the sign of the Boar in my attempts to reconstitute the old Greek zodiac.[20]

6. Heracles and Apollo

The myth of Heracles is as closely associated with the sun as is the myth of Apollo. This is what Jane Harrison perceived when she wrote in *Themis*[21] that the demigod was a solar spirit, daimon of fertility and the annual cycle. She interpreted from this perspective, correctly in my opinion, the story of the combat of Heracles and the river Achelous as told by Deianira at the beginning of Sophocles' *Trachiniae*. She also commented that, at the beginning of the play, the wives of Trachis invoked the sun to obtain news of the hero.[22]

She further mentions that the hero, as the "young sun," struggles with Hades, the setting sun, at Pylos, and that he once used the cup of the sun as a vessel. Let me say in my turn that, when he goes to seek Admetus in the kingdom of the dead, Heracles represents the springtime sun that regenerates the sun of the winter solstice: this comes out clearly in the diagrams. The duration of the labors of Heracles is sometimes given as one lunar/solar year of fourteen months (*Trachiniae*), sometimes as eight years and one month.[23] Eight years is, approximately, one quarter of the mean sun. The extra month, astronomically unexplainable, may symbolize the entry into another cycle.

The affinity between the cycles of Apollo and Heracles is expressed in many details of the legend. Hence, it is said that the god taught the hero the art of archery.[24] The struggle of Apollo and Heracles over Ambracia, judged in favor of Heracles by Cragaleus, takes on all its meaning when one realizes that this city, situated not far from Dodona, is opposite Delos, birthplace of Apollo, in relation to Delphi. Since he had failed to conquer Delphi, would not Heracles, or the group of people represented by this name, have wished to found an oracle at Ambracia, which, as the direct heir to the oracle of Dodona, would have tended to rival Pytho's?

A subsequent rearrangement of the mythical data made Apollo the artisan of the glory of Heracles. It was understood that it was the Delphic oracle who had directed the hero, after he had slain his children and those of Iphitus in a moment of madness, to retire to Tiryns and put himself in the service of Eurystheus, doing the works that the latter commanded, after which he would gain immortality.[25] And Arrian[26] says that Heracles was not given divine honors, either before or after his death, until the god of Delphi had given word to do so. The reconciliation of the two traditions is completed by the apparent triumph of Apollo. But certain Heraclean directions, especially the Sardis-Phlius-mouth of the Alpheus axis, seem to have played quite a prominent role in the oracles of colonization, as will be seen in chapter 19. Heracles appears as the champion and almost as the instigator of Greek expansion, a role which seems natural, bearing in mind the labors and journeys of the hero. And later he appeared on many Sicilian and Alexandrian coins. In all these events, it is as though Apollo, after having supplanted Heracles, had then by compensation favored the spread of his cult throughout the Greek world.

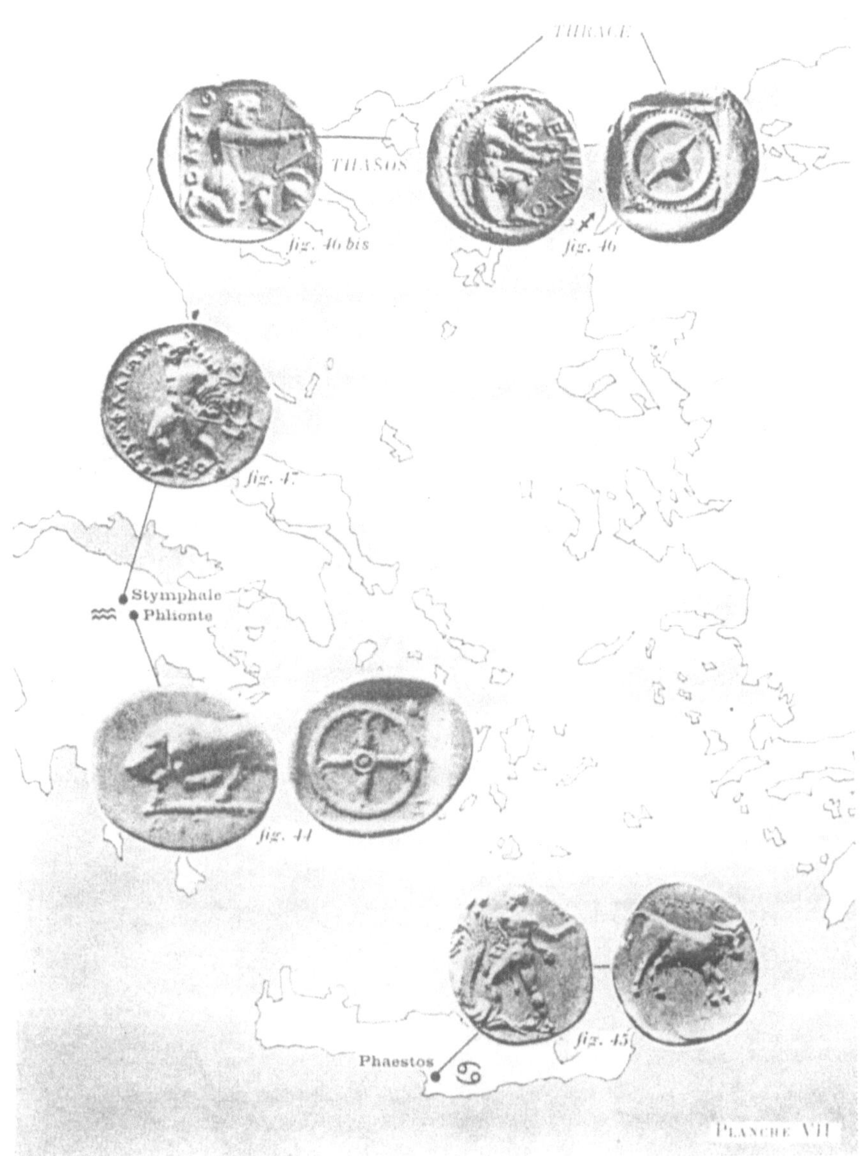

Map 12. ***The Phlius Zodiac: the Calendars of Heracles.***
Figure 44. *Coin from Phlius: symbol of the center and bull of the New Year.*
Figure 45. *Coin from Phaestus: Heracles and the Hydra; bull of the New Year.*
Figure 46A. *Coin from Thrace: Heracles the Archer (Sagittarius) and axial symbol.*
Figure 46B. *Coin from Thasos: Heracles the Archer.*
Figure 47. *Coin from Stymphalus: Heracles fighting the birds of the lake.*

Chapter 11

The Astral Significance of Greek Myths and Heroes

It is now possible to show that a great many mythological stories concerning heroes, demigods, or gods take on their full significance only when they are seen in context of an astral religion that places major emphasis on the figures of the zodiac and the constellations. Here again, as far as geographical locations are concerned, the zodiacal wheels act as keys to decoding, which shows the extreme antiquity of the system. This type of analysis also elucidates the relationships among certain myths and resolves certain apparent contradictions. If the present work is not to take on undue proportions, I cannot undertake to retrace all the great Greek myths, which has already been successfully done.[1] I am therefore assuming that they are familiar, at least in general outline.

Similarly, I make no claim to exhaust an immense subject in a few pages. But I shall try to demonstrate, by means of some specific examples, the advantages of using the diagrams in interpreting the geographic locations that are so abundant (and so apparently arbitrary) in the stories of Greek mythology. For the convenience of the analysis, I will follow the order of the signs of the zodiac.

1. Myths and Rites of the Spring Equinox

a) Cephalus, Eos, Procris. I have already said that the story of Cephalus has the characteristics of an astral myth and that this hero is associated with the island of Cephallenia, which bears his name, and the sign of Aries, which corresponds to the human head (see pp. 12 and 78). The marriage of Cephalus and Procris, a lunar diety, can be explained in context of the sacred geography of Attica. Thorikos, where they reigned, is near the "polar" axis facing the island of Helena, which represents the moon for Attica, and the coastal area around Prasiae and Brauron were also sacred to the moon (see chap. 7). The abduction of Cephalus by Eos (Aurora) describes a movement from west to east along the latitude of Delphi.

This subject is illustrated by a Melian relief from the fifth century in the British Museum (fig. 26). The same scene appears on the hydria of Caere (fig. 23), which I have suggested calling the "vase of the spring equinox."

The expedition with Amphitryon against the Taphians corresponds to the reverse journey from east to west. The very name of the island of Taphos indicates that it must formerly have been considered the tomb of the sun. Strabo[2] mentions a certain confusion between Cephallenia and Taphos. Even a short stay in the Ionian islands reveals that the daily spectacle of the drowning of the sun in the sea is especially magnificent there. Cephalus wanted sons, so in obedience to the Delphic oracle, he coupled with the first female creature he met, who happened to be a she-bear. He must have met her between Delphi and Helicon! She bore him the twins Acrisius and Proetus, the founders of a dynasty of Argos, who symbolize the two halves of the year. The allusion to the pole (Bear) also marked the affinity between the two fire signs of Aries (Cephalus) and Leo (Argos). Acrisius was, incidentally, to be slain by his grandson Perseus.

According to Strabo, it was Cephalus enamoured of Pterelaus who inaugurated the ritual jump at Leucas, and not Sappho rejected by Phaon, as Menander claims.[3]

Thus many details in the legend of Cephalus clearly pertain to spring and to the latitude of Delphi.

b) Olympia: The Olympic Games, the Race of Pelops, and the Feasts of Spring. It seems unnecessary to repeat F. M. Cornford's excellent analyses of

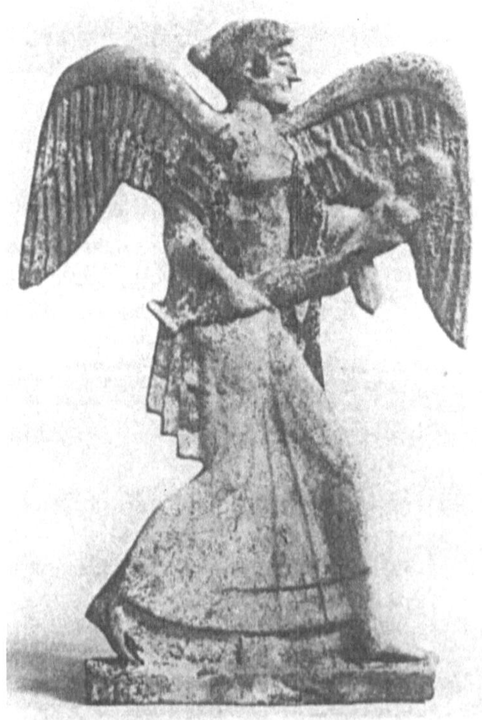

Figure 26. *The abduction of Cephalus by Eos, terra-cotta relief from Milo, circa 460 (British Museum, B 365).*

the origin of the Olympic Games in any detail here,[4] except to emphasize that the Olympian rites suggest a history of the calendar. This author has demonstrated the calendary significance of the myths and rites of Olympia, the date of the games being connected with the lunation of the summer solstice, the probable beginning of the year in Elis. The interval between these two celebrations was alternatively from 49 to 50 months, the complete cycle being a great lunar/solar year of eight years. But the starting point of the calculation was the winter solstice, the probable beginning of a former annual cycle.

Cornford and other analysts have said that the marriage of Pelops and Hippodamia has the characteristics of a sun-moon hierogamy. And it is certainly very obvious that the race of Pelops, which defines a "Heraclean" line, essentially Olympus-Isthmia, is an abstract journey: a chariot race through the mountains of the Peloponnese would not advance further than a few hundred meters!

The Heraea, the most ancient festivals celebrated at Olympia, seem related to a lunar calendar. Everywhere there is testimony to the same sequence: (1) earth calendar, ruled by the rhythm of the seasons; (2) lunar calendar; (3) lunar/solar calendar; (4) solar calendar. At Olympia, as elsewhere, everything in the primitive calendar was ruled by the cycle of vegetation, and the year began with the spring renewal. As already mentioned, the mouth of the Alpheus was in symbolic relation with this time of year. This is why, in the rites of Olympia, there survived a festival of the New Year associated with the month of Elaphios as reported by Pausanias:[5] a sacrifice was made at that time on top of the Hill of Kronos. Cornford thought this had to do with a very ancient spring feast, which was later associated with the date of the equinox. So this is once again the ancient Heraclean system seen in the preceding chapter, whose center was Phlius and which corresponds to a period when the spring equinox was associated with Taurus.

c) The Spring Equinox of the Sardis System: Mount Sipylus. F. M. Cornford has judiciously related the spring sacrifice at Olympia with the festival of Tantalus. He saw in the latter the transposition of a ritual of death and resurrection, and I can do no better than refer the reader to his analysis.[4] What is especially interesting is the location of this festival, which is none other than the peak of Mount Sipylus, a site very near the earth line and west of Sardis, thus establishing a symbolic relationship with both earth and spring. Now, Pelops's throne is on the summit, and the sanctuary of the Great Mother, worshipped here under the name Plastene, according to Pausanias,[6] is a little lower down the mountain.

It seems to me that the rite in honor of Leto, associated with one of the legendary birthplaces of Artemis and Apollo at Ortygia and celebrated on the peak of Mount Solmissus near Ephesus,[7] should be related to a more ancient site that marked the spring equinox in the sign of Taurus in relation to Sardis.

The analogies between this Ephesian rite and those of the Idas of Crete and Mysia, especially the presence of the Dactyls in all these cults, and Aeschylus's "confusion" in having Tantalus reign on Mount Ida of Phrygia, must relate to the Leo-

Aquarius (or Leo-Boar) axes taken as directions of reference, and hence to calendars in which the year began not at the spring equinox but at the summer solstice.

d) The Spring Equinox of the Delos System: Mount Cuckoo and Mount Pron. By analogy, one may assume that a rite or legend should be associated with a mountaintop for each of the main zodiacal wheels. Found so far are the ritual jump of Leucas and the legend of Eos and Cephalus for the Delphic system, the sacrifice on the Hill of Kronos for the system at Phlius, and the festival of Tantalus on the heights of Sipylus for the zodiacal wheel of Sardis. Remaining to be discovered is how the spring equinox was represented in relation to Delos.

It is naturally appropriate to seek this in the neighborhood of Hermione. One only need open Pausanias to find a description of the mountain sanctuaries around Hermione. On top of Mount Cuckoo (the former Thornax) stood a sanctuary of Zeus; on the neighboring mountain of Pron was a sanctuary of Hera[8] as well as a sanctuary of Demeter.[9] This, according to legend, was the site of the marriage of Hera and Zeus in the form of a cuckoo. The latter is a patent reference to both the spring equinox and an ancient calendar of birds. A good many texts since Hesiod attribute this meaning to the cuckoo.[10] As seen earlier, Hermione is where the Mount Ida–Delphi cosmic axis intersects the coast of Argolis.

♦

Incidentally, the geographical connections between the sanctuaries of Hera and Zeus also appear here. At Olympia Zeus supplants the goddess, which is interpreted to correspond to the transition from matriarchy to patriarchy, a sociological explanation that may not be strictly necessary in this context, but the sanctuary of Zeus at Aegina is also on the latitude of the Hera temples. An extension of the Mount Ithome–Nemea line, perpendicular to the Dodona-Aegina line, determines the site of the temple of Hera at Perachora (map 3).

2. Castor and Pollux

Since the cult of Gemini at Sparta was the basis of my statement that Laconia was considered to be governed by this sign of the zodiac, I could be accused of begging the question if I now overemphasized the astrological aspect of the myth. But this is the place to bring out a few details on the subject. One must first remember that Zeus took the form of a swan (that is, the animal that represented the celestial region opposing Gemini in the old zodiac; see p. 144) to couple with Leda and to father Castor and Pollux. It is said that the Dioscuri were born at Pephnos, and they had a heroic tomb at Therapne.

Other sets of twins in the Greek legends are also relevant. The most interesting are the twins of Messenia, Idas and Lynceus, said to be the cousins of the Dioscuri; they represent the memory of the time when the sign of Gemini governed this area. The name Lynceus and his characteristic piercing glance situate the sign of the Lynx in the season of spring in the old zodiac.

The sisters of the twins of Messenia, the Leucippides, Phoebe (the pure, the new moon, priestess of Athena) and Hilaeira (the siren, the full moon, priestess of Artemis) were married to Castor and Pollux, marriages which caused the two pairs of Gemini to quarrel. And as might be expected, Idas and Lynceus, representing a more ancient state of the sky, were eliminated by Castor and Pollux.

The twins who originated in other parts of Greece really symbolize zodiacal opposites: Amphion and Zethus stand for the Taurus-Scorpio opposition (see section 5 below). The twins Pelias and Neleus represent the antagonism and complementarity of the two horse signs of Sagittarius and Gemini: Pelias retires to Iolcus, Neleus to Pylos.

3. Helen and Cancer

Helen is an ancient lunar goddess, particularly associated with Cythera, the island that represents the moon in the Delphic system (see also p. 15). Her legend can be studied as a lunar myth: since the moon travels throughout the zodiac, Helen is wooed by every type of man and especially by Paris, symbol of the Leo-Aquarius cosmic axis (Troy, Mount Ida). Helen is the sister of the Dioscuri, who inhabit the neighboring sign. She is, at least at Cythera, supplanted by Aphrodite, but in fact, it is always the moon that rules the sign of Cancer.

The equivalent significance of Helen and the Cretan Ariadne will be shown in studying the myth of Theseus.

4. The Cancer-Capricorn Axis: Zeus and Typhon

The serpent Typhon represents the world axis and is simultaneously associated with Cancer. The Cancer-Capricorn opposition is often symbolized by the combat of Zeus, whose throne is at Olympus, and Typhon.

5. Orion and the Taurus-Scorpio Axis

Celestially, the constellation of Orion is near the zodiacal sign of Taurus. In fact, Orion seems to represent the Taurus-Scorpio pair of forces.

As for his origin, he is sometimes associated with Boeotia, especially with the cities of Hyria and Tanagra, and sometimes with Euboea. Strabo mentions a para-etymology that relates his name to Oreum.[11]

On a command of the Delphic oracle, reported by Pausanias,[12] Amphiclus led the colonists from Istaia, a city in the north of Euboea, who went to settle at Chios.

The relationship Boeotia-Orion-Scorpio seems to refer to a tradition more ancient than the insertion of Libra in the zodiac. The myth of Orion has affinities with those of Osiris and Gilgamesh, as pointed out by R. Graves.[13] Pausanias indicates a tomb of Orion at Tanagra.[14] But the legend of Orion essentially took place in the system centered at Delos. Orion traveled to Chios in the sign of

Scorpio to court Merope, daughter of Eonopion. The father, unwilling to give him his daughter, blinded him. Orion then sought out Hephaestus, hence to Lemnos on the polar axis of the Delian system, and taking the child Celadon on his shoulders, asked to be pointed towards sunrise; he was then healed. (This may have to do with an ancient medical tradition of treatment by heliotherapy of blindness due to venereal disease, since Scorpio represents human sexuality.) A fragment of the *Minyad*, a poem attributed to Prodicus, a Phocaean author, concerns Orion's death;[15] Phocaea is also situated in Scorpio in relation to Delos.

The association of Orion with Crete seems anomalous and poorly documented, but Crete is also part of the system centered on Delos. It was also said that Orion pursued the Pleiades for seven or nine years. Aurora, having fallen in love with him, brought Orion to Delos, the fixed center of the Delian system. This could also describe the movement of a cult in the Aegean that originated in Boeotia, since Aurora by definition always represents the area to the east of any given place. Incidentally, it was through studying the populating of Chios by the Boeotians that Sakellariou was led to examine the myth of Orion. Here it may already be anticipated that astrology played an important role in the Delphic oracles of colonization (see ch. 19).

Orion attempted violence on the goddess Artemis, so she sent a scorpion to sting him to death. And in the sky the constellation of Orion eternally runs away from Scorpio. Many objects, especially Corinthian vases and bronzes displayed in various European museums, show a winged giant who is, I believe, sometimes Orion and sometimes Ophion (figs. 36 and 157). A certain confusion probably existed between the two characters, who were both associated with Scorpio. When the serpent also appears or when the giant has the beak of an eagle or the mouth of a serpent, the character is evidently Ophion.

6. Cadmus and Harmonia or Scorpio and Libra

Cadmus is the hero whose name is associated with the founding of Thebes. His name is a Semitic word that means "oriental," and his story recalls the migration of an oriental myth to the west. Cadmus has successively been connected with several traditional centers, while retaining the same symbolic sense that associates him with the sign of Scorpio. The places where his history occurs are homologous points in the zodiacal wheels.

a) Phoenicia, Cadmus's country of origin, is in the sign of Libra in relation to Ammoneion.
b) Cilicia—where Cilix, Cadmus's brother, reigned—is in the sign of Scorpio in the same system.
c) Samothrace and Thasos are in Scorpio in relation to Delphi.
d) Thebes is in Libra in relation to Delphi.
e) Budva, on the Illyrian coast, where Cadmus and Harmonia were said to have retired and died, is in Scorpio in relation to Cumae.[16]

It would appear that the character of Cadmus, somewhat confused with an Axiokersos-Hades, had represented one of the incarnations of the ruler of a portion of the zodiac that included Libra and Scorpio (old sign of the Eagle). He is therefore rather similar to Hephaestus. And since Dionysus and Hades are two aspects of the same god, Dionysus's birth in the line of Cadmus is not fortuitous. The dragon that must kill the hero is an image of the chthonian and infernal aspect, the serpent side of the sign of the Eagle.

In the history of Cadmus, the Taurus-Scorpio opposition-complementarity is manifested in several ways. The foundation legend of Thebes associates a bovine with the origins of the city. A Delphic oracle, which is of course known only in late poetic reconstructions,[17] orders Cadmus to follow the cow of the lunar emblems (the moon travels throughout the whole zodiac) and to found a city where it would stop. Twice before Zeus had made alliances with women of this line by taking the form of a bull: first with Io, then with Europa. When the master of the gods marries a mortal, he very often adopts a zodiacal form. Dionysus, a bull-god, son of Semele, would also be born into this family. The marriage of Cadmus and Harmonia may commemorate the insertion of the sign of Libra in the zodiac. Harmonia was originally from Samothrace: in allegorical terms this could mean that the priestly college of that island decided on the zodiacal reform. As one might expect, Cadmus and Harmonia were also venerated at Thebes.

The contrast-affinity of the Theban twins translates the Ares-Aphrodite (Aries-Libra) or Taurus-Scorpio opposition into a masculine register. They are the sons of Antiope-Moon[18] and Epopeus-Helios. One of them, Amphion, is contemplative and musically gifted; the other, Zethus, is an active personality and an ardent warrior.

Amphion and Zethus were born at Cithaeron (on the 0 degree Virgo line). Thebes is near the earth line, at a latitude close to Delphi's, and on the road from that city to Athens, thus occupying a unique position in the Greek world. Only Chalcis was closer to the earth line, but being situated off the main routes of communication, it adopted the eagle as a symbol.

The legend of Amphion must be compared with the *Homeric Hymn to Hermes* and put into relationship with the position of Thebes on the map. Pausanias reports that Amphion had been Hermes' student.[19] To the sound of the lyre, he built the walls of the city, and each of its seven doors corresponded symbolically to a string of his instrument, and thus to a planet. The city of Harmonia was an image of the divine harmony: its very plan is the picture of a lyre.[20]

It seems that the main purpose of the rest of Amphion's story, his marriage with Niobe, the daughter of Tantalus, was to mark Apollo's triumph over the earth and the disappearance or absorption of a more ancient tradition, supplanted by the triumphant cult of the solar god. In the same way that Cadmus had triumphed over the dragon, Apollo and Artemis were to massacre the children of Niobe, an aspect of the earth goddess. The massacre takes place on the earth line at Mount Sipylus, site of an archaic earth cult going back to the Hittite period and site of the festival of Tantalus. This remarkable site thus interconnects several systems of symbolic correspondences.

It was also said that Antiope, driven mad by Dionysus, had been healed by the hero Phocos (eponym of Phocis), who had married her. The tomb of Antiope and Phocos was situated near Tithorea in Phocis. A rite, which still existed in Pausanias's time, marked the memory of a former rivalry between Libra and Scorpio. The traveler relates:

> When the sun is transiting the sign of Taurus [that is, when Scorpio rose at sunset], the people of Tithorea in Phocis like to steal some of the earth from the tomb of Zethus and Amphion and put it on the tomb of Antiope. If this is done at that time the land of Tithorea will yield a fine harvest, while that of Thebes will be less fertile. This is why the Thebans then keep watch over the tomb.[21]

And Pausanias goes on to quote the oracle by Bacis that was the origin of the belief. It seems to me that this belief was really a remnant of the memory of the introduction of Libra into the zodiac and its adoption by Thebes under the name Harmonia. It was a symbolic effort by the people of the Scorpio region to retain supremacy: indeed, Tithorea is very close to the Taurus-Scorpio axis in relation to Delphi.

7. Perseus, Solar Hero and Champion of Athena

All the details of the myth of Perseus connect the hero with the Leo-Aquarius axis and the neighboring Virgo-Pisces axis.

The circumstances of his conception are already characteristic: to meet Danaë, who is locked inside a metal cage, Zeus takes the form of a golden shower. The scene is at Argos which was situated in the sign of Leo; Zeus adopts a shape that characterizes the opposing sign of Aquarius. Similarly, a golden rain had fallen at the birth of Athena. The rain thus represented the sign of the Aquarius-Pisces northwest region, opposite the Leo-Virgo sector. The rest of the legend of Perseus confirms that he is a solar hero associated with Leo. He and his mother are abandoned to the seas in an ark that makes a landfall at the island of Seriphos; this island, long sacred to the sun, is also situated in Leo in relation to Delphi.

Perseus's principal heroic deed took place in the northwest. As already mentioned, the Gorgon represented the ancient guardian of the sign of Virgo and was supplanted by Athena. By eliminating the Gorgons, Perseus is acting as the champion of the ruler of the neighboring sign, and that Athena should come to his aid goes without saying! The three Gorgons represent the three decans of the sign and were replaced by the three Virgins.

Chrysaor, the man with the golden sword, and Pegasus, who were born from the Gorgon's neck, symbolize the beneficial and spiritual side of the Pisces-

Aquarius region. Moreover, all the constellations associated with the myth of Perseus—Cepheus, Cassiopeia, Andromeda, and Pegasus—are situated in this part of the sky. The special association of Pegasus and Aquarius has already been explained (see p. 21).

Ancient mythographers and geographers situate the history of Andromeda and her deliverance by Perseus in "Ethiopia"; specifically, they enchain the princess to a rock facing Joppa, the modern Jaffa.[22] And this city is in the sign of Leo in relation to Sardis. Finally, the struggle of Perseus against Dionysus and his allies, going so far as the supposed murder of the new solar god at Argos, corresponds to a rivalry between characters whose functions are too similar and who cannot bear to coexist because of it. There was a heroic tomb of Perseus, Pausanias tells us,[23] between Mycenae and Argos. But he was especially honored at Seriphos and Athens.

8. Bellerophon, Corinth and Lycia

The story of Bellerophon in many ways duplicates the myth of Perseus, which is illustrated for example by Hesiod's affirmation that the chimaera was slain by Pegasus, aided by the generous Bellerophon.[24] This repeats the image of a solar hero associated with the two great Leo-Aquarius axes in the Sardis and Delphi systems, both of them overlapping Pegasus.

The identity of Bellerophon and Perseus is illustrated by Melian reliefs of the British Museum (figs. 27 and 28). The first shows Perseus riding Pegasus just after he has sliced off the Gorgon's head; the second, Bellerophon on Pegasus, slaying the chimaera.

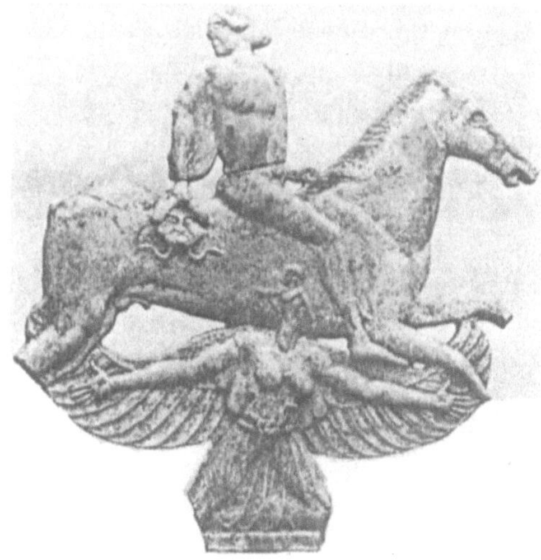

Figure 27. *Perseus mounted on Pegasus slaying the Gorgon (Medusa), terra-cotta relief from Milo, circa 450 (British Museum, B 619).*

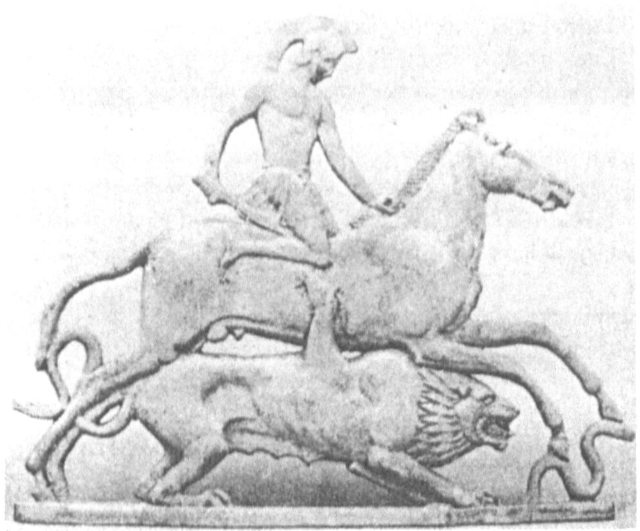

Figure 28. *Bellerophon mounted on Pegasus, slaying the chimaera, terra-cotta relief from Milo, circa 475–450 (British Museum, B 364).*

This is why it is difficult to decide whether the Argive bas-relief, where one sees a hero on horseback killing a serpent, represents Perseus or Bellerophon, although Perseus is here more probable. The identification of Bellerophon with Chrysaor illuminates the connection between them (Chrysaor fathers Geryon and Echidna, that is, the guardian monsters of Taurus and Scorpio, signs on the axis at right angles to the Leo-Aquarius line, these of course being the former solstitial and equinoctial axes). Bellerophon and Pegasus are thus brothers or cousins, both descendants of Poseidon. Perseus was associated with Argolis at Argos, Mycenae, and Midea. Bellerophon is a Corinthian, said to be the son of Glaucus and grandson of Sisyphus. He sometimes meets Pegasus at the fountain of Pirene, at other times on Mount Helicon at the spring of Hippocrene. But Bellerophon would go to Tyrins in Argolis to ask king Proetus to purify him.

Proetus and Acrisius are the sons of Abas, king of Argos, a city situated in Leo in the Delphic system. When their father dies, they fight over the Argive throne. Acrisius pursues his brother, who finds refuge in Lycia, in the sign of Leo in relation to Sardis. Proetus there marries the daughter of King Iobates, who, at the head of a Lycian army, brings Proetus back to Argolis and settles him at Tiryns. The kingdom would henceforth be divided between the two brothers. Acrisius's daughter, Danaë, fertilized by the golden rain, was to give birth to Perseus, another hero of Leo.

The association with Lycia seems specific to Bellerophon. In fighting the chimaera, he is a solar hero struggling with volcanic fire! And as Robert Graves believes, the chimaera probably represents an ancient calendar of three seasons[25] (figs. 28 and 30).

I am tempted to consider that the story of the heroic deeds demanded of Bellerophon by king Iobates in Lycia is fragmentary or distorted as we have inherited it, so the two rival calendars cannot be compared with any certainty. But as a whole, in my opinion, it described the substitution of a calendar of three seasons by a calendar of four. The beginning of the year remained fixed at the summer solstice at the heliacal rising of Sirius, which then occurred in the sign of Leo. This sign relates to the position of Patara in the system centered on Sardis (Athena's aid could also indicate the adoption of an Athenian-type calendar with a slight variation of the beginning of the year when the sun entered Virgo). My analysis of the monument of triple Geryon, found at Cyprus, led me to a similar conclusion, and another case, very close to it geographically, provided me with absolute certainty.

9. The Heroic Deeds of Theseus (Map 6)

a) Theseus Triumphs over the Elements; He is Associated with Leo and Virgo. Theseus is originally from Troezen in Leo, but he is a hero who "specializes" in the sign of Virgo, having deep affinities with Bellerophon. This must be why his mother Aethra was first courted by Bellerophon. Theseus has Aegeus as a mortal father and Poseidon as a divine one. The part of Greece where he was born had a special cult of the sea-god, who was especially venerated at Troezen; the great sanctuary of Calauria stands opposite it on the island of Poros. Troezen was also a center of the cults of Athena and Artemis.

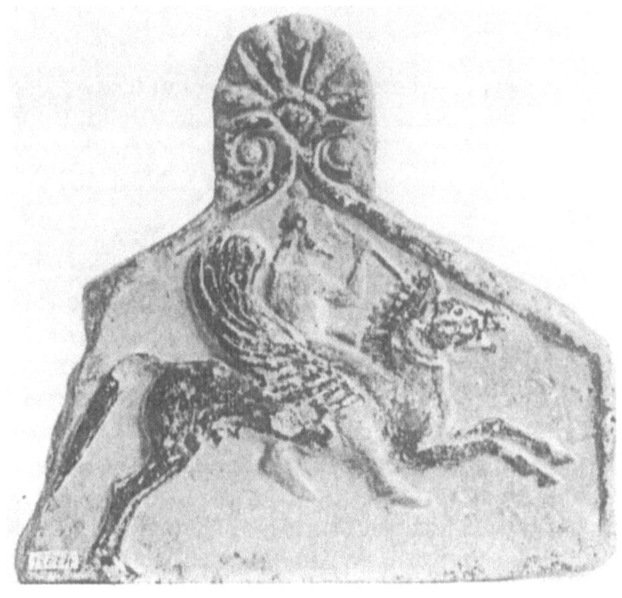

Figure 29. *Bellerophon riding Pegasus.*

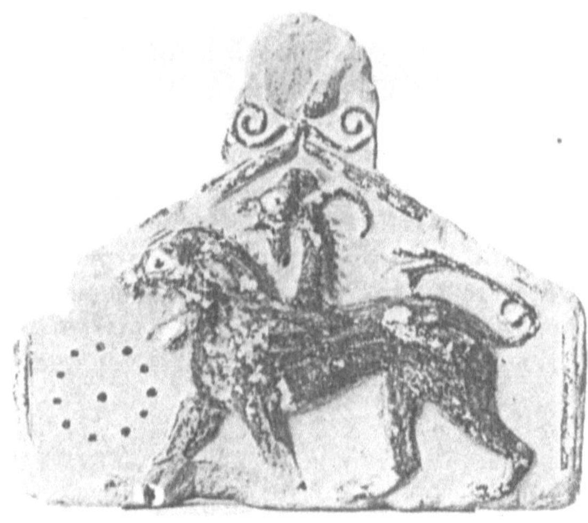

Figure 30. *The chimaera (antefixes of Thasos, Museum of Athens, photos courtesy of École française d'archéologie, Athens).*

Let me immediately mention the important role played in the life of Theseus by the Troezen-Athens-Aphidnae-Scyros line that joins the signs of Leo, Virgo, and the Eagle. The deeds of Theseus on the way from Troezen to Athens have the characteristics of a real journey of initiation; they describe the complex process by which a man born in the sign of Leo becomes the champion and representative of Athena to the point of later being considered the patron of the city of Athens. The beings over whom he successively triumphs seem to represent a series of trials by the elements:

a) At Epidaurus he conquers Periphetes, son of Hephaestus (fire).
b) At Cenchreae, he slays the brigand Sinis, son of Poseidon (the sea). Being himself a son of Poseidon, he had to be purified of this murder.
c) At Crommyon, he kills the sow Phaea, daughter of Echidna and Typhon (the earth).

The episode of the Scironian rocks seems to have a double meaning: it is a trial by air because of the vertiginously high road through the site. The presence of the gigantic tortoise in the sea, who devoured the travelers thrown down by Sciron, marks the transition between the ancient sign of the Tortoise, which also ruled the island of Aegina (see p. 16), and the entrance into Megaris, a vassal province of Athens. The western part of Aegina is visible from the Scironian rocks. Before gaining access to Athens, Theseus must still vanquish the belligerent Cercyon, an enemy he meets at Eleusis, and Damastes-Procustes, a sort of Cabirus. In these events, it is as though Theseus has to transit six initiatory circles before arriving at Athens. The seventh trial would be that of poison, given him on Medea's instigation. He undergoes this victoriously by showing his sword to

Aegeus, who so recognizes him as his son. It is then that the hero really is adopted by the sign of Virgo.

The deeds attributed to Theseus, without being as varied as those of Heracles (they do not comprise a complete solar cycle) have the peculiarity of covering several signs of the zodiac, all having a symbolic relationship with Virgo or Leo. Geographically, they all occur in the interval between the meridians of Delphi and Sardis.

b) The Cretan Cycle and the Minotaur. Theseus has to vanquish Minos the Bull, but not merely in imitation of a heroic deed of Heracles. It is also highly probable that, in a distant past, Athens and Knossos entered into conflict over maritime supremacy. Most of Crete, however, is in the sign of Taurus in the Sardis system.

I do not at present have the means to show how this fact was assimilated to the Cretan bull cult, which is documented by many monuments. But everything indicates that the relations between the various civilizations of the Near East were narrow and frequent, and this from earliest antiquity.[26] What is more, Amnisos and Knossos are on the Delos-Ammoneion axis. But Crete does not seem ever to have had its own zodiacal wheel, the form of the island not lending itself to this very well. If there was such a system, it must have been by divisions along a line of latitude. Perhaps the labyrinth represented something of this sort?[27]

To return to Theseus, a hero who originates in Leo is the natural enemy of Taurus because of the aspect of squaring between the two signs. In going to Knossos, Theseus remains in the region corresponding to Leo in relation to Delphi. In killing the Minotaur, he is the lion of Delphi triumphing over the bull of Sardis. This may also mark an important time in the history of cults and of the calendar. (Transfer of the beginning of the year from the spring equinox to the summer solstice.)[28]

c) Itinerary and Chronology of Theseus's Journey in Crete. Plutarch says that Theseus left Athens for Crete at the spring equinox, on the sixth of Munychion (April–May), and returned to Attica at the autumnal equinox on the seventh of Pyanepsion (October).[29] His symbolic journey thus takes place during the summer half of the year and the areas he travels in are obviously in astrological relationship with that season, covering mainly the signs of Leo, Cancer, and Virgo. When Theseus "forgets" to raise the white sail, Aegeus, the old year, throws himself into the sea: the old year very probably began when the hero left at the spring equinox. Theseus returns at the autumnal equinox, when the sun is opposed to this yearly beginning. His visit to Amphitrite during his journey in Crete[30] represents an attempt to pacify the aquatic powers of the sign of Cancer. It is especially as a hero of Leo that Theseus triumphs over the Minotaur.

d) Ariadne, Helen and the Cancer-Capricorn Axes. The return voyage with Ariane, who represents the softness of the moon and the sign of Cancer, follows an itinerary that is close to the solstitial axis of the Delian system (meridian of Delos). Naxos is thus put into relationship with Cancer, Ariane's "house," and that she should stay there seems quite natural (see pp. 29 and 60). The variations of the legend have the same essential symbolic significance. To say that Theseus abandons Ariane at Cyprus changes nothing of the meaning because Cyprus represents the moon in relation to Sardis (see p. 83) and is the island of Aphrodite. (The name Ariadne designates the goddess, while Ariane is the woman who incarnated the divine principle.)

Helen and Ariadne are two names of a single earth-moon goddess, perhaps of Cretan origin. Their lunar significance explains the number of their paramours.[31] Helen was related to Cancer in the Delphic system, just as Ariadne was in the Delian. There may have been a Helen-Ariadne-Persephone triple goddess, whence would have come Artemis-Hecate.

The alleged murder of Ariadne by Artemis means that the latter was later substituted for the former as the ruler of the sign of Cancer. Similarly, the parallel stories about the deaths of Ariane at Naxos and Helen at Rhodes, both being hanged from trees, refer to the great "world axes," the two north-south axes going through Delphi and Camiros[32] (see p. 67 on the coins of Camiros). From their positions on the zodiacal wheels, Helen and Ariadne, contrary to what Nilsson and Neustadt have thought, cannot be goddesses of spring but are rather goddesses of the harvest associated with the summer solstice[33] and who could be represented as corn dollies.

e) The Crane Dance and Mount Gerania. At Delos Theseus meets up with the sign of Virgo. The crane dance that he introduces there relates simultaneously to the Gorgons, who are sometimes represented as cranes, the zodiac, the labyrinth, and possibly the invention of the alphabet.[34] The crane is also Apollo's bird, since the god takes that shape when he seeks refuge in Egypt. In a calendar of birds it represents the period from the 6th of August to the 2nd of September, which generally corresponds to the sign of Leo.[35] The feast of Apollo on the 7th of Metageitnion (August–September) must have been the day when the crane dance was executed, as G. Thomson believes.[36]

If one now looks at the map of Greece, one will notice the summit of Mount Gerania (1,351 m) dominating the isthmus. The peak is visible from both the Gulf of Corinth and Saronica. Now, the Delphi-Mount Gerania line forms an angle of 135 degrees with the latitude of Delphi. In the zodiacal diagram this gives the exact date of the 6th of August, which marked the entrance of the sun into the sign of the Crane! Even after the adoption of the modern zodiac of twelve signs, certain points of the annual solar cycle probably kept their ancient names: this is a fragment of an ancient calendar of birds. The parallel of the Delphi–Mount Gerania line drawn through Delos is none other than the Delos-Pagasae line mentioned on p. 35 as being indicated by the very orientation of the sanctuary of Apollo at Pagasae. This is a trace of a division into eight of the zodiacal wheels centered on Delphi and Delos.

f) The War with the Amazons. Theseus's participation in the war against the Amazons and the abduction of Antiope have to do with his symbolic relation with Athens and with the sign of Virgo. The Amazons (see p. 46) inhabited the part of Anatolia that corresponds to the sign of Pisces, which opposes Virgo. This is also why legendary history told of a campaign of the Amazons who crossed the Bosphorus and passed through northern Greece to beseige Athens, pushing all the way to Sparta.[37]

g) The Abduction of Helen, the Marriage of Peirithous. I have said that a latent rivalry exists between the Mercurial signs of Virgo and Gemini, and between Athens and Sparta (see p. 15). In Theseus's career this rivalry is manifested by the abduction of Helen, sister of the Dioscuri. But for this he associates himself with Peirithous, a Thessalian hero representing Sagittarius, the sign opposing Gemini. The signs of Virgo and Sagittarius are squared, however, which is marked by Theseus's participation in the massacre of the centaurs during the marriage of Pittheus.

The Dioscuri pursue Theseus and Pittheus to Tegea, a city situated at the latitude of Troezen, where there was a famous sanctuary of Athena. Helen, chosen by lot, is won by Theseus, who keeps her at Aphidnae (north of Athens), whose name means "land of the dead."

h) The Descent to the Underworld. It has often been said that the descent to the underworld of Theseus and Pittheus to take Persephone is something of an imitation of the descent to the underworld of Heracles. Like Heracles, they would have descended at Cape Taenarum, the abode of Cerberus (the Great Dog).

Plutarch, in a strange attempt to rationalize the myth, made Hades (Aidoneus) and Persephone the king and queen of the Molossi![38] But the impudent are kept as prisoners in the underworld.

During their absence, Castor and Pollux occupy Athens, find Helen at Aphidnae through the betrayal of Academus, and capture the mother of Theseus, Aethra ("brilliant sky"), an atmospheric state rather than a person, who was to become the "servant of Helen."

i) The Tomb of Theseus. As already mentioned, the Troezen-Athens-Aphidnae line ends in the northeast at Scyros, where Theseus died and was buried. A Delphic oracle having ordered the return of his ashes to Athens,[39] his tomb was rediscovered by an eagle, symbol of the sign in which it was located.

Thus many details of the legend of Theseus take on their full meaning when they are examined in relation to the astrological wheels.

10. The Heroes of Sagittarius

Thessaly, Pelion, and the Pagasetic Gulf, ruled by Sagittarius, saw the birth of a number of heroes characterized by the dynamism of this sign, who were specially gifted for action and great enterprises, like Achilles and Jason. This is true of the stories of the disciples of the good centaur Chiron, on the one hand, and the descendants of Tyro, daughter of Salmoneus, on the other.

Sagittarius also governs Thrace: Orpheus, ruler of the constellation Lyra, is associated with Mount Pangaeus. The musician Orpheus, whose legendary tomb was at Dium, is also associated with the great north-south axis, and hence with Capricorn.

Conclusions

The following table shows that the great myths that have just been discussed describe the six great zodiacal axes:

Aries-Libra axis:	Cephalus-Eos
	Hera and the Cuckoo
Taurus-Scorpio axis:	The Race of Pelops
	Amphion and Zethus
	Orion
Gemini-Sagittarius axis:	Neleus and Pelias
	The Dioscuri and Pittheus
Cancer-Capricorn axis:	Zeus and Typhon
Leo-Aquarius axis:	Perseus
	Bellerophon
Virgo-Pisces axis:	Perseus
	Theseus

It would thus appear that the locations of the Greek legends are significant, and that their meaning is in fact astrological.[40] The simultaneous consideration of several zodiacal wheels helps to explain:

1. The existence of parallel myths: Helen and Ariadne, Perseus and Bellerophon, Orion and the Theban twins.
2. The multiple locations of certain myths: Orion in Boeotia, in Euboea, at Chios; Bellerophon at Corinth and in Lycia.

Certain cycles, such as those of Theseus and Helen, without having the scope of the legend of Heracles, embrace several signs of the zodiac. But Helen remains associated with Cancer, and Theseus with Virgo and Leo. It will later be seen that the extension of the system of astrological references to the whole of the Mediterannean basin led mythographers to have the gods and heroes of Greece travel widely; something of this sort has already appeared in relation to the last years of Cadmus and Harmonia.

Chapter 12

The Revelation of the Lion of Julis

1. The Lion of Julis

The strange face of the Lion of Julis at Kea (fig. 31) is a great enigma, comparable to that of the Sphinx at Gizeh.[1] The island of Kea, named Ceos or Keos in antiquity, is near the coast of Attica but is not part of the ordinary tourist circuits, and one needs at least two days just to get there and three or four days for a complete visit because it has practically no roads. (For the past few years the American School of Archeology has been pursuing fruitful excavations there despite this.) This relative isolation is surely one of the reasons why the Lion of Kea has been so seldom described. The description most often quoted is in the first volume of *Voyages dans la Grèce* by the Dane P. O. Brönsted, a work first published in German and whose French translation, produced as a large album, appeared in 1828. The traveler's text is illustrated by an engraving which is a rather unfortunate attempt at restoration.

In regard to the lion, Brönsted recalled the legend told by Heraclides Ponticus, which tried to account for the presence of a gigantic statue that was already unexplainable for the ancients. According to this popular story, a lion sent by Zeus pursued the Nereids, who were living on the moist slopes of the eastern part of the city of Kea and were causing death to the women. These nymphs, fleeing towards Carystos, passed by the cape in the northeast part of the island, which was subsequently named "Lion." The existence of such a legend mainly proves the great antiquity of the statue, because the story was obviously invented by a people who knew nothing of its origin and meaning.

Goethe seems to have intuitively felt its importance. After reading Brönsted's work the inspired writer noted in his *Journal*, which is now in the Berlin Library: "The Lion of Kea is the only prehistoric trace of a vanished civilization that was great geographically and remained so psychobiologically, that of Atlantis."[2] The author may possibly have been aware of the position of Kea in relation to Delphi, but I believe that he was wrong in thinking that the lion was the *only* remains of an ancient civilization. And while the myth or hypothesis of Atlantis remains attractive to many minds, I prefer to speak of a Borean or Hyperborean culture, which immediately places the problem in the Greek world.

The great statue, which I visited in 1962, stands on the slopes of a little valley on the north coast of the island near the modern town of Kea, which occupies the site of the ancient Julis. The lion, carved in a mass of schistous

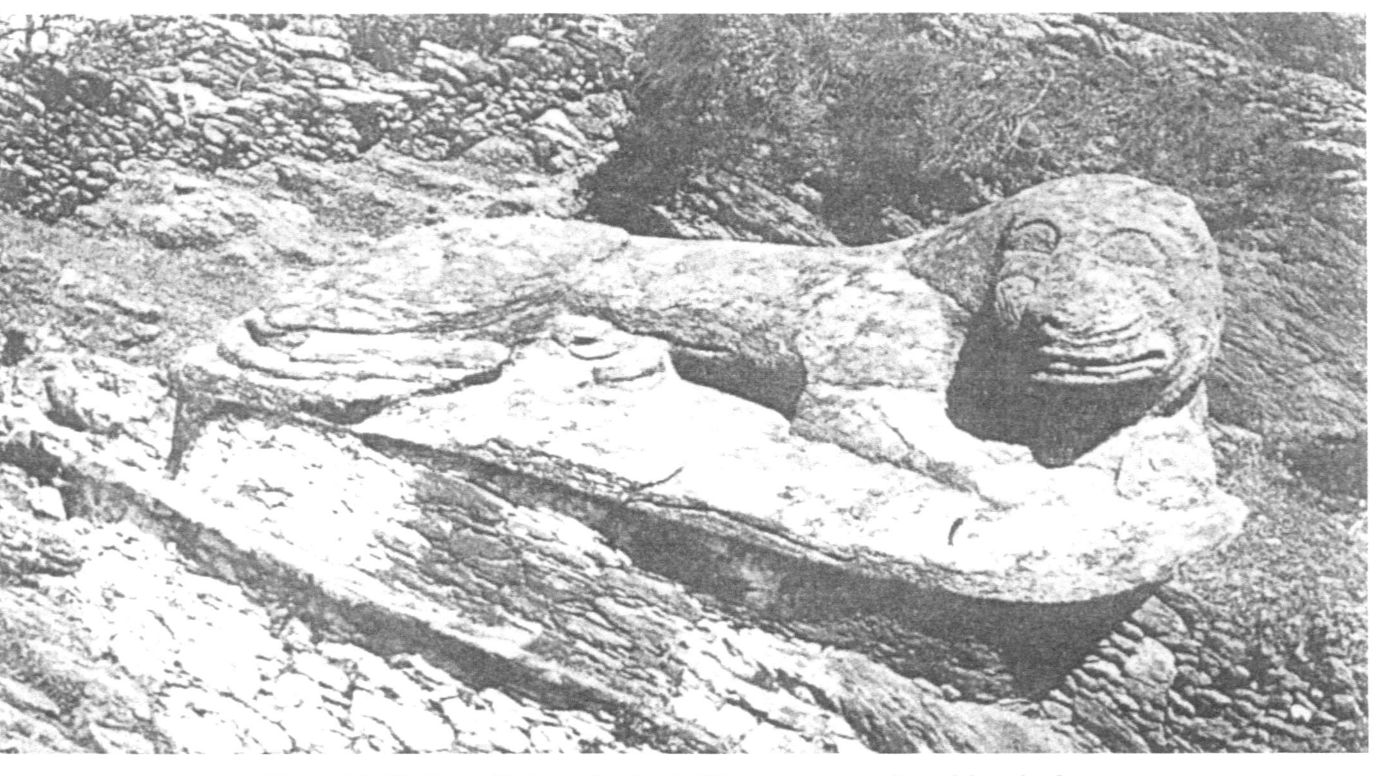

Figure 31. *The Lion of Julis on the island of Kea, ancient guardian of the calendar.*

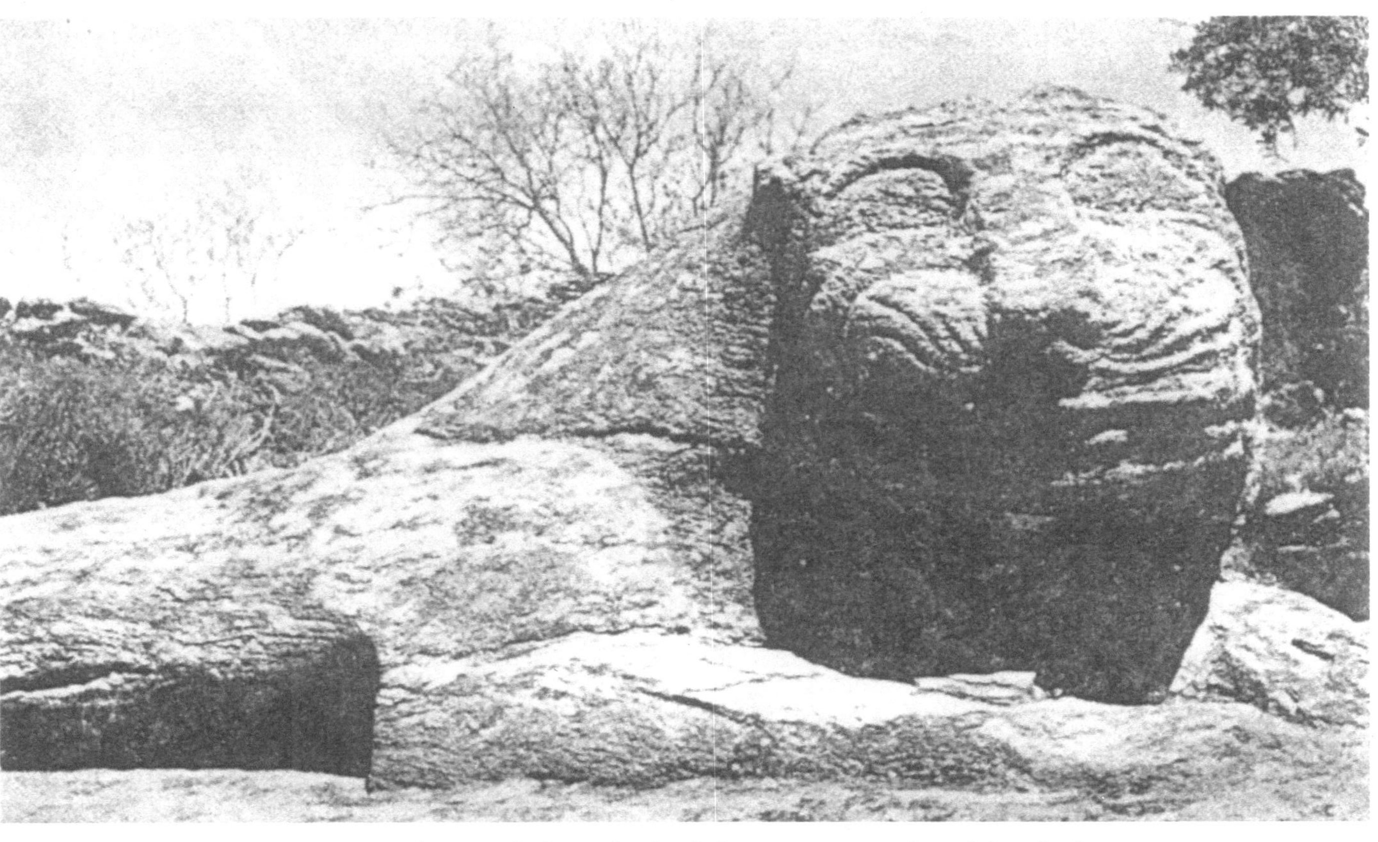

Figure 32. *The Lion of Julis on the island of Kea, ancient guardian of the calendar.*

rocks, is about 6 meters long; it is unquestionably a male. The head looks as much like a human head as a lion's, and the treatment irresistibly suggests certain Egyptian sphinxes. The erosion of time has probably reduced the thickness of the body, but without significantly changing its overall proportions (figs. 31 and 32).

The body of the lion is oriented almost northeast to southwest, and it defines an angle of 120 degrees with the north. The head forms a right angle with the axis of the body and is thus turned towards the south-southeast. In other words, the Lion of Kea is more or less oriented to the solstices and is looking towards the sunrise above the hill at the time of the winter solstice (inset, map 7). An astronomer could undoubtedly date it precisely according to this. Now, in a terrestrial projection of the zodiac where the Cancer-Capricorn axis would theoretically correspond to a south-north line, the point of 0 degree Leo would make an angle of 30 degrees with that line. A simple geometric construction, based on the equality of internal and external angles, allows pinpointing a site that must have played an important role in this system, and it is none other than the summit of Mount Olympus, as will appear if the angular measures taken from the Lion of Kea are transferred to the map of Greece (map 7). As for the lion's body, it seems to indicate the direction of Acria on the south coast of the Peloponnese, where, according to Pausanias, stood the most ancient sanctuary of the Mother of the Gods.

One may suppose that the lion dates from the era when the zodiacal sign that it represented was related to the summer solstice; it must therefore go back to at least 2000 or 2500 B.C. This makes it contemporaneous with the culture whose traces have recently been found at Kea and with the first Egyptian dynasties (the first calendar is said to date from 4200 B.C.).

Gabriel Welter devoted a few pages to the Lion of Julis in *Archäologischer Anzeiger* in 1954. In his article he gives the list, which is rather short, of the travelers who have mentioned it in their accounts since Brönsted. Basing himself on a comparison, which I find rather weak, with a stone lion found at Izmir, he suggested dating the Lion of Julis to about 600 B.C. If such a recent date is considered, the existing lion must have replaced a more ancient one that had the same meaning. The statue is in a sheltered valley, which could have protected it from excessive erosion. Excavations underneath the statue would likely bring interesting revelations, perhaps even the debris of a more ancient statue.

The style of the Lion of Julis is comparable to that of the astonishing terracotta of a woman's head, probably a goddess, recently found by Professor J. L. Caskey on the site of Ayia Irini not far from the statue.[3] This head goes back to at least the Mycenaean era, between 1200 and 1500 B.C., which is already closer to my suggested date for a first lion.

Julius Caesar belonged to a *gens* named Iulius; after his death and apotheosis, the month of his birth, *quin(c)tilis*, was dedicated to him and was then named *Iulius mensis*. As Nicolas Sarafoglou has pointed out, the very name of the place where the Lion of Kea is located, Julis, shows that, during a relatively late period, the statue was still symbolically related to the month of July.

2. The Coins of Kea, the Dog and the Dog-days, the Bull

There seems to have been a long tradition associating the character of Aristaeus with the dog-days that provides interesting geographical and astronomical information. The ancient coins of the cities of Julis and Carthaea bear on one side a dog leaping towards a star, and on the other, the head of Aristaeus (map 9, fig. 6).

The dog is interpreted as that of the dog-days and the star is Sirius. In the Egyptian calendar, which was in use during the whole pharaonic period, the heliacal rising of Sirius, which marked the beginning of the year, occurred when the sun was in the constellation of Leo. The summer solstice coincided with the heliacal rising of Sirius towards the year 3400 B.C., when the spring equinox was in the sign of Taurus. Now, if one draws the parallel of latitude of the Lion of Kea, one will notice that the ancient mouth of the Alpheus, at a short distance south of the modern one, was at the exact latitude of the lion. The river bears a name which in Phoenician means both the first letter of the alphabet and the ox or the bull.[4] It designates the site in the Greek territory that was in symbolic relation with the spring equinox (see p. 80).

R. Graves[5] rightly identifies Orthus, Geryon's dog, with Sirius. He fathered the chimaera, the sphinx, the Hydra, and the Nemean Lion with his own mother Echidna. This is as good as saying that he is the father of the calendar, and especially of symbols of Leo. By an odd transfer, the dog Cerberus, identical to Orthus as a guardian of the summer solstice, but without Sirius, was associated with Taenarum when the summer solstice changed to Cancer.

3. The Alpheus or Taurus, the *Elaphe*

One is led to an oriental origin of the calendar through the very name of the Alpheus. In the *Homeric Hymn to Hermes*, the cave to which the young god drives Apollo's cattle is near the mouth of the Alpheus, close to Pylos (door) of Triphylia. This cave really exists: one only need check Strabo[6] to see that it is very probably one of the caves by the sea mentioned by the geographer. He says that one is called "the cave of the nymphs Anigriades" (from the name of the river Anigrus that empties into the sea there), and the other is associated with the Pleiades and the birth of Dardanus. The Pleiades are situated in the sign of Taurus. So, in my opinion, it is wrong to look for the "cave of the mouth of the Alpheus" towards Pylos of the bay of Navarino farther south, as has sometimes been done. A methodical excavation of the caves mentioned by Strabo at the foot of the heights of Samicon, which corresponds to the ancient coastline, would probably lead to interesting discoveries connected with the prehistoric bull cult.

Because of the phonetic similarity of the words *aleph* and *elaphe*, the stag or the doe are sometimes substituted for the bull, to which they are zoologically close. Since Taurus was associated with the spring equinox and the vernal point, and Artemis ruled the Great Bear and the whole movement of the sky, the doe that usually accompanied her may have represented the new year or the calendar year in general.[7] The legend of the river Alpheus in pursuit of Artemis sets up a relationship of identical meaning. The priestesses of Artemis at Letrini, near the mouth of the Alpheus, painted their faces with gypsum, *alph* also meaning white, the color of an astral and lunar goddess.[8] At Olympia, sacrifices were made to Kronos on the Hill of Kronos by priestesses called queens, at the spring equinox in the month of Elaphios. And Artemis, the moon goddess, is the ruler of the whole zodiac and the calendar, as is her brother Apollo.

One is thus in the presence of a series of consistent indications, and it may be concluded that the Lion of Kea represented the zodiacal guardian of the sign of Leo during a time that seems indistinguishable from the very origins of the calendar. And it is certainly not a coincidence that the lion is looking towards Egypt.

During the same period, the spring equinox was associated with the mouth of the Alpheus. A little later, it would be put in relationship with the mouth of the Achelous, which in its turn would become a river-bull.

Search for the Center. If one assumes that Olympus did not represent the center, but the northern point of this system, one will notice that at the intersection of the Kea-Olympus line and the coast of Thessaly stood the important sanctuary of Apollo at Pagasae. (The Julis-Olympus-Acria figure is a right triangle, incidentally.) If one joins the mouth of the Alpheus to Pagasae, one finds the probable center of the system, which was none other than Trachis. The center was then transferred to Delphi. The summit of Olympus, Trachis, and Delphi are appreciably on the same meridian which finishes at Cape Taenarum and constitutes the great north-south axis of Greece. This axis is perpendicular to the Kea-Alpheus line. After the transfer of the center to Delphi, the Lion of Kea was no longer related to the beginning of the zodiacal sign, but to its third decan.

4. Aristaeus

I will now turn my attention to the character of Aristaeus, associated with Kea and the zodiacal sign of Leo. According to legend, during a plague that was devastating the Cyclades in the season when the star Sirius brings the hottest days of the year, Aristaeus stopped the scourge by making sacrifice to Sirius and Zeus. The latter, touched by his prayers, sent the Etesian winds, which freshened the atmosphere.

Aristaeus is the son of Apollo and the nymph Cyrene. This nymph had won the heart of the god by her conquest of a lion. It has been suggested that Cyrene be identified with the nude goddess of the Middle East who became the lion goddess of Crete and Mycenae.

Aristaeus is also associated with Cer, the bee-goddess, who takes the form of this solar insect to represent the soul of the lion.[9] He is identified at the same time with the Egyptian Thoth, spirit of the dog-days, whence later came the dog-headed Saint Christopher. Iconographical documents show the association of the lion, the dog, and Sirius. One is a fragment of the sculpted calendar of the Small Metropolis in Athens, which comes from the Sarapeum, formerly on the same site, and the other is an illustration from the *Codex Vossianus* of Leiden illustrating the *Phaenomena* of Aratus.[10]

My study of the Lion of Julis seems to indicate the existence in a distant era of a system that symbolically described the first known calendar, of which the main geographical coordinates were the Lion of Julis, the ancient mouth of the Alpheus, Mount Olympus of Thessaly, and Acria. Trachis was probably the center of this system, which included the sanctuary of Pagasae.

I notice that the Trachis-Acria line also passes through Phlius and Lerna. So the system reconstituted from the Lion of Julis merges with the calendar of Heracles for the Peloponnese and continental Greece, which has been described earlier. One could also imagine an ellipse whose two foci would have been at Trachis and Phlius.

5. A Significant Rectangle

Starting with the Lion of Julis and the mouth of the Alpheus, a rectangle whose diagonals cross at Delphi can be constructed, whose angles are defined as follows:

Taurus: Spring equinox. Related to the mouth of the Alpheus.
Leo: Summer solstice. Lion of Julis.
Eagle or Serpent: Autumnal equinox. Small island to the east of Scyros.
Aquarius (Pegasus): Winter solstice. Mouth of the Acheron (formerly, the Boar).

The two long sides of this rectangle are almost identical to the two Hera lines. The two short sides are tangents to a circle whose radius is Tempe-Delphi, with Delphi as the center.

The Mouth of the Acheron. When the great oracle of the dead of Ephyra was instituted near the mouth of the Acheron, the region was probably still in symbolic relationship with the winter solstice, the region of shadow and death. The mouth of the Acheron is symbolically related to the "death of the sun," something like Leucas but on a different plane (the point facing Cape Leucatas, which is associated with the spring equinox, is on the same meridian). Other symbolic correspondences should be noted: the coins of Elaea, a city situated at the mouth of the Acheron, portray Pegasus[11] (Aquarius) (map 9, fig. 14). Nearby, Cape Chimaera evokes the Leo-Aquarius opposition. Ephyra is the former name for Corinth. Finally, a tributary of the Alpheus in Triphylia took on the name Acheron.[12]

As one might expect, each angle of this rectangle is associated with the three others by relationships of affinity or opposition. Thus when Heracles made sacrifice to the Twelve Gods at Olympus, he raised six altars and burned the thighs of the victims on a fire of white poplar wood cut from the trees that grow on the banks of the Acheron.[13] This sacrifice was like a reply to Hermes' sacrifice in instituting the cult of the Twelve, as told in the *Hymn to Hermes*.

6. A Rectangle Centered on Sardis

If one draws a rectangle of the same dimensions as the one just studied, but with the diagonals crossing at Sardis, the sign of Taurus is put into relationship with the sanctuary of the Taurobolium in the island of Icaria, the sign of Leo falls naturally in Caria in the region dedicated to this sign, and the sign of Aquarius seems to correspond to the crater of Ordymnus, an extinct volcano on Mytilene.

The sign of the Eagle is in the kingdom of Midas. In the city of Midas, the remains of a veritable city of blacksmiths have been found, which tempts me to link it symbolically with Hephaestus's forge. Strabo wrote: "Midas drank bull's blood, they say, and thus went to his doom."[14] Since Taurus represents the sign opposing that of the kingdom of Midas, I believe that, rather than a general belief in the harmfulness of the fermented bull's blood, this is an astrological reference to birth and death, and the ancients were establishing an analogy between the cycle of one year and a lifetime.[15]

It is thus manifest how different modes of approach result in consistent conclusions, as much for the sacred geography of Greece as for that of Anatolia.

Chapter 13

Fixed Symbols of the Signs, Directions, and Seasons The Loves of Zeus

Having arrived at this point in my research, I was momentarily alarmed at the abundance of the documentation that was available and the effort of interpretation that it required. Indeed, it seemed that a good number of texts and literally thousands of illustrated documents, in every museum of the world, especially in Europe and North America, had an astrological significance.

In the following chapters, I shall try to indicate some general principles and, by means of specific examples, give the meaning that can be attributed to a series of symbols that appear in Greek sculpture from Mycenaean times to the Classical period. I shall then attempt to interpret more complex imagery and characteristic monuments, from coins to temple pediments.

Just as Ventris and Chadwick's fine discovery has shown that the language transcribed by Linear B is phonetically and morphologically close to ancient Greek, even if there was an apparent break in continuity and loss of the tradition, so while the exact original meaning of certain symbols was lost from view, the symbols themselves were retained through the centuries. The same motifs already appear on Creto-Mycenaean gems and sculptures that were to survive all the way to Classical art (this adjoins the concepts of P. Nilsson, C. Picard, and several others on the persistence of archaic themes in Greek religion of the Classical period). Certain motifs were then transmitted to Byzantine and Roman art, and some symbolic images maintained their meaning from the Assyrian period to sixteenth-century Europe.

1. The Fixed Symbols of the Directions of Space: the Cycles of Four Animals

In chapter 10 on the calendars of Heracles, I examined the Hesiodic symbols of the signs of the zodiac, and I will now complete the table of these symbols from p. 101. In order to establish symbolic equivalences and overlappings of meaning, the directions of space and the signs of the zodiac must be considered as a whole. For example, the griffin is the guardian of the north and Hyperborea, while Aquarius (the Boar) and then Capricorn are the signs of the winter solstice. So they are, as it were, equivalent. Similarly, the chimaera and the lion have closely related meanings.

The Solstices and the Equinoxes

Since Greek astrology was of Babylonian, Phoenician, and Egyptian origins, it is not surprising that the same symbols reappear with identical meanings in the civilizations of the Near East and Greece. A study of these filiations would demand an entire volume. For the time being, I will merely give my conclusions, which are based on the examination of many documents.

The famous plaque of Dudu[1] from Tello, dating from the third millenium and now in the Louvre, shows the symbols of the equinoxes and solstices, while the serpent with four coils on the lower part of the relief seems to describe a year of four seasons. The design of a cylinder from the first millenium B.C. is reproduced as an example. Conserved in the British Museum, it shows a winged horse and a lion; it may be compared with the Lycian coins where one sees the same image of the solstitial axis (map 11, fig. 30). The horse sitting between the lion and the winged horse can represent a Gemini-Sagittarius axis, which are two equine signs[2] (fig. 33).

Another seal from the same period portrays a character who is king of the heavens: he is standing on the sphinxes of the equinoxes and is holding the lions of the solstices in outstretched arms as though they were common chickens.[3]

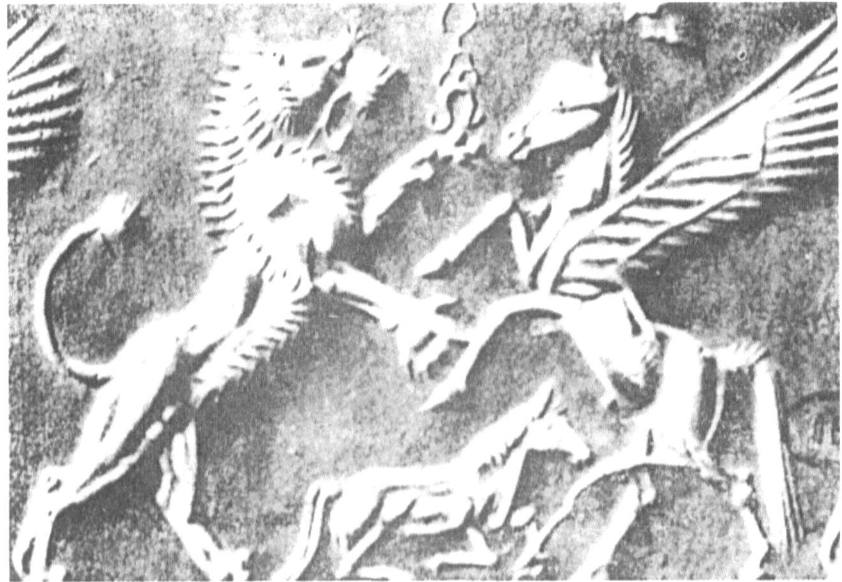

Figure 33. *The Leo-Aquarius axis: Assyrian representation.*

The equinoxes were first symbolized by sphinxes. More exactly, I believe that the spring equinox was a male sphinx and the autumnal equinox a female. This corresponded to a "pre-zodiac" and a year divided into masculine and feminine halves by the equinoxes. In the Akkadian calendar two festivals of the New Year were celebrated, one at each equinox.[4] Later on, the stag either supplanted the sphinx or was superimposed on it to represent the equinox, which could be a borrowing from Hittite civilization,[5] also because of the *elaphe-aleph* word play. A stag stands for the spring equinox, a doe the autumnal.

The overlapping of these symbols sometimes produced rather strange syncretic forms that can explain the fantastic creatures in Cretan sculpture. There is a sort of bull-stag equivalence, but the bull is situated at the beginning of the annual cycle, the doe in the middle, and the stag at the end. One also sees a ram-headed sphinx, which represented the equinoxes in oriental art during the period when the spring equinox was shifting to the sign of Aries.[6]

ZODIACAL SYMBOLS AND ASTROLOGICAL AGES

	1ST PERIOD	2ND PERIOD	GENERAL SYMBOLS
Spring Equinox:	Bull (winged or wingless) Hare Geryon	Ram	Sphinx Stag or Elaphe
GEMINI:	Very often represented as riders or horses.		
Summer Solstice:	Lion Dog (Sirius) Chimaera	Cancer (the spiral) Hydra Octopus Serpent Typhon Goat	Lion
VIRGO:	Succeeds Gorgon (which remains symbolized by Athena's owl).		
Autumn Equinox:	Swan Eagle (Scorpio) Serpent	Phix or Male Sphinx Harmonia	Female Sphinx Doe
SAGITTARIUS:	The Centaurs, and especially, Chiron.		
Winter Solstice:	Siren Boar Pegasus (horse) Chrysaor Bellerophon Lioness	Capricorn (goat) Nereid of Capricorn	 Panther
PISCES:	Sign represented by Triton-Nereus, the Old Man of the Sea.		

(Also see table p. 101)

The ancient symbols of the solstices are the lion, the chimaera, and the dog for summer, and the boar for winter. The winter quarter of the year was sacred to Dionysus as a time of darkness, whence the image of the panther for the winter solstice. In the following astrological age, the solstitial axis was associated with the octopus (Cancer, the spiral) in opposition to the griffin (direction of north) or the goat (Capricorn).

According to whether the emphasis on the symbols of the seasons and the directions is placed on the direction, the zodiacal sign, or the astronomical phenomenon (equinox or solstice), this series of simple correspondences will enable anyone familiar with it to interpret the monuments correctly. The table gives a symbolic alphabet that will provide an accurate reading for thousands of vases and sculptures having, in one way or another, a cult or symbolic significance in relation to the zodiac, the seasons, or the directions of space. It may be surprising that this has never been established before; it is a classic example of mystery in broad daylight.

Greek artists combined the drawings of the symbolic animals that appear on this table in hundreds of ways. The Corinthian workshops seem to have long been the repositories of this tradition, and the most beautiful vases of the "geometrical" style come from Corinth. However, the same images were held in honor throughout the Greek world. A great many examples could be given. Anyone curious will find plenty of them by opening a few volumes of the *Corpus Vasorum Antiquorum*. Also, I believe that there is a direct connection between the frequency of such imagery on Corinthian vases and the fact that ancient Corinth was situated in symbolic relation to the ancient Leo-Aquarius or Leo-Boar solstitial axis. The probable role of Corinth in the spread of the custom of decorating temple pediments with sculpture of symbolic meaning will be dealt with in chapter 17.

Let me take some characteristic examples from H. G. Payne's work *Protokorinthische Vasenmalerei* (Berlin, 1933).

First is the drawing (fig. 34) on an aryballus of the British Museum,[7] composed of the following animals:

Lion—Male Goat—Female Goat—Lioness

I interpret this as being inspired by the history of the solstices, since the lion and lioness represent the earlier solstitial axis, while the male and the female goats designate the one that succeeded the Lion-Lioness or Lion-Boar axis. On this drawing it seems that the male goat, for pictorial reasons, stood for the sign of Cancer!

The drawing on an aryballus from Eretria (fig. 35), also in London,[8] portrays the following animals:

Lion—Male Sphinx—Female Sphinx—Lioness

In my view this corresponds to a change in sex, since the animals are clearly differentiated. This is an image of the equinoxes and the solstices, often reproduced, and which is inspired by the motifs of oriental art.[9]

Figure 34. *Aryballus in the British Museum: the solstices (lions), the equinoxes (goats).*

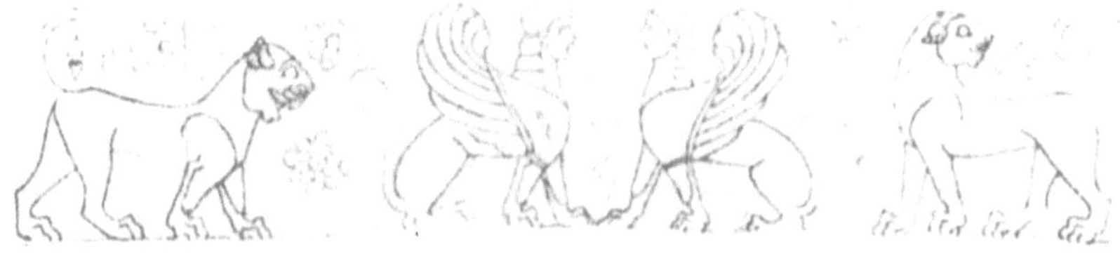

Figure 35. *Aryballus from Eretria (British Museum): the solstices (lion and lioness), the equinoxes (sphinxes).*

Next are two aryballi from the Boston Museum, first published in 1900 by Joseph Clark Hoppin, which are the subject of a plate in H. G. Payne's book.[10] One of them raises a slight question of interpretation that is not resolved by J. C. Hoppin.

On the flanks of this aryballus (fig. 36) the following characters are drawn:

Winged Giant—Chimaera
Character with an Eagle on his Shield—Panther

According to the table on p. 135, the chimaera and the panther represent the solstitial axis. Slightly anticipating what will be said in chapter 15, the armed character must be Geryon. His shield bears an eagle because he is opposed to the sign of the Eagle, being himself associated with Taurus. If one refers to the table of the Hesiodic guardians of the signs on p. 101, one will see that the great winged giant associated with the sign of the Eagle can be none other than Ophion, whose very name means serpent, and who is simultaneously the eagle and the serpent.[11] So this is a representation of two perpendicular axes, since Geryon and Ophion stand for Taurus and Scorpio, respectively, hence the earlier solstitial axis.

A Theban aryballus (fig. 37) offers a drawing that is easier to read:[12]

Male Sphinx—Chimaera—Bellerophon on Pegasus—Female Sphinx

The stars disseminated here and there clearly show that this is an astral scene, and the caduceus (there is really only one on the vase) alludes to the

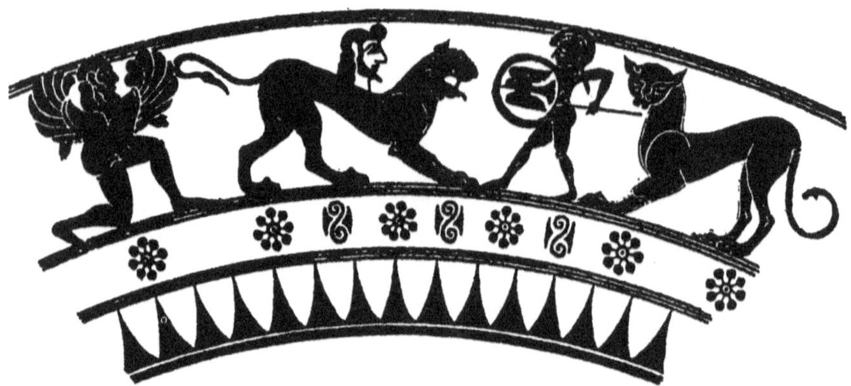

Figure 36. *Corinthian aryballus in Boston: Ophion, chimaera, Geryon, and panther (the equinoxes and the solstices).*

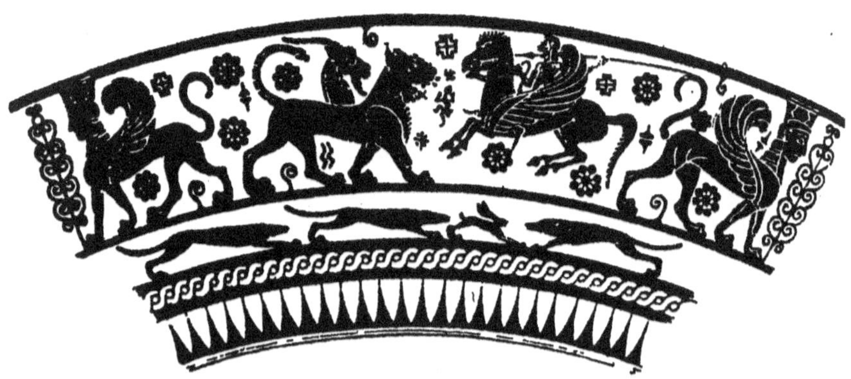

Figure 37. *Theban aryballus: equinoxes and solstices. Above, sphinxes and chimaera; Bellerophon and Pegasus; caduceus and lizards, stellar symbols. Below, hare and three dogs.*

seven planetary orbs. Not only do the equinoxes and the solstices appear, but again, in the middle of the drawing, a little lizard stands for the constellation of the Dragon where the former Polestar was located (see p. 181). This vase gives the opportunity to explain an image that frequently appears in various ways on Corinthian vases, which is the hare being chased by dogs. When there are four animals, they stand for the four seasons. When there are more, the hare represents the first month of the year followed by as many months as there are animals or subjects in the frieze. Here the hare (Taurus) stands for spring, and the three dogs the three other seasons.

A vase from Syracuse[13] (fig. 38) bears the following drawings:

1st register: Calydonian Hunt (Boar)—Stag—Sphinx—Male Goat
2nd register: Dog—Hare—Dog—Dog

This decor combines the different symbols of the equinoxes and the solstices in an unusual way, because in reality the boar and the goat never symbolized the winter and summer solstices simultaneously!

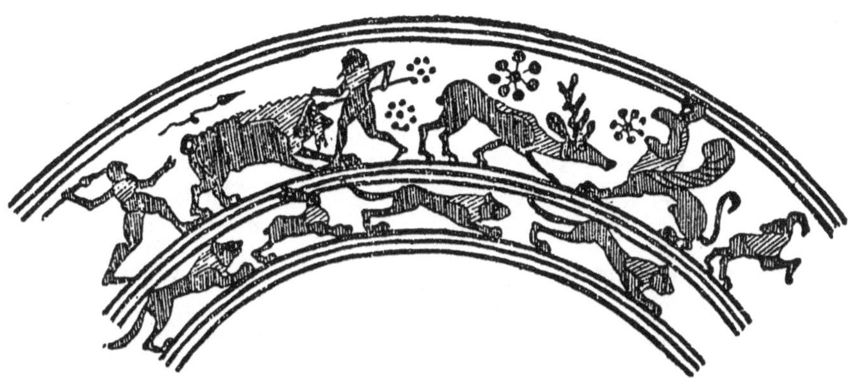

Figure 38. *Vase from Syracuse: above, the Calydonian hunt, stag, sphinx, and goat. Below, hare and three dogs.*

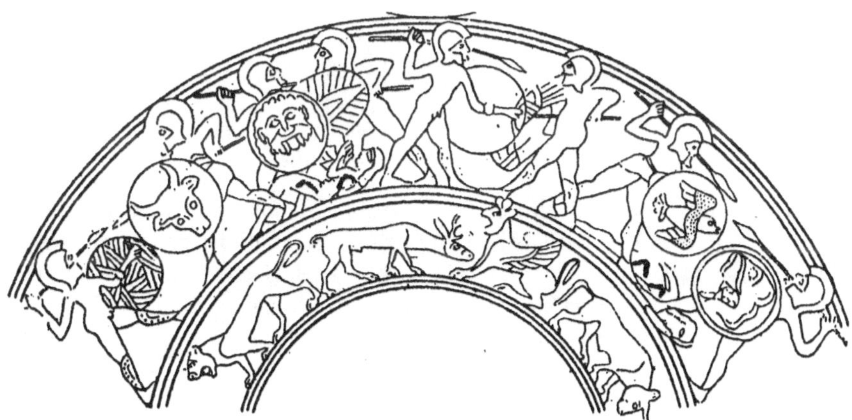

Figure 39. *Double representation of the seasons: above, shield devices. Below, lion, stag, sphinx, and bull. Notice the combination of images belonging to two successive periods in figs. 38 and 39.*

On another vase (fig. 39) one sees the combination:

Lion—Stag—Griffin—Bull

accompanied by scenes of combat which seem to refer to the history of the calendar.[14]

On many Greek vases of every origin as well as on Etruscan vases, these symbolic animals are employed to decorative ends. One often finds the winter solstice represented by a swan placed between two sphinxes[15] (the equinoxes), or else the spring equinox symbolized by a hare between two lions (the solstices). The lion, the panther, and the ram, either singly or in association, appear on hundreds of vases.[16]

The following equivalences may be kept in mind:

Summer Solstice—Day—Lion.
Winter Solstice—Night—Lioness, Panther, Boar
Spring Equinox—Male Principle—Male Sphinx
Autumnal Equinox—Female Principle—Female Sphinx

On many cups and vases appear four animals, in confrontation or in pursuit, that represent the four seasons of the year.[17] It can happen, by the way, that the direction of their movement is retrograde; this is true of a vase in the Museum of Arta (Church of the Panaghia Parigoritissa), which reads:

Hare—Panther—Swan—Dog

Sometimes the animals are arranged so as to be apparently directed towards the point considered as the beginning of the year. There are obviously several cycles of equivalent meaning. Among the most common are:

Bull—Lion—Swan—Lioness

Or else:

Hare—Lion—Swan—Panther

The goose is often substituted for the swan. One must beware of confusing the dogs in pursuit of a hare, which appear on a separate frieze in most cases, with the dog of the constellation Canis, which is associated with Sirius and the sign of Leo, just as one must distinguish between the horse representing Aquarius and the same animal associated with Gemini.

A Cylix of the Solstices. I believe that the drawing on a black-figured cylix in Munich (fig. 40) has never been correctly interpreted. I cannot agree with Jane E. Harrison that this is no more than a grape harvesting scene in which serpents, daimons of fertility,[18] would be participating. In my opinion, half of it represents the goats of Capricorn, and the other half, where one sees serpent-headed beings, suggests Hydra and the sign of Cancer. I think that the form of

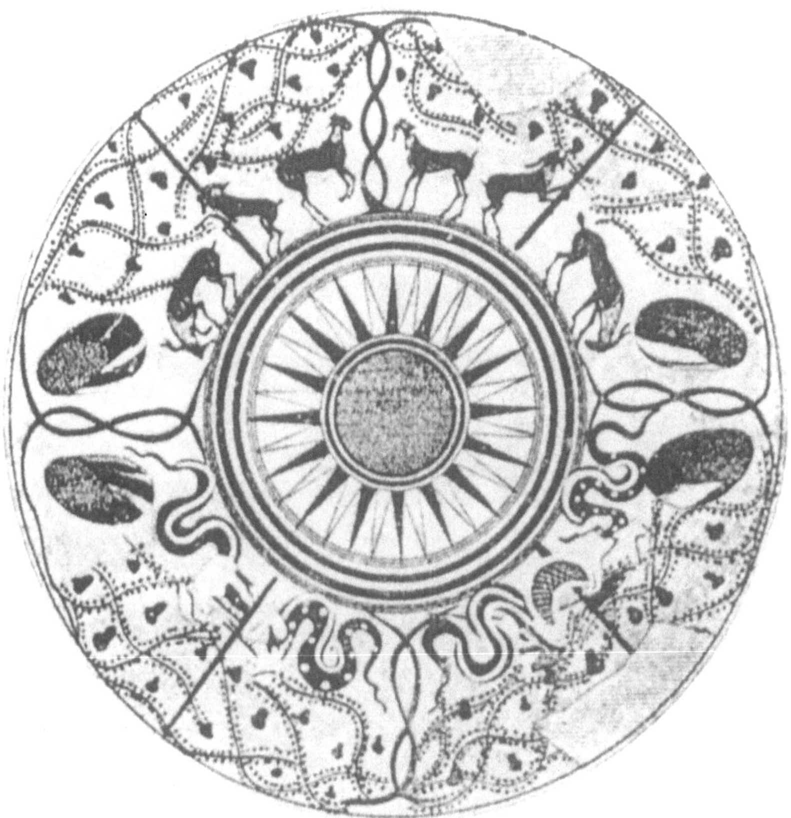

Figure 40. *Cylix of the solstices: goats and female hydras among vines (which seem to describe a year beginning at the winter solstice).*

the object held by two of these beings is more important than its supposed purpose (is it really a basket for gathering grapes?) because, even if this is seen as a grape harvesting scene, I can't help but notice that the object is shaped like a lunar crescent. Now the moon is traditionally associated with Cancer, which is its house. The vine gives a decorative and Dionysiac unity to the cup. Dionysus is associated with Aquarius, the goat, and the winter solstice. The drawing on this cylix must therefore, I believe, be seen primarily as a symbolic image of the solstices.

A Phrygian Vase. I think it interesting to here reproduce a Phyrgian vase (fig. 41) with a handle from seventh-century Gordium, now in the Archeological Museum of Ankara, which was brought to my attention by Jacques Hure.

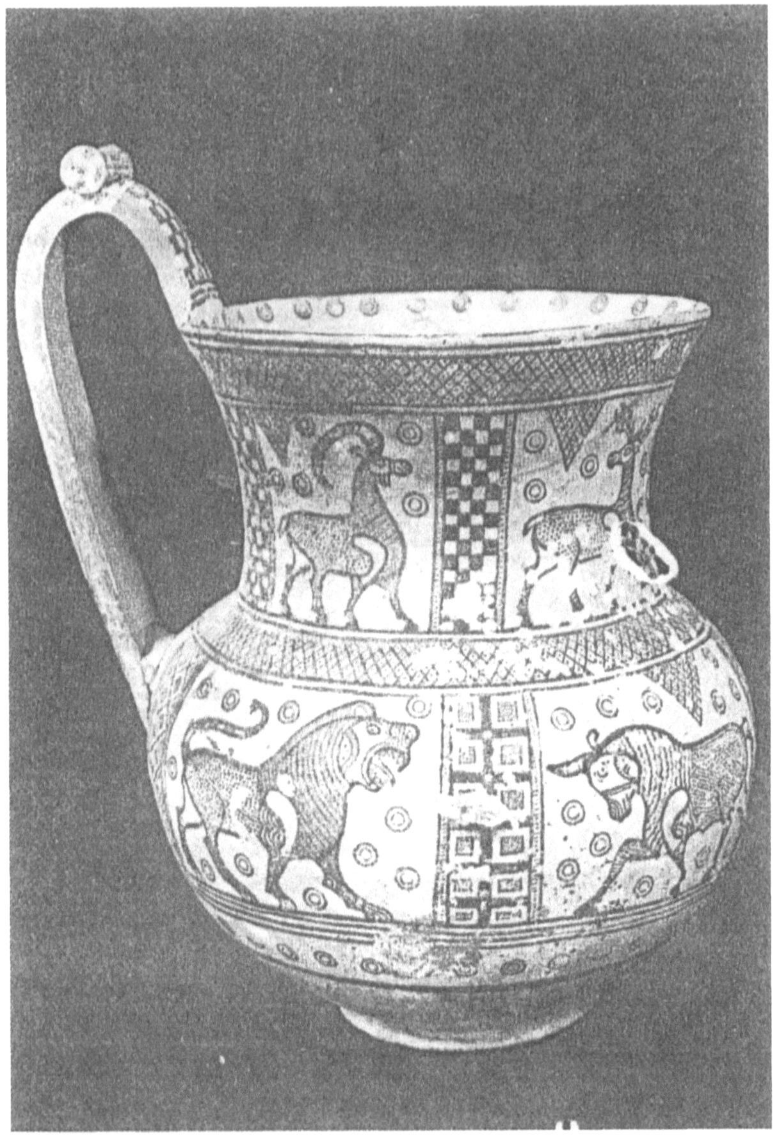

Figure 41. *Phrygian vase of the seventh century found at Gordium (Museum of Ankara).*

This vase is especially interesting in that it simultaneously describes the zodiacal signs, the solstices, the equinoxes, and the four seasons. Both sides being similar, the vase as a whole defines a period of two years. This gives the following arrangement:

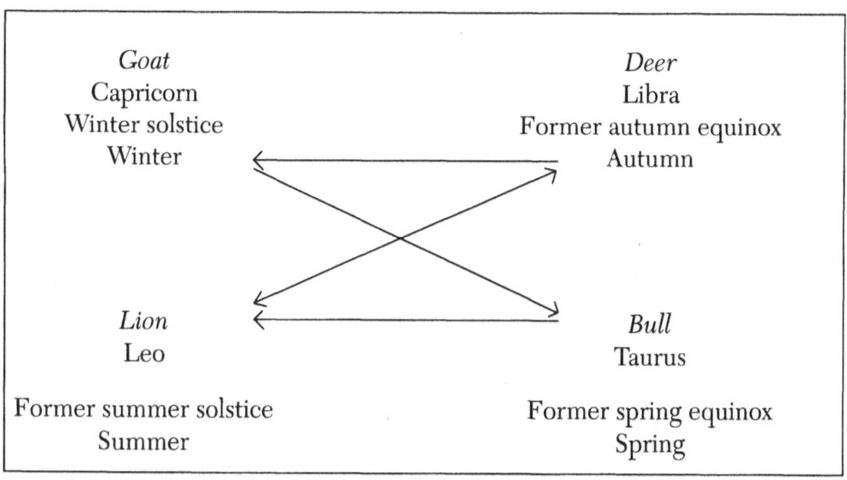

This vase confirms that the deer was the Anatolian symbol for autumn. The presence of the goat may be surprising (one would rather expect the boar). However, this becomes understandable when one realizes that the little pointed circles represent stars. One would therefore be dealing with a calendar established on the fixed stars of first magnitude, which sets up the following correspondences:

Goat: Alpha of Capricorn, *Giedi* (*Uz* of the Akkadians)
Lion: Alpha Leonis or Regulus
Bull: Alpha Tauri or Aldebaran
Cervidae: Alpha Librae or Zubenelgenubi, the southern claw of the Scorpion.

If this set of four animals is put into relationship with Sumero-Akkadian mythology, the following correspondences appear:

God of the waters: EA: goat (Capricorn)
God of the underworld: NERGAL: lion
God of the earth: ENLIL: wild ox or bull
God of the sky : ANU: stag.

The god Nergal-Rasap, or Nergal-Rešef, prefigures Apollo in many respects (both are associated with Leo). According to J.-E. Dugand (*Chypre et Canaan*, Nice, 1973, p. 231) the statue found at Enkomi in 1949 that portrays the celebrated god wearing a headdress with two long horns is a Tešef-Mikal that prefigures Apollo Amyclaeus.

Let me finally comment on the cruciform arrangement: the solstices are to the left, the equinoxes to the right. The twelve squares between the lion and the bull may stand for a year of twelve months.

2. The Loves of Zeus

The amorous adventures of the king of the gods, who took on various shapes, have an astral meaning closely connected with the zodiac and also with Greek sacred geography. This is easily shown. One only need apply the principle of the complementarity of opposing signs. In every case Zeus adopts a zodiacal form that relates to the sign opposite the one governing the region where he unites with a mortal.

I here bring together what I have already partly said on the subject:

The Pole. Zeus united with the bear Callisto, which represents the center and the pole. From this union Arcas was born, who gave his name to Arcadia, the central region of the Peloponnese.

Taurus-Scorpio Axis (and Libra). In a bull's shape, Zeus unites with the Theban Antiope, who is associated with the Libra-Scorpio sector. Antiope gives birth to the twins Amphion and Zethus (see p. 115). Harmonia, daughter of Electra and Zeus, is associated with Samothrace, and thus with the same zodiacal area.

Sagittarius-Gemini Axis. For his love with Leda at Sparta in the Gemini region, Zeus takes the shape of a swan, which represents Sagittarius. From this union are born the Dioscuri (Gemini) and Helen (Cancer).

Leo-Aquarius Axis. Zeus, as drops of golden rain (Aquarius), fertilizes Danaë at Argos (sign of Leo); she gives birth to Perseus, a Leonine hero.

It is sometimes said that Zeus approached Antiope in the form of a satyr (which would represent Aries). He took on a human form with Alcmene, when substituting for Amphitryon, which makes the latter a sort of Ganymede! Aquarius is often a man.

The Eagle. A zodiacal meaning may be attributed to Ganymede's eagle only if this image is associated with a system centered on Delphi wherein Mysia and the Troad would be represented by the sign of the Eagle. Because of the particular nature of this union, the god does not take on the form of the opposing sign but that of the sign itself. It is once again manifest how zodiacal symbolism is intimately connected with the sacred geography of Greece.[19]

Chapter 14

Double Symbols
Syncretic Forms
Fighting Animals, Dynamic Symbols of Seasonal Variations
The Calendar of Xanthus

1. Double Symbols

In a short work entitled *Greek Geometric Art, Its Symbolism and Its Origin,*[1] Anna Roes has assembled some interesting documentation, but has not really taken full advantage of it because she did not perceive the zodiacal nature of the symbols, which she qualifies uniformly as "solar." This adjective, although correct, is too general in meaning.

Referring to the interesting illustrations in her book, I will discuss in this chapter a very important aspect of Greek art, inherited, as is clearly established by Roes, from Iranian art. (It might be as true to assume a common tradition for the origins of both.) The point which I will first consider is the frequent appearance of double animal symbols. Sometimes the animals are represented whole; sometimes only the front halves of their bodies are shown.

This is an example of the phenomenon that has already been observed in the preceding chapter in speaking of the sphinx and the stag, symbols of the equinoxes. For reasons that are at least partly aesthetic and for convenience of representation, a single animal, shown twice, has the function of representing the axis of the solstices or the equinoxes. Thus instead of having a horse-lion couple for the solstitial axis, one will have either a double lion or a double horse. But these symbols are not absolutely equivalent because their choice depends on the time taken as the beginning of the year. The following is a table of these principal double forms ("double" can here apply to two animals or to two protomes of animals).

a) Earlier Solstitial Axis:
   Year beginning in Spring: Double Bull.
   Year beginning in Autumn: Double Sphinx.
b) Earlier Solstitial Axis:
   Year beginning in Summer: Double Lion (or Lion-Lioness) or Double Rooster.
   Year beginning in Winter: Double Horse.

c) Later Equinoctial Axis:
   Year beginning in Spring: Double Ram (or Double Monkey).
   Year beginning in Autumn: Double Stag (or Stag-Doe).
d) Later Solstitial Axis:
   Year beginning in Summer: Double Spiral.
   Year beginning in Winter: Double Goat (or He-goat and She-goat).

So one has, astronomically, the following equivalences:

1ST PERIOD	2ND PERIOD
Double Bull	Double Ram or Double Monkey
Double Sphinx	Double Stag
Double Lion	Double Spiral
Double Horse	Double Goat

These simple keys open the way to understanding the symbolic meaning of a great number of objects of all kinds: terra-cottas, bronzes, coins, ornaments, jewelry, tripod bases, chariot ornaments, etc.

To take a simple example, the golden diadem of Athens (fig. 42), in the collection of the Louvre (Inv. 93), illustrates what I mean: there on either side of a kid or a female goat (winter solstice) are two stags being devoured by lions. I believe that this must be interpreted to symbolize a year which probably began at the winter solstice, divided into two halves by the solstitial axis.

I think, however, that an important reservation concerning double zodiacal symbols must be made. It is likely that in some cases this doubling is purely decorative, and the two confronted symbols describe the beginning and the end of a single zodiacal sign. To be convinced of this, one only need look at the plaque from the temple of Hera at Samos (fig. 28, p. 51), where it is very clear that the two kneeling bulls represent the beginning and the end of the sign. Thus the image of two confronted roosters most often represented only the sign of Leo.

2. A Syncretic Form: the Hippalectryon

I can now give a rational explanation for many of the mysterious syncretic symbols whose meaning has never been clearly understood. The best known is the hippalectryon, which was specifically but ephemerally in vogue during the sixth

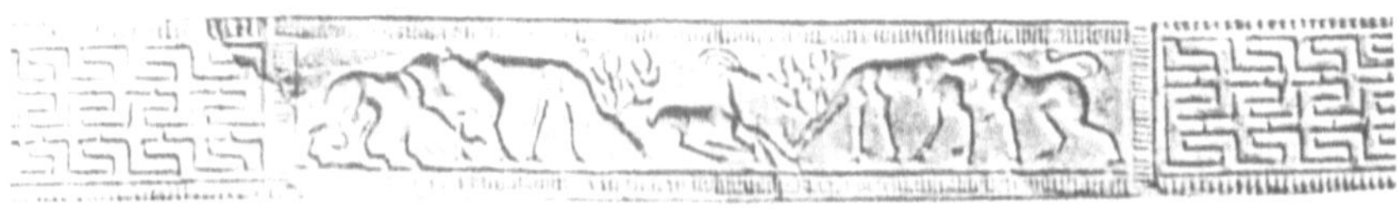

Figure 42. *Golden diadem from Athens: goat of Capricorn and stags being devoured by wild animals symbolizing the equinoxes and solstices (Louvre Museum).*

century.[2] This strange monster is composed of the front part of a horse to which the artist generally added the legs of a rooster with spurs and a rooster's tail. In *The Frogs* of Aristophanes, Euripides (uninitiated) mocks Aeschylus (initiate of Eleusis) for having spoken of the hippalectryon. Aeschylus, in a verse of his play *The Myrmidons* had apparently mentioned a "horse-rooster the color of fire."

The rooster, which for the Greeks long remained the "Persian bird," is quite obviously a solar fowl. Symbolically, it was very quickly taken to represent Leo. On the acropolis of Athens stood a sculpture of a hippalectryon with a rider, about which P. Perdrizet has written:

> If, towards the year 500, an Athenian had dedicated a hippalectryon to the goddess on the acropolis and if the authorities had given their approval, it was because this offering, which seems strange to us, was not so for the Athenians of that time; on the contrary, they must have considered it appropriate and beneficial. I can explain this only by assuming that the image of the hippalectryon was endowed with magical virtue, that it was an ἀποτρὸπαιον.[3]

In the remainder of his article, P. Perdizet emphasized the rooster's funerary significance, which derives from its zodiacal symbolism, as I will show in my second volume. It is, in fact, not difficult to deduce that the hippalectryon, which associates the front part of Pegasus with the tail of the rooster, symbol of Leo, represents the Leo-Aquarius solstitial axis.

Some of the monuments inventoried by Perdrizet confirm this by allowing me to establish that the hippalectryon, symbol of the Leo-Aquarius axis, is consistently associated with the signs of Leo, Aquarius, and Pisces. Here are some of them:

a) On a plaque of the British Museum (fig. 43), from Eleutherae, dated to the seventh century, one sees two rearing hippalectryons facing one another. Between them in the center is a radiating circle or a pointed rosette, an evident

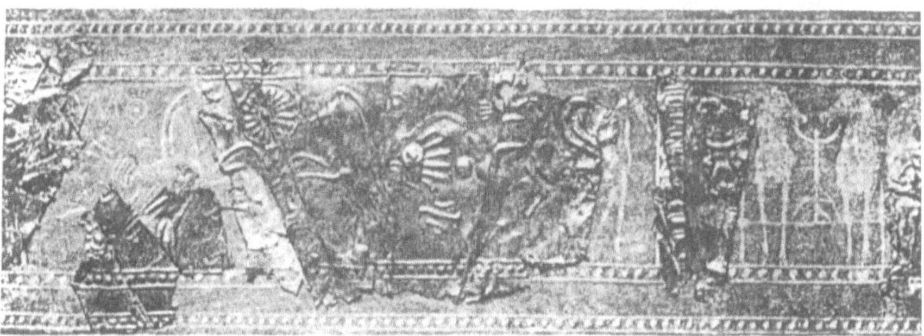

Figure 43. *Plaque from Eleutherae with two confronted hippalectryons and a winged horse (British Museum).*

solar symbol. To the right, in better condition, are a zigzag that suggests the glyph for Aquarius, a bird, and the hindquarters (the only remaining part) of a winged horse. All this supports my interpretation.[4]

b) On an amphora in Munich are two scenes of a zodiacal nature: on one side, one sees an *ephebus* with a lance and a coat mounted on a hippalectryon (symbol of the Leo-Aquarius axis), on the other, a centaur throwing a block of stone on the lapith Caeneus (Gemini-Sagittarius opposition).[5]

c) On an Attico-Corinthian amphora in the University Museum of Bonn that is believed to come from Aegina appear two hippalectryons framed by two sirens, symbol of Aquarius. An analysis of the decoration on this amphora, according to Hermann Thiersch's description,[6] must begin with with the symbolic animals on both sides. There one sees panthers (Aquarius), sirens (Aquarius), hippalectryons (Leo-Aquarius axis), roosters (Leo), and rams. Aquarius is symbolized no less than sixteen times. Now, on the map of Greece, Aegina is in Leo. Leo appears four times. Aries, a fire sign like Leo and having special affinity with it, is represented seven times.

The main scenes on the amphora are, on one side, a battle of Amazons, allusion to the Pisces-Virgo axis, and on the other a battle of hoplites. Although the exact interpretation of the latter is unknown, I think that it would doubtless prove to be another reference to the Leo-Aquarius axis.

d) Some have wondered[7] whether certain coins from Lampsacus did not represent hippalectryons. Lamer, after having considered this hypothesis, rejected it, with insufficient reason, in my opinion. It is all the more probable because Lampsacus is on the Leo-Aquarius axis in the system centered on Sardis (see p. 45 and the coin of map 11, fig. 36).

3. Other Syncretic Forms

The other syncretic forms comparable to the hippalectryon may be divided into two categories, which have always been confused through misunderstanding their distinguishing characteristics.

Many examples of syncretic forms will be found in John Boardman's *Greek Gems and Finger Rings*, 1971, where one notices, from the Creto-Mycenaean period onwards, the frequency of groups of fighting animals. In such groups the attacking griffins always represent the winter solstice and the direction of north.

a) Forms of General Astrological Meaning. These forms appear on vases or gems. Several represent the solstitial axis and have the same meaning as the hippalectryon: the boar-rooster, the panther-rooster, and the young woman-rooster.[8] A bird with the head of a hare symbolizes the Taurus-Eagle equinoctial axis.

b) Forms of Horoscopic Meaning. But other forms, of which there are generally only single examples, have a horoscopic meaning related to the hour and the season of birth of an individual person. They appear exclusively on gems and intaglios. Thus a chalcedony in the Cabinet des Médailles in Paris features a she-goat-rooster, an association of Leo and Capricorn. A gem in the British Museum depicts a bull-rooster (the Taurus-Leo square). Also known are the rooster with a donkey's head (a Leo-Cancer association that refers to the constellation of the Donkey in that zodiacal region), and the bird with the head of a he-goat (Eagle and Capricorn). The dog-headed bird describes the Eagle and Sirius; the griffin bird with a rooster's head synthesizes the Eagle, the North, and Leo. The lion-headed rooster is a Leo to the second power. It could describe an individual born at dawn in summer.[9] Gnostic gems were to inherit this astrological tradition and featured complex monsters that combined a set of signs in a condensed form of multiple meaning, whose purpose was to provide effective and specially calculated protection for the bearer of the object thus decorated (the hare-headed bird can obviously also have a horoscopic meaning).

4. Associations of Zodiacal Symbols

It can also happen that the zodiacal symbols are juxtaposed in the images without being merged. The hare, as I have said, is often used to represent Taurus. As a result of this, an eagle snatching up a hare in its talons stands for the Taurus-Eagle opposition. One animal has been substituted for another to produce a zoologically acceptable image. This ancient figuration of the equinoctial axis was in use all the way to Byzantine and Roman art.

Although not directly on the subject, not being part of the Greek world, a very attractive image from Iran deserves some attention, because it illustrates the symbolic mode of thinking that is being examined.

It appears on Iranian bronzes that represent an eagle perched on a doe. No one seems to have noticed that this image is a charming image of the autumnal equinox (fig. 44). The doe itself symbolizes the equinox, the perched eagle the precarious balance of nights and days at that time of year. Momentarily, it will fly away and engage in a hopeless but valiant struggle against the serpent of night.[10]

5. Dynamic Symbols of Seasonal Variations

Certain symbols of simple meaning do not seem ever to have been correctly interpreted. These also relate to the animals that designated the four quarters of the year towards 2500 B.C., and they are dynamically combined. Several of them, incidentally, were borrowed by the Greeks from the Orient and are found in Mesopotamia and Phoenicia before making an appearance in Crete and then in Greece.

The symbols:

1. The period from the spring equinox to the summer solstice was the time of the triumph of Taurus. Its principal symbols were the winged

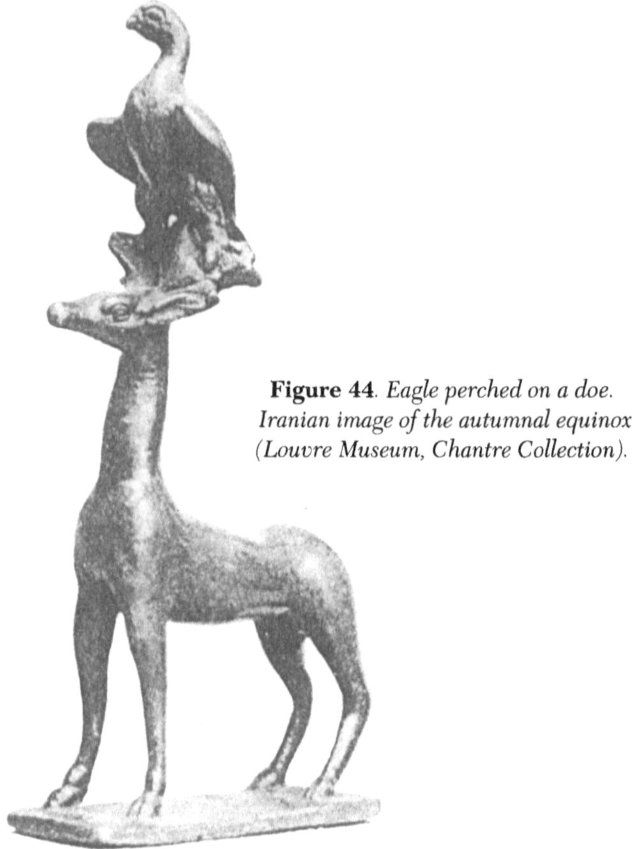

Figure 44. *Eagle perched on a doe. Iranian image of the autumnal equinox (Louvre Museum, Chantre Collection).*

bull, the stag, and the hare. During this time, the weather gets increasingly hotter, which was symbolized by a lion or lions devouring a bull.

2. The period from the summer solstice to the autumnal equinox is the time of the hottest weather. The heat then begins to progressively diminish. This season was symbolized by a lion attacking a stag or a hind.

   During a certain period, the winged bull seems to have stood for spring and the southwest quarter, and the lion or lions attacking a bull stood for summer and the southeast quarter of Greece.

3. From the autumnal equinox to the winter solstice the days become progressively shorter. The battle of night and day, of what increases and what decreases, was symbolized by the dramatic fight between

the eagle that flies high towards the light of the sky and the serpent that crawls low in the shadows. The best image of this part of the year is the serpent raising its head, because it is then that the shadows become dominant.

4. From the winter solstice to the spring equinox, the days get longer and longer, symbolized by the winged horse, the panther (either alone or attacking a kid or a stag), and the boar eating a fish.

Oddly enough, the symbols of the seasonal variations remained unchanged even after the precession of the equinoxes had led to the substitution of Aries for Taurus, Cancer for Leo, Libra for Scorpio, and Capricorn for Aquarius. The only exception seems to have been the symbol of the winged goat for the beginning of the year, when the winter solstice was taken as the origin.

Antiquity of These Symbols

A whole volume could be devoted to the study of the symbols of seasonal variations showing how they were transmitted from one civilization to another while retaining their astral significance. Frequent in the religious imagery of Assur or Sumer, whether on ivory tablets or bas-reliefs, they reappear with consistent meaning in Byzantine and Roman art. For four thousand years, their universal value as well as their intrinsic plastic value led every civilization that flourished on the shores of the Mediterranean to adopt them.

To establish the great antiquity of these fighting animals, I will give only one example from André Parrot's book on Sumer, a bas-relief from third-millenium Kish, now in the Museum of Baghdad, representing a lion attacking a deer.[11] It is difficult to know when the exact meaning of such images was lost from view. But their frequency, the orientation of the sites chosen for such imagery, and the judicious reemployment of ancient sculptures in many churches, such as the stones embedded in the walls at Saint-Benoît-sur-Loire or the reliefs from the ancient Sarapeum of Athens incorporated into the decor of the Church of the Small Metropolis, suggests that their meaning remained intelligible until the dawn of "modern times."

I will simply mention a few characteristic examples of these oriental and Phoenician images, since this inquiry is limited in principle to the Greek world in the present volume. As might be expected, the symbols of seasonal variations are often associated in Cretan and Greek art with those of the spatial directions, especially with griffins and sphinxes.

The similarity of certain Minoan objects, seals or ivories, for example, with those of Sumer, Egypt, or Phoenicia is such that it is sometimes difficult to decide whether they were imported or produced by local workshops in imitation of Crete or Mycenae, faithful copies of an oriental or "orientalizing" style. But the probable unity of Creto-Phoenician civilization must be taken into account if, as is generally believed today, the Philistines were Mycenaeans who inhabited the coast of Phoenicia.[12] Without being forced to choose between these theories, I will merely point out the striking similarities between the ivories of Megiddo and the Creto-Mycenaean ivories found, for example, in Crete, at Pylos, in the tombs of Argolis (at Mycenae or at Midea) and at Spata or at Menidhi in Attica. The symbols of the seasonal variations are ubiquitous. The objects of Megiddo date from the thirteenth century B.C. and are thus contemporaneous with late Minoan and Mycenaean III (late Helladic).

A beautiful ivory coffer found at Megiddo[13] features the combination of a lion and a human-headed sphinx. That is, it describes the solstitial and equinoctial axes (fig. 45). Other ivories from Samaria show sphinxes (sometimes described as "cherubs" because of their human heads), ram-headed sphinxes similar to those of Arslan Tash, a lion attacking a bull[14] (fig. 46), etc.

One only need compare these objects with the ivory plaques found at Spata[15] (fig. 47), for example, to perceive the identity of their inspiration.[16]

Dozens of gems from Crete or the islands have the same motifs.[17]

Documents Showing the Various Meanings of the Symbols of Seasonal Variations. Most interesting are the Greek monuments which put these symbols into relationship with a season of the year or a direction of space. I will review some of them.

The symbol of the confronted bull and lion appears on the most ancient known coins, those of the kings of Lydia. It seems to specifically designate the southeast quarter of Anatolia and could be related to the Phoenician or Babylonian origin of Lydian culture.

The sculptures from various temple pediments that show one or two lions devouring a bull will be studied in an upcoming chapter. This motif seems to have symbolized the southeast quarter (bearing in mind my earlier comment on a certain irresolution between the symbols for spring and summer).

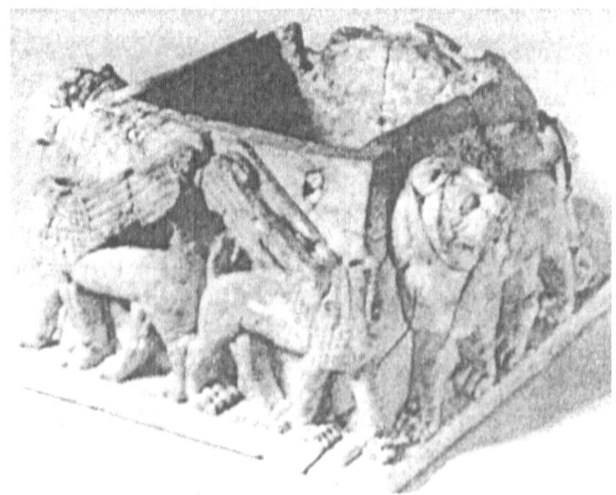

Figure 45. *Coffer from Megiddo: lions and sphinxes (solstices and equinoxes).*

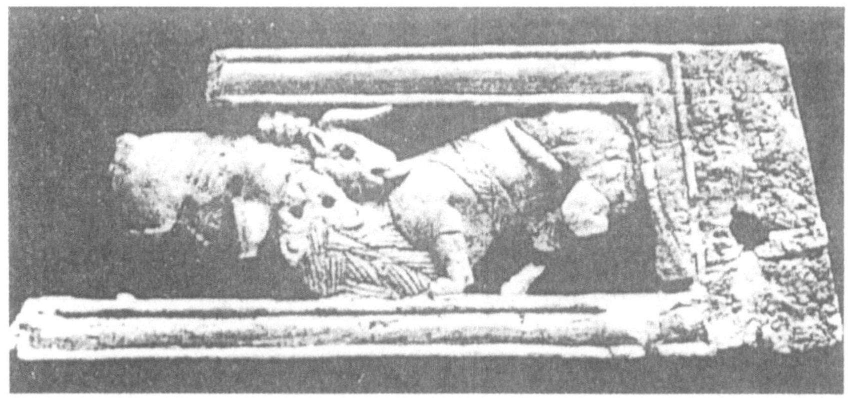

Figure 46. *Ivory from Samaria: lion devouring a bull.*

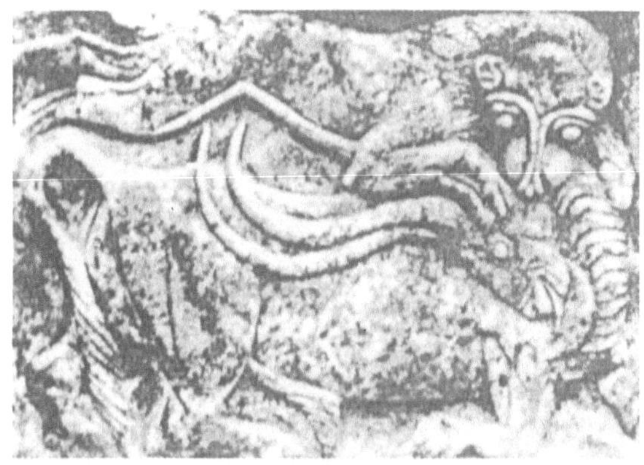

Figure 47. *Ivory from Spata (Attica): lion devouring a bull.*

It is, however, surprising to find images of a lion attacking a bull on coins from Acanthus, a city of Macedonia, whose geographical position cannot explain such a symbol.[18] But this becomes understandable when one realizes that Acanthus was a colony of Andros. The image describes the position of this island put, like Kea and Thera, into symbolic relationship with the high heat of summer.

The symbol of the eagle attacking a serpent appears on coins from Chalcis. In keeping with the law of the equivalence-complementarity of opposites, it is found on the coins of Olympia (see p. 19).

On a vase conserved in Berlin, Thetis is bringing to Achilles a shield whereupon is painted an eagle with a serpent in its talons and four stars.[19] And indeed, Achilles is associated with the northeast quarter of the Greek territory in the Delphic system.

The most frequent symbol for the northwest quarter is the panther. I know of only one figure of a head of a winged boar holding a fish in its jaws. The vase where it appears is a good example of a vase with astrological meaning, which is why I will describe it briefly. It is a black-figured Attic vase now in Berlin[20] (fig. 48). The drawing that concerns us is the device on Athena's shield in a scene where the goddess is opposing Ajax and defending Cassandra. The dynamic symbol describes the part of the sky opposed to the sign of Virgo and simultaneously alludes to the Leo-Boar solstitial axis. Ajax is here identified with the sign of Pisces, opposed to Virgo (in the Delian system, Salamis, where Ajax reigned, is in the sign of Pisces).

On the other side of the vase is another scene, complementary to the first as to astrological meaning: one sees Theseus, hero of the sign of Virgo and of Athens, slaying the Minotaur. But rather than a symbol of the Taurus-Leo square (Theseus came from Troezen) or the Taurus-Virgo trine, I believe that this must refer to the Taurus-Eagle equinoctial axis that complements the symbolism of the solstitial axis in the other drawing. (The tomb of Theseus was at Scyros.)

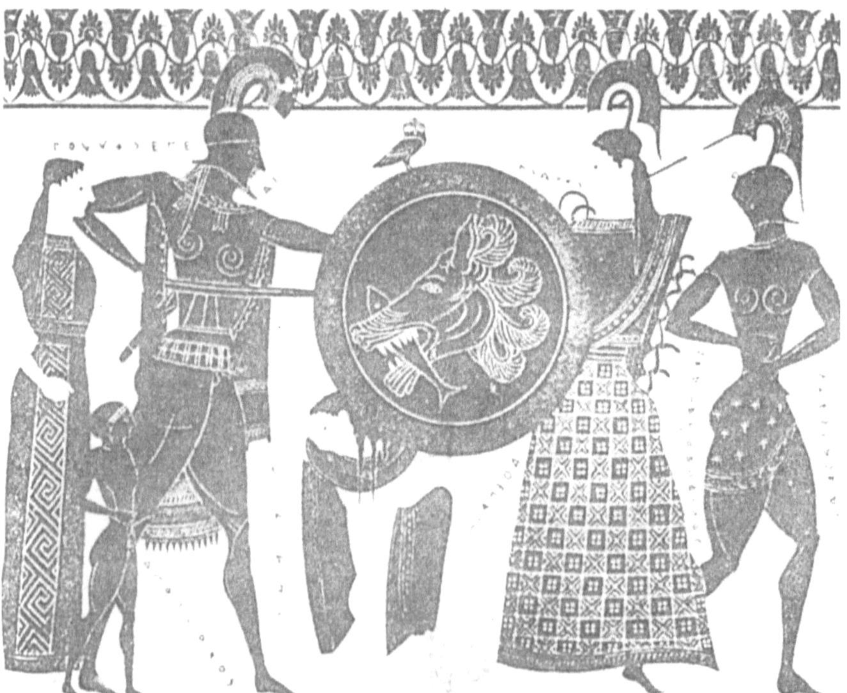

Figure 48. *Attic black figure vase in Berlin: shield device of the head of a boar devouring a fish (symbol of the northwest and winter).*

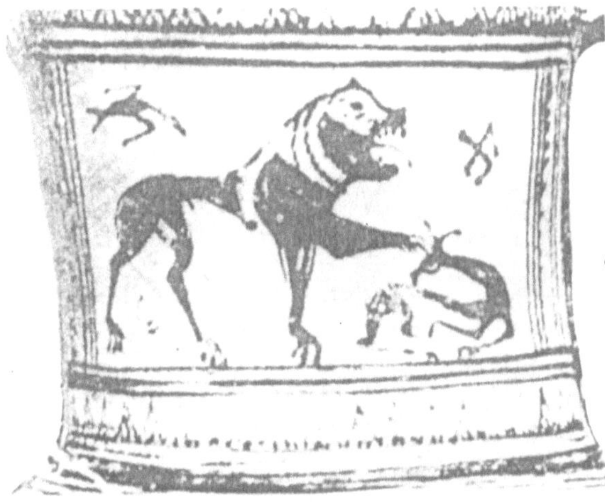

Figure 49. *Neck of an amphora of the geometric period in the British Museum: bird, lion and deer; swastika.*

It is enough to leaf through the album of Arias and Hirmer (*The Greek Vase*) to see that, from the geometric period onwards, the symbols of seasonal variations often appeared on vases, especially on their necks (fig. 49), accompanied by swastikas, i.e., solar symbols. They are on the famous "François vase" of Florence, whose symbolism will be studied separately in another volume.

It can also happen that the symbolic scene on one side of a vase indicates the timing of the scene on the other. Thus, on the columned krater B. 360 in the British Museum, found at Armento, one sees two lions attacking a bull on one side and on the other a departure of warriors.

One might think that the lions suggest the idea of combat, but in my opinion this combination really means that the departure of the warriors took place in spring or summer.

6. The Calendar of the Acropolis of Xanthus

In the British Museum there is a group of sculptures in the form of quadrangular blocks, which were brought back by Charles Fellows from the acropolis of the city of Xanthus in Lycia. Their exact original order being unknown, they are currently arranged for display in the following order:[21]

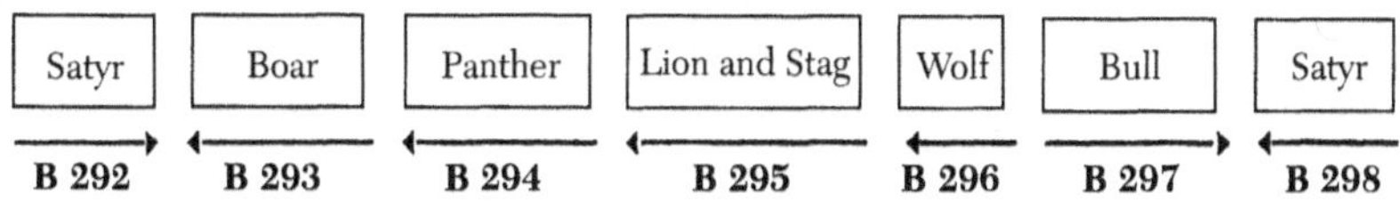

According to my previous deductions, this must be a calendar. I suggest a scheme (fig. 50) that corresponds to a division of the year into six. Could this be the ancient three-season calendar already suggested in discussing the myth of Bellerophon? (See p. 118)

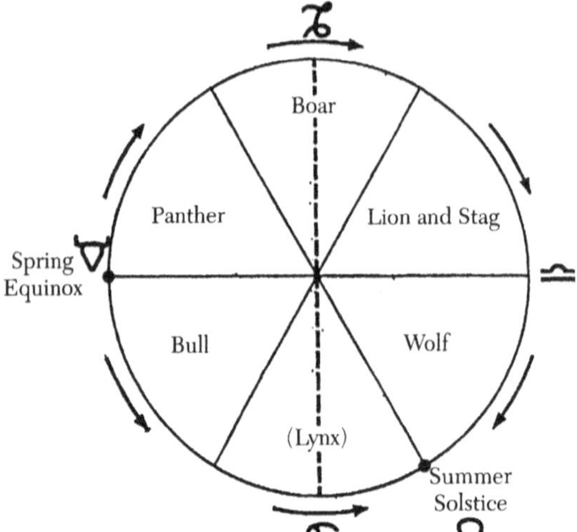

Figure 50. *Diagram of the calendar of Xanthus.*

It is unlikely that the satyrs represent a part of the sky and of the year. They are spirits of fertility, which here symbolize the earth, since the changing seasons affect the life of the planet—the vegetation, animals, etc. They act as earthly guardians of the calendar. The fact that the bull is the only figure facing to the right indicates that it commanded the series and that the year began at the spring equinox.

The animal of uncertain identity is more probably a wolf than a lioness through the etymology (or para-etymology) of the name Lycia. One element is missing in the series, which should be a horse, a lynx, or an octopus.

I was at this stage in my reasoning when I consulted the second volume of the publication of the Xanthus excavations by Henri Metzger: *Fouilles de Xanthos, l'Acropole lycienne* (1963).

One reads in this work (paraphrasing one sentence):

> Among the blocks reemployed in the Byzantine wall of the southern slope and brought to London by Fellows, [some can be of help in reconstructing a terrace wall—these are] sculpted blocks where have been recognized a satyr brandishing a pine branch, a boar running to the left, a leopard, a lion devouring a doe, and a panther or a lynx walking to the left [N.B.: In my opinion, B 294 is a panther and not a leopard, and B 296 is a wolf and not a lynx or panther.] We can now add to the London documents a fragmentary block (Relief 3341), taken from the slopes of the acropolis, where we see a leopard walking to the right."[22]

This relief, that completes the group so propitiously, was very probably a lynx. The animal's head is missing, but several arguments can be put forth to support this interpretation.

The main thing, in my opinion, is that the animal is facing to the right like the bull. It therefore very probably also stood for one or two months of the beginning of the year.

What is more, each animal is treated separately, regardless of the relative dimensions of the various animals: the panther, boar, bull, and wolf are all the same height, that of the stone blocks on which they are carved.

My suggested reconstruction is thus the following:

1. B 292 Satyr to the right	
2. B 297 Bull to the right 3. Relief 3341 of Xanthus [Lynx] to the right	Spring—1st season
4. B 296 [Wolf] to the left 5. B 295 Lion devouring a stag to the left	Summer—2nd season Autumn—2nd season
6. B 293 Boar running to the left 7. B 294 [Panther] to the left	Winter—3rd season
8. B 298 Satyr to the left.	

So this would indeed be the three-season calendar also described by the myth of the chimaera.

The series of six figures is thus probably complete. Each sculpture represents two months (fig. 51), an arrangement perfectly suitable for the decoration of an agora.[23]

The Roosters of Xanthus. A group of sculptures of roosters in the British Museum also comes from Xanthus, which is in the sign of Leo in relation to Sardis. This decorative group also has a symbolic meaning related to the solar significance of the bird.

I can very well imagine a section, on one side of the calendar that I have just reconstituted, reserved for a symbolic motif of roosters.

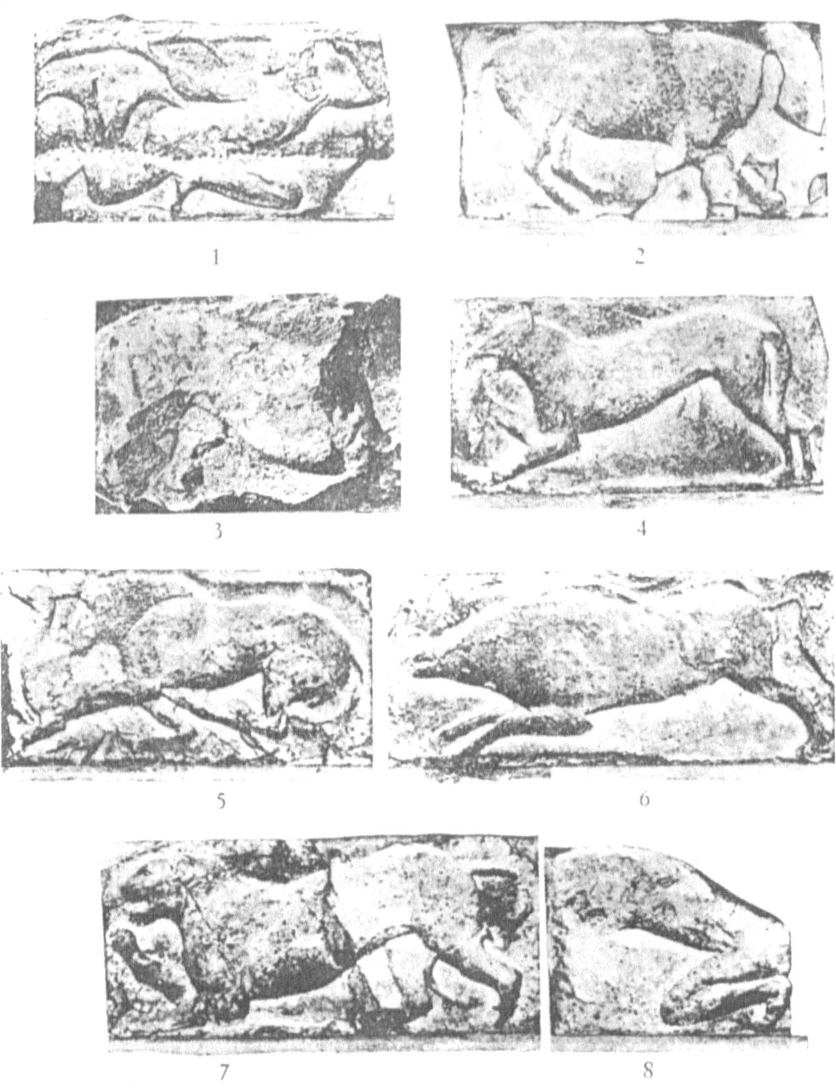

Figure 51. *Proposed reconstruction of the bas-reliefs of the acropolis at Xanthus: (1) Satyr, to the right; (2) Bull, to the right; (3) Lynx, to the right; (4) Wolf, to the left; (5) Lion devouring a stag, to the left; (6) Charging boar, to the left; (7) Panther, to the left; (8) Satyr, to the left.*

Chapter 15

Shield Devices
The Common Origins of Blazons and Monetary Symbols
The Complementarity of Opposites
Plaques from Delphi
Study of Vases

1. Shield Devices

To my knowledge, the only study of the decorative motifs that appear on shields, which are known through depictions on vases and monuments, is George Henry Chase's already old work cited in note 19 of the preceding chapter.[1]

This was the starting point for my own research, which was to yield very fruitful results. It quickly became clear that almost all these symbols refer to gods or signs of the zodiac and may be interpreted in terms of astrology.

The archaic motifs categorized by Chase as decorative or "terrible" emblems: the bull's head, the crab, three crosses, the octopus, and the wheel all have an astral significance.

Appearing on the shields are the signs of the zodiac, the circumzodiacal constellations, the circumpolar constellations, and the gods, represented by their attributes. The following is a concise table set up according to Chase.

SIGNS OF THE ZODIAC

ARIES:	Ram, Ram's head, Young boy on a Ram
TAURUS:	Bull, Protome of a Bull, Bull's head, Bull's horns, Hare
GEMINI:	Horseman, Horsemen, Horses, Pilos (pointed cap of the Dioscuri)
CANCER:	Crab, Polyp, Cuttlefish, Octopus
LION AND SIRIUS:	Lion, Winged Lion, Lion's head Protome of a Lion Wolf (can also represent Capricorn) Dog, Dog's head, Rooster, Chimaera
VIRGO:	Gorgon, Serpent, Owl
LIBRA:	Double Lighting, Sphinx, Stag, Winged Stag, Protome of a Stag

SCORPIO: Eagle, Eagle with Serpent in its talons, Scorpion
SAGITTARIUS: Swan, Dolphin, Centaur in various positions
CAPRICORN: Goat, Goat's head, Protome of a Goat
AQUARIUS: Boar, Siren, Pegasus, Horse (winged), Protome of a winged Horse, Panther
PISCES: Fish, Nereids

OTHER CONSTELLATIONS
Stars in a Cross: Orion
Seven Stars: Pleiades
Bow of a ship: Argo Navis

CIRCUMPOLAR CONSTELLATIONS
Dolphin, Wolf, Swan, Boar
The Boar relates to Aquarius, the Swan (or Goose) and the Dolphin to Sagittarius.

SYMBOLS OF THE NORTH-SOUTH AXIS
Griffin, Plane leaf, Fig leaf, Palm leaf, Trees

POLAR SYMBOLS
Swastika, Triskele, Wheel, Winged Wheel

DIVINE SYMBOLS
Apollo: Bow, Tripod, Laurel leaf, Crow, Scarab, Rat
Artemis: Doe, Fawn, Quail
Heracles: Club
Demeter: Ear of Grain
Dionysus: Panther, Silenus, Winged Phallus, Ivy, Cantharus, Vine
Zeus: Lightning, Eagle
Poseidon: Trident, Anchor, Horse
Aphrodite: Tortoise, Dove
Athena: Owl
Helios: Human head surrounded by rays, Sun

Numerical symbols (1, 2, 3, 4, 5, 6, 8, 9 balls; 2, 3, 5 crescents), rings, and rosettes are in a separate category. Some could refer to the calendar and to months, assuming that the balls represent the sun and the crescents the moon. Some symbols seem to allude to a function or a victory. Others are in all probability really symbols of deities: a chariot or a helmet can stand for Athena or Ares, as ivy or a cantharus stands for Dionysus.

The conclusion that may immediately be drawn from this table is that the symbols on coins and on blazons had a common origin, and that this origin was astrological.

2. The Complementarity of Opposites. The Lesson of the Vases

Frequent examples have been seen in earlier chapters of zodiacal symbols placed according to the great axes (six per center) as well as certain equivalences and complementarities coming into play. It has even been suggested that the use of complementaries may have been a magical or prophylactic practice, each sector warding off the adverse influence of the opposing sign.

Similarly, it would appear that the decor of a shield sometimes appertained to the person, to fate, to the family, to the actions of the bearer of the shield, and sometimes to the enemy he was fighting.

G. H. Chase saw this complementarity, but only in the case of giants. He mentioned the centaur on the shield of Caeneus, who fought the centaurs (loc. cit., p. 88 and LXVII, I), and he interpreted the presence of the Gorgon on the shield of Enceladus (ibid., CXXI) as a reference to his defeat by Athena. He also noticed that there is sometimes a horse on the shield of Ephialtes, Poseidon's enemy.

A quick glance at a few volumes of the *Corpus Vasorum Antiquorum* or a book of photographs of Greek vases will reveal many examples, not only for the giants but a variety of characters, and notably for Heracles.

The shields of characters painted on vases, in fact, very often bear the symbol of their enemy. Here again I could give many examples. Anyone can find them. I will mention only a few of the most conclusive, considering them in two groups: "The Labors of Heracles" and "Other Scenes."

a) The Labors of Heracles.

1. *Heracles and Geryon:* The black-figure paintings on a Chalcidian amphora from Vulci,[2] now in the Cabinet des Médailles, show the struggle of Heracles, assisted by Athena, against Geryon. The triple Geryon, who represents Taurus, is protecting himself with a shield whose device is an eagle, symbol of the sign opposing Taurus (and also the sign of Chalcis) (fig. 52).
2. On the amphora of Exekias (black-figure vase) in the Louvre,[3] Geryon is protected from Heracles by a shield decorated with a leonine head of Heracles; Heracles is here considered as a hero of the sign of Leo.
3. On a cup from Munich,[4] Geryon, who is fighting Heracles, has a boar painted on his shield, a reference to the Leo-Boar axis, in squared aspect to the Taurus-Scorpio (or Taurus-Eagle) axis with which the triple monster is associated.
4. *Heracles and the Lion:* On an Attic-style red-figure krater with colonettes in the Villa Giulia of Rome, found at Falerii Veteres (Civita Castellana),[5] we see Heracles fighting the lion. Athena, who is assisting him, has a shield decorated with a chimaera.

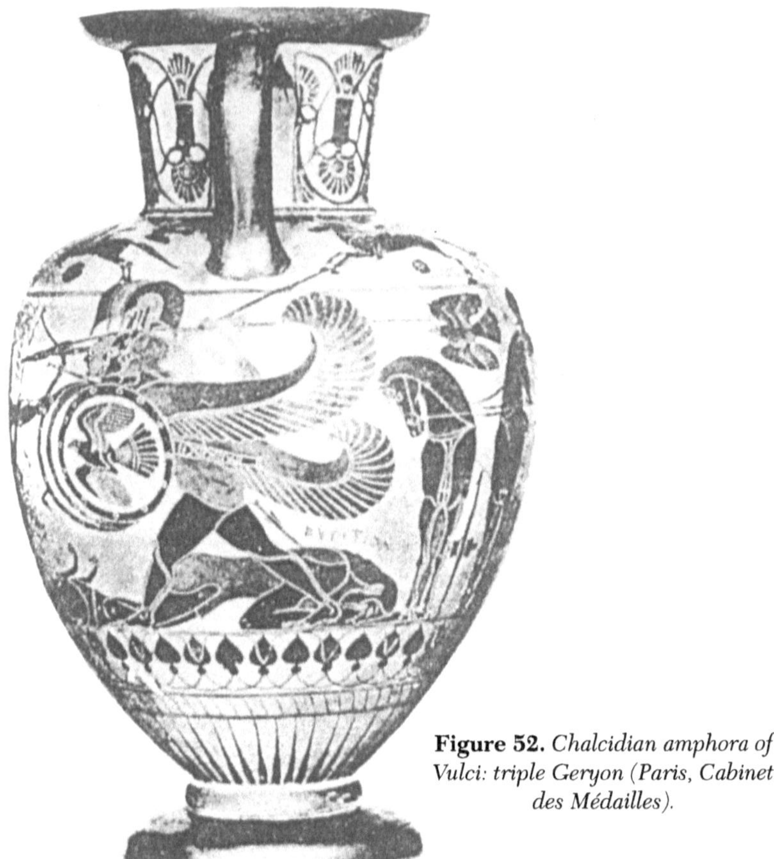

Figure 52. *Chalcidian amphora of Vulci: triple Geryon (Paris, Cabinet des Médailles).*

It would an easy matter to add to this list.

b) Other Scenes of Combat:

1. Very frequently, especially on Panathenian amphoras, Athena's shield features one of the symbols of the Pisces-Aquarius sector, opposite Leo-Virgo, and often the figure of Pegasus.[6]
2. As G. H. Chase has observed, Caeneus's shield bears the image of a centaur on the Harrow vase where Caeneus is shown fighting the centaurs.[7]

   Let me mention here that Caeneus ("the new"), to be seen again in studying the west pediment of the temple of Zeus at Olympia, could refer to a very ancient calendar in which the solar year began in Gemini.

3. On a vase in Naples, also mentioned by G. H. Chase,[8] where a Gigantomachy is drawn, a Gorgon appears on the shield of Enceladus, who is doing battle with Athena. What is more, there is a griffin on the goddess's shield, which associates Enceladus with Olympia and the direction of north.
4. On a vase from Boston[9] that depicts the battle of Achilles and Athena against Memnon, who is allied with Eos, Achilles' enemy has a Gorgon on his shield.

Here again many more examples could be given by a detailed analysis of all the vases where shield devices appear. But the same principle is applied everywhere: the shield, a defensive weapon, is in another sense an image of the celestial vault and displays to the enemy a symbol that reflects him.

3. Symbolic Scenes Showing Zodiacal Oppositions: Plaques Found at Delphi

It would seem, from deduction to deduction, that the ancient Greeks employed three or four parallel series of zodiacal symbols, and that most of the battle scenes, parades, or processions of characters with decorated shields, animal figures, mythological scenes, and scenes from the *Iliad* are subject to receiving an astrological interpretation.

Besides the zodiacal signs figured in the usual way, it is appropriate to consider from this point of view the ancient Hesiodic guardians who were defeated by heroes, the heroes who supplanted them, the gods, demigods, and the Homeric characters, whose significance is connected with their place of origin.

The result of all this is that a considerable number of Greek works of art have astrological meaning, and it appears that for centuries this civilization was completely imbued with astrological beliefs. Many works which have not yet been understood will take on far greater meaning if the set of keys I am now offering is willingly used, and apparently heterogeneous images will then take on their full significance and synthetic value.

It seems to me that the bronze plaques found in all the great sanctuaries of Greece deserve special attention. They sometimes have lateral holes that suggest that they could be sewn onto clothing. Now, all of them have a zodiacal meaning, and I think that some were used to decorate priestly robes or cult objects, which should not be surprising if, as I am led to believe, Greek religion was pervaded by astral beliefs. Others appeared on the armlets of shields, where they probably had a magical function.

Most of the decorated plaques of this type are unfortunately fragmentary. Let me nevertheless mention one from Dodona showing the labors of Heracles.[10] A series that is almost complete comes from the excavations at Delphi[11] (figs. 53 and 54). I shall attempt an interpretation. It had six symbolic scenes, of which five are extant. On each one are two or three characters; in four cases out of five, these are scenes of duals or conflict.

Figure 53. *Bronz plaques found at Delphi (upper part). Scene 2: Zeus, Hera, Hephaestus (Cancer-Capricorn axis). Scene 3: Achilles and Penthesilea (Gemini-Sagittarius axis). Scene 4: Ares and Aphrodite (Aries-Libra axis).*

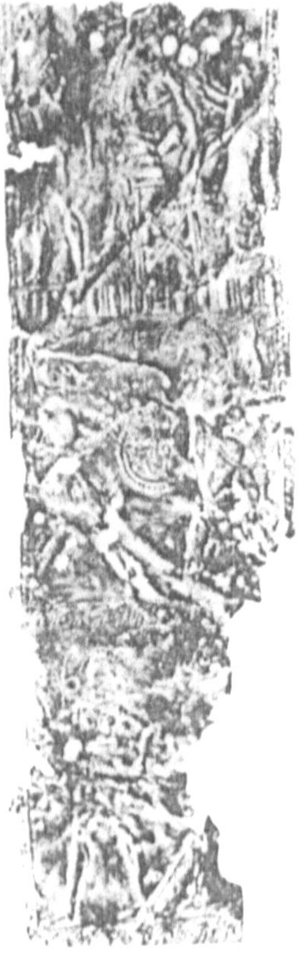

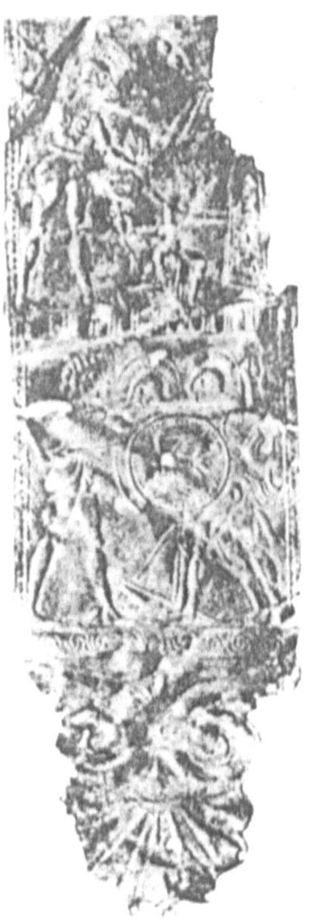

Figure 54. *Bronz plaques found at Delphi (lower part). Scene 5, with the lizard: Ajax and Cassandra before the Palladium (Virgo-Pisces axis). Scene 6: Heracles and Geryon (Taurus-Scorpio axis).*

a) At the top, one register is missing. I will return to this.

b) The second register depicts a scene at Olympus. There is some doubt as to the characters shown, but they are probably Zeus, Hera, and Hephaestus. Such a scene is a reference to the Cancer-Capricorn axis.

c) The third register shows the struggle of Achilles and Penthesilea (whose name is indicated on the plaque). Achilles, the student of Chiron, represents Sagittarius; Penthesilia, Gemini (in the Sardis system).

One is therefore dealing with the Gemini-Sagittarius axis.

d) The fourth register shows a scene of abduction. The warrior is evidently Ares, ruler of the sign of Aries, the woman, Aphrodite, who rules Libra. This scene describes the Aries-Libra axis.

e) The fifth register is of Ajax and Cassandra before the Palladium. The frequent occurrence of this scene on vases teaches us that it is a common image of the antagonism between Virgo and Pisces.

The lizard appearing between the two characters stands for the constellation of the Dragon. A look at a star map will show that the star Thuban or Alpha in Draco, the Polestar in the age of Taurus, is on the Pisces-Virgo axis.

Let me mention, while we are on the subject, the very frequent association of the lizard with images of the Pisces-Virgo axis. The animal also appears on the neck of a bronze krater in the Louvre, where one sees Perseus slaying the Gorgon.

f) The sixth and last register shows the struggle of Heracles and Geryon, that is, the Taurus-Scorpio axis.

Only the Leo-Aquarius axis is missing in this series. It is easy to deduce that it must have appeared on the missing part. Oddly enough, a silver plaque, which is smaller and from another similar object, was also found at Delphi[12] (fig. 55). On it are two lions and a little character who can be none other than Chrysaor, the man with the golden sword, whose name also happens to be an appellation of Apollo.[13] This is, undeniably, a representation of the Leo-Aquarius cosmic axis,

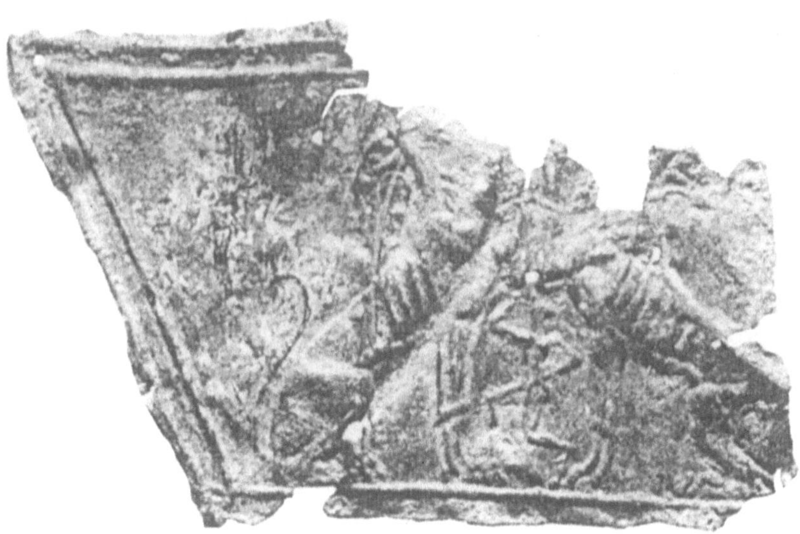

Figure 55. *Bronze fragment found at Delphi: Chrysaor between two lions or the Leo-Aquarius axis.*

which propitiously completes the documentation on the Delphic images of the zodiacal lines. These plaques contribute important support to my theories by demonstrating the role that astrology must have played in the religion of Delphi.

The order in which the six axes are described is not random. Beginning with the sign of Leo (summer solstice), the series turns in a clockwise direction, retrograde in the zodiac, that is, in the celestial order of the signs, which gives the following: Leo, Cancer, Gemini, Aries, Pisces, etc.

The break that puts the Taurus-Libra axis at the end could be interpreted as a reference to the victory of Heracles over Geryon, corresponding to the rejection of the ancient calendar which began with Taurus and its substitution by one beginning with Leo. I have studied this series of scenes here, because the symbolism seems to have a more general meaning than that of the armlets of shields to be examined in the next chapter, which I believe had a more specific horoscopic significance related to the place of origin of the bearer of the shield.

4. Zodiacal Aspects on Vases. Principles of Interpretation. Oppositions and Squares

Readers who have read this far have probably already felt on several occasions that each chapter could have been the subject either of an entire book or of an individual monograph and that I am only giving the essential, reserving the possibility of returning later to certain aspects of this research.

Let me now say that, in order to establish a science of Greek vases, it would be necessary to begin with the three following premises:

First Premise. All Greek vases are not merely decorative, but are also objects with a unified significance. There is an organic link between the different scenes on a vase, and the vase as a whole has a global and synthetic meaning.

Second Premise. The connection between the various scenes on a vase is most often symbolic.

Third Premise. Very often—in about a third of the cases, it would seem—this symbolic link is of astrological nature, either directly or through sacred geography.

More specifically, many scenes on vases represent the astrological aspects of opposition or squaring. I shall restrict myself to a few examples, four of which come from the large album by P.-E. Arias and M. Hirmer, *Le Vase grec.* (In this book alone three times this number could be analyzed.)

a) Amphora of Nessus

This is a well-known Proto-Attic amphora in the Museum of Athens from the necropolis of Dipylon. The main scene on the bulge of the amphora represents the triple Gorgon; Perseus does not appear, although he has just beheaded the monster. This symbolizes Virgo, the sign of Attica, with reference to the Leo-Virgo sector in opposition to the Pisces-Aquarius sector. An eagle above the beheaded Gorgon and a frieze of six dolphins under the main subject allude to the northeast region, in squared aspect to the main subject.

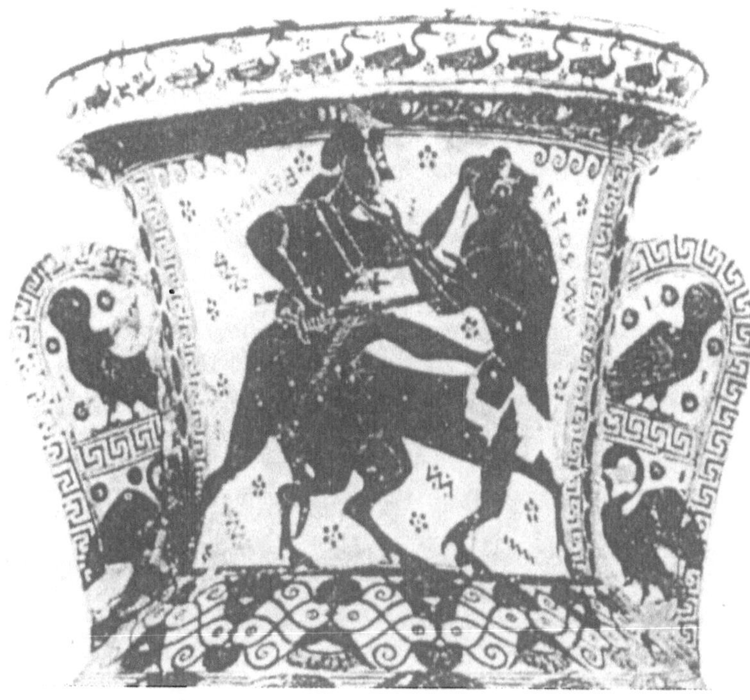

Figure 56. *Amphora of Nessus (Museum of Athens).*

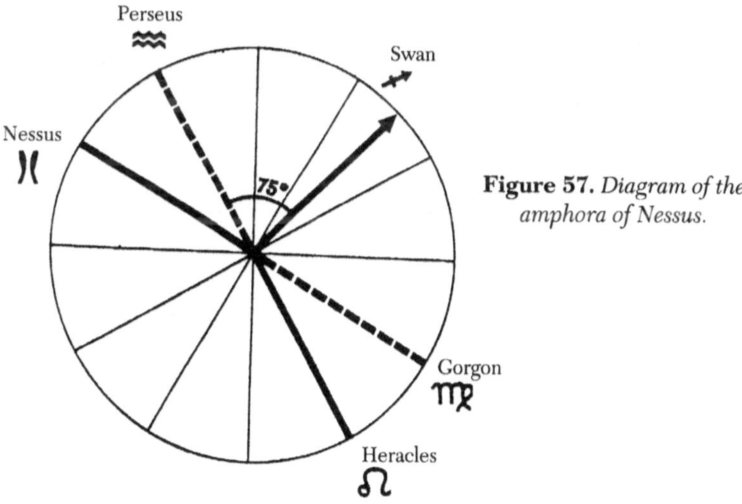

Figure 57. *Diagram of the amphora of Nessus.*

On the neck of the vase, one sees Heracles killing Nessus, which illustrates another Leo-Pisces opposition, since Nessus is associated with Aetolia. On the handles are owls, the birds of Athena, and swans. These birds describe Sagittarius, region of the centaurs, situated in squared aspect to the main opposition. Finally, the upper frieze, composed of sixteen little swans, could refer to a calendar in which the year was divided into sixteen lunar months beginning in Cygnus[14] (fig. 56).

I thus arrive at the following zodiacal scheme (fig. 57) (which puts Cygnus at 15 degrees Scorpio).

b) A plate from Rhodes in the British Museum,[15] where the same Gorgon-Swan association appears, confirms my interpretation of the amphora of Nessus. It is found on many other vases.[16]

The character represented is in fact a Gorgon and not an Artemis Mistress of Beasts as is sometimes claimed (there is the same confusion concerning the pediment of the Gorgon in the temple of Artemis at Corfu). The monster is holding a swan in either hand, which once again describes the Virgo-Sagittarius square.

c) This is the same Virgo-Pisces and Gemini-Sagittarius square of axes described by a great krater with volutes in the Museum of Palermo (fig. 58).[17] But this is a later symbolism, because the two perpendicular axes are on two separate registers, one representing a Centauromachy and the other an Amazonomachy. Such images will be found again in the tympanal decoration of temples.

d) A beautiful image of the Sagittarius-Virgo square is provided by a fragment of a bas-relief that showed, it is believed, the struggle of Achilles and Penthesilea, that is, in astrological terms, the Sagittarius-Virgo square (fig. 59).[18] Only the character of Achilles is extant, and his shield bears an enormous Gorgon, symbol of Virgo.

The fallen warrior is named Aenia. This is the name of an Aetolian city which is in the Pisces sector of the Delphic system, opposed to Virgo (Gorgon). In Quintus of Smyrna's *Posthomerica* (XI, 79), there is mention of an Aenus/Ainios, who is a Cetii slain by Ulysses. He is one of the people, allied with the Trojans, who bore the name of the cetaceans, and who lived near the river Cetius. (This may be the modern Havra which empties into the Gulf of Adramyti.) In any case, one finds the region of Mysia, which corresponds to Pisces in the Sardis system.

5. The Vases of Exekias

Here is how I was led to study the role of astrology in the vases of the great painter Exekias.

An Attic hydria of the fifth century in the Louvre (fig. 60) shows Achilles and Ajax playing with dice. Athena is standing between them. The glance of the goddess and the direction of her lance indicate her hostility to Achilles and,

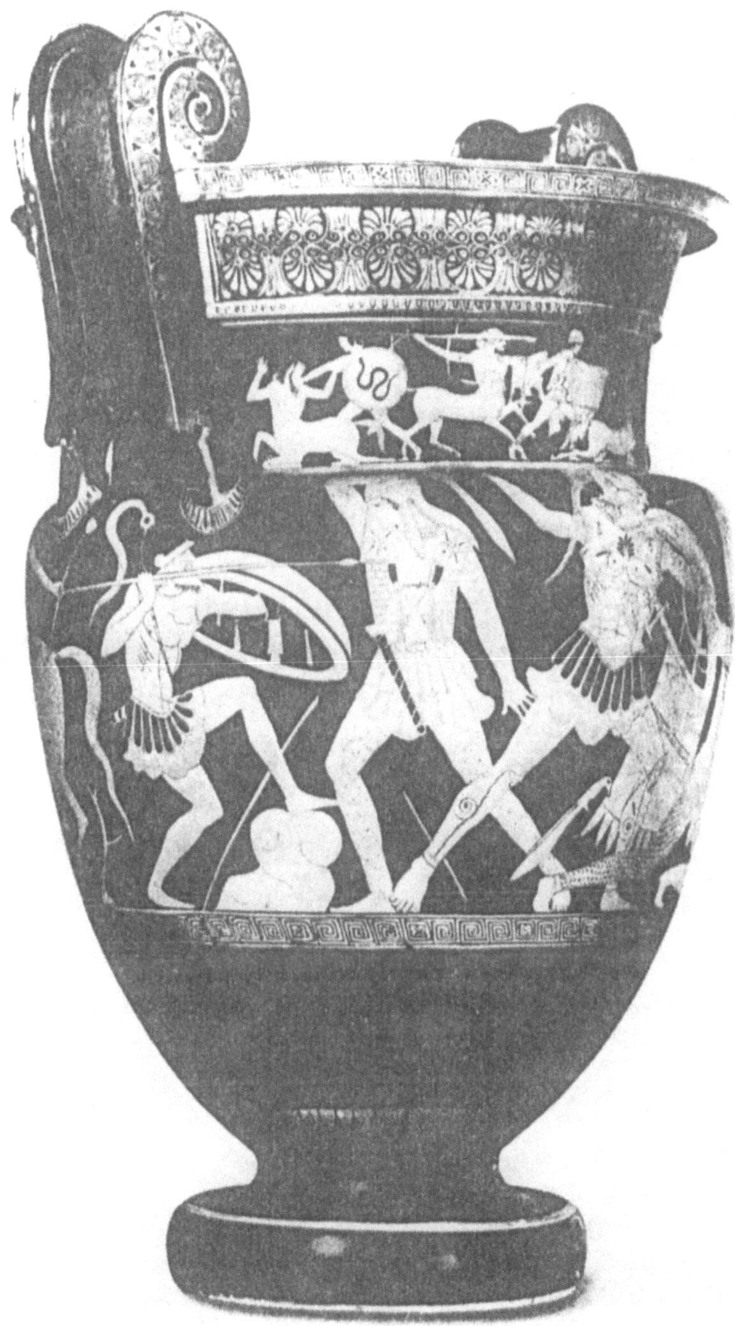

Figure 58. *Krater with volutes (Museum of Palermo).*

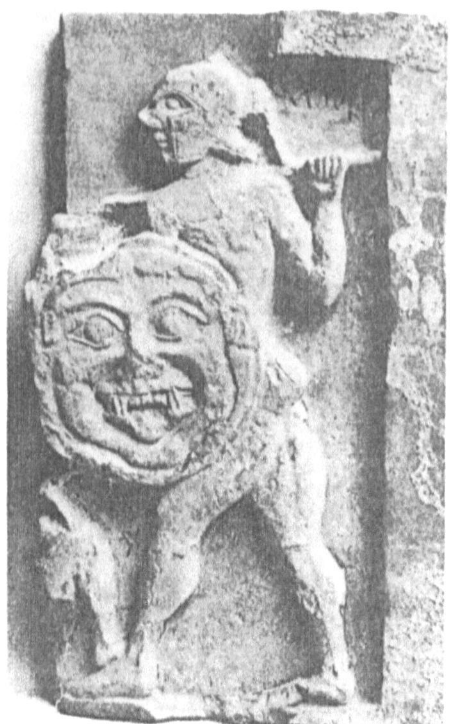

Figure 59. *Achilles bearing a shield with the head of the Gorgon (terra-cotta, New York).*

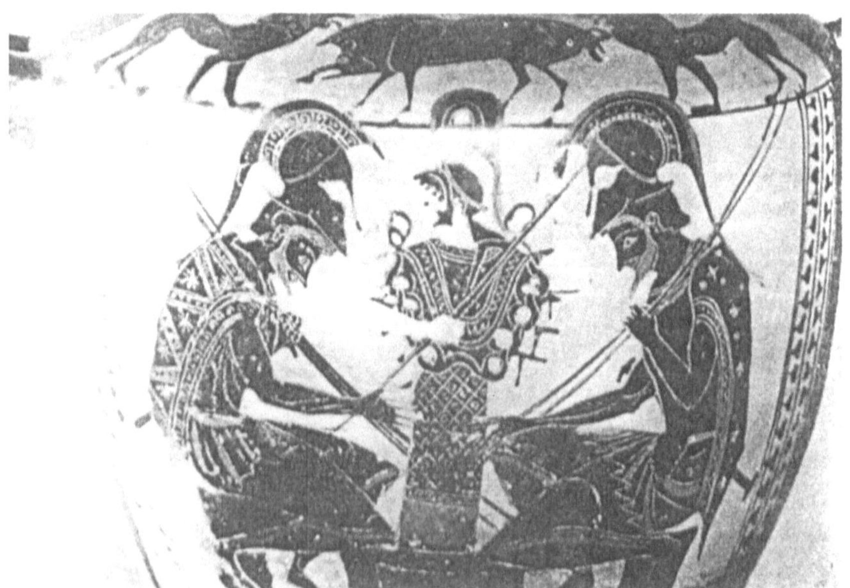

Figure 60. *Achilles and Ajax playing dice; between them stands Athena (Virgo-Sagittarius square), fifth century Attic hydria.*

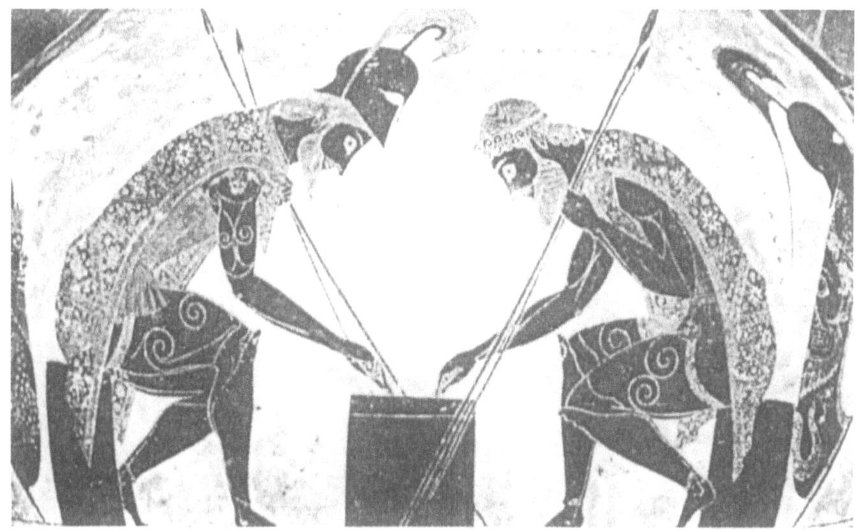

Figure 61. *Amphora of Exekias from Vulci.*

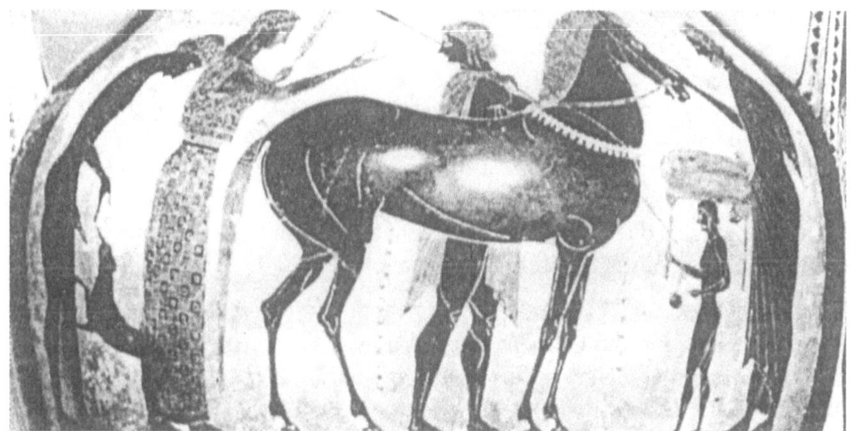

Figure 62. *The other side of the amphora: the Tyndaridae.*

accordingly, her support of Ajax. This drawing corresponds to the following diagram (bearing in mind the boar and the lions on the hydria's neck) (fig. 63).

This scheme seems to relate to the half of the year from the summer solstice to the winter solstice, with special emphasis on the Virgo-Sagittarius square, important for the Athenians since their city was under Athena's protection.

a) Amphora of the Vatican: the Sagittarius-Gemini Opposition. The design of an amphora by Exekias (sixth century), from Vulci and in the Vatican Mu-

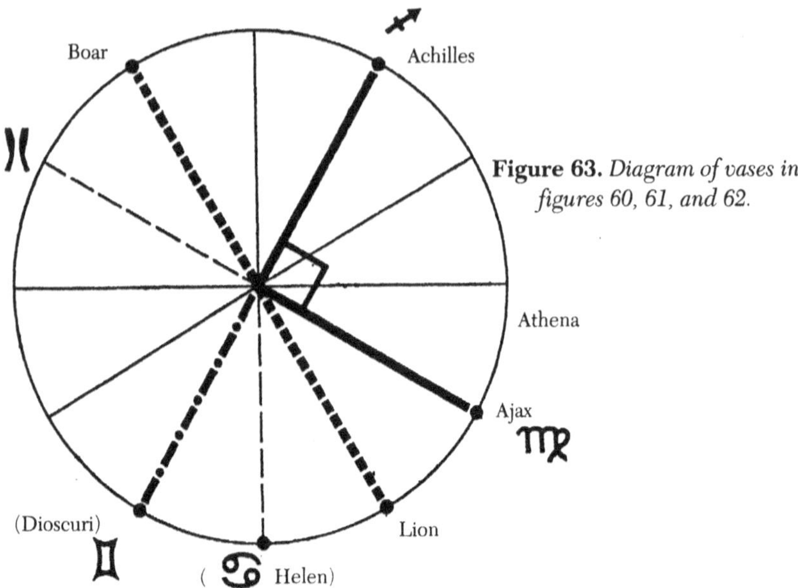

Figure 63. *Diagram of vases in figures 60, 61, and 62.*

seum, upon which Achilles and Ajax are also playing dice obviously has the same meaning (fig. 61).

Arrived at this stage in my reasoning, rather simple as one can see, and not even knowing if Exekias's vase was painted on the other side, I had drawn up a list of the subjects that would best complete the design from the point of view of astrological symbolism, and this list was as follows:

1. The Dioscuri (Gemini)
2. Perseus and the Gorgon (Pisces-Virgo axis)
3. Heracles and Nereus (Pisces-Virgo axis).

No. 2 and 3 had the disadvantage of entailing a double partial use, Virgo already being represented by Ajax, king of Salamis. I then saw that the first subject, and hence the most probable, appears on the other side, where one sees not only the Dioscuri, but the whole family of Tyndaridae (fig. 62). It would seem that Exekias, the great Athenian artist of the third quarter of the sixth century, was also an initiate and spoke the language of both the many and the few.

To achieve certainty on this, I consulted the work of Werner Technau, where the main works attributed to Exekias are listed.[19] It immediately became clear that, of the few vases whose subjects have been identified, several are apt to receive a simple astrological interpretation.

b) Amphora with Neck from Vulci: the Leo-Aquarius Axis. This is an amphora conserved in Berlin (Berlin, 1720). On one side Heracles is strangling the Nemean Lion, which is a figuration of the sign of Leo.

In application of the rule of the complementarity of opposing signs, one may expect to find characters associated with Aquarius on the other side. And indeed, on the obverse, Exekias has painted two horsemen named Demophoon and Acamas. These are two sons of Theseus who played an important role in the Trojan war. They are particularly associated with the removal of the Palladium and were among the warriors inside the Trojan horse.[20] They are very appropriate characters for representing Aquarius, of which this horse is a symbol, as will be seen in chapter 19.

c) Amphora from Vulci in the Louvre: Solstices and Equinoxes. An amphora in the Louvre (F. 53) from Vulci depicts the battle of Heracles and Geryon on one side. This is a conventional representation of the former Eagle-Taurus equinoctial axis. On Geryon's shield is figured a leonine head of Heracles, which refers to the affinities of Heracles, solar hero, with Leo.

The drawing on the other side of the vase describes Aquarius: one sees the hero "Antiphus" on his chariot. I believe this to be Antiphus, son of Priam, a Trojan hero. The presence of a siren confirms this interpretation. Finally, the lid of the vase is decorated with three stags alternating with three sirens, also symbols of the equinoxes and solstices (the number three could refer to the number of months in each season).

d) Amphora with Neck in the British Museum: Squares and Sextiles. An amphora in London (B. 210) from Vulci, dated to about 525 B.C., shows on one side the struggle of Achilles and Penthesilea, an image of the Sagittarius-Virgo square (fig. 64).

On the other side are Dionysus and his son Oenopion, king of Chios: Dionysus represents Aquarius, Oenopion, Scorpio (fig. 65). This design therefore describes another square. One obtains this layout (fig. 66):

The signs are in a harmonic relationship with the two others according to these aspects:

> sextile (aspect of 60 degrees) Sagittarius-Aquarius, or Achilles-Dionysus,
> sextile Virgo-Scorpio, or Penthesilea-Oenopion.

To better understand how certain correspondences are established, one could imagine substituting Penthesilea by another character associated with Virgo, Theseus for example. Now Oenopion is the son of Theseus. This kind of scheme brings out the "force fields" of the zodiac very clearly.

e) Amphora with Neck in the British Museum: Harmonious Aspects. On this amphora of London (B. 209), Exekias has painted the struggle of Achilles and Penthesilea on one side, or the Sagittarius-Virgo square.

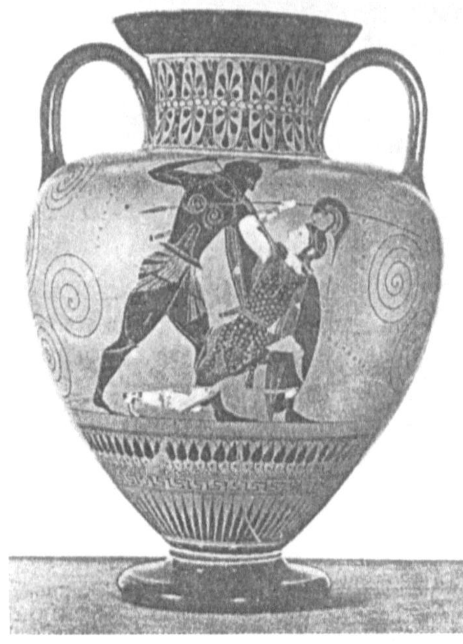

Figure 64. *Conflict of Achilles and Penthesilea.*

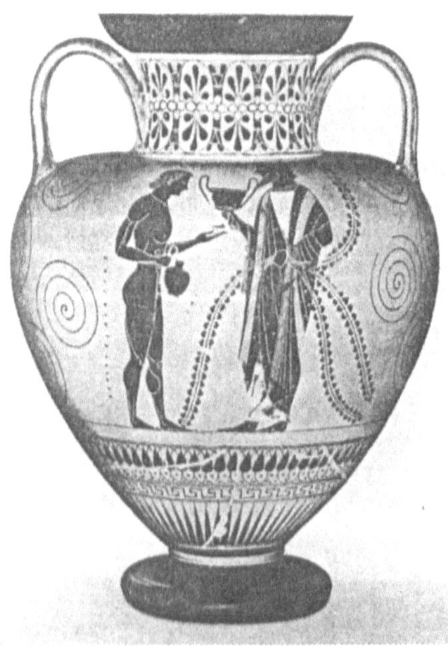

Figure 65. *Dionysus and his son Oenopion.*

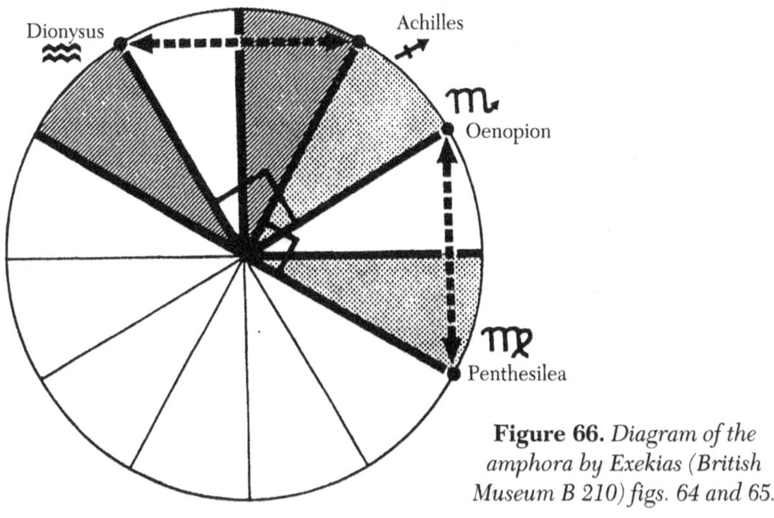

Figure 66. *Diagram of the amphora by Exekias (British Museum B 210) figs. 64 and 65.*

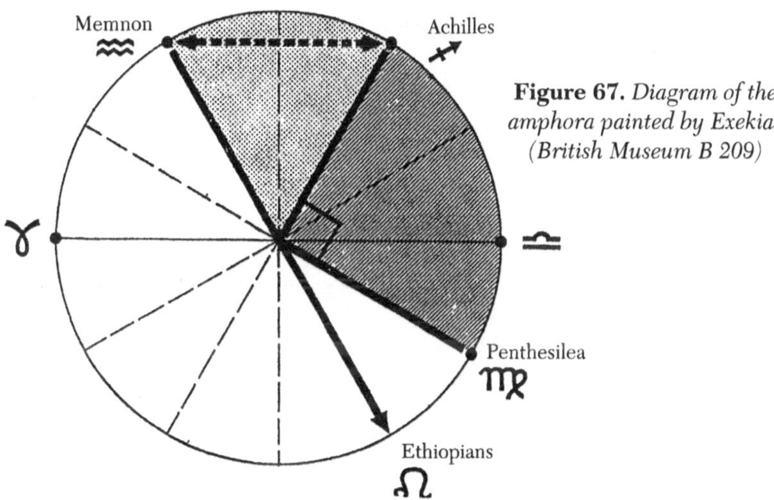

Figure 67. *Diagram of the amphora painted by Exekias (British Museum B 209)*

The other side shows Memnon, son of Aurora, defeated by Achilles at Troy. Memnon is commonly given as a king of the Ethiopians; he alludes to the Leo-Aquarius axis. But his defeat is really a victory, since Aurora obtains immortality for him. The equinoctial points are in harmonic relation with Sagittarius as well as with Aquarius. As for the Achilles-Memnon relationship, it stands for the Sagittarius-Aquarius sextile. The vase as a whole relates to the half of the year from the summer solstice to the winter solstice (fig. 67).

Through these five examples taken from a single artist, one can appreciate the variety of meanings derived from astrological symbolism, which set up subtle connections between different myths.

What has just been established for the individual case of Exekias can also be demonstrated for other important painters, in particular the painter of Amasis[21] and Sakonides.[22]

To avoid overloading the present work with too many similar examples, I reserve the possibility of devoting special monographs to these painters should the occasion arise.

6. Images of the Solstices and the Equinoxes on Vases

A considerable number of vases refer to the axes of the solstices and the equinoxes. Often they curiously superimpose various kinds of symbolism. I will give three typical examples that complete what I said in chapter 13 about the cycles of four animals.

1. The two sides of a hydria from Caere, reproduced in the book by Arias and Hirmer *Le Vase grec*,[23] seem at first glance to represent scenes very foreign to one another. On one side Heracles is bringing the triple Cerberus to Eurystheus, who is hiding in panic in an earthenware jar. On the other side one sees a hare between two birds of prey.

The table of symbolic correspondences on p. 135 provides an immediate reading for these images. Heracles at Taenarum and Heracles overcoming Cerberus are associated with the summer solstice; he leads Cerberus to Tiryns, which means that the new summer solstice pays an ironic tribute to the old (in Leo). We have seen that Cerberus is in fact a memory of the Great Dog, Procyon, having lost its astronomical significance.

On the other side is a clear representation of the old equinoctial axis: the hare represents Taurus and the two eagles stand for the sign of the Eagle or Scorpio.

2. Let me also mention the beautiful cup of Achikles and Glaukytes from Vulci, dated to about 540 B.C., in the Museum Antiker Kleinkunst in Munich.[24] On one side appears the hunting of the Calydonian boar (fig. 68), on the other Theseus slaying the Minotaur (fig. 69). These are the two earlier solstices (Leo-Boar) and the equinoxes (Taurus-Eagle), with special reference to the Taurus-Boar square. The sphinxes on either side of each scene are images of the equinoxes. All the characters are named on the cup; even the sphinxes and Athena's lyre are clearly labeled. An almost identical piece is in the Museum of Athens.

3. In the Los Angeles County Museum there is an antique black-figure amphora dating from about 500. On both sides appears what is described as a "winged victory," perched on a bull and holding a vine[25] (fig. 70). In reality, this is an unusual superimposition of equivalent symbols—the victory is a siren representing the sign of Aquarius, as is confirmed by the vine, the Dionysiac plant, that she is

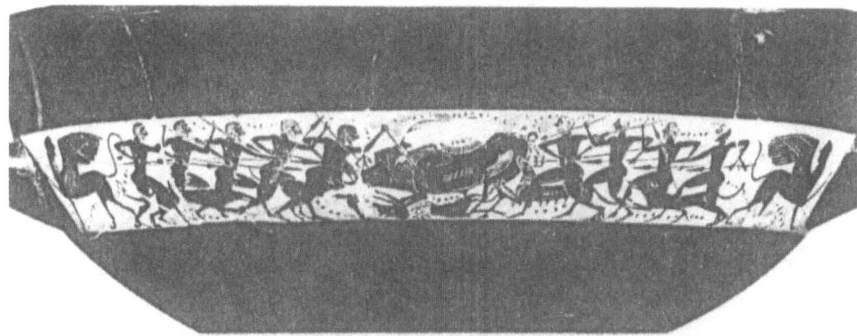

Figure 68. *The hunting of the Calydonian boar.*

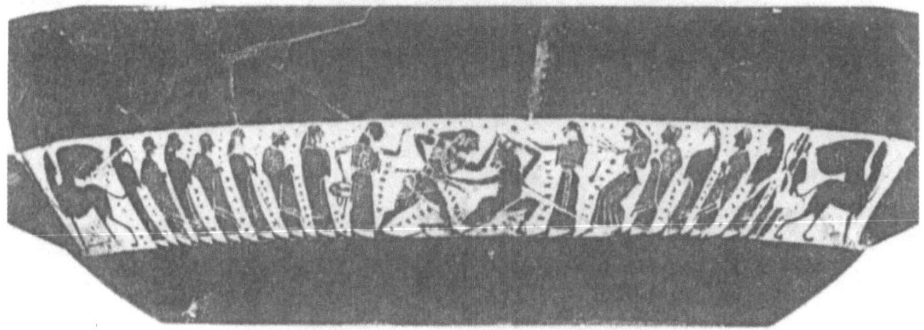

Figure 69. *Theseus and the Minotaur.*

holding. So I believe that this must be a representation of the Taurus-Aquarius square with additional allusion to the spring equinox and the winter solstice (and perhaps to the period from the winter solstice to the spring equinox).

Here again I will refrain from giving more examples, which could easily be done.

7. A Corinthian Aryballus of Astrological Design

a) The design of a Corinthian aryballus in the Louvre (fig. 71) deserves some special attention.[26]

On it are warriors whose shields bear the following drawings: bull's head from the front, bull's head in profile, eagle, and lion's jaws. Now, an examination of the distribution of these decorated shields around the circumference of the aryballus clearly shows that this must be an astrological scheme. The warriors, in all the drawings but one, are opposed in pairs. The drawings summarize, in an order that is not random, all the possible relationships of the right isoceles

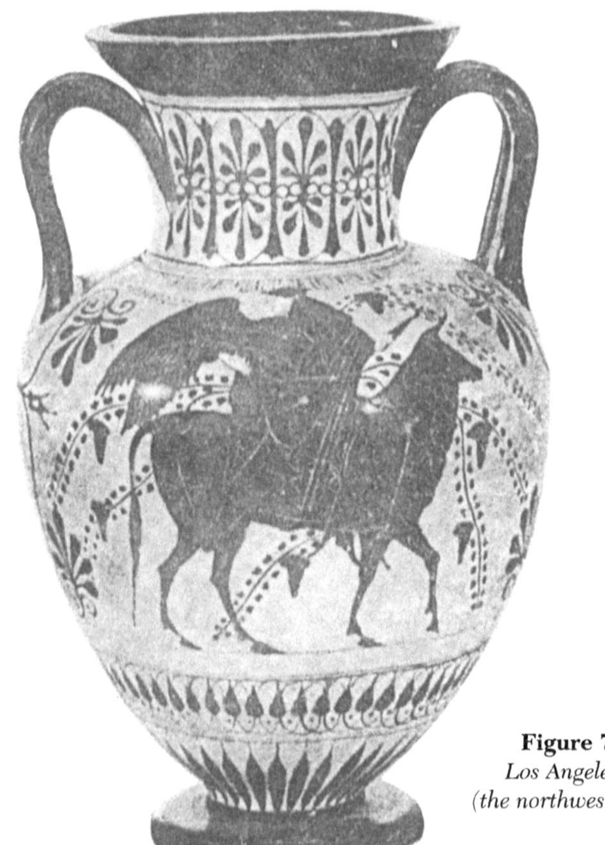

Figure 70. *Amphora of Los Angeles: siren on a bull (the northwest quarter or winter).*

triangle defined by the zodiacal signs of Taurus, Leo, and the Eagle (Scorpio). One has, starting from the woman's nose that serves as the mouth of the vase, and going in a counterclockwise direction, these scenes of conflict: (1) Lion-Eagle (fig. 72), (2) Lion-Bull in frontal view (figs. 71 and 74), (3) Eagle-Bull in profile (fig. 74).

A fourth scene (D-A and D-T) is formed by a composition, obviously central in intention and position, placed just under the woman's nose, and which is not lacking in humour (figs. 72 and 73). It depicts a warrior, either wounded or dead, whose shield bears the jaws of a lion. A warrior with a shield decorated with a bull is pulling off his helmet, while a warrior with an eagle is removing his *cnemidae* (footwear). This is a pleasant allegorical image of the Taurus-Leo and Eagle-Leo double square. The general scheme is as follows (fig. 76):

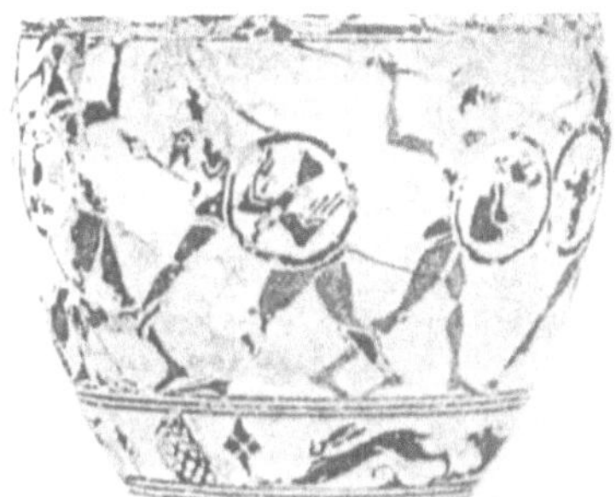

Figure 71.

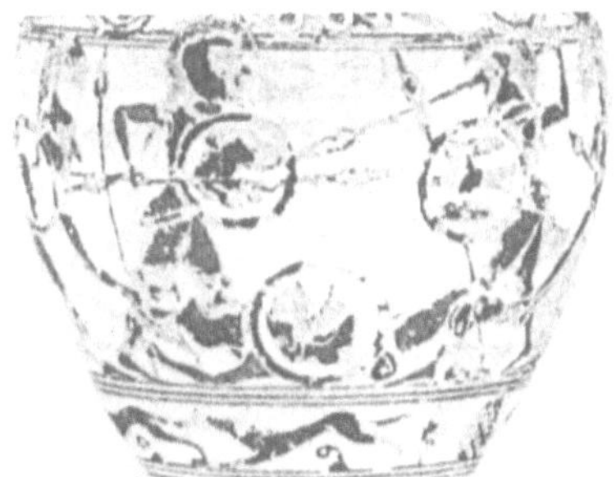

Figure 72.

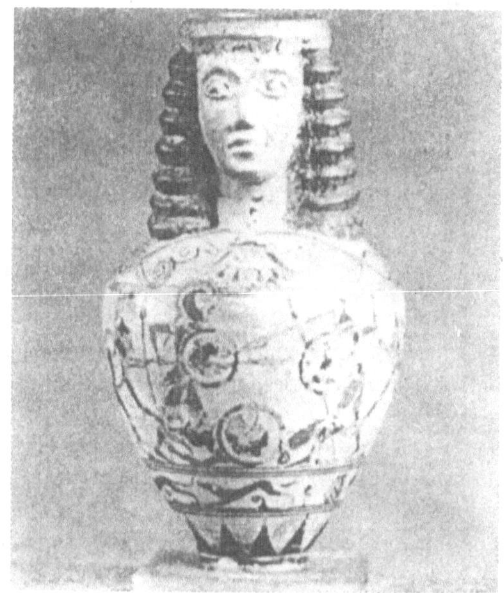

Figure 73.

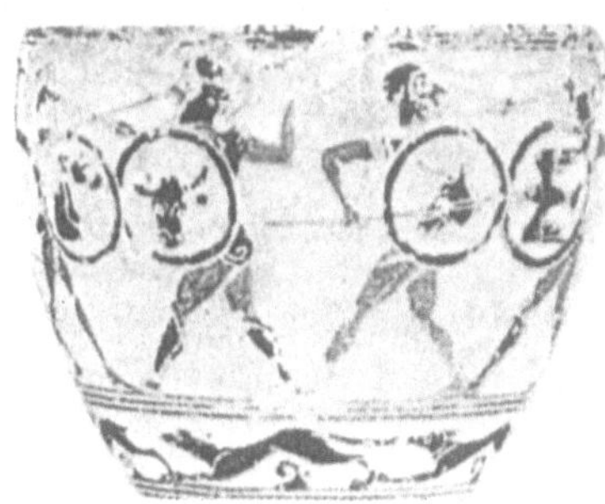

Figure 74.

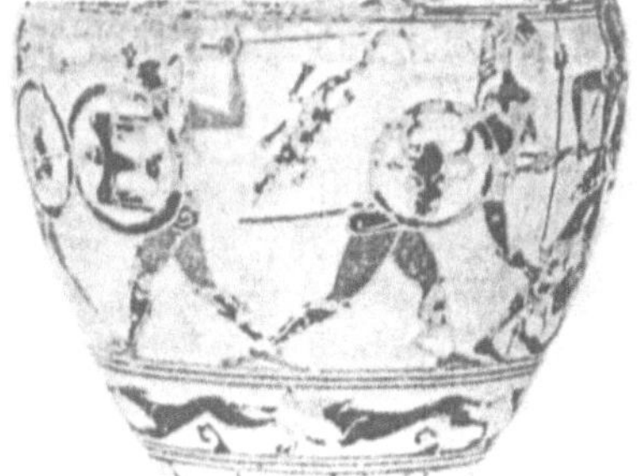

Figure 75.

Figures 71, 72, 73, 74, & 75. *Corinthian aryballus in the Louvre Museum describing the geographical position of Corinth.*

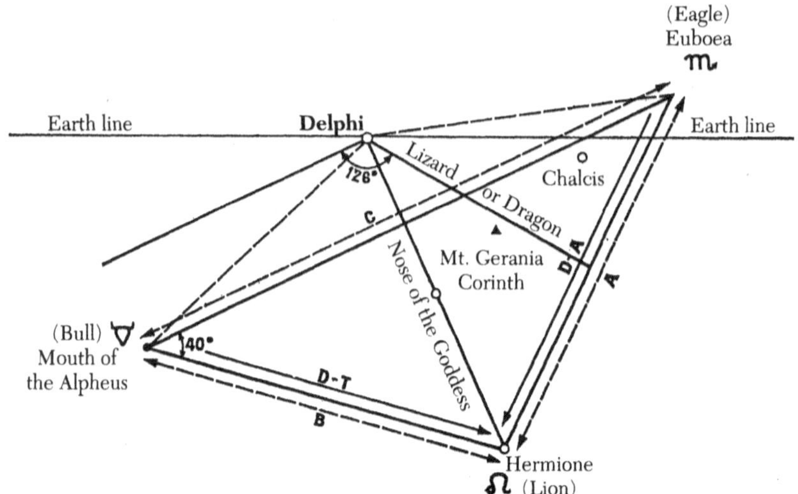

Figure 76. *Geographical significance of the Corinthian aryballus.*

b) Thus the drawings review all the possible relationships among the three signs. This cannot represent an alliance between Taurus and the Eagle in league against Leo, since the Taurus-Eagle opposition is indicated by drawing C (fig. 74).

In reality the power relationships so described are of a permanent nature and the concept of the design is purely astrological.

The geographical diagrams will once again be of great help.

The layout obtained can in fact be easily found on the map of Greece. One only need draw an isoceles triangle between the mouth of the Alpheus–Hermione–Euboea, with the Delphi-Hermione line as the height. This triangle is identical to the one described by the aryballus.

Corinth is on the Hermione-Delphi height of this triangle, on the Leo-Aquarius cosmic axis, as seen in chapter 2. This height divides the considered triangle into two equal right triangles. So in the design of this vase, the lion represents Corinth, the bull Elis, and the eagle Chalcis and Euboea. (The coins of Chalcis were stamped with an eagle.) Chalcis is very near the Earth line (latitude of Delphi). Here again one is dealing with symbolic geography: this Corinthian aryballus describes the geographical position of Corinth in terms of astrology.

This is not a specific historical situation because, during the course of the Peloponnesian Wars, the Corinthians never fought the people of both Elis and Euboea simultaneously.

Such a vase probably had a ritual use in the cult of Apollo as ruler of the calendar and master of the seasons.

c) The rest of the vase's design supports my interpretation. Incidentally, by its very nature, a vase opens in three-dimensional space and so better lends itself to the description of cosmic symbolism than a flat painting.

Now, the vase was conceived in such a way that the nose which serves as the spout is orientated according to the Leo-Aquarius cosmic direction (fig. 73) (with at least an implicit pun on and ὑδρία and ὑδροχοεύς.

It would undoubtedly not be pushing the interpretation too far to suggest that the woman's head really represents Ge. This would mean that on all similar vases having zodiacal imagery, a neck shaped as a woman's head always represents the earth, upon which the zodiacal symbols are projected. When one realizes that the very material of the vase is fine clay, one can appreciate the depth of this symbolism.

I will now show how certain details of the vase's design describe the harmonious superimposition of astral symbolism and geographical meaning.

In examining the charming frieze of animals in pursuit running along the base of the aryballus, one might at first be tempted to see in it an artistic fantasy. But since the vase as a whole is so highly structured and planned, it would be astonishing if it didn't contribute to the overall unity. Now, this frieze is in fact also strictly calculated and meaningful. One sees a hare being pursued by four dogs one behind the other, giving five animals in all. The hare, I have said several times before, is a hieroglyph for the sign of Taurus (simply because the constellation of the Hare is in the zodiacal region of Taurus). The frieze in question therefore represents the hare of the New Year (the first month) followed by four months. In fact, when the year began in Taurus, the Greeks employed a zodiac of ten signs, as was seen in chapter 10. The frieze represents the five months going from the spring equinox to the autumnal equinox, the period defined by the preceeding diagram, which includes the part of the year in symbolic relation with the southern half of Greece (Taurus-Eagle opposition). The animals are moving in the order of the sequence of the months, as is normal.

Remaining to be explained is the rather unusual presence of a lizard (fig. 75) at the level of the gap between the third and fourth dogs. In a zodiac divided into ten parts, each sign corresponds to 36 degrees. The angular distance described is therefore of 126 degrees in relation to the beginning of the sign of Taurus. It is enough to look at a star map to see that this lizard refers to the celestial Dragon and is thus a polar symbol, like on the plaque from Delphi studied earlier[27] (cf. p. 165).

Beginning with very simple principles, which are understandable within the context of my deductions, and applying them with a "geometrical" rigor that is not lacking in humor in treatment of detail, the designer of this little vase seems to have achieved a kind of masterpiece of the symbolism of astrological geography. Such a vase probably had a ritual function: one might imagine a combination of astrology and hydromancy.

It is not by chance that I am ending this chapter with the study of a Corinthian vase which is outstandingly significant through its association of zodiacal symbolism with sacred geography. In the next chapter, I will examine the probable role of the solar city in efforts to unify astrological imagery. It remains evident, however, that the origin of the system must be sought at Delphi.

8. Symbolic Formulas

It is henceforth possible, in very many cases, to write an equation or formula for the meaning of a Greek coin, a vase, a shield, or a bas-relief using the conventional signs of astrology.

Fifty different examples could be given. To take only a few from the fourth and sixth sections of the present chapter, one may write:

Section 4. a) Amphora of Nessus:

♒ ☍ ♌ | ♍ □ ♐
♓ ☍ ♍ |

c) Krater of Palermo:

♓ ☍ ♍
♊ ☍ ♐

d) Bas-relief of Achilles: ♐ □ ♍

and

Section 6. 2. Cup of Achikles and Glaukytes: 3. Amphora of Los Angeles:

♌ ☍ ♒ | ♉ □ ♒ ♉ □ ♒
♉ ☍ ♏ |

The same astral meanings can obviously be described in ten or fifteen different ways, which leaves an appreciable range to the choice and taste of the artist. Studies of the frequency of images of certain zodiacal and planetary aspects would undoubtedly show that, here again, the choice of subjects is often related to the place where the vase was made.

Section 7. The vase studied in this paragraph has the formula:

<table>
<tr><td rowspan="2">♁</td><td rowspan="2">▽ ☍ ♏</td><td>▽ □ ♌</td></tr>
<tr><td>♌ □ ♏</td></tr>
</table>

which describes the position of Corinth in the Delphic system.

Chapter 16

The Horoscopic Meaning of the Armlets of Shields

My study of the bronze plaques from Delphi that may have been part of the armlets of shields led me to the masterly study by Professor Emil Kunze, director of the Institute of German Archeology at Athens, entitled *Archaische Schildbänder*,[1] which essentially describes the armlets of shields from Olympia.

From the very beginning, I marveled to see that all the scenes on these armlets had a zodiacal meaning. To be convinced of this, one only need read the table of contents in Professor Kunze's book, where all the subjects and symbols seen in the preceeding chapters are to be found. Without giving the complete list, here are the principal symbols: first are animals, in confrontation or in pairs, lions, panthers, sphinxes, and sirens, which are symbols of the equinoxes and solstices and, by extension, the four directions. Then come mythical creatures; the chimaera and the Gorgon are ancient Hesiodic guardians of the zodiacal signs. To this list may be added images of the labors and adventures of Heracles, Theseus, and Perseus. The mythical scenes on the armlets of shields, which are limited in number, all have a zodiacal significance and have already come up in earlier chapters (e.g., birth of Athena, Zeus and Typhon, Gigantomachy). A series of scenes having to do with the Trojan War describe Aquarius and the relationship of various signs of the zodiac with the Leo-Aquarius axis. In the album of plates that accompanies the work, there is a reproduction (pl. 73) of the shield armlets that are wholly extant. From these documents, I was able to attempt an interpretation of the symbolic scenes appearing on them.

First of all, it was necessary to distinguish the fixed symbols of the directions of space, which most often appear at the beginning and at the end of the metallic bands, from other mythical scenes that establish relationships among various signs. The structure and function of the shield caused the armlet to be divided into two unequal parts: the longer one, which generally included five or six scenes, was below, the shorter one, with generally one scene less than the other, was above. The two metallic parts of the armlet, joined together by a leather handle, almost always showed the same sequence of scenes. However, very often one scene placed at the level of the warrior's heart appeared only once; the symbolic meaning of this scene must therefore have been particularly important.

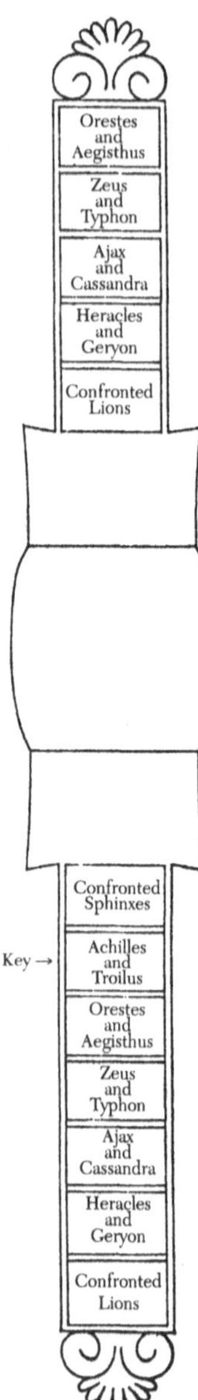

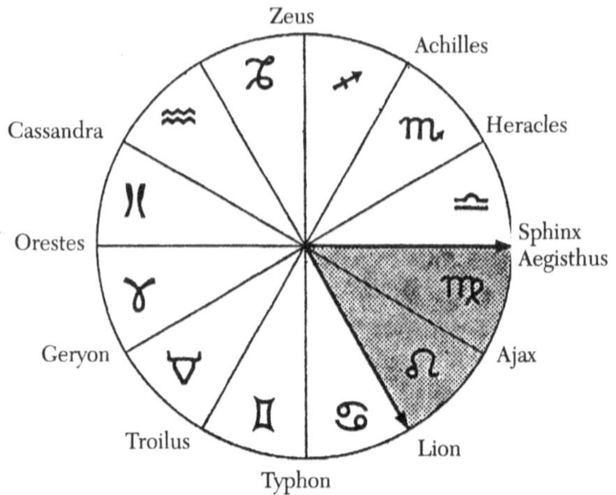

Figures 77 & 78. *To the left, a type I shield armlet. Above, zodiacal diagram corresponding to fig. 77; it describes Argolis, Corinthia, and Attica.*

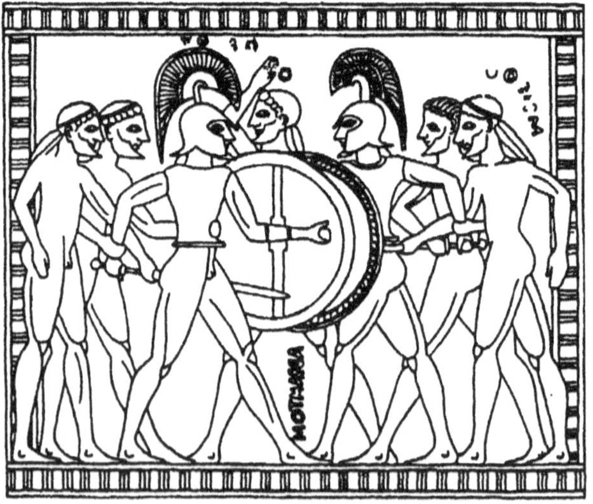

Figure 79. *Combat of Amphiaraus and Lycurgus.*

Since these sets of symbols very probably had horoscopic significance, I had to draw the figure and the theme in each case, while bringing all my previous deductions into play.

I was led to formulate two hypotheses:

1. The fixed symbols (confronted animals or simple symbols) described the area of origin of the bearer of the shield by defining a zodiacal region in relation to Delphi: sometimes a quarter of the country, sometimes a specific zodiacal sign. As a result of this, each group of confronted animals described a single zodiacal sign and not an axis.
2. The scene that was often unique, placed at the level of the heart, was more highly important. It designated the period of birth of the warrior in some cases, assuming that the shield was really individual. Thus I am almost certain that the armlet inventoried by E. Kunze as type IV belonged to the shield of a Nemean chief born in summer.

In other cases, the scene having the determining value had a more general meaning. This was true if the shield could be borne by any native warrior of a city or region. But because of the type of protection that it aimed to provide, the design of the armlet allowed me in several instances to distinguish a single zodiacal sign inside the group of three signs symbolized by the groups of confronted animals (see types IV, V, VII, VIII).

These were, in short, zodiacal symbols that afforded magical protection. So, besides a science of interpreting zodiacal symbols on vases, here was the opportunity for a similar science for the armlets of shields. Beginning with the complete groups described and reproduced by E. Kunze, I recomposed a few diagrams. On the following pages are the results of this work for eight different examples. For each one I give a sketch of the sequence of scenes on the armlet, my suggested zodiacal scheme, and a brief commentary.

Type I. Three examples (fig. 77) of this model are known.[2] The sphinxes and lions define the southeast quarter of Greece, including Argolis, Corinthia, and Attica. The warrior who bore the shield must therefore have been from one of these provinces (fig. 78).

The bearer of the shield was placed under the protection of Achilles, as is shown by the position of the scene representing Achilles and Troilus. Sagittarius is in squared aspect to the area defined by the sphinxes and lions.

Type IV. This armlet, of which there is only one example, is especially interesting.[3] The combat of Amphiaraus and Lycurgus, who can be identified with certainty because of an inscription[4] (fig. 79), is shown twice on plaques that are larger than the other scenes. It specifically refers to the theater of the struggle: Nemea.

The sign of Leo is evoked no less than five times (fig. 80): by confronted lions, the combat of Heracles and the lion (which again alludes to Nemea), twice

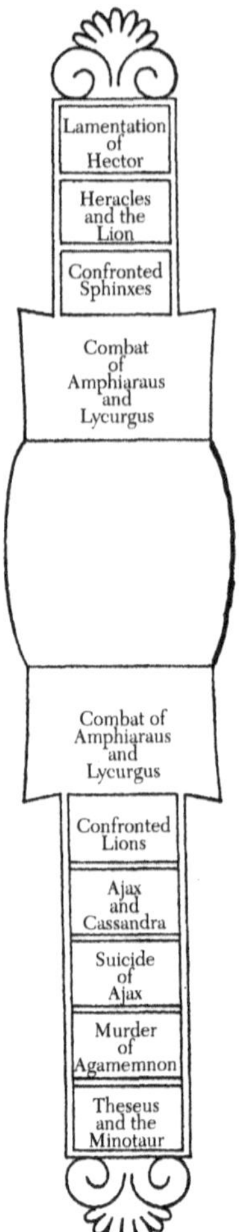

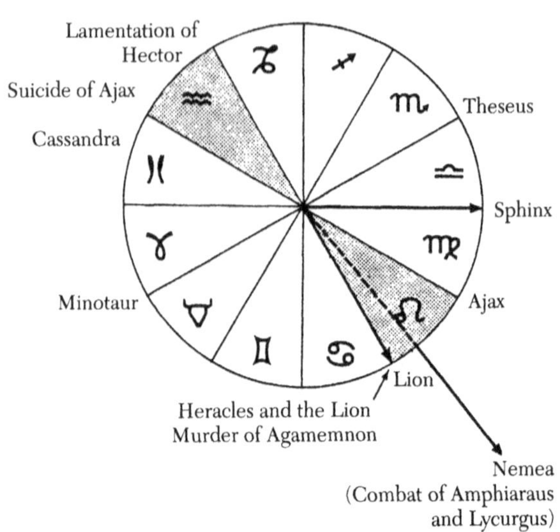

Figures 80 & 81. *To the left, a type IV shield armlet. Above, zodiacal diagram corresponding to fig. 80. It emphatically describes Nemea.*

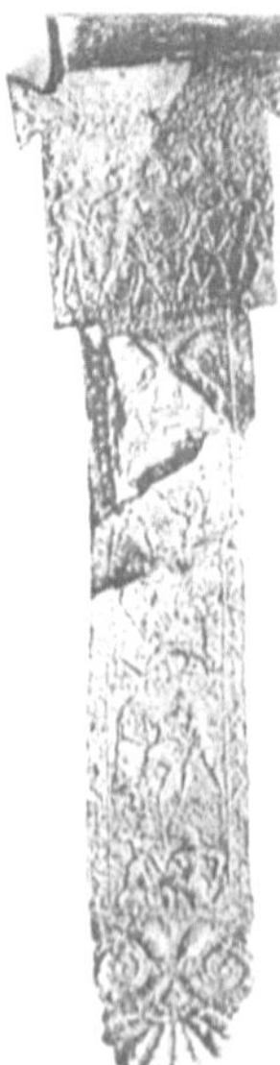

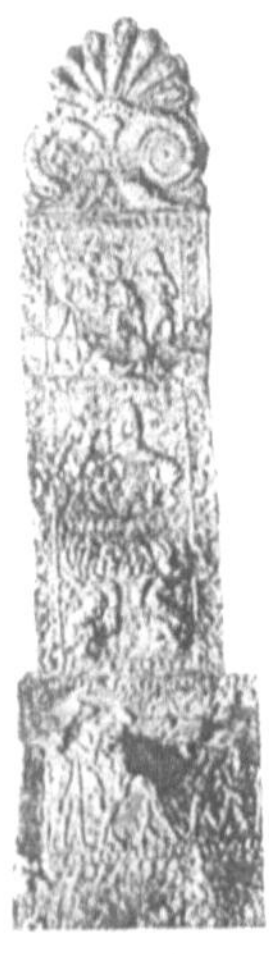

Figure 82. *Views of armlet type IV (above, and left).*

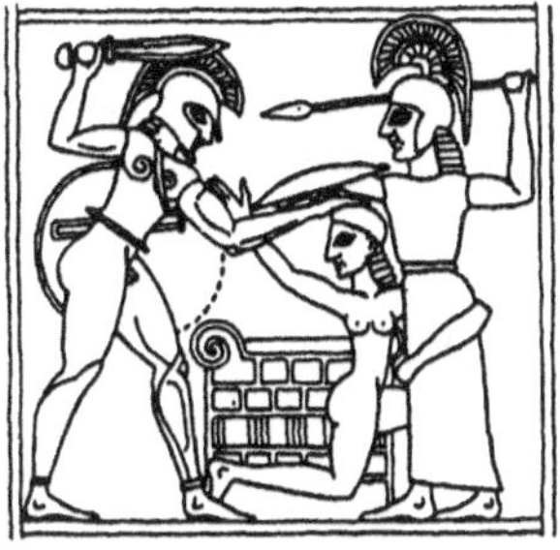

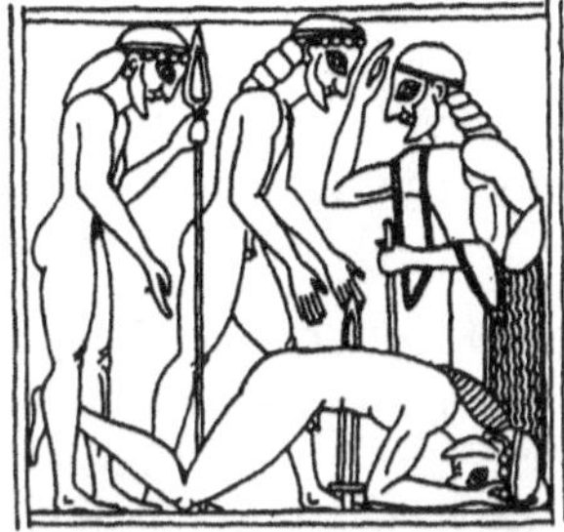

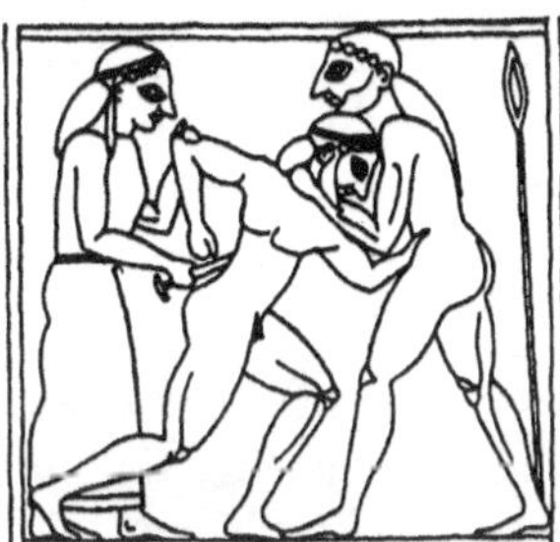

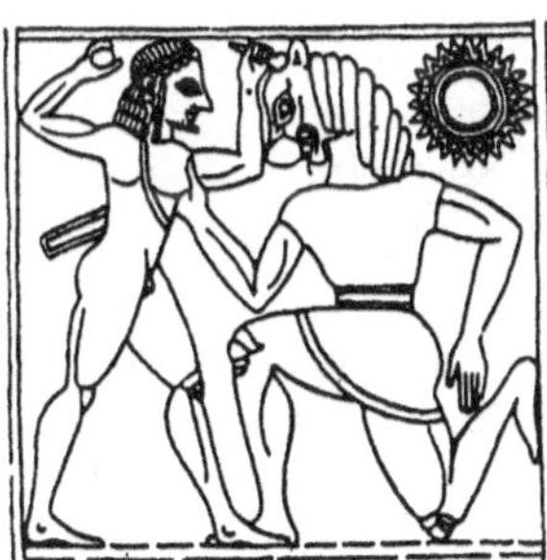

Figure 83. *Details of the motifs of type IV.*

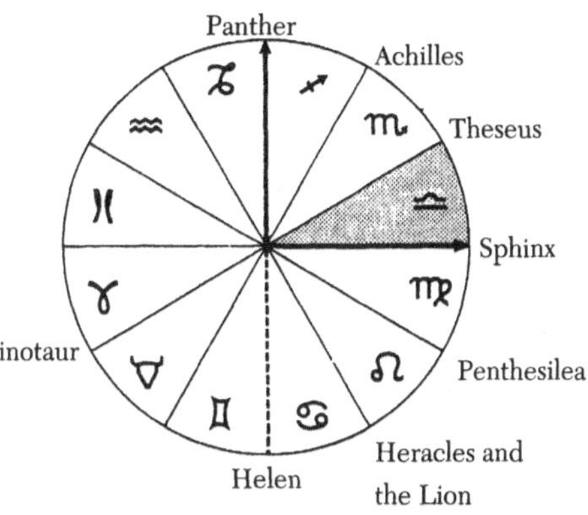

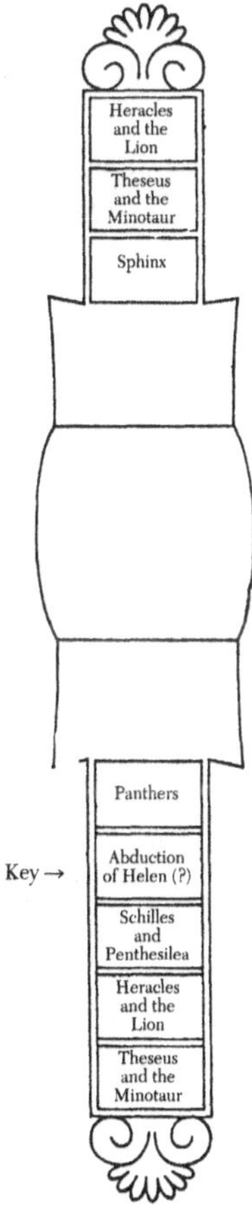

Figures 84 & 85. *To the right, a shield armlet of type V. Above, zodiacal diagram corresponding to fig. 84; it describes the northeast quarter in relation to Delphi, especially Boeotia and Phthiotis.*

by the struggle of Amphiaraus and Lycurgus, and finally by the murder of Agamemnon, which traditionally took place at Mycenae. Several photos and drawings of this very interesting type are reproduced here to give the reader an idea of this kind of object (figs. 82, 83 and 79). Since the lions and the sphinxes define the southeast quarter in relation to Delphi, one may deduce from the design as a whole that this is the armlet of a shield of a Nemean chieftain who was probably born towards the summer solstice. For magical reasons that are easily understood, the signs of Aquarius, Taurus, and Scorpio also appear, placed respectively in opposition and in a square to the sign of Leo (fig. 81).

Type V. Kunze mentions three examples of this kind of armlet[5] (fig. 84). The Panther-Sphinx delimitation describes the northeast quarter. The scheme as a whole suggests that shields with this type of armlet belonged to warriors from Boeotia or Phthiotis. Helen, associated with Cancer, represents the Cancer-Libra square (fig. 85).

Type VII. This shield, of which Kunze mentions only one example[6] (fig. 86), must describe an individual horoscope. The Gorgon and the lions define the sign of Leo; this was doubtless the shield of an Argive or a Corinthian warrior. The horseman refers to the Dioscuri and could concern a native of Gemini, and thus the end of spring (fig. 87).

Type VIII. This model is also known through a single armlet[7] (fig. 88). The lions and the Gorgon encompass the sign of Leo, therefore, once again Argos or Corinth. Eurystheus could specifically mean that Tiryns was the warrior's place of origin (fig. 89). As in type IV, the main symbols are grouped in Leo; this suggests summer as the season of birth of the bearer of the shield.

Type IX. There are two extant examples[8] (fig. 90). The siren symbolizes the Aquarius region: these must be shields that came from Epirus (fig. 91). (I don't believe that the law of complementarity of opposites is applicable here.)

Type X. The model is known by a single example[9] (fig. 92), but it must be a shield that could be borne by any soldier of the same troup. The most important image, the conflict of Heracles and Geryon, opposes Boeotia to Elis (fig. 93). The Cancer-Capricorn axis, in harmonious relationship with Scorpio, is represented four times.

The winner of the struggle is Heracles, hence, the Boeotian. In this particular case, an inscription on the shield confirms its Boeotian origin.[10] Such a confirmation should be noteworthy to readers who, having arrived at this chapter, might still have some reservations as to the merit of my concepts. This also shows that there is justification in attributing special importance to the scene situated at the level of the warrior's heart, particularly when it appears only once in the design of the armlet, which is indeed the case for type X.

Type XIII. The arrangement[11] (figs. 94 and 95) again defines the area of Argos and Corinth, while also describing the opposite region of Aquarius and the signs of

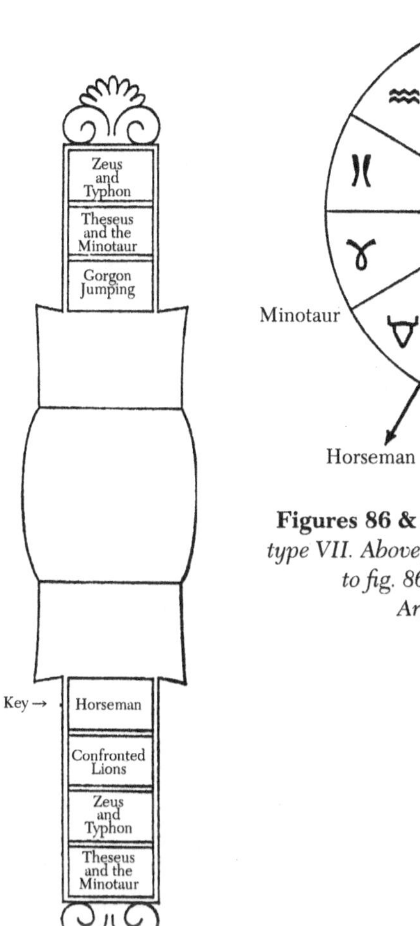

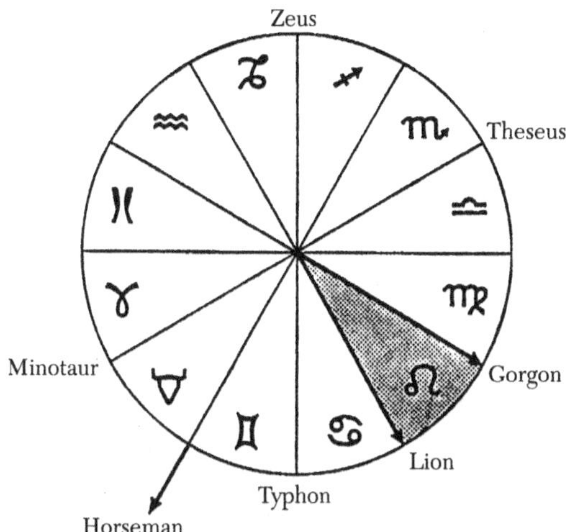

Figures 86 & 87. *To the left, a shield armlet of type VII. Above, zodiacal diagram corresponding to fig. 86; it specifically designates Argolis and Corinthia.*

Sagittarius and Gemini, in squared aspect to the Leo-Aquarius axis. The scene of Ajax with the corpse of Achilles (which could also symbolize Aquarius, since the scene is at Troy) seems to refer rather to a Virgo-Sagittarius square.

As to its significance, this type of armlet greatly resembles types I and IV, but with the meaning extended to Attica.

I will confine my discussion for the time being to these eight examples. Interested readers will find several others in Kunze's book that can be at least partially interpreted.

It will have been noticed that types I, IV, VII, VIII, and XIII, or five of the eight examples of those armlets sufficiently well preserved to establish an

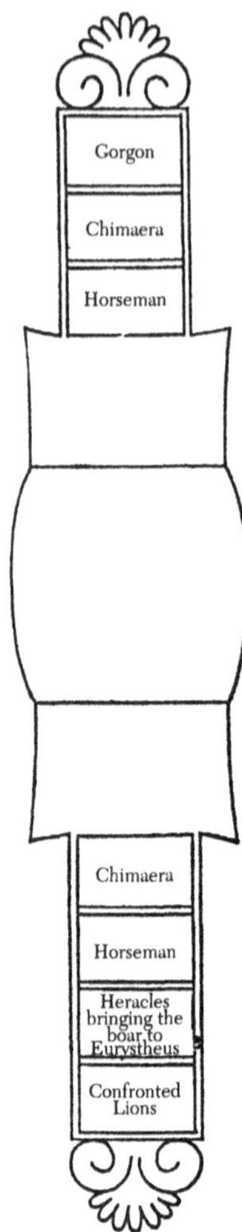

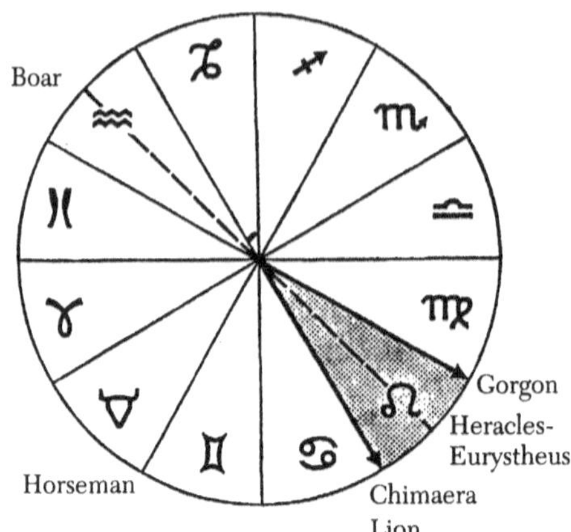

Figures 88 & 89. *To the left, shield armlet of type VIII. Above, zodiacal diagram corresponding to fig. 88; it refers to Argolis and Corinthia and especially Tiryns.*

astrological diagram without great difficulty, describe the sign of Leo, that is, Corinth and Argolis in the Delphic system.

During the course of a conversation in October 1963, I communicated the results of this interpretative work to Professor Kunze. I learned from him at that time that twelve examples of the same dedication had been found at Olympia, by which the Argives had dedicated to Olympian Zeus a major booty taken from the Corinthians.[12]

Since the shield inscribed with zodiacal and planetary symbols was conceived as an image of the celestial vault, the symbolic function of the armlet was

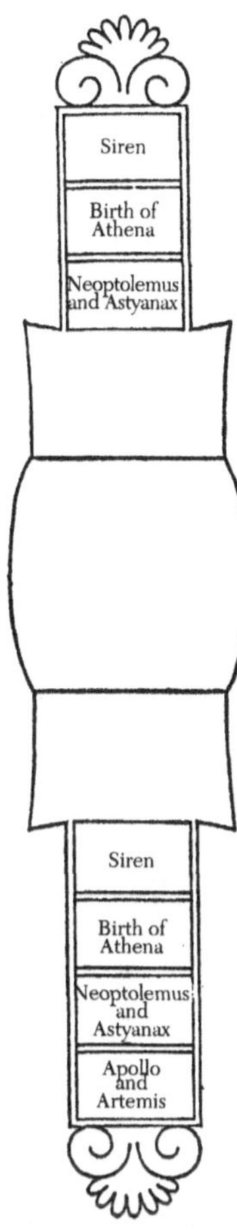

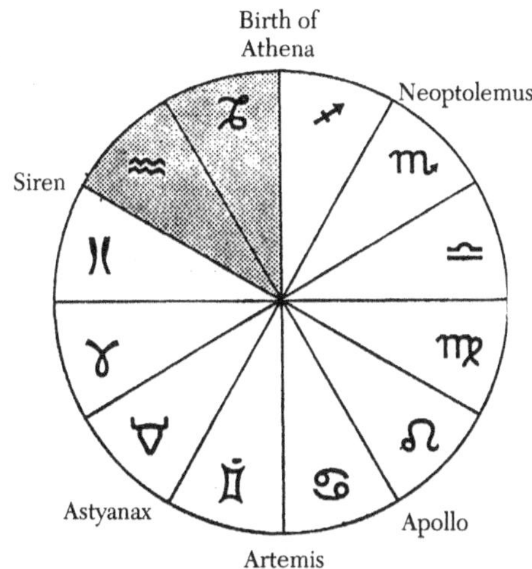

Figures 90 & 91. *To the left, shield armlet of type IX. Above, zodiacal diagram corresponding to fig. 90; it describes the northwest region (Epirus).*

to establish the connection between the cosmos and the individual. Despite their conventional and stereotyped nature, the skillfully rendered symbolic scenes placed the individual first in his spatial context, then in his city (by means of fixed symbols) and, if necessary and probably in the case of chiefs, expressed the reality of individual destinies with the complexity and variety of life itself.

Let me end this chapter with one last suggestion. There may have been one symbolic scene per decan, that is, a set of thirty-six or maybe seventy-two symbolic scenes for the zodiac. (This would mean than only three or six of the scenes of the fall of Troy would concern Aquarius alone.) If this is indeed the case, it should be possible, starting from the illustrations in Professor Kunze's book and the *Corpus Vasorum*, to reconstruct the whole system. Others after me may

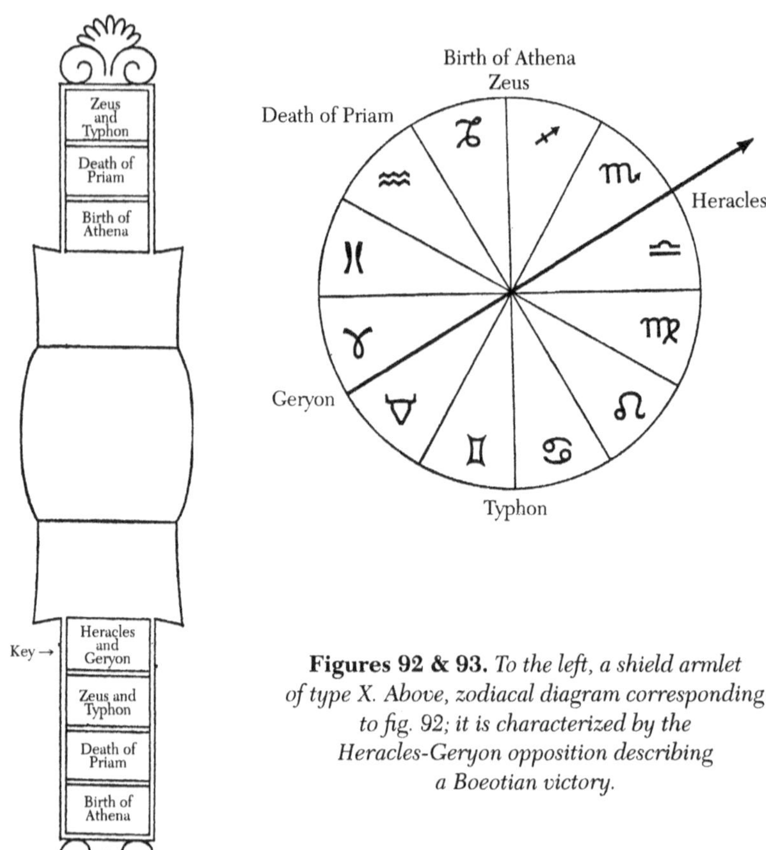

Figures 92 & 93. *To the left, a shield armlet of type X. Above, zodiacal diagram corresponding to fig. 92; it is characterized by the Heracles-Geryon opposition describing a Boeotian victory.*

perhaps achieve this. All the evidence shows that there was, with respect to the preparation of the armlets of shields, a genuine sacred science that obeyed definite laws and comprised a direct application of the principles of sacred geography in combination with horoscopic considerations.

A comparable fact exists in a neighboring geographical area. It seems to me that a strong similarity exists between the armlets of Greek shields and the ornamental quiver covers from Luristan, which are also bronze plaques with several registers featuring mythological figures.[13]

It is highly probable that in both cases these are magico-astrological images designed to protect either the bearer of the quiver or the bearer of the shield.

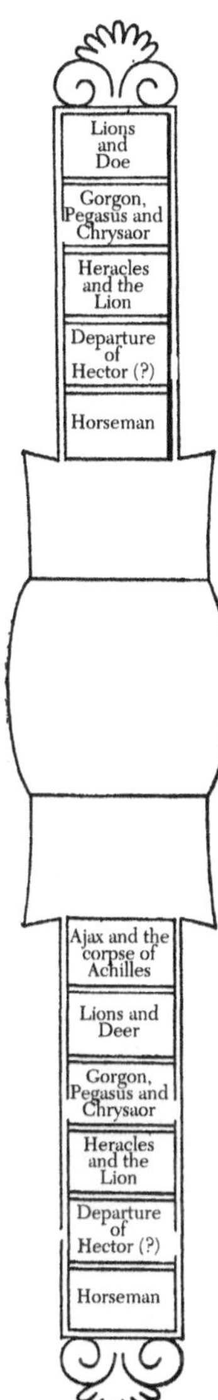

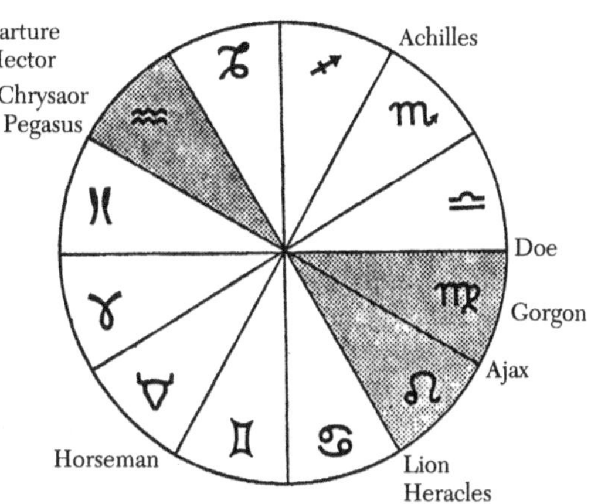

Figures 94 & 95. *To the left, shield armlet of type XIII. Above, zodiacal diagram corresponding to fig. 94; it seems to designate the Leo-Virgo region (Argolis, Corinthia, and Attica).*

Chapter 17

Greek Temples: Sculpted Pediments and Zodiacal Geography The Structure of Sanctuaries

After having deciphered the principal zodiacal and calendary symbols employed in Greece from at least the eighth century to the Age of Alexander (and probably to the Byzantine era), I shall now attempt to show that the decoration of temple pediments is directly related to this symbolism and always describes the temple's position in the system to which it was attached.

The pediments will be examined from this point of view in an order that associates chronology and geography. The book from which my essential information will be drawn is by Étienne Lapalus, *Le Fronton sculpté en Grèce des origines à la fin du IVe siècle.*[1]

Lapalus started with the astonishing assumption, which is very widespread today, according to which aesthetic considerations would have always been more important than symbolic meaning in the decoration of temples. To anyone possessing, even in the slightest degree, a sense of the sacred, it is quite obvious that the opposite must have been true. Does anyone really believe that, in a society of the traditional type, the priesthood could have been subordinate to the artisans and sculptors? In reality, religious considerations, and especially the importance of sacred geography, were never forgotten, and often outweighed questions of aesthetics and plastic values.

This approach will provide a coherent and consistent interpretation of both symbolic and religious scope. The scenes on one or both pediments of a temple very often seem to have no apparent connection. But their relationship can be established without any difficulty on the level of astrological symbolism, and this has a spatial significance; it always situates the temple and relates it to a whole. Since the geographical position and the overall symbolic meaning of the sanctuary are defined by the decoration of the pediments, the decor may have no immediate bearing on the cult of the god worshipped in the sanctuary. But rather frequently, at Tegea or at Aegina, for example, local legends are skillfully interwoven with a far-reaching order that encompasses all of Greece.

It will also be seen, which is of major importance, that my code of interpretation is valid not only for the sanctuaries of Apollo, but for all the great temples.[2] In reading this chapter, readers may refer to the preceding maps and to map 8.

To establish a first basis for this, a characteristic example will be discussed, the pediment of the Gorgon at Paleopolis in Corcyra. This is one of the best preserved archaic pediments, and its reconstruction has never been a problem. The sculptures form a block with the background slabs, so they could be reassembled without any difficulty. This example will already allow me to formulate specific rules for interpreting the symbolic meaning of pediments. Next a complementary pediment will be analyzed, that of the first Hecatompedon of Athens. A series of examples that are part of the Delphic system will then be looked at, reserving for the end of the chapter the pediments of the temple of the Athenians at Delos, those belonging to the Heraclean system of Phlius, the sanctuary of Olympia, and finally, the temple of Samothrace.

1. Corfu and Athens

a) Corcyra. There is a considerable bibliography on the pediment of the temple of Artemis at Paleopolis in Corfu.[3] This is the great pediment of the Gorgon, dated to 585 B.C., where one sees the Gorgon, accompanied by Chrysaor and Pegasus, flanked by two panthers (fig. 96).

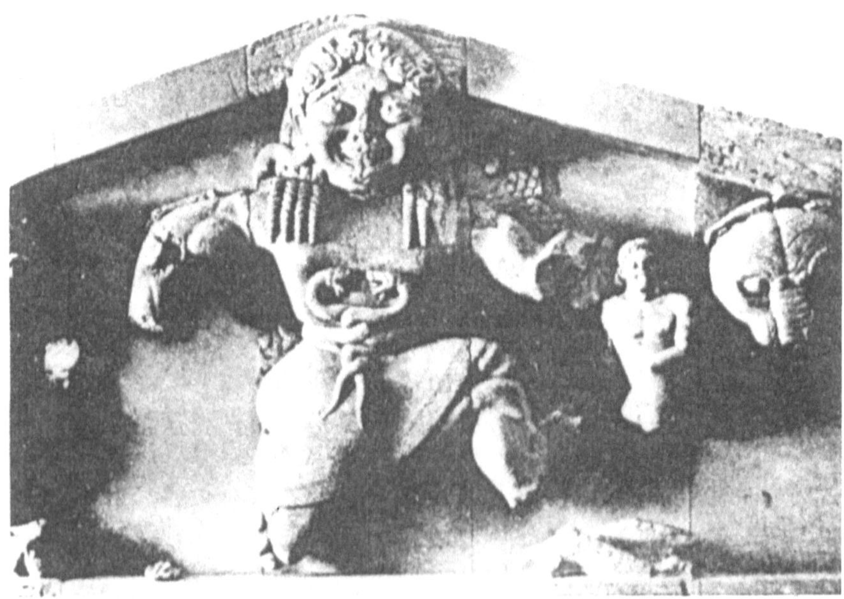

Figure 96. *Pediment of the temple of Artemis at Paleopolis in Corcyra: Gorgon, Chrysaor, Pegasus, and panthers.*

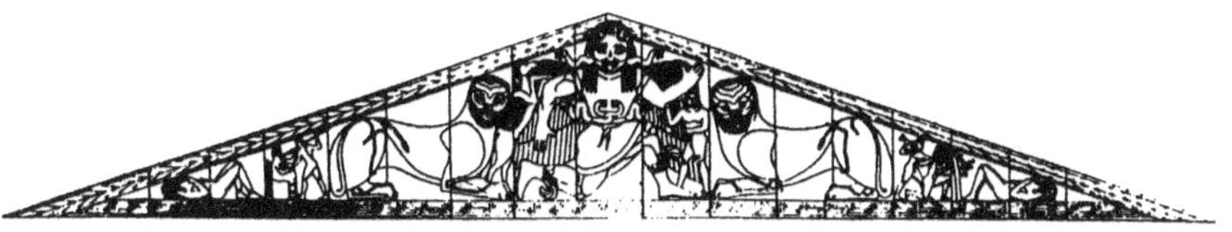

Figure 97. *Drawing of the pediment of the temple of Artemis at Paleopolis, describing the northwest quarter in relation to Delphi.*

Paleopolis of Corcyra was situated near the Virgo-Pisces zodiacal axis. If the law of complementarity of opposing signs is applied, it will seem quite normal to see the Gorgon on this pediment as the ancient guardian of the sign of Virgo. There is no reason to assume, as certain archeologists have,[4] that this Gorgon "really" represents an Artemis Mistress of Beasts, a supposition essentially based on the fact that the temple was very probably sacred to the cult of Artemis. The panthers in fact represent and describe the northwest quarter of the Delphic system. This quarter naturally includes the three signs of Pisces, Aquarius, and Capricorn.

The Gorgon designates the Virgo-Pisces axis. Chrysaor and Pegasus relate to the neighboring sign of Aquarius, hence to Corfu and the part of Epirus situated opposite the island (Paleopolis was in Aquarius, slightly east of the Virgo-Pisces axis).

Remaining to be interpreted are the two scenes of conflict on plaques on either side of the Gorgon, which have caused much ink to flow and inspired widely divergent theories. According to one of them, the scene of Iliupersis (the fall of Ilium) represents Neoptolemus, son of Achilles, striking old Priam, who is seated. The other scene is of Zeus hurling lightning at a giant. It has been stated, again and again, that these two scenes, whose presence on this pediment is unexplained, bear no relationship to the central subject and to the panthers[5] (fig. 97).

However, despite appearances, the series of scenes is coherent and perfectly constructed, if one is willing to adopt my point of view. These images have a hieroglyphic meaning; they complete and support what is being said by the Gorgon, Chrysaor, Pegasus, and the panthers.

The scene of Iliupersis refers to Troy and, by analogy, to the sign of Aquarius (Troy is in Aquarius in relation to Sardis). The scene of Zeus and the giant takes place on Olympus, and therefore stands for the sign of Capricorn (fig. 98). In the angles of the pediment are two defeated giants, which have the same meaning. Scenes of Gigantomachy symbolize a polar direction, most often corresponding to north, which is here the case.

The Corfu pediment as a whole, which at first glance seems quite strange and incoherent, describes in a precise and detailed manner the northwest quarter

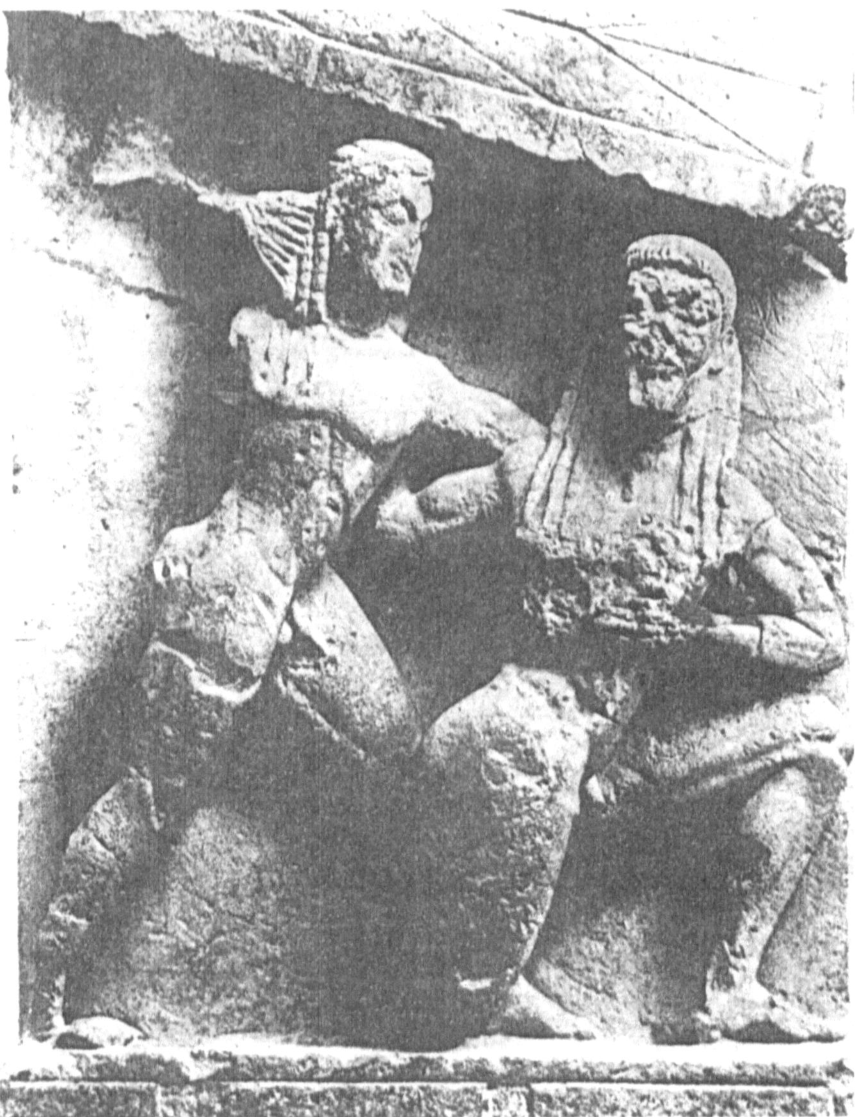

Figure 98. *Zeus striking a giant with lightning. Pediment of the Gorgon, Museum of Corfu.*

of Greece, where Corcyra is located, and the three zodiacal signs (Pisces, Aquarius, Capricorn) corresponding to this quarter. This may be summarized as follows:

1. The panthers describe the northwest quarter.
2. The Gorgon designates the Virgo-Pisces axis.
3. Chrysaor and Pegasus symbolize Aquarius.

4. The scene of Iliupersis also concerns Aquarius.
5. Zeus and the giant related to Capricorn.
6. The giants in the angles refer to Olympus and also to Capricorn.

Only astrological symbolism can provide a coherent and logical interpretation for this artifact, which has always been so baffling to commentators.

Beginning with this outstanding example, I can compose some rules of interpretation which establish a method that is both logical and organic for deciphering and explaining the decor of all the pediments of Greek temples.

b) Principles of Interpretation. The symbols previously described as the symbols of seasonal variations, such as panthers, lions killing a bull, lions attacking a stag, or serpents, which are categorized by archeologists as "terrible" or "apotropaic" symbols, are determinators in the decoration of pediments that always represent a quarter of the Greek territory in relation to Delphi.

Each quarter so defined necessarily includes three signs of the zodiac. The rest of the tympanal design always indicates, in one way or another, the temple's position in one of these three signs. Two main procedures may be followed for this purpose:

1. When the temple is situated on a zodiacal line or in immediate proximity to it, the tympanal decor refers to the zodiacal axis in question and to its neighboring signs.
2. When the sanctuary is situated in the middle of a sign, its position is defined by signs, symbols, and symbolic scenes describing the two axes that border it. This is true, for example, of the sanctuaries of Apollo at Eretria, Aphaia at Aegina, and Asclepius at Epidaurus.

c) The Hecatompedon of Athens: the Old Man of the Sea. By virtue of the principle of the complementarity of opposites, if there was a temple pediment at Corfu showing the Gorgon with Pegasus and Chrysaor, there must have been a pediment at Athens dedicated to Nereus, the Old Man of the Sea, ancient guardian of the sign of Pisces (Nereus was also known as Triton, which recalls Athena's association with Lake Tritonis). This assumption immediately proves to be true: at least two pediments on monuments of the acropolis, contemporaneous with the sanctuary of Artemis at Corcyra, depicted the conflict of Heracles and Nereus. One, dating from about 580 to 570, belonged to a monument located southeast of the Parthenon. This is the "red pediment," of which only three fragments *in poros* are extant.[6] Another pediment of the same date is more complete: it was part of the first Hecatompedon Peripteros. Its fragments clearly show that it defined the southeast quarter of Greece in the Delphic system.[7] The central motif on the main pediment was composed of two lions, lying down face to face, with serpents on the pediment wings. One of the serpents may have stood for the north-south axis and Cancer, the other the earth line, intersecting the north-south axis to the north, and the Eagle-Serpent region. The two confronted lions

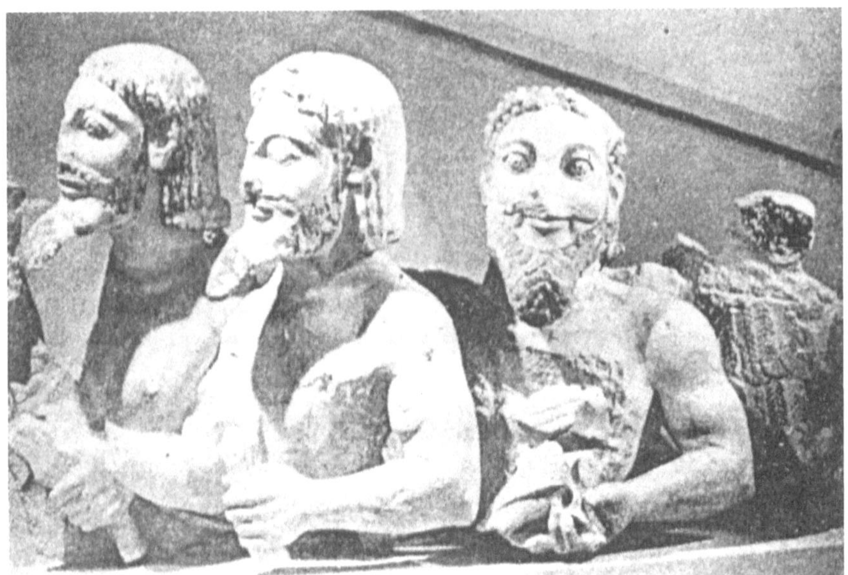

Figure 99. *Athens, Museum of the Acropolis: the three-headed old man of the first Hecatompedon, contemporaneous with the temple in Corcyra. This figure expresses, in relation to fig. 96, the complementarity of opposites (Pisces-Virgo opposition-complementarity).*

described the sign of Leo; the two lions devouring a bull, the southeast quarter as a whole.

Remaining to be discussed is the Heracles-Triton group, which occupied the left wing of the rear pediment, and the old man with three heads (fig. 99) that appeared on the right wing, according to the generally accepted reconstruction.[8] Heracles, hero of Leo, was portrayed struggling with the guardian of the sign of Pisces. The guardian of Pisces was clearly represented by the triple "bluebeard," whose three heads corresponded to the three decans of that sign (or if it was Typhon, which is rather improbable, to the three decans of Cancer). If, as some believe, this old man was Proteus being consulted by Menelaus,[9] the latter, son of Atreus, also represents the sign of Leo in conflict with Pisces.

I thus arrive at the following arrangement:

1. Serpents of Cancer and Scorpio: the southeast quarter.
2. Confronted lions: Leo.
3. Lions attacking a bull: the southeast quarter.
4. Triton-Nereus: the Virgo-Pisces axis (also symbolized by a Gorgon's head on the peak of the roof) or else Typhon: the sign of Cancer.
5. Heracles and Menelaus: Leo.
6. Menelaus, husband of Helen, is also associated with Cancer.

The complementary pediments of Corfu and the Hecatompedon of Athens are certainly impressive: each describes a quarter of the year and of the territory of ancient Greece. May one not assume, then, that towards the same period there could have been two sanctuaries related to the Gemini-Sagittarius axis, whose pediments, conceived along the same principles, described the two other quarters of Greece? The most likely sites for such pediments seem to be Olympia and Pagasae. Similar symmetrical sanctuaries may have existed all over Greece, but it remains improbable that there had been a series of twelve describing a complete zodiac. The existence of the pediment of the Gorgon is no doubt due to Corinthian influences.

2. Temples of the Delphic System

The extrapolation I have just made may seem bold, but what some readers may still consider a working hypothesis is soon to be definitively proved.

a) Athens. Some pediments of other monuments of the acropolis will now be looked at, those of the "Ur-Parthenon," the Hecatompedon of the Pisistraditae, and the Parthenon.

ANCIENT PARTHENON. The very existence of such a monument remains problematical. It would have been built toward the end of the seventh or the beginning of the sixth century. The pediment which has been found featured two confronted lions, each one devouring a bull.[10] Again, this stands for the southeast quarter of the Delphic system.

THE HECATOMPEDON OF THE PISISTRADITAE. This temple would date from about 520.[11] It is assumed that a Gigantomachy was figured on the east pediment, which would describe the north-south axis. Attributed to the west pediment of this building is a marble group of two lions attacking a bull (another image of the southeast quarter).

THE PARTHENON. The pediments of Phidias continued to honor the ancient principles: the birth of Athena described the north-south axis, and both pediments as a unit were conceived for the glorification of the ruler of Virgo in the Delphic system.

b) Sparta. Sanctuary of Artemis Orthia. In the ruins of the sanctuary of Artemis Orthia at Sparta, a group of two sitting confronted lions has been found, which seems to have been part of a pediment.[12] This image must have related to the sign of Leo and been part of a pediment that described the southeast quarter of Greece.

c) Eretria. The central subject of the west pediment of the temple of Apollo Daphnephoros at Eretria, dating from about 500, was Athena. From the pediment as a whole, which is believed to have been an Amazonomachy, there remains a group showing a scene of abduction, probably Theseus carrying away

Antiope.[13] This scene seems to refer to the two axes that delimit the region of Eretria: Theseus, hero of Virgo, abducts Antiope, heroine of Libra. Athena rules Virgo, and the Amazons also share the sign's characteristics.

d) Aegina. The pediments of the temple of Aphaia at Aegina (second decade of the fifth century) are believed to have shown battle scenes around a central Athena.[14] The west tympanum would relate to the Second Trojan War; the east would illustrate the expedition of Telamon, assisted by Heracles, against the Trojan king Laodemon (First Trojan War).

Heracles is especially associated with Leo, as was seen in chapter 10. Telamon represents Aegina, and Troy the sign of Aquarius; the whole symbolizes the Leo-Aquarius axis.

The geographic position of the island of Aegina is described as follows:

1. Heracles: Leo
2. Expedition of Telamon against Troy: Leo-Aquarius axis
3. Athena: Virgo
4. Telamon: Aegina.

e) The Temple of Hera at Argos. Knowledge of the sacred geography of Greece can bring elements of resolution to certain controversial points. One example is the west pediment of the Heraion at Argos.[15] This sanctuary is situated near the Leo-Aquarius axis (in the Phlius system, it is in Leo).

The east pediment represented the birth of Zeus with Rhea, nymphs, and Curetes. The scene is on Mount Ida, point of origin of the Leo-Aquarius axis. On the west pediment was a scene of the fall of Troy. In examining the figures that have been found, one hesitates between Ajax dragging Cassandra away from the altars and the meeting of Menelaus and Helen. The former seems more probable as another reference to the sign of Aquarius, in opposition to Leo. The great Ajax, son of Telamon, reigned over Salamis, and he is here associated with Leo (it has been seen earlier that he sometimes stands for Virgo because of the proximity of Salamis and Athens). The two pediments of the Hera temple would therefore symbolize the Leo-Aquarius axis.

A scene between Menelaus and Helen is less likely: it would represent either a Leo-Cancer association (Menelaus is the son of Atreus and is associated with Mycenae and Leo) or else a connection between the two neighboring signs of Gemini and Cancer (Menelaus is the king of Sparta).

f) Epidaurus. The east pediment of the temple of Asclepius at Epidaurus was decorated with an Iliupersis around a central Andromache. Local healing heroes may also have appeared in this scene.[16] The subject of the west pediment was an Amazonomachy.

In regard to these pediments, E. Lapalus had no qualms in writing: "At Epidaurus in the fourth century, the theme [of the Amazonomachy] can be considered as having no symbolic value, and it was chosen only for aesthetic reasons, for the vitality and human pathos of its scenes."[17] Such a statement can be explained in the case of Epidaurus by the fact that the pediments constitute a sort of extreme case. While elsewhere a rather complex interplay of mythical scenes and religious traditions is encountered, here the symbolism is purely spatial through references to zodiacal geography. The first pediment defines the Leo-Aquarius axis, the second the Virgo-Pisces axis. Together they precisely define the sign of Leo, to which Epidaurus belonged in the Delphic wheel. The system of description employed is the same as the one encountered in the temples of Apollo at Eretria and Aphaia at Aegina.

◆

From studying the different pediments attached to the Delphic system, I conclude that temple decoration was fundamentally in harmony with the zodiacal sector where the temple was located. The Corinthian workshops that produced geometrical vases played a prominent role in implementing pediment decorations with zodiacal symbolism.

In various parts of his study, E. Lapalus emphasizes Corinth's role in the very invention of the pediment: "The Corinthians," he writes, "inventors of the architectural pediment, were in all probability also the first to cover the tympanal field with a plastic ornamentation in painted terra-cotta."[18] Truly, it does seem quite natural that this city, situated on the cosmic axis, whose coins bore Pegasus and the solar swastika, should have played a major role in unifying pediment symbolism.

3. Delphi: the Pediments of the Temple of the Alcmaeonidae

One would anticipate that the principles which inspired and guided the design of the pediments of the other sanctuaries in the Delphic system should have found a special application in the site of the omphalos. Simple reasoning shows that one should expect to see at Delphi:

I. An image of the four seasons, which simultaneously refers to the four quarters of Greece.

II. A representation, by means of symbolic scenes, of the two great axes that cross at Delphi:

1. The east-west axis.
2. The north-south axis.

The pediments of the temple of Apollo of the Alcmaeonidae from the sixth century, studied according to the generally accepted reconstruction (fig. 100), will contribute a fine confirmation to my theories. The two will be looked at separately, without losing sight of the fact that the global meaning is expressed by the unity of both. It is generally agreed that they are contemporaneous.

a) The Symbols of Seasonal Variations and the Four Quarters. The design of the pediments was conceived so that the symbols of the four seasons, and thus

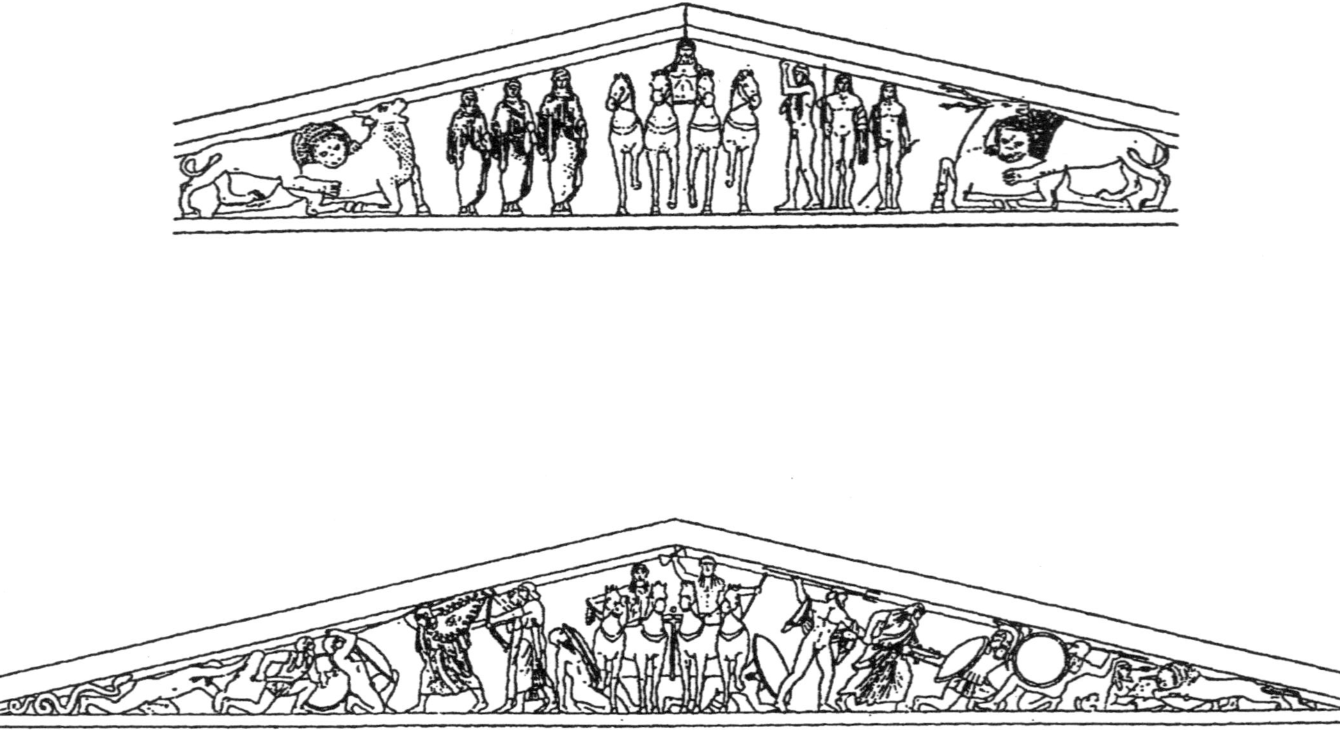

Figure 100. *Reconstruction of the pediments of the temple of Apollo at Delphi: the four seasons.*

of the four quarters of Greece, were placed at the corners of the temple as follows:

Southeast angle: lion attacking a bull, spring
Northeast angle: lion devouring a stag, summer
Northwest angle: serpent, autumn
Southwest angle: panther, winter.

The temple was orientated to the summer-sunrise winter-sunset solstitial axis (northeast to southwest direction) in such a way that there could not be exact correspondences between the symbolic animals in the pediment angles and the four directions of space. I will soon show why one of the meanings of these statues was relatively sacrificed.

The so-called terrible or apotropaic symbols obviously have the same meaning whether they appear in the middle of the pediment or in the angle, and there is no reason why these ancient symbols of oriental origin, transmitted from one civilization to another throughout the Middle East, should have suddenly changed meaning at Delphi to symbolize Apollo's "wild earth" mentioned in the prologue of Aeschylus's *Eumenides*. This is, nonetheless, the point of view adopted by E. Lapalus:

> The decoration of this pediment illustrates a basic fact of the Delphic religious tradition, the arrival of the civilizing deity Apollo upon the wild earth of Parnassus, whose barbarity is symbolized by the two angular groups of fighting animals.[19]

Elsewhere in the same book this author suggests another interpretation for the pediment angles:

> In introducing in the angles of the Delphic pediment these great groups of animals, whose apotropaic value was certainly no longer essential, and in giving them dimensions which at first glance can seem out of proportion to the central scene, the decorators were mainly concerned with giving the tympanal composition a strong foundation.[20]

This is a typical example of the prejudice I spoke of earlier that places aesthetic considerations above religious or cult significance.

b) The East Pediment. The east, or rather northeast, pediment of the temple showed the epiphany of Apollo and his chariot, an obvious allusion to sunrise, the east-west axis, and the daily path of the sun. Primarily, this pediment represented the triumph of the solar deity entering the sign of Leo at the summer solstice. To the right of the god, in the space which I ascribe to spring, stood three *kores*, and to his left, three *kouroi*, in the part corresponding to summer.[21]

The *kores* could possibly represent the signs of Taurus, Gemini, and Cancer, and the *kouroi* could be an image of Leo, Virgo, and Scorpio. Knowledge of the specific attributes or weapons of each statue would certainly settle the question. Nevertheless, what I am suggesting is a very good explanation for the welcoming gesture of the largest of the *kouroi* symbolizing Leo, since that sign is the astrological house of the sun and relates to the dog-days, which are especially intense in the blazing heat of Delphi in summertime. The weapons of the other youths would be significant if, as it is believed, the second bore the lance of Athena, ruler of Virgo, and the smallest the hammer of Hephaestus, master of Scorpio. The year changed sex at the summer solstice, as already mentioned (p. 102).

c) The West Pediment. On the west pediment in central position were Zeus and Hera in a chariot. The master of the gods was brandishing his lightning. The Zeus-Hera association directly alludes to the Cancer-Capricorn axis, which is confirmed by the choice of a Gigantomachy for the entire pediment. The presence of the Letoidae, Athena, Poseidon, and Hephaestus should not be surprising, since they are all zodiacal deities. The overall diagram could facilitate a more exact reconstruction of the pediment (fig. 101).

In the concept of the pediment design, priority has been given to the two central figures, Apollo and Zeus, who were placed precisely on the Leo-Aquarius symbolic axis, one looking towards the solstitial summer sunrise, the other the winter sunset. This was achieved to the detriment of the exact positioning of the animal figures, of which two could have occupied their correct positions if they had been in the middle of the tympanum, like in the archaic pediments. In that case, the lion and stag group would have been placed in the middle of the east pediment, and one or two panthers would have appeared in the central part of the west pediment, but once the decision had been made to put the animal figures in the angles, a better approximation of the squaring of the circle could

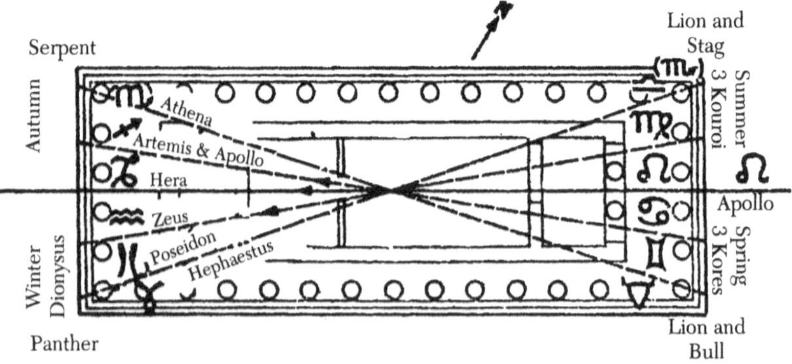

Figure 101. *Delphi: plan of the temple of Apollo and the zodiacal division of the pediments.*

not be obtained. This marks the transition from one type of symbolism to another, the deeper meaning remaining unchanged.

4. Delos: the Pediments of the Temple of the Athenians

Readers who have followed my reasoning can easily infer that, if there were any surviving pediments from a temple of Apollo at Delos, these should feature a spatial symbolism similar to that of the Alcmaeonidae at Delphi, that is, describe the two perpendicular axes corresponding to the east-west and north-south directions. This is because Delos, like Delphi, was an omphalos. Now, it so happens that major fragments of sculpted groups that were part of the pediments of the Athenian temple of Apollo at Delos have been found[22] (fifth century). This hexastyle temple had its entrance to the west like the great temple of Apollo.

At the peak of the west pediment stood a group which, according to the most generally accepted interpretation, represented the abduction of Cephalus by Eos. As was seen at the beginning of chapter 11, this scene symbolizes both the Aries-Libra axis and the east-west direction. At Delphi, where the entrance to the temple was to the east, it was the group on the east pediment that represented the east-west axis. At Delos, on the east pediment of the temple of the Athenians, there was another scene of abduction, that of Oreithyia by Boreas. One can reasonably see in this a reference to the "kinship" of the Athenians with Boreas. The cult of Boreas at Agrae, on the banks of the Ilissus (see chap. 7), associated him with the Lesser Mysteries and with the symbolic polar axis of Delos-Athens-Delphi (0 degree Virgo direction in the Delphic system).

Delos is situated both on this line and on the meridian of Mount Haemus, homeland of Boreas, the "gateway of the gods" of the Delian system (the cult of Boreas was nevertheless generally believed to be of Libyan origin).

The name of the nymph Oreithyia means "she who rages on the mountains," but the place of her abduction was said to be the banks of the Ilissus. The choice of this second group for a monument donated by the Athenians was therefore very significant: it pertained both to the Delos-Mount Haemus direction—hence to the north-south axis—and to the symbolic polar direction of Delos-Athens-Delphi.

5. The Pediment of the Hydra at Athens

Although I cannot review all the pediments of the Greek world, if the present chapter is not to become unduly long, it is highly probable that most of them could be interpreted in terms of sacred geography. The omphalos only needs to be found in each case.

For example, the pediment of Heracles and the Hydra, which by its dimensions must have belonged to a rather small building, relates to the sacred geography of Attica. The remains were found on the acropolis, southeast of the Parthenon, hence in the direction of Agrae. It could therefore have been situated on the Delos-Agrae-Acropolis-Eleusis-Delphi line, the polar direction for Attica, and stood for the Capricorn-Cancer axis (see chap. 7).

6. Temples in the Phlius System: Tegea and Calydon

The pediments of the temple of Athena Alea at Tegea in Arcadia are a rather special case. The sculptures are from a fairly late period (middle of the fourth century). Pausanias's description[23] mentions their subjects. It seems to me that they took up themes that had been treated in the decoration of a much more ancient temple. In fact, the decor only has meaning in the system centered on Phlius (see map 6: The Calendars of Heracles), in which Tegea is situated on the Gemini-Sagittarius line.

The west pediment of Tegea showed the combat of Achilles and Telephus. This was closely watched by the fathers of the fighters, Peleus and Heracles. Telephus was the hero representing Tegea. Legend was to make of him the father of Tarchon and Tyrrhenus, thus associating him closely with the origins of Rome. This confirms his affinity with the sign of Gemini. (Also near Tegea is Pallantium, the native town of the colonizers who named the Palatine, according to another story).

Achilles and Peleus symbolize the sign of Sagittarius, opposed to Gemini. Heracles usually represents Leo, and his presence recalls the Leo-Boar axis. The hunting of the Calydonian boar in fact appeared on the pediment of the façade.[24]

As was seen in chapter 10, there was a sign of the Boar, in the Heraclean system of Phlius, whose sanctuary was at Calydon. The similarities among Calydon, Phlius, and Tegea are striking. The sites of Phlius and Calydon are on orientated hillocks, the latter including a major earthwork (fig. 102). The sanctuaries of Artemis and Apollo at Calydon are both turned towards Erymanthus and Phlius. If one draws the Calydon-Phlius and the Tegea-Phlius lines on the map, one will observe that they more or less form a right angle. The purpose of this aspect of physical geographic squaring is, I believe, to express the relationship between the two sanctuaries. The astrological aspect between Gemini and Leo is a sextile (60 degree angle). The apparent discrepancy is understandable when one considers that the Phlius system is really a zodiac of ten signs. During a period before the invention of tympanal design as a system of reference, symbolic relationships between the various sanctuaries were indicated by their orientation. This system was later abandoned, no doubt because it was too complicated to execute.

7. Bassae

Something of this sort probably appears at Bassae, built on the site of a more ancient temple, while retaining its orientation to Delphi. Since the work of W. B. Dinsmoor,[25] it has been generally accepted that the pediments of the temple of

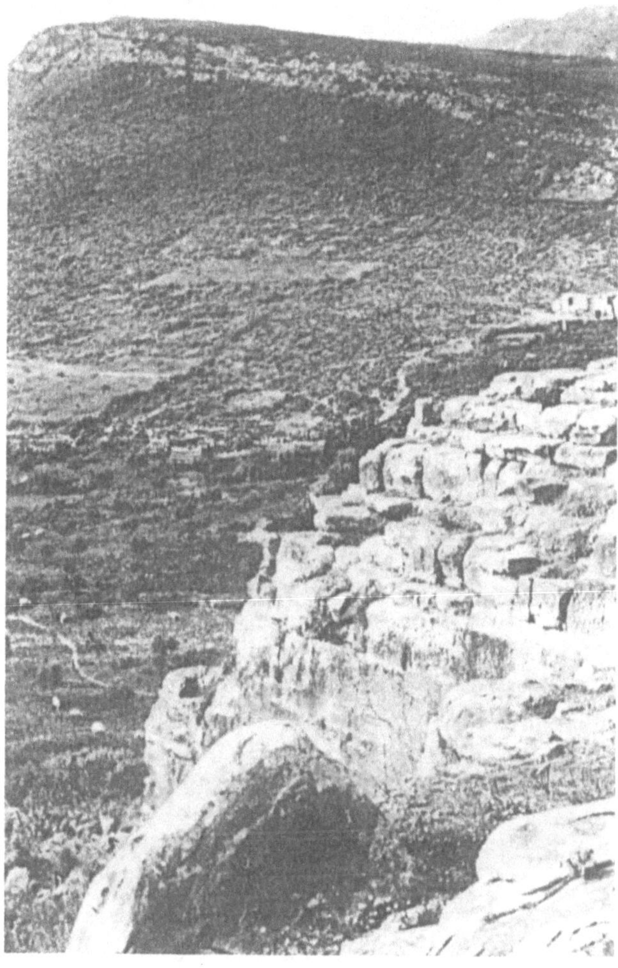

Figure 102. *The terrace of the temples of Calydon, southwest angle. (Photo J. R.)*

Apollo Epicourios at Bassae showed the history of Niobe and the death of the Niobidae under the arrows of Artemis and Apollo. Niobe was the daughter of Tantalus, who reigned at Smyrna. The scene of the death of the Niobidae takes place on Mount Sipylus; it alludes to the earth line that passes through Delphi, near Thebes, by ancient Smyrna, and the mass of Mount Sipylus (Niobe is the sister of Pelops and the wife of Amphion).

To situate the temple in the Delphic system, the four walls of the *cella* had been decorated with a frieze of the wars of the Greeks against the Amazons, the centaurs, and the lapiths. Some of these sculptures, now in the British Museum, appertain to the Virgo-Pisces axis, others to the Gemini-Sagittarius axis. These two perpendicular axes indicated that Bassae was located in the sign of Gemini in relation to Delphi.

8. Olympia

I have reserved the pediments of the temple of Zeus at Olympia for now, because these famous fifth-century pediments, admired by every visitor to Greece, set particular problems and feature what may be a unique combination of two systems of coordinates. This is probably attributable to an accumulation and superimposition of religious traditions in a prominent site (see chap. 11). The east pediment represents the preparation for the nuptial race of Pelops. This scene symbolizes a solar rite and the history of the calendar, and it refers to the omphalos of Phlius. The orientation of the temple indicates the Olympia-Phlius-Isthmia line, which is the equinoctial line of the Peloponnese (map 6). It is therefore not surprising that the Alpheus should appear in the angle of this pediment, since it designates the alpha, the bull, and spring. Pindar, in his telling of the founding of the Olympic Games by Heracles (*Olympian Odes*, X, 45), says that the Alpheus was honored at Olympia "as one of the twelve sovereign gods" (which here must be understood as "one of the rulers of the twelve signs of the zodiac").

The west pediment shows the battle of the lapiths and the centaurs, that is, the Gemini-Sagittarius axis, like the frieze of the *cella* at Bassae. This pediment describes the position of Olympia in relation to Delphi at a relatively late period. (Olympia was formerly in the sign of Taurus.) The west pediment therefore seems to be part of a more recent tradition of spatial symbolism than the east. The presence of a Centauromachy can also be explained as an allusion to the centaurs of Mount Pholoe, which play a role in the history of Heracles.

♦

The pediments of the temple of the Alcmaeonidae of Delphi are dated to about 505, and those of Olympia from 470 to 456, so they are almost contemporaneous.

The temples of Apollo at Delphi and Zeus at Olympia are oriented to the summer sunrise-winter sunset solstitial axis.

Both pediments of these temples have an astonishing character of complementarity: at Delphi, Apollo occupies the center of the east pediment, in the same position as Zeus at Olympia. The Apollo of the west pediment at Olympia is a symmetrical answer to the Zeus of the west pediment at Delphi.

I shall once again suggest a zodiacal arrangement, while recognizing a greater margin of doubt for the interpretative details of the pediments at Olympia. The temple was hexastyle, which corresponds well with the proposed layout.

Pausanias's description of these pediments[26] must be carefully examined—he says "to the right" for the right of an observer facing the pediment. Here is the essence of his text:

> On the front pediment is the scene, just before the chariot race between Pelops and Oenomaus, where both parties are preparing for the competition. An image of Zeus has been carved towards the middle of the pediment; to the right of Zeus is Oenomaus, who is wearing a helmet and standing next to his wife Sterope, one of the daughters of Atlas. Myrtilus, the charioteer of Oenomaus, is there too, sitting in front of the horses, of which there are four. After him are two men, who are nameless, but who must be in the service of Oenomaus to take care of the horses. At the very edge lies the Cladeus, the river which, in other ways also, the Elaeans honor most after the Alpheus. To the left of Zeus are Pelops, Hippodamia, the charioteer of Pelops, horses, and two men who seem to be Pelops's grooms. Then the pediment narrows again and in this part is represented the Alpheus.

If a zodiacal scheme is set up according to this information, the following correspondences emerge (fig. 103).

The Alpheus and Pelop's charioteer = Taurus
Pelops = Gemini
Hippodamia = Cancer
Zeus and Oenomaus = Leo
Sterope = Virgo
Myrtilus (charioteer) and the river Cladeus = Libra

In order to obtain an exact correspondence between the positions of the signs and the characters on the pediment, Hippodamia would have to appear between Pelops and Zeus, which does not agree with the rule of perfect

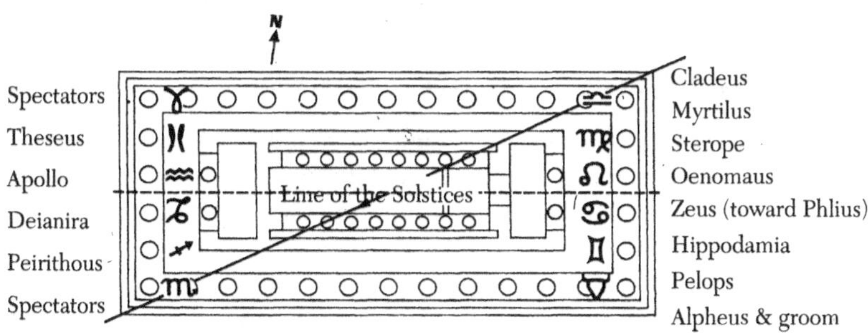

Figure 103. *Zodiacal scheme of the hexastyle temple of Zeus at Olympia.*

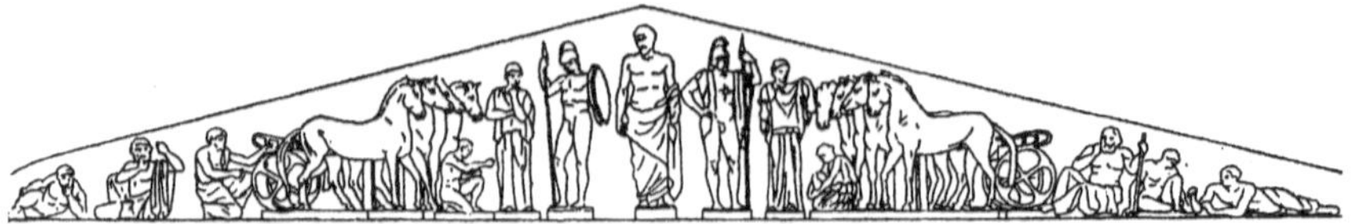

Figure 104. *The east pediment of the temple of Zeus at Olympia.*

symmetry applied in reconstructing the pediment, but which is not in itself impossible (fig. 104).

The Cladeus, opposed to the Alpheus in this scheme, is a tributary stream which, in geographical reality, flows from the north and empties into the Alpheus near Olympia. Its course is perpendicular to that of the Alpheus.

Now, here is the description of the rear pediment, showing the battle of the lapiths and the centaurs, as Pausanias gives it:

> In the middle of the pediment is Peirithous. On one side is Eurytion, who has seized Peirithous's wife, with Caeneus coming to the aid of Peirithous—and on the other side is Theseus defending himself against the Centaurs with an axe. One Centaur has grabbed a young girl, another an adolescent in the bud of youth. I think that Alcamenes must have sculpted this scene *because he had learned from Homer's poem that Peirithous was a son of Zeus, and because he knew that Theseus was a great-grandson of Pelops.*

If the zodiacal scheme is developed, these correspondences come forth for the west pediment:

Female spectators and anonymous fighters = Scorpio
Peirithous = Sagittarius
Deianira (or Caeneus) = Capricorn
Apollo (Peirithous, according to Pausanias) = Aquarius
Theseus = Pisces
Female spectators and anonymous fighters = Aries

These figures oppose and complement one another from one pediment to the next. They describe the zodiacal axes, and not the succession of signs like at Delphi, because in order to find the signs in the order of terrestrial projection, one must go diagonally from the northeast angle to the southwest (an astronomer could decide if this diagonal indicates the solstitial direction for the foundation date of the sanctuary). I believe that the sentence emphasized by Pausanias had the express purpose of showing that one had to look for the symbolic relationships among the characters on both pediments.

With a real penetration of the deeper meaning of Greek mythology, Robert Graves wrote: "Oenomaus, who represented Zeus as the incarnate Sun, is therefore called a son of Asteriё, who ruled Heaven . . . Queen Hippodameia, by marriage to whom he was enroyalled, represented Hera as the incarnate Moon."[27] According to this concept, Hippodamia is both the daughter and spouse of Oenomaus-Zeus. I refer the reader to the works of Cook and Cornford on the origin of the Olympic Games and the identification of the winner with Zeus.[28]

All this corresponds closely to the scheme I am suggesting: Hippodamia in the sign of Cancer symbolizes the moon, and Oenomaus-Zeus in Leo can be identified with the summer sun.

To return to Pausanias's text, he associates Peirithous with Oenomaus-Zeus, that is, the Gemini-Sagittarius axis and the Leo-Aquarius cosmic axis according to the figure. He also associates Pelops and Theseus, or once again the Gemini-Sagittarius axis, and its perpendicular axis of Virgo-Pisces. Olympia is close to the Gemini-Sagittarius axis in the Delphic system. This axis is elsewhere described by the very subject of the battle of the lapiths and the centaurs. Such correspondences cannot be a series of coincidences but, in my opinion, express deliberate intentions.

Pausanias apparently made an extraordinary "mistake" in declaring that Peirithous appeared in the center of the west pediment of the temple. Émile Cahen thought this could be explained by the visual memory of a painting in the Theseum of Athens, where Peirithous was shown giving a centaur a punch on the jaw. This gesture, "spiritualized," would have been the origin of Apollo's gesture at Olympia and would have caused Pausanias's confusion.[29]

Is such a confusion in fact possible? By supposing that it is, isn't one underestimating the great traveler's intelligence, who so often shows a profound and unique understanding of rites and cults in his writings? I believe that, for the ancients, it must have been obvious that the character in the temple axis and symmetrically opposed to Zeus could only be one god, and that god had to be Apollo. Pausanias's error would therefore have been intentional, meant to stimulate curiosity and thoughtfulness in visitors to Olympia. On the east pediment appears a Zeus associated with the summer sunrise, thus playing the same role as Apollo on the east pediment at Delphi. He is at the same time Oenomaus. At the center of the west pediment is an Apollo associated with the winter sunset, like Zeus at Delphi. Apollo is the ancestor of the lapiths, but Pausanias tells us that he is Peirithous, that is, the sun near the Gemini-Sagittarius axis. The reason for this is the geographical position of Olympia in relation to Delphi.

The presence of Caeneus on the west pediment, reported by Pausanias, seems to refer to a solstitial calendar (which was true of the later calendar of Olympia), because Caeneus, "the new," represents the New Year, as has been established by Robert Graves.[30] Apollo, we are also told, was venerated in the grove of Altis under the appellation Thermios. This name alludes to the sanctuary of Thermus in Aetolia, in the sign of Pisces in relation to Delphi (Theseus-Pelops relationship indicated by Pausanias, see map 8).

At Thermus a sanctuary of Apollo from the geometric period has been discovered, which shows the great antiquity of the cult of the god in that site. A fragment has been found from the painted pediment of the temple, one of the most ancient pediments known, which is believed to have represented a Centauromachy. The painted metopes of the temple show Perseus with the Gorgon's head, a head of a Gorgon, Chelidon and Aedon, and Orion. This again in all probability is a calendar. These scenes in fact describe in the following order: the ancient solstitial axis, Virgo, spring, Scorpio, or the equinoctial axis.[31] This temple was orientated to the southwest, that is, towards Olympia and the mouth of the Alpheus (vernal point of the system).

At Delphi, like at the temple of Zeus in Olympia, the east pediment, associated with the summer half of the year, features static scenes, while the west pediment, related to the winter half, shows dynamic scenes.

The ancients may have thought that the greater vitality taken from the hot season could be transferred to the cold, at least symbolically. I suggest seeing in the alternation of the Apollonian and the Dionysiac a more general application of the principle of the complementarity of opposites, of which so many examples have already been seen.

9. The Temple of Hera at Samothrace: the Structure of the Sanctuary and the Pediment; Victory and the Ship

How the cults of Samothrace, of which little is known, might be included in the zodiacal wheels long eluded me. The island is still difficult to get to, mainly because there are no fast boats between Alexandropolis and Kamarotissa, and I was unable to travel there until 1964 towards the time of the summer solstice. First let me define the island's position in the three zodiacal wheels of the Aegean.

1. In the Delian system, it is in Sagittarius, near the Cancer-Capricorn axis.
2. In the Delphic system, it is in Scorpio.
3. In the Sardis system, it is in Aquarius, not far from the ancient solstitial axis (fig. 105).

The group of cults particular to Samothrace must be put into relationship with the zodiacal wheels. The two Cabiri, in the same category as the Dioscuri, refer both to Mount Ida of Mysia and to the Gemini-Sagittarius axis of the Delian system. The myth of Harmonia and her marriage to Cadmus have to do with the Libra-Scorpio sector of the Delphic wheel, which is confirmed by the presence of the sphinx on certain coins from Samothrace. The myth of Dardanus describes the Leo-Aquarius axis of the Sardis system.

The astral nature of the cults of Samothrace is beyond any doubt. In speaking of the first degree of initiation, Diodorus declared that the initiates were

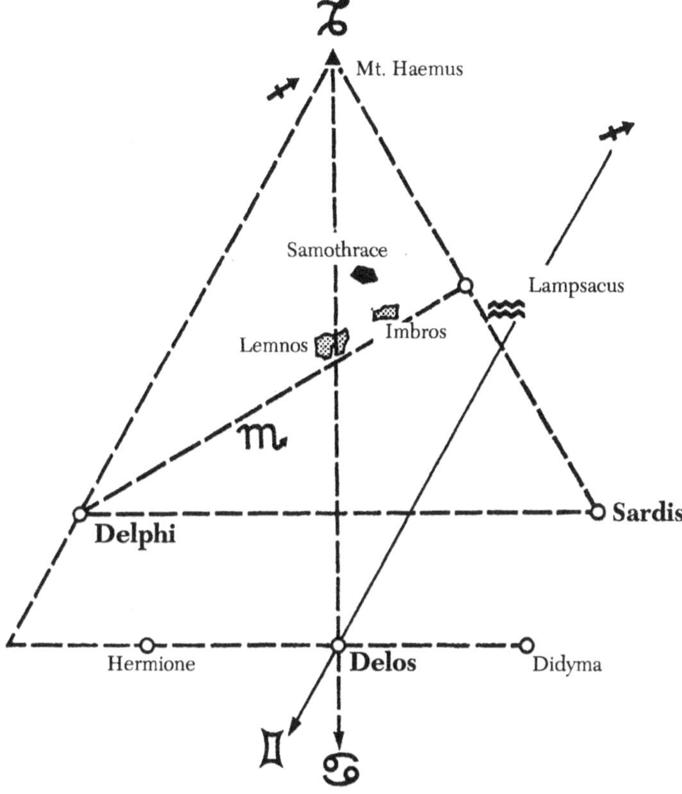

Figure 105. *Position of Samothrace in relation to the zodiacal wheels centered on Delphi, Delos, and Sardis.*

shown symbolic objects that "represented heaven and earth." Naturally, it was the Hera temple, the most sacred place of all, where certain privileged Mystae became Epoptae, that must have been most highly charged with symbolic meaning. A visit to the sanctuary of the great gods allowed me to reconstruct the probable zodiacal arrangement of the Hera temple which, such as it remains, is from the Hellenistic period, but was built according to a more ancient plan. Two details caught my attention: the presence of a marker cross on the Hellenistic wall, contemporaneous with the Heraion, and the position, which seemed strange at first glance, of the foot of the torch where candidates to initiation were questioned (the number of lamps found during the course of excavations suggests that the ceremonies of Samothrace were nocturnal).

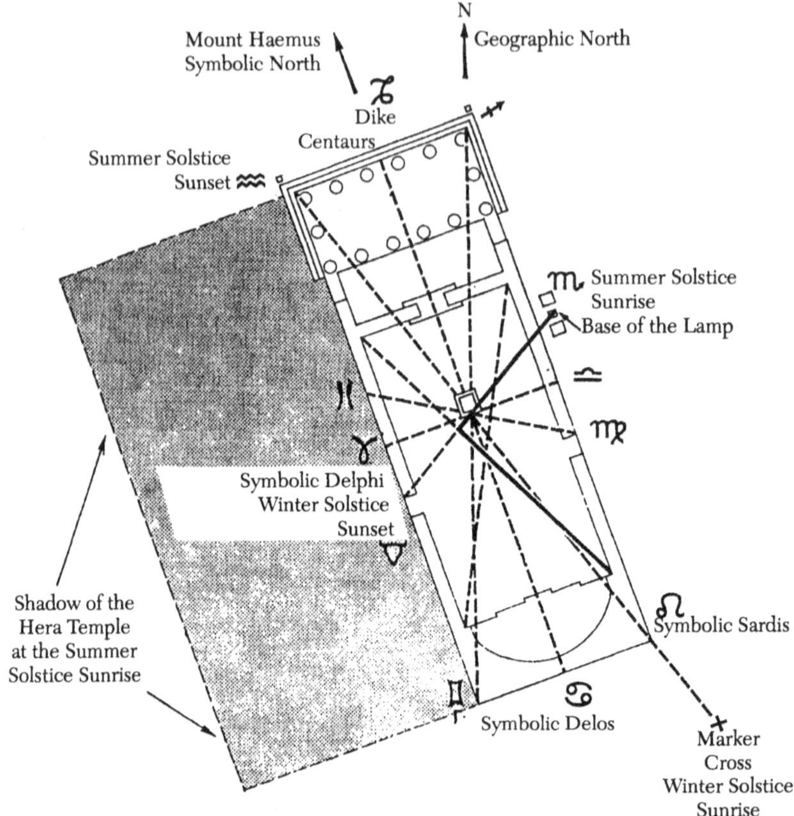

Figure 106. *The zodiacal structure of the Hera temple at Samothrace.*

By comparing the orientation of the sanctuary with the diagram of the island's position, I was able to rediscover the zodiacal structure of the Heraion (fig. 106):

1. The axis of the temple, a symbolic polar direction, corresponded to a Cancer-Capricorn direction and was directed towards Mount Haemus.
2. The marker cross, appearing in relief on the wall of the southern enclosure, corresponded to the diagonal of the temple, both diagonals crossing at the altar. This direction indicated the Leo-Aquarius axis of the Sardis system and the summer sunset.
3. From the diagonal in the ancient part of the sanctuary, a right angle struck through the altar, center of the sanctuary, determined the

position of the base of the lamp. It thus symbolized the summer sunrise. The feasts and rites of initiation must therefore have taken place around that time. I was able to verify that towards that date, at sunrise, the columns of the anastylose cast a single shadow from the structure of the building.

The axis of the temple and its perpendicular struck from the altar determined four points. The perpendiculars to the diagonals defined four others, and with the four angles, I could then situate the twelve signs of the zodiac: three before, six around the altar, and three behind the Hera temple. In this zodiacal layout, the torch was associated with Scorpio, the sign towards which Samothrace is located in relation to Delphi, and with the autumn equinox.

The Pediment. In the Museum of Samothrace I had seen the work of Phyllis Williams Lehmann on the pediment of the temple of Hera.[32] I took a good look at this book; it was an interesting opportunity to see whether the reconstruction suggested by Lehmann supported my theories.

This pediment is rather different from those seen until now. These are late sculptures, probably from the middle of the second century B.C., the front of the Heraion not having been completed until then. Its single pediment tended to condense the meaning of the temple as a whole, while in the tympanal designs seen earlier, the meaning was shared by both pediments. All this suggests that the island had been one of the last refuges of an ancient tradition.

While generally agreeing with Lehmann's fine reconstruction, which is based on an examination of all the known fragments of sculpture (among which, providentially, are many right feet!) and on a study of the literature on Samothrace, I would like to add a few comments.

Let me quote the lines in which Lehmann states her conclusions:

> Its primary theme was the Nurturing of Aëtion. The infant destined to establish the Samothracian mysteries appeared in the center of the pediment in the arms of a mighty striding figure, probably Dike, who bore him to the Horai, attended by the Charites or Moirai, to be reared. His elder brother and sister reclined in the corners of the gable: Dardanos, who later carried the rites to Troy, and Harmonia, whose marriage to Kadmos was celebrated in the annual festival. Between these prime characters in the Samothracian legend lay two pairs of reclining figures: to the right, Saon, eponymous hero of the islanders, and Mount Saoce, personification of the grandiose mountain [Phengari or Mount Juna] that dominated their land; to the left, two counterparts, possibly Okeanos and Tethys, life-giving forces associated with islands. All four turned to regard this auspicious moment in Aëtion's life, as did their neighbors, Harmonia and Dardanos.[33]

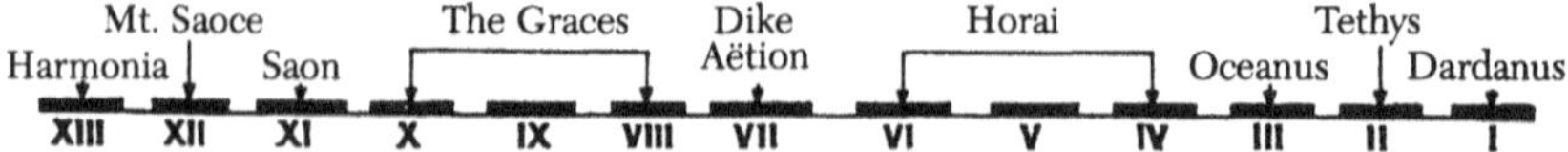

Figure 107. *Diagram of the pediment of the Hera temple of Samothrace.*

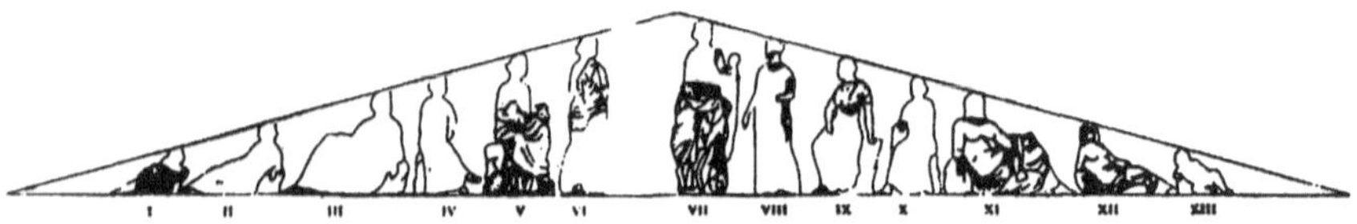

Figure 108. *Reconstitution of the pediment of the Heraion at Samothrace by Phyllis Williams Lehmann, drawing by Philip Oliver Smith.*

The arrangement corresponding to this description, using Lehmann's numbering, and with the same orientation as in the preceding figure, is illustrated in figure 107.

Figure 108 shows Lehmann's reconstitution of the Hieron of Samothrace but with the orientation in frontal view (north). In order to find the names of the characters represented, fig. 107 must be read from right to left.

The absence of the Cabiri-Dioscuri on this pediment may at first seem surprising, but it becomes understandable when one remembers that they had their own sanctuary and that there were statues of them in the Anaktoron, seat of the Lesser Mysteries.

The Central Dike. Lehmann believes that the central character of the pediment was Dike cradling the young Aëtion in her arms, one of the children of Zeus and Electra and the future founder of the mysteries of Samothrace.

This agrees admirably with the symbolic polar direction of the temple axis. To be convinced of this, it is enough to read Jane Ellen Harrison's pages on Dike in *Themis*,[34] especially on the association of Dike with the celestial wheel. Dike, we read in this work, is the way and the order of the universe, the Tao. Let me quote a few relevant lines:

> Dike is the way of life of each natural thing, each plant, each animal, each man. It is also the way, the usage, the regular course of that great animal the Universe, the way that is made manifest in the Seasons, in the life and death of vegetation; and when it comes to be seen that these depend on the heavenly bodies, Dike is manifest in the changes of the rising and setting of constellations, in the waxing and waning of the Moon and in the daily and yearly courses of the Sun.

In at least one text, Euripides' *Medea* (verse 410), Dike represents the circular course of the entire cosmos. In the general reversal of all things:

> Upward go the streams of the living rivers,
> Dike and all things are turned about.[35]

If after reading this quotation, one returns to the prominent position of Dike on the pediment of the Hera temple at Samothrace, several important details are apparent. Dike is associated with Capricorn, the pole, and the winter solstice. She is the wheel; she is the way; she shows the path that leads to the gateway of the gods, which is Mount Haemus here, homeland of Boreas. The initiate was symbolized by the child Aëtion carried in her arms.

Dike is also the season of winter in its infernal but not necessarily maleficent aspect, as discussed by J. E. Harrison, which is associated with her role as guardian of the threshold and ruler of the universal order. On this point, I would like to add a little to what Lehmann says. She believes that only three seasons were symbolized on the pediment of the Heraion, and it is possible that during an ancient period a three-season calendar was employed. But during the late period when this pediment was carved, Greek calendars had four seasons. The marker cross that allowed me to discover the zodiacal structure of the sanctuary in fact shows that the year was divided into four.

The law of alternation that one observes in the distribution of the various figures must have governed that of the seasons. Statue V, with its great cluster of grapes, undeniably symbolizes autumn. I suggest the following distribution:

IV: Spring (Thallo)
V: Autumn (Carpo)
VI: Summer (Auxo)
VII: Dike (who is also winter).

The transition from a calendar of three seasons to a calendar of four would have been made in this way.

Lehmann very convincingly suggests that the two children appearing on the two angles of the temple pediments are the other children of Zeus and Electra associated with the mysteries of Samothrace, to the west Harmonia and to the east Dardanus. Harmonia is on the side of Thebes; Dardanus, representing the Troad, is on the east side. Exoteric geographical considerations therefore dictated the choice of position for these statues.

The Harmonia-Dardanus or Libra-Aquarius relationship is a trine, the supremely harmonious astrological aspect. The law of complementarity is seen to occur here if one considers that Harmonia occupies the place that belongs to Aquarius in the layout. This inversion was perhaps meant to conceal one of the secrets of initiation, since the pediment could be viewed by anyone.

Remaining to be discussed are the centaurs[36] on the caissoned ceiling of the *pronaos*. It is easy to see how they were related to the zodiacal scheme of the temple, since they stand for the sign of Sagittarius. They also represent the true polar direction of the Heraion and the position of Samothrace in the Delian system.

On view in the Museum of Samothrace is a sculpture on loan from the Louvre, whose exact origin is unfortunately unknown. It represents griffins attacking a stag, which describes the northeast quarter in relation to Delos and the Sagittarius sector in particular.

Mystery in Broad Daylight or Victory and the Ship. No one thinks it surprising to see acroteria in the shape of victories pouring libations from every angle of the Hera temple[37] or a victory standing on the prow of a ship on some of the coins of Samothrace. No one knows what historical victory the famous monument commemorated; several have been suggested, none of which are convincing.

I think that in order to find the meaning of the Winged Victory of Samothrace, one must begin with the ship on which it stands. It describes the constellation of the Ship (Argo), which succeeded the Great Dog as a marker of the solstitial axis. On a star map, one can easily see that the star α in the constellation of Argo is very close to the Cancer-Capricorn axis. This direction is identical to the Mount Haemus–Delos line in the Delian system which includes Samothrace.

If one now looks at the general plan of the sanctuary[38] (fig. 109), one observes that the prow of the ship and the Winged Victory, installed in a fountain, had been deliberately placed on the bias in such a way that the Victory was looking northwards, a fresh reference to the gateway of the gods and a purely spiritual victory. Orientated in this way, the impetus and the glance of the statue ended exactly at the northeast angle of the anaktoron, the most sacred angle of the building, where initiation was given.

In the concerted unity of a great sanctuary of antiquity, anything hazardous or fortuitous seems to have been excluded. Now, all the buildings essential to the cult, the anaktoron, the temenos, the Heraion and its dependencies, are almost entirely situated to the east of the symbolic south-north line that goes from the Winged Victory to the northeast corner of the anaktoron. All these buildings are oriented to the northwest, that is, towards Mount Haemus, so that the whole arrangement is a reduced image of the position of Samothrace in the Delian system (fig. 105).

The temple of the Cabiri, as one would expect, was placed to the west of this line, since the Cabiri were equated with Gemini. The position of the area excavated by Conze, in relation to the whole sanctuary, rather suggests that that area may have been sacred to the cult of Cadmus and Harmonia. The position of the statue of Harmonia on the western part of the pediment of the Hera temple would seem to support this point of view.

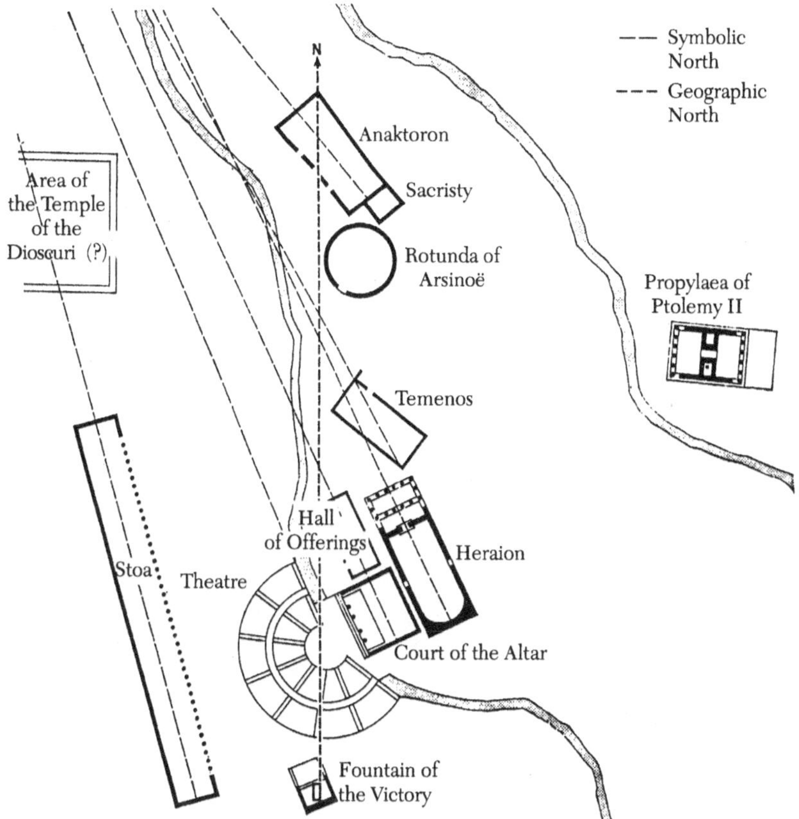

Figure 109. *The general plan of the sanctuary and the south-north axis (compare with fig. 105).*

To sum up my study of the Heraion and the sanctuary of Samothrace, let me say that everything seems to underscore the leading roles played by both the real and the symbolic polar axes.

It may be concluded that this was a cult that attributed prime importance to astrolatry and the solstices. The orientation of the Hera temple, the central Dike on its pediment, and the orientation of the famous Winged Victory are so many references to the pole and to the Cancer-Capricorn solstitial axis.

And baptism by the blood of a ram or a bull, of which there seems to be evidence at Samothrace, can only have meaning in relation to the symbols of the zodiac and a ritual of the New Year.

Chapter 18

Greek Temples of Asia Minor The Decor of the Temple of Assos in the Troad

Several developments could be introduced here, but I shall restrict myself to comparing the orientations of the sanctuary at Didyma and the temple at Bassae, and to proposing a detailed reconstitution of the sculpted decor of the temple of Athena of Assos in the Troad, because it provides the opportunity for an outstanding practical application of the theories explained in the sequence of these chapters.

1. Didyma and Bassae

It is enough to compare the two zodiacal wheels centered on Delphi and Sardis to see that the sanctuaries of Apollo at Bassae and Didyma occupy homologous points, since they both correspond to the sign of Gemini. I have explained (p. 3) how the "abnormal" orientation of the temple at Bassae was, for one thing, the starting point for my research. The very name Didyma means "twins," and the deities venerated in the sanctuary of the Branchidae were the divine twins Apollo and Artemis.

If the plans of orientation of the two sanctuaries are compared (Didyma was rebuilt during the Hellenistic period around the more ancient temple and is gigantic), the analogy in their implantation is certain.

A diagonal of the temple at Bassae (fig. 110) is orientated exactly south-north, and as I have measured myself on site, the entrance and therefore the axis of the temple are exactly orientated to Delphi.

At Didyma (fig. 111) the entrance is to the northeast, and a diagonal of the temple corresponds to the direction of Sardis. There is a difference of about 2 degrees 30 minutes between the orientations of the archaic sanctuary and the Hellenistic temple, which suggests a probable bearing taken on the heliacal rising of the constellation of Gemini. The enormous Gorgons' heads, which were part of the decor of the frieze, refer to the Pisces-Virgo axis, perpendicular to the Gemini-Sagittarius line.

In both cases, the orientation to the north refers to the omphaloi.

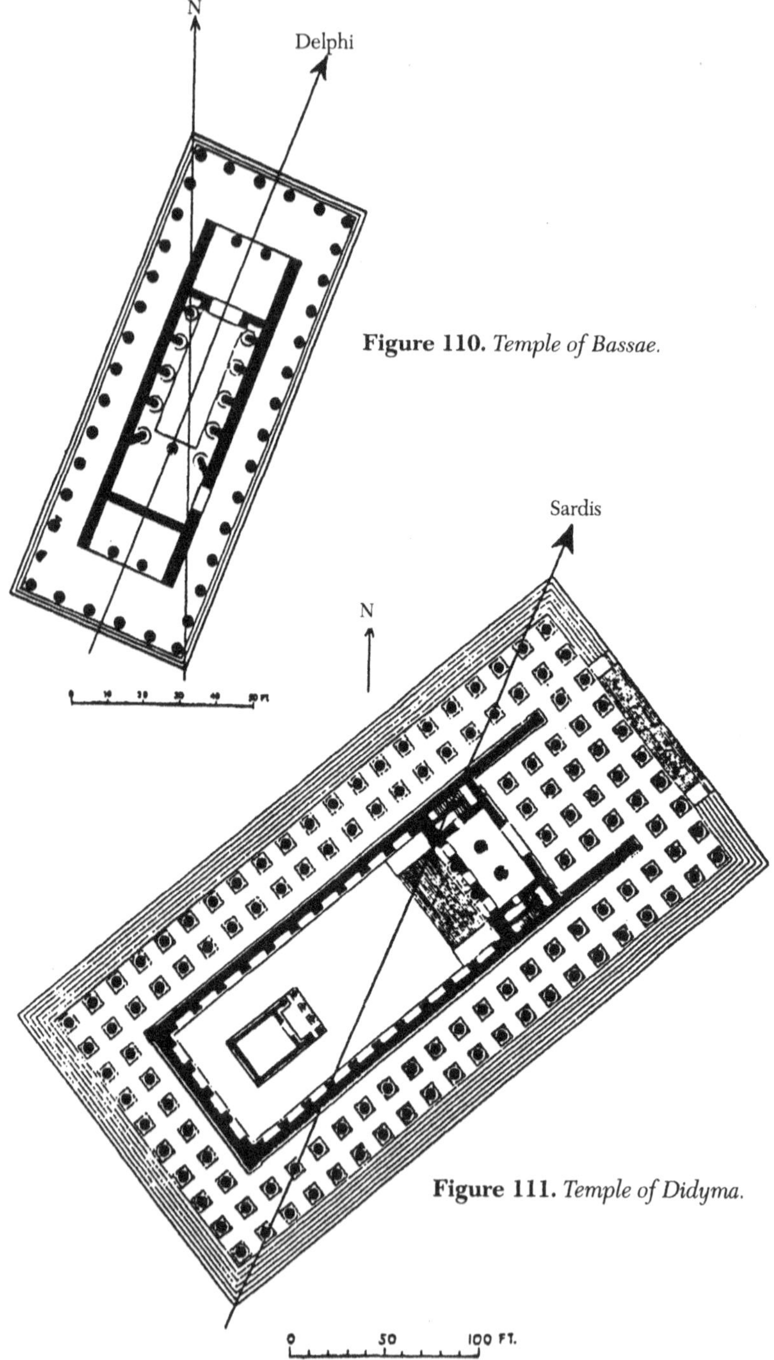

Figure 110. *Temple of Bassae.*

Figure 111. *Temple of Didyma.*

2. The Decor of the Temple of Assos in the Troad[1]

The temple of Athena of Assos in the Troad, one of the two Doric[2] sanctuaries of Asia Minor, contrary to what has sometimes been claimed, is genuinely archaic, probably from the sixth century B.C., and not an "archaizing" style temple. Its decorative sculptures, now divided among the Louvre and the Museums of Istanbul and Boston, are of great interest and support the practical value of my theories, as will be shown. Among them are:

1. The main decor of the two façades
2. The symbols of the equinoxes (confronted bulls and sphinxes)
3. Metopes describing the zodiac
4. Groups of animals that, in my opinion, describe the four seasons, which must have been located in the four angles of the building.

It is extremely probable that the decor of the east façade described the beginning of the year (spring and summer) and that of the west the autumn and winter. The general arrangement thus suggested is analogous to the one already established for the temple of Delphi (fig. 101).

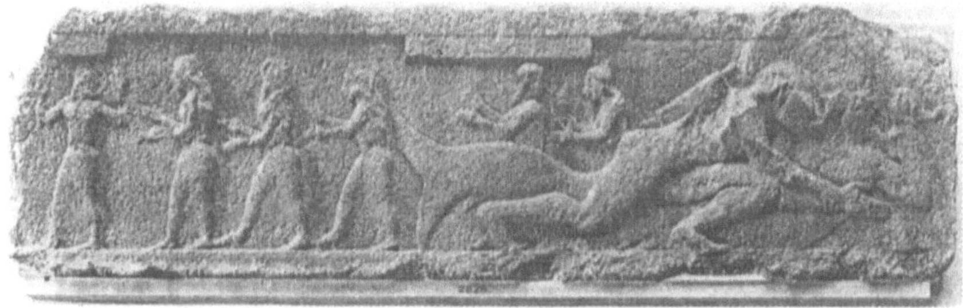

Figure 112. *Heracles and Triton. Mysian women celebrating the hero's victory: sign of Pisces.*

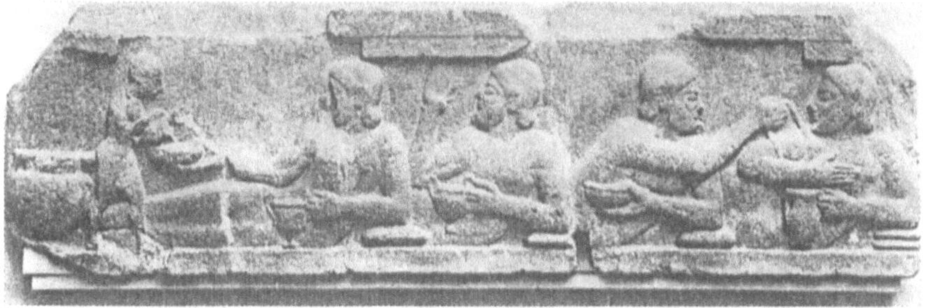

Figure 113. *Heracles giving Eurystheus the belt of Hippolyte, Queen of the Amazons, during a banquet; sign of Virgo and Virgo-Leo sector.*

1. Symbolic Subjects on the Façades

It appears that the temple of Assos was considered to be on the Pisces-Virgo line of the Sardis system. The two main scenes chosen to illustrate the pediments were taken from the legend of Heracles. On the west pediment must have appeared the struggle of Heracles with the marine monster that guarded Hesione. To the left are Mysian or Trojan women applauding the hero's victory (fig. 112).

The east pediment must have shown the scene in which J. T. Clarke suggests seeing the feast during the course of which Hercules gives Eurystheus the belt of Hippolyte, Queen of the Amazons (see table p. 100). The belt would be the object that is clearly visible between the two guests to the right (fig. 113).

So, with these two complementary scenes, this would be a representation of the Virgo-Pisces axis. Since the temple wasn't orientated to Sardis, it probably was orientated in relation to the heliacal rising of Spica (fig. 132).

It was therefore in all likelihood a temple of Athena. The direction of Sardis is given by the line joining the northwest angle to the middle of the east façade.

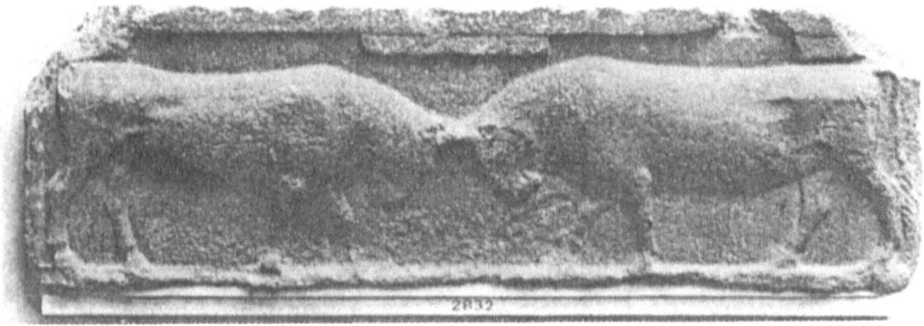

Figure 114. *Spring equinox.*

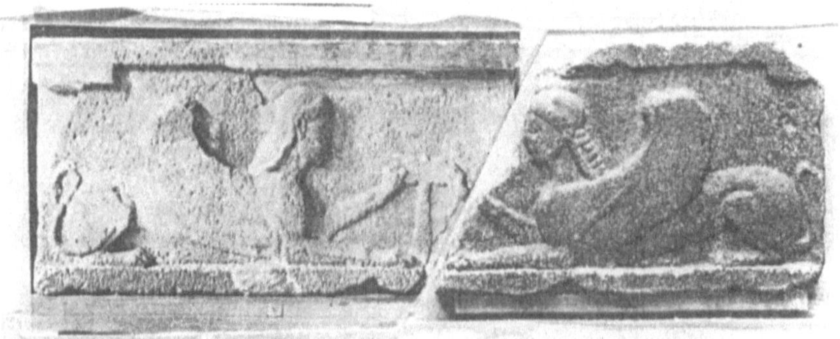

Figure 115. *Autumn equinox.*

2. Symbols of the Equinoxes

Two groups of confronted bulls (fig. 114) and two groups of sphinxes in the "hieratic position" have been found, some intact, others in fragments (fig. 115). The bulls describe the spring equinox and the sphinxes the autumn. It seems to me that the most probable position for the bulls is at either end of the west pediment and, for the sphinxes, on the ends of the east pediment, which agrees with the usual placement of equinoctial symbols. Since there are two groups of each type, the central positioning proposed by Bacon and Clarke is completely out of the question, although attractive from the aesthetic point of view. Each group of two bulls or two sphinxes was 2.5 meters long. As a result, the groups of fighting animals are automatically excluded from the ornamental friezes of the façades.

F. Sartriaux (op. cit., pp. 112–13) suggested placing the sphinxes on either side of one façade, but oddly enough, he did not use the confronted bulls for the other. Itier (op. cit., pp. 118–19) is alone in distributing the bulls and the sphinxes as I have. But since he did not have a principle for his classification, he grouped the scenes of Heracles with Triton and the banquet with the bulls, and he put three blocks of centaurs on the other façade with the sphinxes. In the latter case, I wonder whether he might not have glimpsed the zodiacal meaning of the design.

This decor has remarkable affinities with those of Corcyra (Corfu) and the Hecatompedom of Athens, which have been studied on pages 198 to 203 (it is also helpful to look at figs. 96, 97, 98, and 99).

THE CENTAURS. It seemed that there was a special problem with regard to the sculpted blocks of centaurs and that they should be distributed on both façades, which is supported by the fact that two different types of centaurs are figured. The symbolic structure of the temple in fact requires the representation of the sign of Sagittarius on the northwest façade. The two blocks (figs. 116 and 117) describing the extermination of the centaurs of Mount Pholoe by Heracles must have appeared there (Pholoe is a plateau situated between Elis and Arcadia). The conflict was brought on by drunkenness and ultimately caused the death of the centaurs. By nature they were semihuman, as is shown by at least three of them (fig. 116) having a pair of human legs. For the three others (fig. 117), it is impossible to say, because the lower part of the sculpture is missing.

In Anatolia, the centaurs sojourned in the region of Olympus of Bithynia (see p. 45 and map 11, fig. 34), which is situated to the northeast of Assos. I think this is why it was deemed necessary to place other centaurs (figs. 118 and 119) of a more primitive nature on the southeast façade, as is shown by the fact that they have four horse's legs.

Let me add that solutions must be researched that would take into account a change of orientation of the characters situated in the middle of the façade. This is true of the one I am proposing.

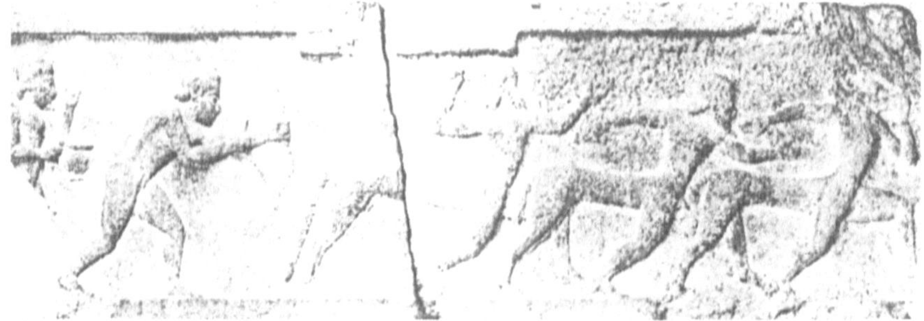

Figure 116. *Heracles and the centaurs of Mount Pholoe.*

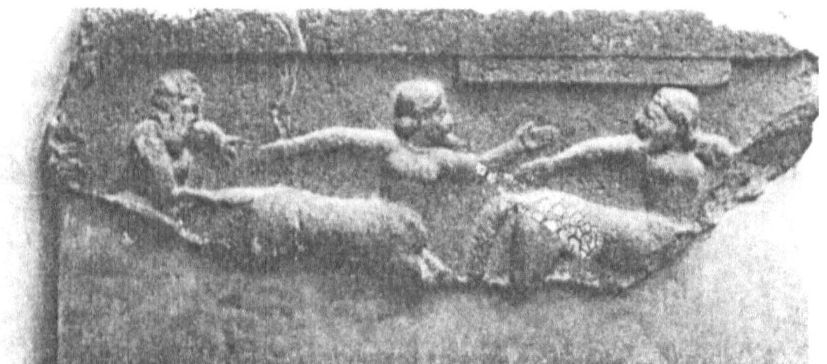

Figure 117. *Centaurs.*

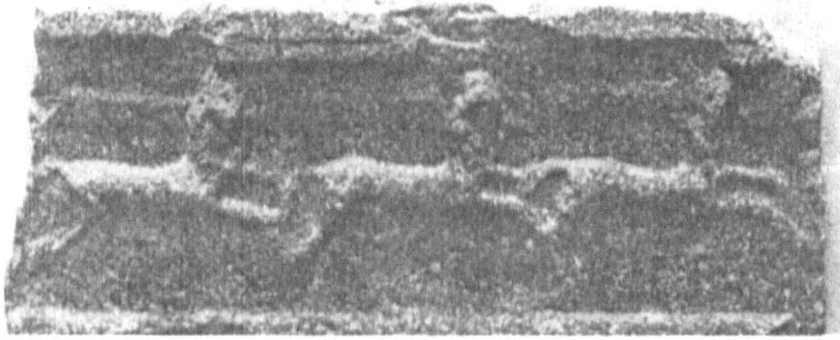

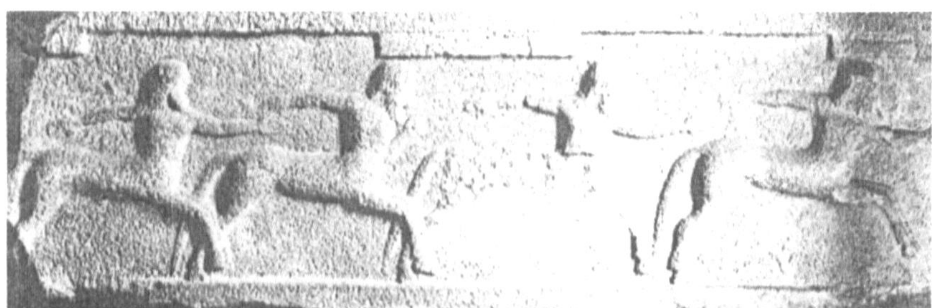

Figure 118 & 119. *Centaurs of Bithynia.*

3. The Signs of the Zodiac on the Metopes

There were probably seven signs of the zodiac on the east façade and five on the west, each sign being, insofar as possible, symbolized by an animal alternating with human characters. But this was not an absolute rule, since for Sagittarius, for example, there was a second centaur of which a fragment is extant. A comparison with the scenes on the shield armlets studied in chapter 16 (especially figs. 77 and 78) suggests the following identifications:

Two running men: the Dioscuri.
Fighting men: one visibly stabbing the other, these are probably Orestes and Aegisthus.
A bearded man pursuing an *ephebus*: Heracles and Hylas.
On the east façade must have appeared Taurus, Gemini, Cancer, Leo, Virgo. Extant are:
Europa on the bull: Taurus (fig. 120).
The Dioscuri running: Gemini (fig. 121).
Confronted sphinxes: Libra (fig. 122).
Orestes and Aegisthus: Libra (fig. 123).

The west façade must have symbolized Scorpio, Sagittarius, Capricorn, Aquarius, and Pisces. Of these remain:

Galloping centaur: Sagittarius (two identical metopes) (fig. 124).
Heracles and Hylas: Capricorn (fig. 125).
Grazing boar: Pisces (fig. 126).

Twelve metopes out of a total of twenty are missing. The metope depicting Heracles and Hylas must have been in an almost central position on the west façade. One quarter of the zodiac, from Sagittarius to Aquarius, was thus described by means of the myth of Heracles and, in addition, the Leo-Virgo sector.

A griffin's foot has been found that was no doubt part of an antefix. This mythical animal designates the direction of north and is a sort of guardian of the cosmic order. Many coins from Assos bear an image of Athena on the front and a griffin on the back, which describes the northwest quarter of Anatolia (more specifically, the sector between the Pisces-Virgo line and the Sardis-Olympus of Bithynia or Sardis-Cios line). Because of the position of Olympus, the Sagittarius direction in the Sardis system takes on a polar significance: this sheds some light on why so many centaurs were present in the decor of Assos.

By comparing the metopes of the temple of Assos with those of the Sicyonian treasury at Delphi (see *Delphes, Délos et Cumes*, pp. 88 to 94) and by referring to the table on p. 100, it is possible to suggest the subjects of the twelve missing metopes. They probably were, in the order of the signs of the zodiac:

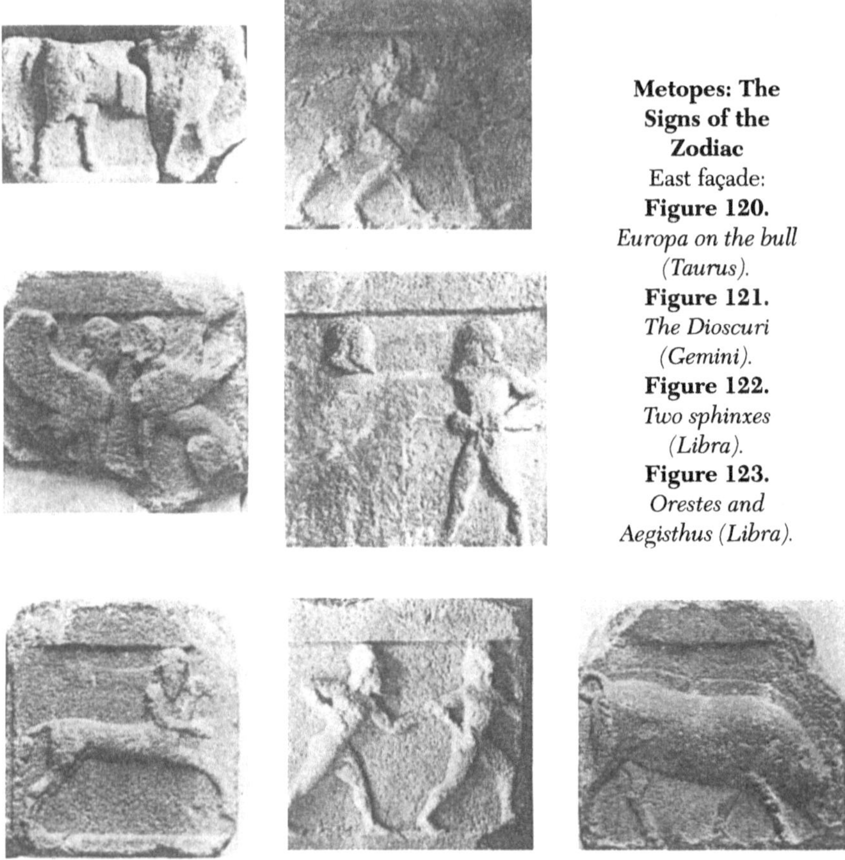

Metopes: The Signs of the Zodiac
East façade:
Figure 120. *Europa on the bull (Taurus).*
Figure 121. *The Dioscuri (Gemini).*
Figure 122. *Two sphinxes (Libra).*
Figure 123. *Orestes and Aegisthus (Libra).*

West façade:
Figure 124. *Centaur (Sagittarius).*
Figure 125. *Heracles and Hylas (Capricorn).*
Figure 126. *Grazing boar (Pisces).*

On the east pediment:

Aries: Phrixus on the Ram
Gemini: Ida and Lynceus
Cancer: the ship Argo
Cancer: Heracles and the Lernaean Lion
Leo: Heracles and the Nemean Lion (or Bellerophon and the chimaera)
Virgo: Perseus slaying the Gorgon

On the west pediment:

Scorpio: the child Heracles strangling the serpents
Scorpio: Ophion
Capricorn: marine goat (or Ceryneian hind)
Aquarius: Stymphalian birds
Aquarius: suckling cow
Aquarius/Pisces: Zeus and Ganymede.

Some of these metopes may subsist in fragments, while others were perhaps incorporated into various buildings at Assos.[3]

In examining the proposed reconstruction of the façades as a unit (fig. 127), the asymmetrical character of the two friezes, similar on both façades, is noticeable. In each case, there are two groups of centaurs orientated to the right, then a group turned to the left. (Even if the combat of Heracles and Triton adopts an orientation to the right, the women are facing left). The whole is a good expression of the Virgo-Pisces opposition, inscribed in the distribution of the zodiacal signs that I am reconstituting.

4. Groups of Animals Describing the Seasons

It would seem that I am the first to suggest that the groups of fighting animals representing the seasons must have appeared at the returns of the long sides in the angles. In this respect a comparison with the pediments of the temple of the Alcmaeonidae at Delphi is conclusive (even if, at Delphi, the groups are at the ends of the pediments). The temple orientation must also be taken into account. I propose the following placement for these groups:

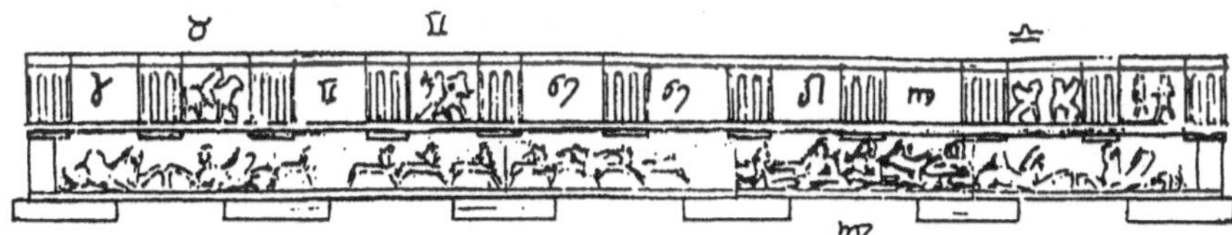

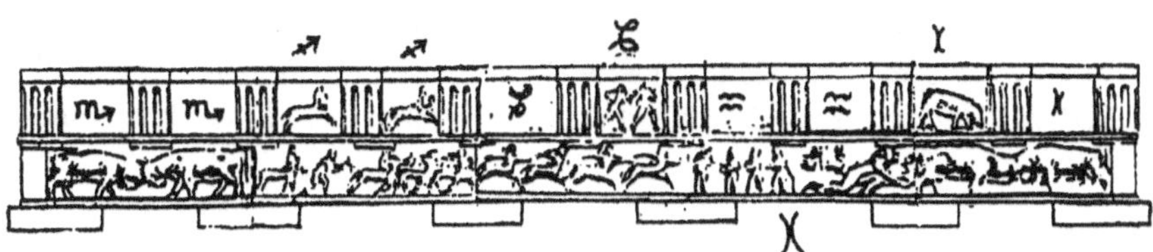

Figure 127. *Temple of Assos: reconstruction of the decor of the façades. Above, east façade; below, west façade. (Twelve metopes are missing.)*

The Seasons, in trigonometric order:

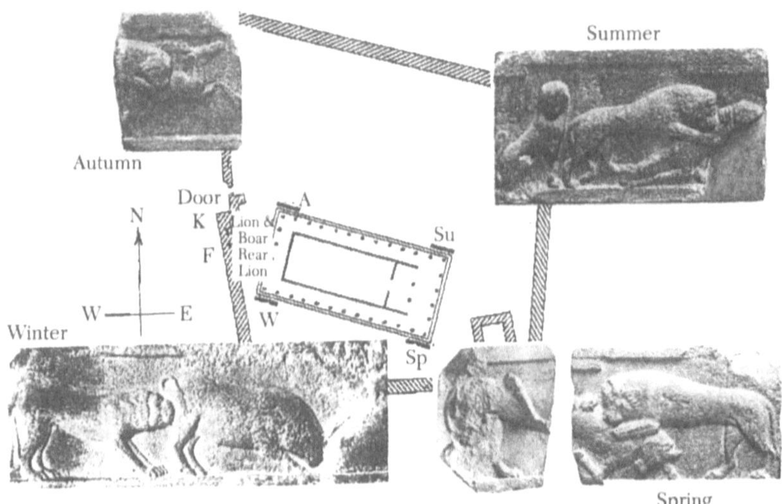

Figure 128. *Lion devouring a bull and hindquarters of another lion: spring*
Figure 129. *Lion devouring a deer and young lion: summer*
Figure 130. *Lion devouring a gazelle: autumn*
Figure 131. *Lion and boar: winter*

Figure 128: Southeast corner: lions devouring a bull: spring. (I agree with Clarke that the hindquarters of the lion that has been found separately belonged to a second beast that was part of this group.)
Figure 129: Northeast corner: lions and deer: summer.
Figure 130: Northwest corner: lion and gazelle: autumn.
Figure 131: Southwest angle: lion and boar: winter.

Let me point out that all four groups include lions (two for the spring and summer), which is a way of emphasizing the Leo-Virgo region.

These groups, which must have been 2.1 meters long each, do not fit the friezes of the façades anywhere. They were thus probably placed on the returns, in other words, on either side of the two long sides of the temple at the level of the friezes. Figure 132 is a drawing of my reconstituted plan of the whole temple.

3. Conclusions

The study in which I have just been engaged allows me to state a few conclusions.

a) "Abnormal" temple orientations are explained by the fact that the temple is turned towards another sanctuary in the same system or else towards the omphalos of the system to which it belongs. This method of construction was probably very ancient and was employed until the invention of tympanal decoration. Some orientations of this type were conserved by religious traditionalism through the ages (Bassae, Calydon, Olympia, Thermus).

b) At a later period the east-west orientation was almost always employed, but the zodiacal coordinates of the temple were clearly indicated by its pediments.

c) In the tympanal decor of temples are the Hesiodic guardians of the signs and the labors of Heracles, as well as the symbols for the seasons and the four quarters. At a later period appear myths of astral significance and scenes of combat, which consistently have the same zodiacal meaning:

Centauromachies stand for the Sagittarius-Gemini axis.
Gigantomachies designate the Cancer-Capricorn axis.
Amazonomachies represent the Pisces-Virgo axis.
Scenes of the Trojan Wars, by analogical reference to the sign of Aquarius in the Sardis system, symbolize the Leo-Aquarius axis.[4]

The series of symbols already seen in the design of vases reappears in the decoration of pediments, and in the same chronological order. These also comprise the inventory of themes employed in the design of friezes.[5]

The pediments of the seventh and sixth centuries prominently feature monsters and guardian animals of the seasons by placing them in central position.[6] In

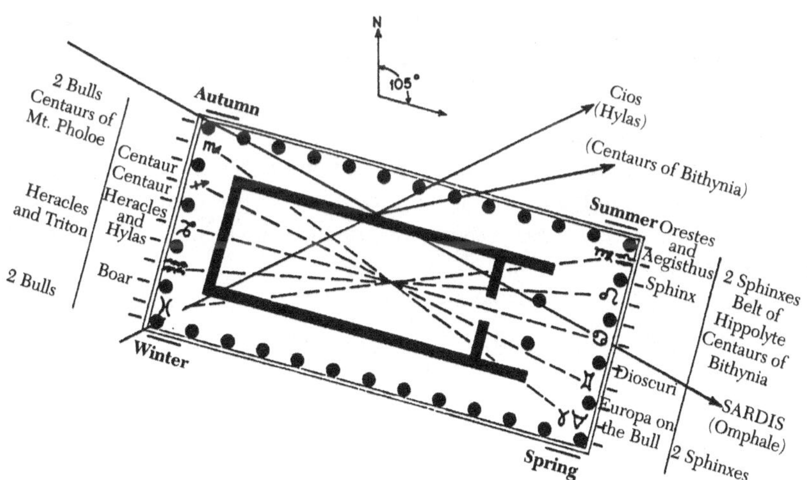

Figure 132. *Temple of Athena at Assos; diagram of the reconstruction of the sculpted decor.*

later centuries, while retaining their meaning as spatial "determinators," they lose their importance in the decoration and are replaced by scenes from legends or heroic deeds.

All these relationships, all these deductions have, I hope, communicated a vision of the poetic rigor and the suppleness of concept and interpretation that the ancient Greeks drew from the astrological meaning of their myths. These must have been known to a fairly wide group of the élite. I think it probable that the artisan foremen and the great sculptors were aware of the true and profound meaning of the images that their hands and tools brought forth from the stone. There must have been genuine brotherhoods of initiated sculptors who were capable of giving temple decoration the value of both a sign and a magical imposition.

The temple as a whole, together with its decoration, was conceived as an organic unit, in which the plan, the arrangement of the columns, the metopes, and the pediments responded to and mutually complemented one another. In this the Greeks were following the example of their predecessors, particularly the Sumerians and the Egyptians.

To illustrate this by a single example, it is obvious that the metopes of the labors of Hercules in the sanctuary of Zeus at Olympia were related to the Heraclean system centered on Phlius, as did the pediment on the façade. What I have here indicated should open the way to developing a science of interpreting the decoration of antique temples and of rediscovering in every case the exact position of any detail of their sculpted decor, especially the metopes.

By now it should be plain that all the temples that were part of a zodiacal wheel during a given period were conceived as a harmonious whole, arranged in the image of the cosmos. And a unifying concept, in which zodiacal symbolism also played a role, must have governed the selection of sites for the various buildings in the great sanctuaries at Delphi, Olympia, or Samothrace.

4. Symbolic Formulas

As I said earlier with regard to coins, vases, and other objects, it is possible to set up an equation or symbolic formula for a region, a city, or a sanctuary, using the conventional signs of astrology. The more complete the formula, the clearer the symbolic equivalences will be.

To describe a sanctuary, one may write:

1. The initial of the considered omphalos:

D	Delphi
Δ	Delos
S	Sardis
Φ	Phlius
A	Athens

2. The zodiacal signs or zodiacal axes considered.
3. The god venerated in the sanctuary.

Here are a few examples:

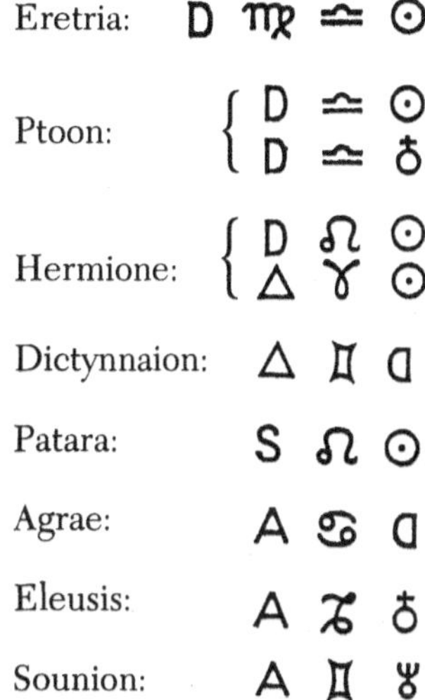

Even for relatively complex cases, the symbolic notation is simple:

Olympia: { D ♊ ♑ / Φ ▽ ♃

Samothrace: { D ♏ ♁ / Δ ♑ ☉ / S ♒ ☉

Chapter 19

The Delphic Oracle and Colonization
Animal Guides
The Trojan Horse

> Most markedly conspicuous of all, again, will be localities which are the homes of some supernatural influence, or the haunts of spirits who give a gracious or ungracious reception to successive bodies of settlers. A sagacious legislator will give these facts all consideration a man can, and do his best to adapt his legislation to them.
>
> —Plato, *Laws*, 747

1. The Oracle and Significant Alignments

The zodiacal wheels, the omphaloi and some of the alignments that have been determined, especially the Heraclean directions, played an important role whenever the Delphic oracle advised the people of a city to venture forth and establish colonies in Asia, Africa, Italy, or Sicily.

The material in Parke's work on the role of Delphi in Greek colonization will serve as the starting point for this chapter. The exact date of the composition of each oracle is not very important, and I could even say that, from my point of view, an oracle would be as significant if it had been composed some time after a colony had been founded!

a) Manto, Thebes, and Claros. The founding of Claros and the oracle of Clarian Apollo were traditionally associated with a colony led by Manto, daughter of Tiresias. She had been captured during the siege of Thebes by the Epigoni, who consecrated her to Delphic Apollo along with other prisoners, keeping their vow to offer the god the best of their spoils. The god gave Manto to Rhacius and ordered him to lead a colony to Asia Minor.[1] The system of zodiacal wheels will here again act as a key to decoding, revealing analogies and parallels.

The position of Claros in relation to Delos matches that of Thebes in relation to Delphi, at the end of the sign of Libra and the beginning of Scorpio, with some ambiguity between the signs in both cases.

b) Magnesia of Greece and Magnesia of Maeander. After analyzing all the oracles concerning the founding of Magnesia of Maeander, Parke concludes: "The Delphians had originally received the Magnesians as a tithe from North Greece, and had sent them away as settlers abroad with this obligation of hospitality [towards them]."[2] The Magnesia of Greece–Magnesia of Maeander line is parallel to the Delphi-Delos line (map 2). Magnesia of Thessaly is located in Sagittarius, and Maeander is in the opposite sign in the Sardis system, on the Gemini-Sagittarius axis. This is another example of the complementarity or equivalence of opposing signs. Both these signs are associated with the symbol of the horse (see p. 14).

c) An Astrological Oracle: The Founding of Aegae (Edessa). The foundation oracles of the city of Aegae are considered to rest on an etymological pun:

> Be sure, divine Caranus, to keep my words in mind. Leave Argos and Hellas of the beautiful women and go to the sources of the Haliacmon. There, where first you see goats grazing, it is your destiny to remain, very envied, you and all your family.[3]

Another oracle gives more details:

> For the pious sons of Temenos there is royal power on a rich, abundant earth. Zeus who bears the aegis grants this. But go quickly to the land of Bottia of the many herds. There, where you see goats, white as snow, with shining horns, fast asleep on the soil of this land, make sacrifice to the favored gods and found the citadel of a city.[4]

A text of Diodorus of Sicily that tells a legend of the origins of Delphi, in which goats stand for the sign of Capricorn, has already been mentioned (see p. 20). I believe that the present oracle also has etymological meaning, but that the very etymology conceals an astrological significance associated with the system of alignments and locations.

The Argos-Aegae line passes through Delphi and is almost identical to the south-north Heraclean line, Lerna-Delphi-Trachis. Caranus comes from Argos in the sign of Cancer; Aegae is in Capricorn. The name of the heroic founder derives from Κἀρανύω, which mean "to bring something to its zenith," in this case the region of the winter solstice. From the very wording of the second oracle we know that Zeus's aegis represents Capricorn and the winter solstice. The coins of Edessa are quite naturally stamped with a goat[5] (map 9, fig. 13).

d) The Foundation Oracle of Thasos. This oracle reads: "Announce to the Parians, Telesicles, that I command you to found a prominent city in the island of Aeria (the Misty)."[6]

The Paros-Thasos line is parallel to the Argos-Aegae line (map 2) and has an identical symbolic meaning in the Delian system, reinforcing the Cancer-Capricorn solstitial axis. But because of the geographical positon of the two islands, the line does not intersect Delos.

e) Sami and Samos. "Ancaeus, I bid you found Samos in the place of Sami, an island in the sea. It is now called Phyllas."[7] It seems that, as a result of this oracle, Samos was thought for some time to correspond to Cephallenia and to the sign of Aries, which may perhaps be due to an error in the estimation of latitude. This would explain the presence of the ram on some of the island's coins (see p. 41).

f) Thera and Cyrene. Several Delphic oracles[8] told the inhabitants of Thera, the modern Santorini, to go forth and found a colony on the African coast. The people were apparently reluctant to do so, and the order was repeated with a surprising insistence. I wonder whether Delphi's intention might not have been to establish a colony that would extend the north-south axis south of Delphi, by analogy with Thera, situated just south of Delos, perhaps to rival Ammoneion, or else to complete the existing system.

While this was not exactly achieved, because of a probable error in the estimation of latitude, Cyrene is nevertheless on the extension of the Delos–Dictynnaion of Crete line.

Thera had represented Sagittarius in relation to Ammoneion see (p. 94). The fact of the Delphic oracle sending the people of Thera to found Cyrene against their wishes was a way of imposing the moral domination of Delphi on the African coast and meant that Ammoneion's role had come to an end. Also, Thera is in the sign of Leo in relation to Delphi, and Cyrene is in Aquarius in the Ammoneion system. Both cities are thus associated with Leo-Aquarius axes.

The oracles that have been analyzed seem to have emphasized the symbolic connection between areas ruled by the same or by opposing signs. Whenever this process of deciphering applies to a text of the Delphic oracle, chances are probably excellent that the text is authentic.

This does not mean, however, that all the other extant oracles of colonization are necessarily false, because other religious or political considerations may have come into play.

2. Animal Guides

In one of his works,[9] F. Vian has assembled a series of references on the role of animal guides in the foundation legends of Greek cities. The animals in these legends fall into two categories that exactly parallel the symbols on shields. Some of them designate the planetary deities: Apollo's crow, Zeus's eagle, Aphrodite's dove;[10] others relate to zodiacal symbolism. In a good many cases, relationships with the diagrams and hence with sacred geography can be established.

A) Zodiacal Symbolism

I. CAPRICORN AND THE GOAT. In the preceeding section, I quoted the foundation oracle of Aegae, where goats are the animal guides for a city that was to mark the direction of Capricorn in relation to Delphi. I also mentioned the role of goats in the selection of Delphi itself, according to Diodorus of Sicily.

The wolves devouring a sheep associated with the founding of Athamania, which was either a city to the northeast of Ambracia or a plain in Thessaly,[11] also represent Capricorn, the ancient sign of the Wolf. The more probable location is therefore Thessaly.

II. THE COW, THE BULL, THE HARE. The animals that symbolize Taurus are associated with cities in the Taurus sector or else in the opposing Scorpio-Libra region.

a) This is true of cities in Boeotia: the founding of Thebes by Cadmus, Mycalessus, Tanagra, and Plataea[12].

b) I have already mentioned that Illyria is in the equivalent zodiacal region in a system centered on Cumae (see p. 114). Hence the legends of the founding of Buthoe and the journey of Cadmus and Harmonia in a chariot drawn by heifers, a legend which may later have spread to Epirus. This journey would have made the connection between Boeotia and Illyria.

c) According to Pausanias, the founding of Boeae, a city whose very name means cattle, on the peninsula southeast of the Peloponnese, is associated with a hare sent by Artemis. This city is exactly on the 0 degree Taurus line in the Delian system[13] (map 2).

III. THE EAGLE. The eagle is associated with the founding of several cities: Seleucia, Laodicea, Antiochia, and Apamea.[14] These are all in the sign of the Eagle in the Ammoneion system or near the 0 degree Eagle axis (map 5).

These examples show that the identity of the animal guide is related to sacred geography. Many legends about the founding of ancient cities describe a foundation ritual associated with astral beliefs. Here is an interesting one: Seleucus Nicanor slays a boar that suddenly emerges from the reeds and draws the perimeter of Laodicea with its blood.[15] Since Laodicea is in the sign of the Eagle (Scorpio), the purpose of the boar sacrifice is to ward off forces hostile to the city's good fortune, a situation represented by the Eagle-Boar aspect of squaring.

B) Animal Guides and Planetary Lines. The symbolic animals associated with the gods appear in sites located on the planetary lines. This is especially true of sites and sanctuaries associated with the earth line and the solar line.

a) THE EARTH LINE. Earth monsters are associated with the foundation legends of Thebes (struggle of Cadmus and the dragon), Delphi (Apollo and the serpent Python), and various places in Boeotia.

b) THE SOLAR LINE. According to a legend transmitted by Libanius, Artemis demanded that the Miletus expedition be accompanied by a dog (a symbol of the dog-days).[16] Many coins of the city are stamped with a lion and the star Sirius.

Since Miletus is not related to the sign of Leo in any of the zodiacal wheels, I believe that this must be interpreted to mean that the city, whose very name indicates that it had ambitions of being a center, was very close to the Hermione-Delos-Didyma solar line.

3. The Trojan Horse

This is the place to ask why the Achaeans built a wooden horse in order to penetrate Troy rather than, for example, a bull or a lion, a castle or ship. The answer to this question is simple. In chapter 4 it was seen that the Troad was in Aquarius in the Sardis system. Coins of Scepsis and Lampsacus bore a winged horse or possibly a hippalectryon (map 11, figs. 36 and 37). According to Quintus of Smyrna[17] (*Posthomerica,* XII), the siege of Troy had been going on for ten years when Calchas, after observing the birds and the stars, counseled the use of trickery and the construction of the horse. Epeus then enters the scene (whose name means horse),[18] an expert carpenter and a pupil of Athena (ibid., 81–83).

The goddess, ruler of the Leo-Virgo region, opposed to the Aquarius-Pisces sector, appears to the carpenter in a dream and assures him of her support (ibid., 106–12). Pegasus was born from the neck of the Gorgon, so the winged horse belongs, to some degree, to the Virgin.

The better to deceive the Trojans, the Greeks retire to Tenedos and entrust Sinon to stay by the horse. Sinon is a heroic volunteer who, braving torture, was to courageously lie and convince the Trojans that the wooden horse was an offering to Athena, meant to appease the goddess who had been angered by the removal of the Palladium.

The character of Sinon reappears in Book II of *The Aeneid.* Virgil eliminates the torture that was inflicted by the Trojans, who in his predecessor's story had cut off Sinon's nose and ears. Sinon reports a supposed speech of Calchas and, in verse 188, Virgil introduces a very interesting detail. This verse reads, "*Neu populum antiqua sub religione tueri.*" I hesitate to comment on this verse in which Virgil once again seems to be the guardian of certain secrets.

If, in regard to the horse, one is dealing with the idea of not restoring an ancient cult,[19] this cult must necessarily have existed sometime at Troy, which was being beseiged by the Achaeans. Such a reference, in my opinion, can only concern the ancient astral deities who can be identified with the Hesiodic guardians of the zodiacal signs, by reference to the list given in the *Theogony*. Naturally, one can object that it is nowhere stated that the Trojan horse had wings. But I believe that Pegasus derives from a more ancient symbol, a wingless horse that represented the winter solstice (see chap. 14).

I therefore think that the horse built by the Greeks to conquer Troy was the image of an astral deity that was associated with the ancient winter solstice and which was a protector of Troy. The horse was, as it were, the totemic animal of the city. As has already been seen, a good number of the scenes taken from episodes of the fall of Troy describe the sign of Aquarius.

Wood is a living, organic material. The Achaeans are protected by Athena who blinds their enemies. Inside the wooden horse, the Achaeans are already magically in the very heart of the city. Symbolically, they have conquered Troy in advance.

♦

An important illustrated document supports this interpretation. This is the design on a Corinthian aryballus in the Cabinet des Médailles of the Bibliothèque Nationale in Paris[20] (fig. 133). In the painting one sees, next to the Trojan horse, a colossal beast in frontal view, either a lioness or a panther, and a great aquatic bird, a swan or wild goose. The three animals obviously have a single nature: they are symbols defining a section of the zodiac from Sagittarius (ancient sign of the Swan) to Aquarius. The quasi identity of the symbols of the horse and the panther, both representing the sign of Aquarius and Troy, is emphasized by the horizontal lines on which the fighting warriors are standing, that connect the gigantic animals to one another. Only my suggested interpretation can, I believe, justify the presence of a panther and a goose on this drawing!

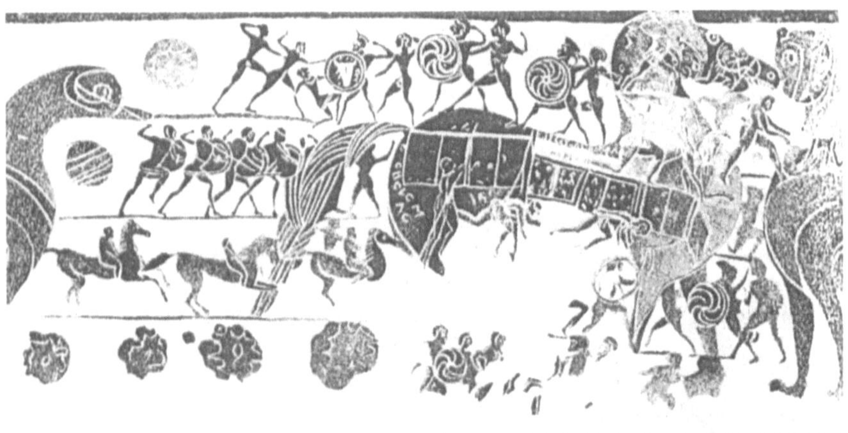

Figure 133. *The Trojan horse as a zodiacal figure (Corinthian aryballus of the Cabinet des Médailles).*

Chapter 20

Zodiacal Imagery at Mycenae The Great Uranian Goddess The Inquiry Continues

I've arrived at Mycenae to hear someone say: "Mr. Schliemann has had a field day!"

—*Maurice* Barrès, *Journey to Sparta*

1. Zodiacal Imagery at Mycenae

Today it seems that very few people examine the original report written by Henry Schliemann on his excavations at Mycenae. I am using the American edition (*Mycenae*, Arno Press, New York, 1976) of Schliemann's work published in 1880. It was in chapter 12 of this book that I found indisputable proof of the use of a zodiac, probably of oriental origin, in ornaments for clothing, small pieces of golden jewelry found in a series of royal tombs, dated to the middle of the second millenium B.C..

Schliemann always gives, whenever possible, the position of the holes through which the ornaments were attached. In the absence of such holes, he assumes very credibly that the ornaments were glued onto fabric. In some cases, he has proof that the figurines were double-sided, and they are often double on a single side.

Figures 134 and 135. The most remarkable feature of this piece is the presence of the bird goddess, which describes the Gemini-Sagittarius axis and refers to the period when the colure of the equinoxes coincided with this axis, celestially visible as the Milky Way. The latter was symbolized by the thick plumage of a divine bird, pigeon, goose, or swan. This refers, therefore, to the distant period of 6500 to 4500 B.C., and hence the zodiac employed antedates by far the construction of the fortress of Mycenae. The gesture of fecundity that the goddess is making, commented on by Schliemann, must be related to the season of spring. The three birds can correspond to the three decans of the sign of Gemini, and the goddess symbolizes a year that begins at the spring equinox.

Figures 136 and 137. The horse also stands for the sign of Gemini; the seahorse can designate Pisces.

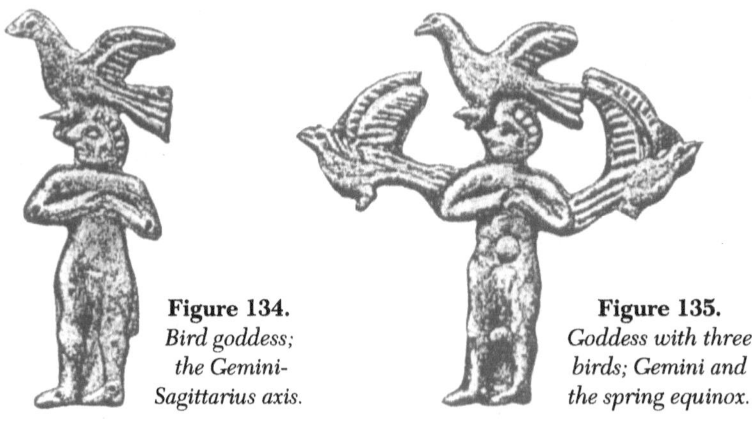

Figure 134.
Bird goddess; the Gemini-Sagittarius axis.

Figure 135.
Goddess with three birds; Gemini and the spring equinox.

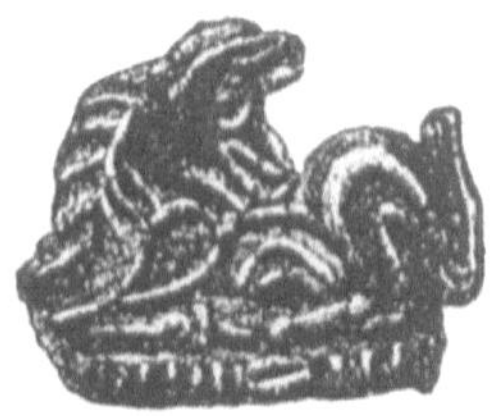

Figure 136.
Horse; sign of Gemini.

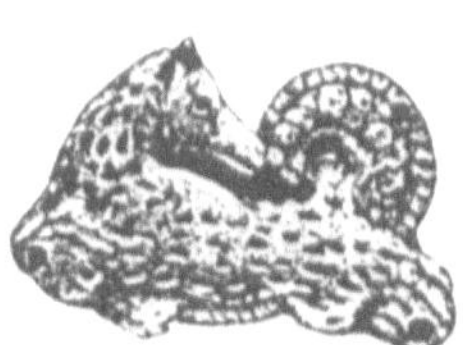

Figure 137.
Sea-horse; Pisces.

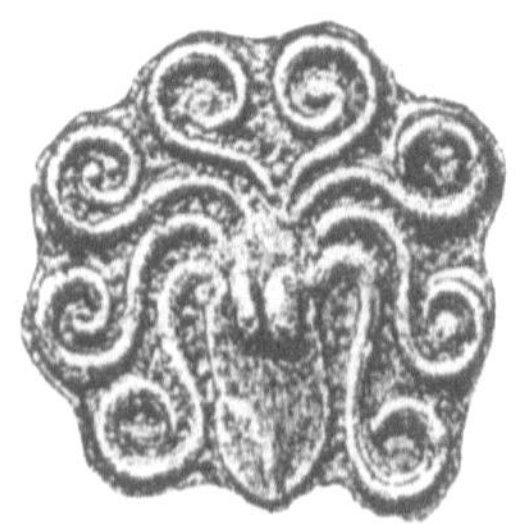

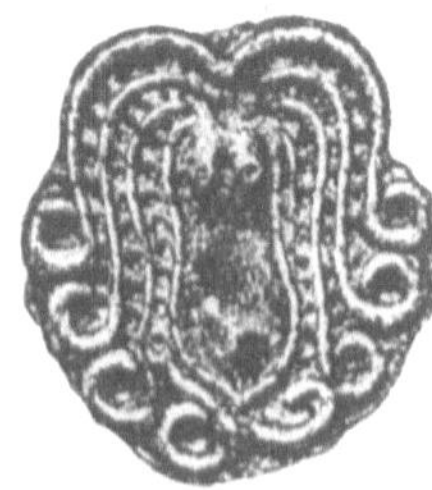

Figures 138 & 139.
Octopodes; sign of Cancer.

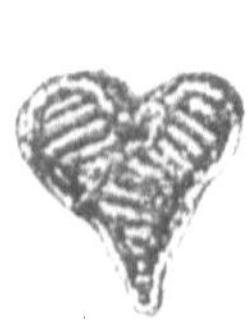

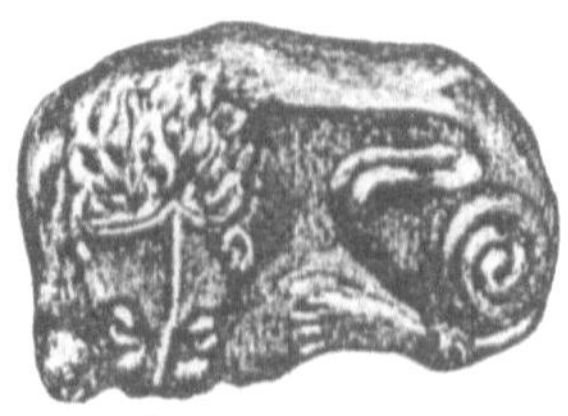

Figures 140 & 141.
Lion and heart; sign of Leo.

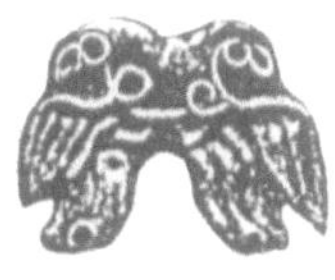

Figure 142.
Owls; Virgo.

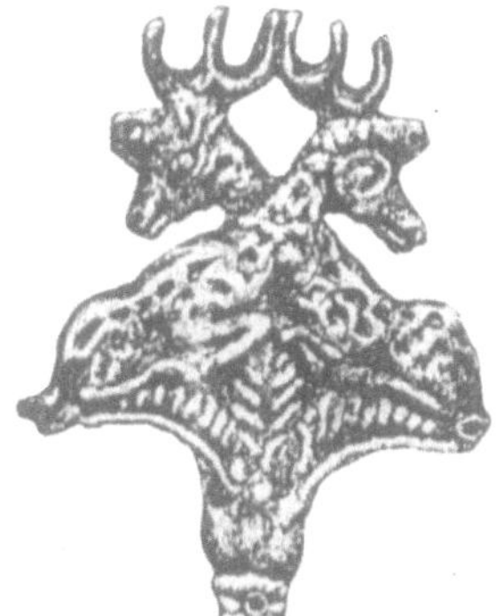

Figure 143.
Deer and palm tree; sign of Libra.

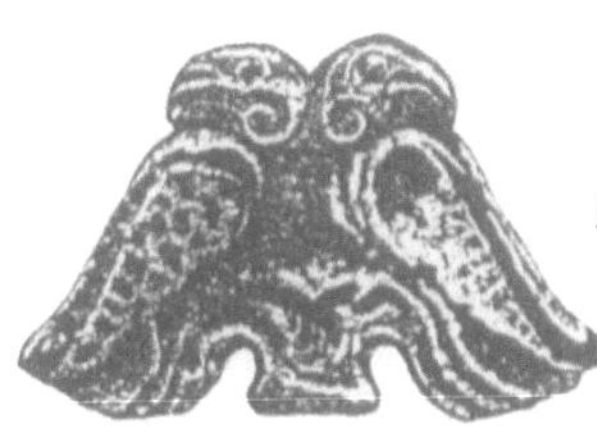

Figure 144.
Falcons; Scorpio.

Figures 138 and 139. There are, among all the figurines, many images of octopodes (frequent elsewhere in Cretan art) that refer to the sign of Cancer.

Figures 140 and 141. One finds several depictions of lions. Very interestingly, in at least one tomb they are accompanied by a heart, which establishes the antiquity of the association of this zodiacal sign with that part of the human body.

Figure 142. The sign of Virgo is present as owls.

Figure 143. Libra, in accordance with the Anatolian traditon, is symbolized by deer whose long horns rise above a palm tree, its three branches representing the three decans of the sign.

Figure 144. Falcons stand for the sign of Scorpio.

Figure 145. The image for Sagittarius is a goddess with a bird above her, which is reminiscent of certain Cretan goddesses and also prefigures Leda (fig. 134), and two swans side by side (fig. 145).

Figures 146 and 147. Here the griffin, guardian of treasures and the direction of north, carries the meaning of Capricorn. Many such images are to be found in Cretan and Mycenaean art.

Figure 148. The butterfly also refers to Capricorn, considered as the gateway to the celestial spheres.

Figure 149. The young panthers symbolize Aquarius, the sign of Dionysus. Pisces may be represented by the sea-horse, if, as Schliemann suggests, figure 136 or 137 shows this animal.

Figure 150. The sphinx refers to the Aries-Libra axis. It most likely stands for Aries.

Figure 151. The three-horned bulls above three palm leaves represent Taurus and its three decans (on the three-horned bull, see my *Géographie sacrée dans le monde romain*, p. 111).

Figure 273 of Schliemann's classification is problematic. It would probably be appropriate to insert it into the zodiac. If the figure is a goddess of the apple-harvest, a sort of "meliad," she should be associated with autumn; however, the presence on her breast of a disc that may be lunar would refer rather to Cancer (fig. 152).

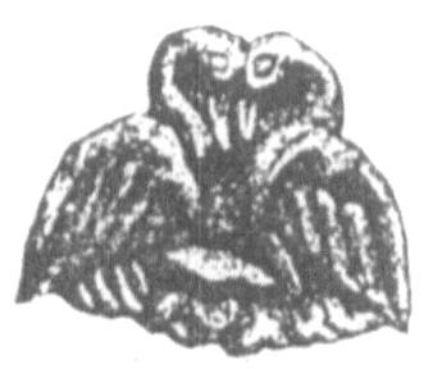

Figure 145.
Swans; Sagittarius.

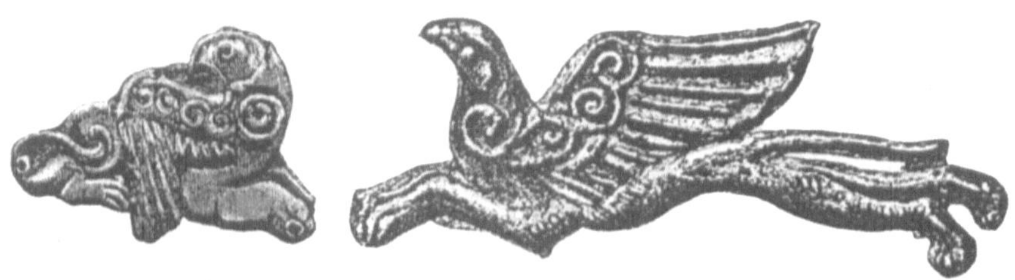

Figures 146 & 147.
Griffins; sign of Capricorn.

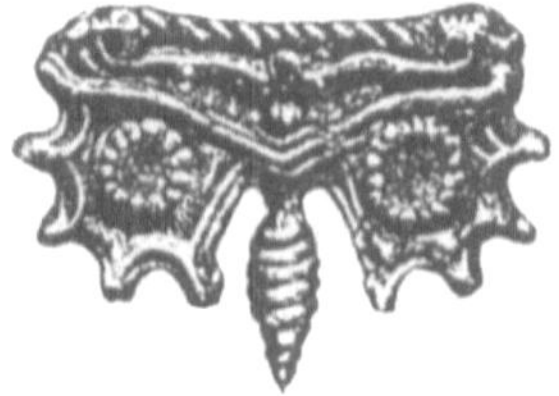

Figure 148.
Butterfly; Capricorn.

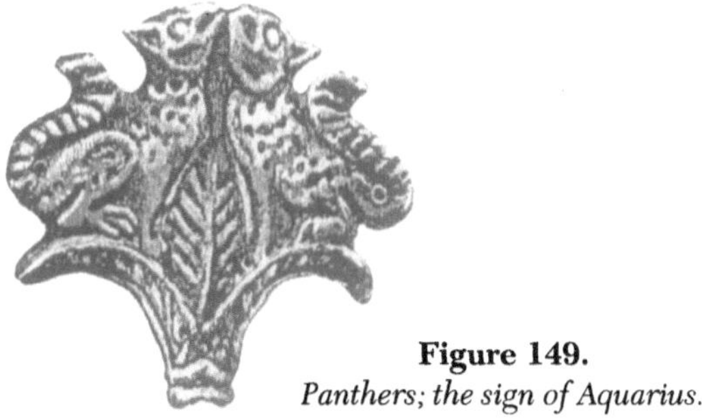

Figure 149.
Panthers; the sign of Aquarius.

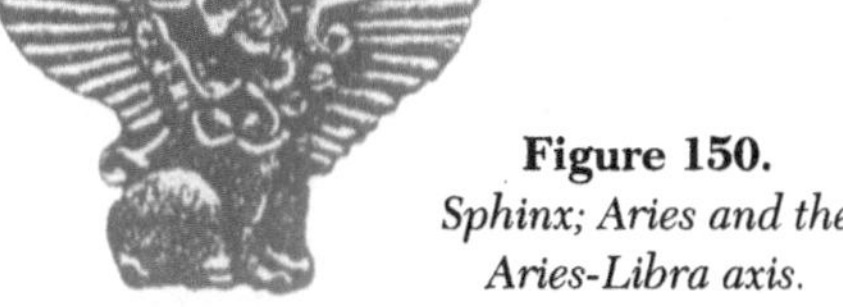

Figure 150.
Sphinx; Aries and the Aries-Libra axis.

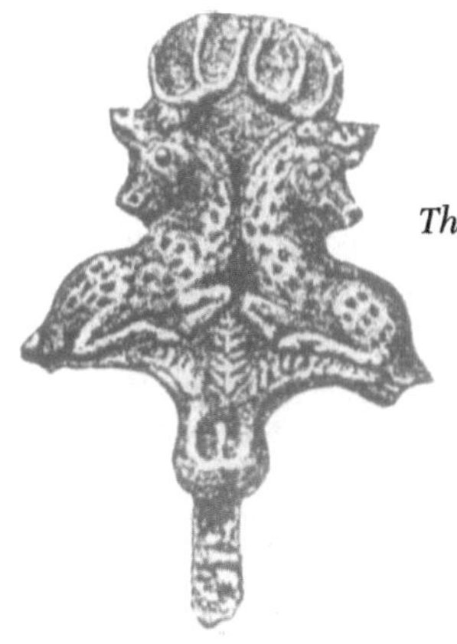

Figure 151.
Three-horned bulls and palm leaves; Taurus.

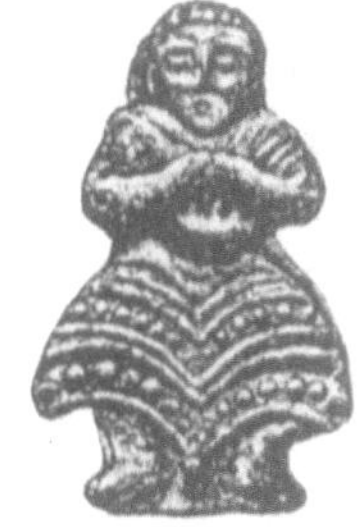

Figure 152.
Goddess of the apple harverst with disc.

The existence of genuine pre-zodiacs has been noted in Crete and Santorini. The set of figurines that has just been quickly examined shows that, before the adoption of the Phoenician zodiac in the Greek world, which occurred toward the ninth century B.C., the Mycenaeans employed a zodiac that may have been partly of Anatolian origin, which is suggested by the use of deer as a symbol of Libra, and panthers for Aquarius, but which also incorporated orientalizing elements such as the griffin and the sphinx. The material published by Schliemann is lacking the familiar symbols for Aries, Gemini (the Dioscuri), Libra (Harmonia), Capricorn (the goat), and Aquarius (Pegasus).

The funerary use of these figurines raises an interesting problem regarding the religious beliefs of the Greeks. It is quite likely, in fact, that they had a magical and apotropaic function, and that in every case they were selected according to the character and the earthly life of the deceased. This suggests the possibility of a Mycenaean astrology. What is more, if readers have followed my thinking, it will be understood that the Cretan images where one sees a goddess with a bird above her head are really a variation on the theme of the Great Uranian Goddess, or the Mistress of the Three Worlds.

In George Mylonas's book, *Mycenae Rich in Gold*, (Athens, 1983), plate 22 shows a funerary necklace composed of identical elements, ten in number, representing falcons.

2. The Great Goddess

The Great Uranian Goddess, Artemis, Harmonia, or Dike, ruler of the law of the pole and guardian of the cosmic order, has been encountered at various times during the course of this research. I believe that images of this goddess, in Greek archaic art from the seventh century onwards, are much more frequent than is generally recognized, but have not been identified for what they are. Artemis is a goddess of complex origins in whom at least three more ancient goddesses were merged: an earth-moon goddess, a Mistress of Beasts of Anatolian origin (already associated with the archaic Apollo), and a Cretan goddess (see chap. 5).

The moon, like the sun, travels through the whole zodiac. That the lunar goddess and the "Mistress of Beasts" are really one and the same seems to have escaped notice because the animals with which she is associated are really symbols of the zodiac (or even a pre-zodiac).

a) On many objects of ivory or pieces of gold jewelry from the sanctuaries of Artemis at Delos and Sparta[1] there is a Great Goddess, who is most often winged (that is, celestial) and holding two lions (like the Babylonian deity); the animals symbolize the solstices. The object as a whole must have afforded magical protection.

b) Such images also appear on vases from the geometrical period onwards. One example is the neck of a vase[2] in the Museum of Athens (see fig.

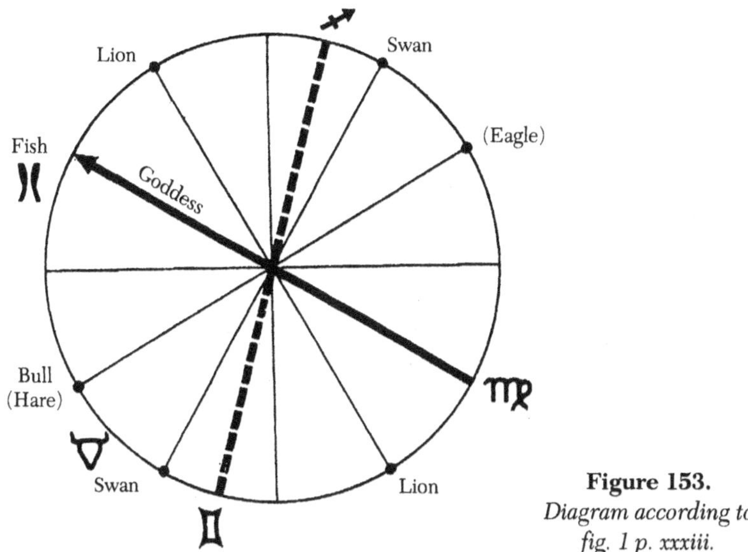

Figure 153. *Diagram according to fig. 1 p. xxxiii.*

1, p. xxxiii), which includes a series of zodiacal symbols whose scheme is as follows (fig. 153):

I conclude from this scheme that the goddess, whose body coincides with the Pisces-Virgo axis, is a "Mistress of Beasts" identifiable with Athena, and that the vase must have been found in Attica or Boeotia.[3]

And in fact, the vase does come from Boeotia.

The drawing on the obverse is of a bird of prey and a hare, an image that is immediately recognizable as the equinoctial axis, with a possible additional reference to a calendar in which the year began at the autumnal equinox.

c) A bronze plaque in the "Greco-Oriental" style of the seventh century, found at Olympia and now in the Museum of Athens (fig. 154), also portrays the Great Goddess. A diagram of the plaque reveals its meaning (fig. 155):

It would seem that the three perched birds, which comprise the most enigmatical register, very probably represent the part of the zodiac associated with the winter solstice and the three signs of Sagittarius, Capricorn and Aquarius.

d) The Lion Gate of Mycenae. The goddess standing on two lions above the famous entrance gate of the fortress of Mycenae has the same celestial significance as the lion goddesses on bronzes and vases. The central pillar symbolizes the cosmic axis and the world tree, associated with the geographical position of Mycenae, which is near the Leo-Aquarius axis of the Delphic system. This sculpture has often been compared with similar figures on Mycenaean or Cretan[4] gems, which sometimes include an image of the celestial vault.

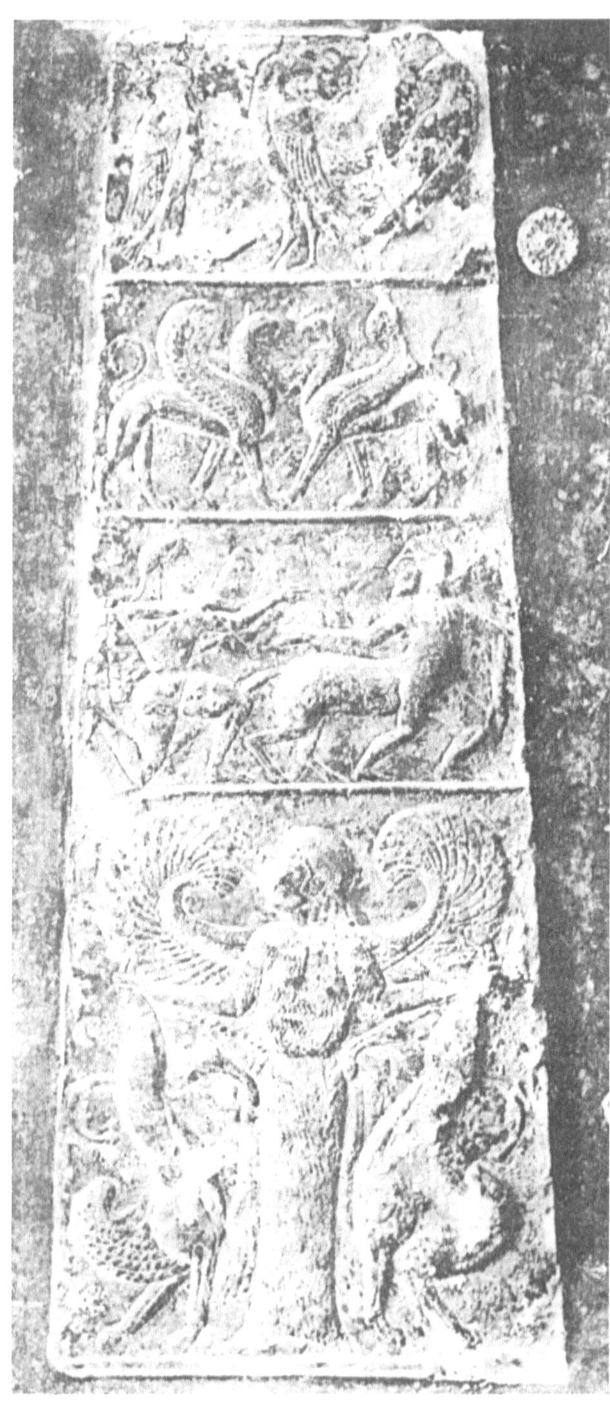

Figure 154. *Bronze plaque found at Olympia. From below to above: winged goddess with animals, centaur and Sagittarian, griffins, birds.*

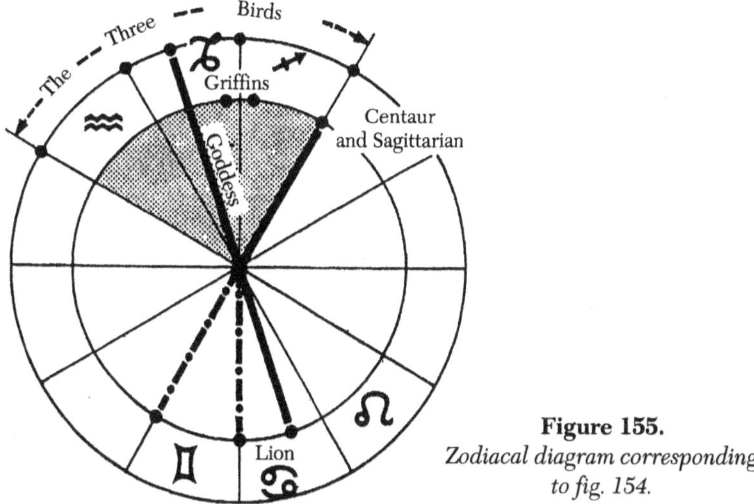

Figure 155.
Zodiacal diagram corresponding to fig. 154.

3. The Handles of Hydrias

A hydria is a vessel made of metal that can be heated, and vapor escapes from it. It can be thought of as symbolizing the union of the four elements: earth, water, fire, and air. This may be why the Great Uranian Goddess, who makes her influence felt on our sublunary world, often appears on the handles of hydrias. There is no corpus on this, which would be very useful and interesting to compile.[5] For the time being, let me simply mention a few outstanding examples.

a) First is the famous handle on the bronze vase found near Graechwill, now in the Historical Museum of Bern[6] (fig. 156). In the center one sees a winged goddess standing on a shell. This shell, which represents Cancer, the sign of the moon and the south-north axis, will be found on many similar representations. It was later associated with Aphrodite-Cytheraea. The shell is winged, making its celestial character overt. The animals surrounding the goddess, lions, serpents, eagle, and hare, are familiar; they describe the equinoctial and solstitial axes.

b) I will now examine the handle of a hydria, in the collection of the Royal Museum of Brussels, which has been recently published[7] (fig. 157). Here one finds closely related imagery. In this case the goddess is no more than a shell, and the lions again stand for the solstices. H. Hoffmann, who published this bronze, was unable to identify the "winged demons" standing on serpents. The presence of the serpents shows that they symbolize Ophion, guardian of the sign of Scorpio. The two "demons" are therefore acting as representatives of the equinoctial axis (see also fig. 36). This imagery could refer to a year beginning at the autumnal equinox.

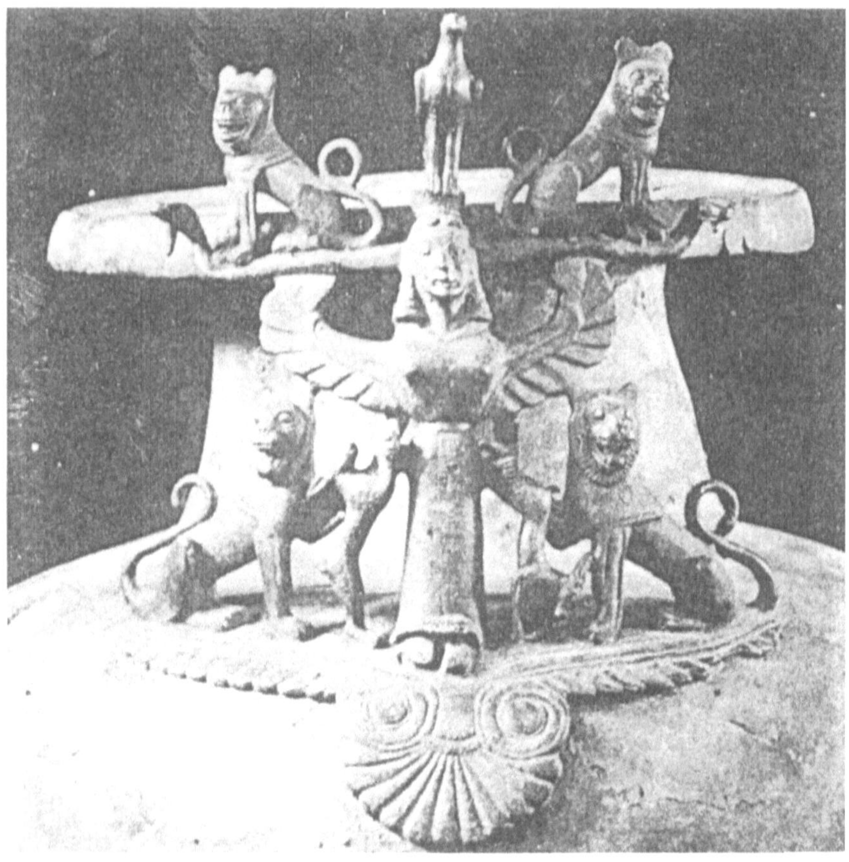

Figure 156.
Handle of the vase of Graechwill (Historical Museum of Bern): winged goddess with shell, eagle, lions, hares, serpents (symbols of the equinoxes and the solstices).

Even when the goddess is absent, the handles of hydrias and urns are often decorated with zodiacal symbols. The Gorgons on the krater of Vix are widely known. One sometimes sees sirens, as on the funerary urn from Ceramicus now in the Museum of Athens. The funerary significance of the zodiacal symbols is, however, another question and should be studied separately. The same symbols were finally transferred to a Master of Animals wearing a winged helmet, a sort of Apollo-Ares-Hermes, who appears on bronze handles displayed in various Italian museums.[8] Oddly enough, he continued to be associated with the shell of Cancer.

4. The Inquiry Continues

During the course of the present work I have hinted at various times that I do not consider my work of interpretation, nor even my research, as being com-

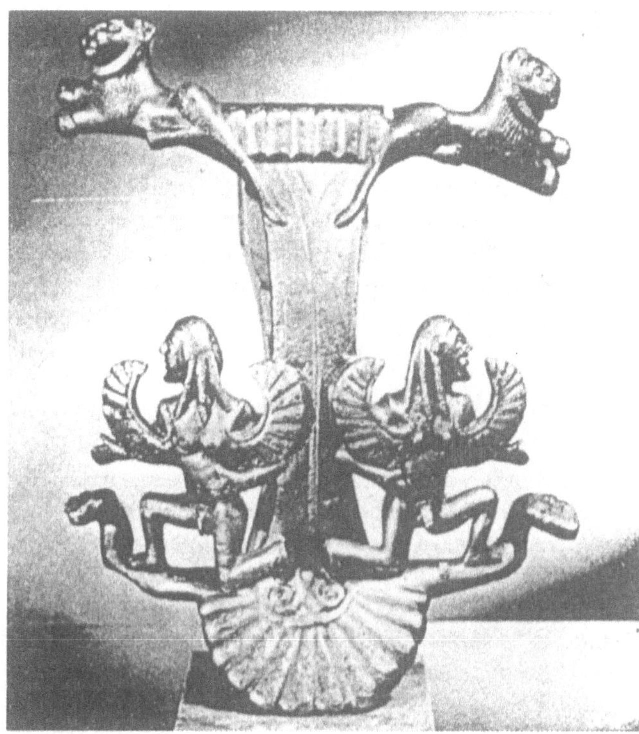

Figure 157. *Handle of a hydria (Royal Museum of Brussels): shell, Ophions, lions (equinoxes and solstices).*

plete. These pages give no more than the rudiments of the language spoken by the monuments of the Greeks, their temples, coins, vases, and shields. It seemed to me that these were often more eloquent than the textual evidence and gave a clearer understanding and a better reading of the latter.

The focus of the present volume is the symbolism of the Greek temple. The second will delve into the history of the calendar, which is closely connected with the history of zodiacs. The significance of an artifact like the Triple Geryon, found at Atheniau in Cyprus and now in the New York Metropolitan Museum, has never been appreciated from this point of view. I will also study some outstanding monuments: the throne of Amyclae, the François vase, and the temple of Hera at the mouth of the Selinus.

In studying certain vases, I have glimpsed the possiblity of reconstructing an ancient calendar of birds and perhaps a calendar of trees. These calendars have many similarities with the Celtic ones and give fresh meaning to the notion of a "Borean tradition" in Greece. I shall also examine the relationship of Greek calendars and festivals with sacred geography. It would seem that, in every city and sanctuary, the New Year and the dates of the great festivals were closely associated with the location of the city or temple and its position in relation to the omphalos.

Astral beliefs are reflected in the institutions themselves, whether at Sparta or Athens. It will be easy to show, for example, that at Sparta and then at Rome, the myth of double royalty is directly connected with the fact that these cities were considered to be ruled by Gemini.

My investigations will not stop there. The influence of sacred geography was in fact very widespread. Astrology, associated with the functioning of the Delphic oracle, played a role in colonization. Through studying the coins and deductive reasoning, it is possible to reconstruct the diagrams that were influential in the colonization of Greater Greece (the southern part of modern Italy and Sicily) and Pontus (which sheds new light on the story of the Argonauts). Indeed, it would appear that all the great cyclical poems of antiquity, *The Epic of Gilgamesh*, *The Iliad*, the *Odyssey*, *The Argonautica*, and *The Aeneid*, rest on a foundation of astral beliefs. These affect the nature of the characters and many episodes, and even determine the very structure of the poems. The great Newton said that the story of the journey of the Argonauts was more like a description of a procession or a calendar than the undertaking of a conquest.

Little by little, the system that I have reconstituted was applied to the whole of the Mediterranean world and then to Europe. It apparently attained its greatest extension in space during the Roman era. The Phoenicians and the Etruscans quite probably contributed to its spread. The great statues of Artemis wearing zodiacal necklaces, the "Carian" statues of Aphrodite, and the statues of Heliopolitan Jupiter contribute consistent supportive evidence. I will show that the zodiacal sign prominently displayed on the breast of the goddess or appearing on the statue of the god always expressed a symbolic relationship with the site where the statue was erected. In this way, each sculpture was individualized. Here again, I was able to predict what type of statue should be found in a given place and to verify these predictions. The importance of a system centered on Cumae[9] will be shown from this point of view. The geometric and geographic relationships among the centers, which have already appeared in regard to Delphi, Delos, Sardis, and the oasis of Ammon will be further examined. And lastly, I will show that astrology was, as it were, the common denominator of the religions of the ancient world. It will be shown, in brief, that the association of astral beliefs with zodiacal geography profoundly influenced the customs and institutions of Greco-Roman civilization, thus uniting them with the basic beliefs common to all the peoples of antiquity and perhaps even earlier.

A noteworthy proof will be supplied by funerary monuments, which display symbols of the zodiac, the seasons, and the four quarters of space. I will be able to interpret many Lycian, Greek, or Roman monuments from this perspective, from the Tomb of the Sirens at Xanthus to the cameos in the Cabinet des Médailles in Paris and countless Greek funerary urns and sculptures on sarcophagi. The various tables of symbols that have already been given can in fact be used to read Byzantine and Roman artifacts. I shall also have to devote a special study to the migration and the persistence of symbolic motifs through several millenia. Many

Hellenistic or Byzantine mosaics describe calendars by means of hunting scenes, and the groups of fighting animals that symbolize the seasons appear in church sculpture. The plan of the second volume, such as it has just been outlined, may seem ambitious. At the time of this writing, the work in question has already been partly written. If I publish the present work now, it is not in a spirit of haste, but because I think that some of the comments that will be made about this volume will enable me to approach the next with fresh insight. For the time being, I hope to have clearly revealed that Greece is intimately linked to the great traditional civilizations and that its people, deeply religious, endeavored for centuries to make their land into the very image of the heavens, to which hundreds of monuments bear silent witness.

—Athens, Quimper, Stanford, 1958–65

Abbreviations

PERIODICALS

A.J.A.: *American Journal of Archaeology*, Princeton.
B.A.G.B.: *Bulletin de l'Association Guillaume Budé*, Paris, Les Belles-Lettres.
B.C.H.: *Bulletin de Correspondance hellénique*, Paris, de Boccard.
Jahrbuch: *Jahrbuch des Deutschen Archaeologischen Instituts*, Berlin, W. de Gruyter.
M.H.: *Museum Helveticum*, Revue Suisse pour l'étude de l'antiquité classique, Basel, Schwabe.
R.A.: *Revue archéologique*, Paris, Presses Universitaires.
R.E.A.: *Revue des Études anciennes*, Bordeaux, Féret.
R.H.R.: *Revue de l'histoire des religions*, Paris, Presses Universitaires.

BOOKS ON COINS

B.M.C.: *Catalogue of Greek Coins in the British Museum*, by B. V. Head, G. F. Hill, etc.
Brett: Agnes Baldwin Brett, *Catalogue of Greek Coins*, Museum of Fine Arts, Boston, 1955.
Cahn: Herbert A. Cahn, *Monnaies grecques archaïques*, Basel, Amerbach, 1947.
Gardner: Percy Gardner, *The Types of Greek Coins*, 1883.
Head: Barclay V. Head, *Historia Numorum*, Oxford, 1911.
Seltman: Charles Seltman, *Greek Coins*, London, 1933 (1960 ed.).

Notes

FOREWARD

1. I have verified some of the alignments with rudimentary means. The angular measurements, when these are essential, should be taken with the proper scientific equipment.

2. The attentive and sustained study of the work of the poet Gérard de Nerval was a discipline that accustomed me to taking a comprehensive view of complex systems.

3. This first chapter of my book was published in *Le Nouveau Commerce*, a publication directed by André Dalmas, no. 4, autumn 1964.

4. As early as 1883, Percy Gardner methodically studied the most ancient types of Greek coins and concluded that all the symbols appearing on them have religious or cult significance, and he established many interesting relationships. However, he did not see the fundamental role of the signs of the zodiac (of which many, as I will show, had never been identified as such).

From the astrological point of view, the most interesting coins are those bearing two zodiacal symbols, which thus refer to a zodiacal axis (e.g., a coin of Lycia with a lion on one side and a winged horse on the other, which describes the Leo-Aquarius axis) or else those bearing a zodiacal sign and a planetary deity (e.g., Theban coins with Harmonia or Libra on one side, and on the other the shield of Ares, ruler of the opposing sign of Aries) (map 9, fig. 9 and map 11, fig. 30).

5. Other similar anecdotes may be found in the introduction to *Delphes, Délos et Cumes*.

6. See the comments on this subject by J. E. Harrison in *Themis*, p. 390.

7. Cyrus H. Gordon, *The Common Background of Greek and Hebrew Civilization*, 1962 and 1965.

8. The example of Cook's *Zeus*, an immense work of research taken up time and again, which my own inquiry overlaps in several places, is an example of how difficult it is to achieve an overall vision of Greek religion.

In *The Earth, the Temple and the Gods: Greek Sacred Architecture* (Yale University Press, 1962), Vincent Scully gives an extensive photographic documentation that is relevant to the present work. He especially emphasizes the relationship of the temple to landscape features.

9. *Discourse on Method*, Discourse 2, trans. F. E. Sutcliffe, Penguin Books, 1968.

PREFACE

1. See Rupert Gleadow, *Les Origines du zodiaque*, French trans., 1968 (1971), pp. 88–89, according to A. Rehm. Also see the lists given by G. Thiele in *Antike Himmelsbilder*, 1898.

2. Cyril Fagan, *Zodiacs Old and New*, London, 1951, p. 40 *et passim*.

3. Giorgio di Santillana and Hertha von Dechend, *Hamlet's Mill*, Boston, 1969.

4. *Les Cycles du retour éternel*, 2 vol., P., 1963.

5. Op. cit., pp. 63 and 258.

6. *The Greek Myths*, 62, n. 2.

7. See Robert Graves, *The White Goddess*.

8. P. Chantraine, *Dictionnaire étymologique de la langue grecque*, articles on καρ and καρα.

9. See O. R. Gurney, *The Hittites*, London, 1952, p. 191, which refers to the works of H. G. Güterbock.

10. Ruth B. Edwards, *Kadmos the Phoenician*, Amsterdam, 1979.

11. While a more detailed study is anticipated, see in the meantime my article "Thèbes ou la Lyre d'Amphion," *Cahiers astrologiques*, Nov.–Dec. 1965, where I have tried to reconstruct the plan according to the text of *The Phoenicians* by Euripides.

12. See J.-E. Dugand: "De l'étymologie du nom d'Aphrodite" in *Hommage à P. Fargues*, no. 21 of the *Annales de la Faculté des Lettres et Sciences humaines de Nice*, 1974, pp. 73–98, and *Chypre et Canaan*, Centre de recherches comparatives sur les langues de la Méditerranée ancienne, Faculté des Lettres de Nice, doc. no. 1, 1973.

13. Some notes on astrology are given in n. 2, chap. 2, p. 265. For further details, see H. Beer's excellent *Introduction to Astrology*.

CHAPTER 1

1. I am referring to the present state of the sacred site. Historically, the cult of Gaia and Themis preceeded that of Apollo. At Delphi, however, Athena's cult under various names (Ergane, Zosteria, Eileithyia, Hygiea) is also more ancient than the solar god's. See the work of P. Amandry, *La Mantique apollinienne à Delphes* (1950), especially chap. 18, "L'Oracle de la terre."

2. Mircea Eliade: *The Forge and the Crucible* (1962), trans. Stephen Corrin, Rider and Co., p. 21.

3. At Delphi, F. Creuzer essentially said, Minerva is the Provident, born from the heart of the sea, who guided Latona, Night in labor, in the island of revelation at Delos, where burned the torches of day and night. She stands be-

fore the temple: she announces the coming of the god and watches over him unceasingly.

On Athena Pronaia, see also n. 19 of chap. 5.

Eileithyia, who helped Latona, was thought to be of Hyperborean origin. The people of Amnisos, near Cnossos in Crete, claimed this goddess, then considered as Hera's daughter (Pausanias, I, 18, 5).

4. On most extant or reconstituted maps, there are major distortions on the east coast of the Peloponnese, which the ancients extended to the east instead of the southeast.

5. The "cutter" or "hewer" (*rafti*) that stands on an islet opposite Porto Rafti would be a statue of Demeter, another example of the association of the cults of Apollo and the Earth-Mother.

However, Cornelius C. Vermeule's article (*Hesperia*, vol. xxxi, 1962, pp. 62–81) indicates that there was another statue, whose site is still visible on the neighboring islet of Raftopoula. In my opinion, this could well have been a statue of Athena for the reason given in chap. 5 (Athena, like Artemis, would have derived from a great earth-moon goddess).

6. Has it been noticed that, in Pausanias's narrative, Apollo appears in the triple terrestrial, celestial, and infernal aspects that the gods of the Greek pantheon sometimes took in imitation of the Mesopotamian? (The triple Hecate comes to mind.) The original temple made of laurel branches evokes the loves of Zeus with the nymph Daphne; this earthly hut of perishable materials succeeds the oracle of Gaia. Then comes a sublimation by music and song, related to an Apollo-Helios, father of the arts and master of the celestial spheres. This is what is indicated by the temple made of beeswax and feathers, which suggests both the buzzing insect's harmonious activity, and the winged and celestial song birds; also, the root μελι found in the words for "honey" and "bee" is very close to μελ, "melody."

Finally, the resonant bronze temple and its golden singers recalls Hephaestus, the smith-god, protector of the Athenians. He gives the sanctuary a subterranean dimension. The three temples, whose very existence has a fabulous and symbolic nature, are really one, simultaneously terrestial, celestial, and infernal, laurel, wax, and bronze. What is more, the phonetic closeness of χηρόσ, "wax," and χῆρ, "heart," may allude to the symbolic correspondence between the heart and solar energy.

Marie Delcourt says, "The temple of wings is a flying temple" (*L'Oracle de Delphes*, p. 162): a celestial temple, I believe.

7. M. Eliade, op. cit., pp. 39–40.

8. Ibid., pp. 41–42. The initial Δ in the names Delos and Delphi, often reproduced on their coins, is naturally an equilateral triangle.

9. Most of the sanctuaries named and considered later in this study already existed in the sixth century B.C. at the latest, several of them going back to the seventh and eighth centuries. Bassae, built towards 420, seemed relatively

recent. Greek excavations, however, have just revealed that the present temple succeeded a more ancient sanctuary. Pausanias (VIII, 41, 7) informs us on this: "On the mountain is a place called Bassae, and the temple of Apollo the Helper, which, including the roof, is of stone. Of the temples in the Peloponnesus, this might be placed first after the one at Tegea for the beauty of its stone and for its symmetry. Apollo received his name from the help he gave in time of plague, just as the Athenians gave him the name of Averter of Evil for turning the plague away from them. It was at the time of the war between the Peloponnesus and the Athenians that he also saved the Phigalians, and at no other time; the evidence is that of the two surnames of Apollo, which have practically the same meaning, and also the fact that Ictinus, the architect of the temple at Phigalia, was a contemporary of Pericles, and built for the Athenians what is called the Parthenon." (trans. W. H. S. Jones).

This text implies a unity of belief among the Greeks, independent of internal wars. What is more, it establishes a kind of kinship between Bassae, Tegea, and the Parthenon. The Corinth-Bassae line is almost parallel to the Athens-Tegea line.

10. C. Picard, *Polyth.*, II, p. 25; quoted by Jean Humbert in a note to the *Hymne à Apollon.* (Homère: *Hymnes*, 1936, p. 99.)

11. J. Carcopino: *De Pythagore aux Apôtres* (1956), pp. 39–41.

12. Strabo, X, 2, 9. This ritual fall has the characteristics of a trial by both air and water.

13. Pausanias, II, 35, 1.

14. Plutarch, *Isis and Osiris.*

15. F. C. Penrose and W. B. Dinsmoor have devoted several articles to the question of dating temples in function of supposed astronomical markers. See in particular F. C. Penrose's article, "On the Results of an Examination of the Orientation of a Number of Greek Temples," in *Philosophical Transactions of the Royal Society of London*, vol. 184 (1893), pp. 805–34.

But the problem had too many variables. The heliacal rising of Spica may well have played a role in the orientation of the temples of Themis and Nemesis at Rhamnus, these being situated in the sign of Virgo of the zodiacal wheel centered on Delphi, as will be seen, but there is little likelihood that the same phenomenon could have come into play in the orientations of the Heraion of Olympia or the temple of Apollo at Bassae.

I believe that one must theoretically begin with the astronomical phenomena that could have played a role in the orientation of a given sanctuary. Thus the heliacal risings or settings of Spica must be influential at Athens or Delos, for example, but at Olympia one should look for the Pleiades, at Ptoon, Scorpio or Libra, etc. (See the following chapters.)

Moreover, it is likely that only temples at the site of an omphalos or especially important ones were orientated to celestial markers. I believe that the less important sanctuaries were orientated according to more ancient temples that were already in existence. In chapter 17, I will be able to give partial answers to these questions.

Most of the relationships suggested by F. C. Penrose in the article cited seem unacceptable to me, except for the temple at Rhamnus, orientated to the rising of Spica, and the temple of Zeus at Nemea (heliacal setting of Aquarius).

CHAPTER 2

1. Charles Seltman, *Greek Coins*, London, 1933; I am using the 1960 edition. Pl. XIII, 14; B.M.C., vol. 1, p. 24, and Pl. XIV, fifth century.

2. For readers unfamiliar with traditional astrology, the following are some basic correspondences to which I will refer in different parts of this study.

1. Symbolic correspondences between the zodiac and man as microcosm:

Aries: head
Taurus: neck
Gemini: chest, lungs, bronchial tubes
Cancer: breasts, stomach
Leo: heart, back
Virgo: intestines, nervous system
Libra: kidneys
Scorpio: sexual organs, bladder
Sagittarius: thighs, ears
Capricorn: knees, bones
Aquarius: legs, circulation of humours
Pisces: feet

2. Planetary houses:
Each "planet" traditionally has two houses. The network of lines of force thus formed greatly resembles a magnetic field.

Sun: Leo
Moon: Cancer

The sun and moon have only one house each, Leo and Cancer together constituting a single force field with a double polarity.

Mercury: Gemini, Virgo
Venus: Taurus, Libra
Mars: Aries, Scorpio
Jupiter: Sagittarius, Pisces
Saturn: Capricorn, Aquarius

The places of exaltation, fall, and exile of the planets may be found in a treatise on astrology. These concepts will, in any case, not be referred to in the present work.

3. B.M.C., vol. 9, Pl. XVI, 9, 10. Strabo indicates (X, 2, 9) that while Menander affirms that Sappho was the first to jump from the cliff at Leucas, others say it was "Cephalus, son of Deioneus, enamoured of Pterelaus."

4. C. Seltman, op. cit., Pl. XXXV, 5, 6, 7. Coins from Olympia, with the effigy of Hera, starting from 420; B.M.C., vol. 9, coins of Elis.

5. Theognis, *Elegies*, 1086, trans. Dorothea Wender.

6. Pausanias, III, 26 (Pephnos where there were statues of the Dioscuri on an islet near the coast), and III, XIII, 1 (Tomb of Castor).

7. For the coins, see B.M.C., vol. 9, pp. 124ff.; Pl. XXIV and XXV. On the Dioscuri, consult the work of George Lanoë-Villène: "Castor," *Le livre des symboles*, 1929, pp. 24–32; see also article on "Horse," pp. 152ff.

Pausanias (III, 20, 4) reports that horses were sacrificed to Helios on Taletus, one of the peaks of Taygetus, and also (III, 20, 9) that Tyndareus made the suitors of Helen swear to defend her and her husband on the body of a sacrificed horse in a place near Sparta which was named "the tomb of the horse" for that reason.

Coins from Cleitor, a city situated on the 0 degree Gemini line, bear the head of a horse facing right and a Dioscurus on horseback. Babelon, *Traité*, II, 1, p. 879, no. 1253.

8. Pausanias, II, 22, 5, and III, 16, 1.

9. Pausanias, III, 22.

10. See Jane Harrison, *Prologomena to the Study of Greek Religion*, the pages on Aphrodite, 1955 ed., pp. 307–15. The hydria of Genoa being discussed is reproduced on her p. 310.

The coins of Cythera show a head of Aphrodite, B.M.C., vol. 9, Pl. XXI, 14, 15.

11. See Marcel Detienne's article, "La légende pythagoricienne d'Hélène," R.H.R., Oct.–Dec. 1957. In a more ancient system Thalamae corresponded to Cancer. Hence the sanctuary of Helios and Pasiphae (the moon) in this locality, mentioned by Pausanias (III, 26, 1).

12. B.M.C., vol. 9, Pl. XXVII, 9.

13. The fact also has a simple astronomical explanation: it is impossible to observe the stars during the day, and when the sun occupies a zodiacal sign, it is the opposite sign that rises in the east soon after sunset.

14. Bouché-Leclerq, *L'astrologie grecque*, note p. 137.

15. *Dictionnaire* of Daremberg, article "Apollo."

16. Agnes Baldwin Brett: *Catalogue of Greek Coins, Museum of Fine Arts, Boston*, 1955, Pl. LXVI, nos. 1287 and 1288; text p. 170.

17. In his study *Saint Christophe successeur d'Anubis, d'Hermès et d'Héraclès* (1936), P. Saintyves has brought out some unusual and striking symbolic and calendary correspondences.

This author writes: "[The star Sirius] was the object of a sacrificial cult in the island of Ceos. From the account of Heraclides of Pontus, the inhabitants watched for the moment of its rising and, according to whether it appeared bright or veiled, in a pure sky or one filled with vapors, they made predictions for the abundance or the sterility of the year. (Cicero, *On Divination*, I, 57.) They made sacrifice to this star (*Schol. Apoll. Rhod.*, II, 526), which was held in high honor in local traditions (Diodorus of Sicily, IV, 82). Hence the image of the radiant dog, which may be seen on the medals of Ceos and its three cities of Julis, Carthaea and Coressia. (Letronne, *Nouv. Rech.*, p. 27 and n. 1.)" (Op. cit., p. 43.)

Byzantine icons and frescoes regularly give Saint Christopher the head of a dog or a lion, and his feast, in the Roman Catholic as well as in the Eastern Church, falls on 25 July. See the important documentation assembled by Walter Loeschcke in *Sanctus Christophorus Canineus* (Sonderdrück aus Edwin Redslob zum 70. Geburstag), Erich Blaschker, Berlin, 1955, and from the same author, *Neue Beitrage zur Darstellung des kynokephalen Hl. Christophorus in Osteuropa*, Berlin, 1957 (Forschungen zur Osteuropaïschen Geschichte, vol. 5). I here thank M. Chatzizakis for introducing these publications to me.

18. See, for example, *Voyages dans la Grèce*, of P. O. Brönsted, vol. 1, 1826, pp. 31 and 78–79, with the quote from Heraclides of Pontus about this lion.

19. Callimachus, *Hymn to Delos*, 36.

20. Cited by Marie Delcourt, *L'Oracle de Delphes*, 1955, p. 158.

21. Cf. J. Harrison, op. cit., pp. 286–92. Contrary to what Plutarch stated, who is quoted by this author in support of her concepts, there were three Artemises (the triple Hecate) and three Demeters (the Arcadian trinity venerated at Lycosura). What is more, Zeus, Apollo, and Dionysus also form a triad.

22. B.M.C., vol. 8, Pl. XI, 8. Partial reproduction of this coin in *Themis* by J. E. Harrison, p. 444. Coins with names of magistrates, period 196–87 B.C. (Series Sokrates-Dionysodos, op. cit., p. 72.)

23. On the three Graces, see Pausanias, IX, 35, 3.

24. René Guénon wrote: "The word *Tulâ*, in Sanskrit, means 'balance,' and it particularly designates the zodiacal sign by that name; but, according to a Chinese tradition, the celestial Balance was originally Ursa Major—for other peoples, Ursa Major and Ursa Minor were assimilated to the two plates of a scale—the symbolism of Ursa Major is naturally linked in the narrowest way to that of the Pole. . . . It would also be appropriate to examine the potential relationship between the polar Balance and the zodiacal Libra; the latter is in effect regarded as the 'sign of Judgement.'" (*Le Roi du monde*, 1939 ed., pp. 115–16.)

In his article on "Le Sanglier et l'ours" (*Études traditionnelles*, Aug.–Sept. 1936, anthologized 1962 in *Symboles fondamentaux de la Science sacrée*), R. Guénon indicated that the transfer of Libra into the zodiac is associated with the transition from equinoctial to solstitial symbolism, connected with a change in the beginning of the annual cycle. The change from the north to the west refers to the Atlantean period. The Pleiades, daughters of Atlas, are also called the Atlantids.

25. B.M.C., vol. 1, p. 72, Pl. XII, 10, fifth century.

26. Pausanias, IX, 16.

27. J. Carcopino, *De Pythagore aux Apôtres*, 1956, p. 25, n. 7.

The shield on Theban coins, as Percy Gardner has indicated, stands for the god Ares: he had a sanctuary at Thebes and governed the sign of Aries, opposed to Libra.

28. H. W. Parke, *A History of the Delphic Oracle*, Oxford, 1939, p. 322.

29. A. Volguine, in *L'Ésotérisme de l'astrologie*, 1953, p. 159, indicates that the substitution of the Eagle by Scorpio is linked to the superimposition of an eight-part division of the zodiac over twelve signs. He writes on this: "The fixed signs of the zodiac: Taurus, Leo, Scorpio, and Aquarius which mark the half-seasons . . . have a very special importance." He indicates that the symbols for these signs are the four animals of the Apocalypse and represent the four Evangelists.

A note on the same page usefully points out: "The sign of Scorpio is frequently associated in symbolism both with the serpent, sexual symbol of the Earth, and with the Eagle, who personifies Air or the Sky and the elevated side of this sign, whose esoterism consists of the sublimation of sexual energy. The union of these two images in the eagle holding a serpent in its talons or beak is really universal, because it is found not only in pre-Columbian America (even appearing in Mexican heraldry), but also on a twelfth-century capital of the Romanesque basilica of Saint-Benoît-sur-Loire, as well as on the obverse of several Carnute coins." I shall return to this question.

30. Coins of Olympia, circa 500, Pl. XIII, 9, 10, 11, 12.

B.M.C., vol. 1. Coins from Chalcis. Eagle holding a serpent in its beak and talons, or else, eagle fighting an erect serpent. (In both cases, the symbolism is evidently the same.) Pl. XX, 9, 14, 15, 16, 17; Pl. XXI, 2, 5, 6, 7; circa 350.

On certain coins of the neighboring city of Eretria, the octopus seems to allude to the division into eight of the zodiacal circle where the Eagle replaces Scorpio.

31. C. Seltman, op. cit., Pl. XXXIV, 5–11.

32. Barclay V. Head, *Historia Numorum*, p. 300. Coin of the Magnesians: 197–146 B.C.

33. G. Dumézil (*Le Problème des Centaures*, 1929), convinced that the centaurs are related to the spring equinox, quickly dismisses the texts that relate them to the winter solstice. However, the "yearly renewal" with which he quite rightly associates them does indeed occur, it seems to me, in the very heart of winter.

A text by Teucer, mentioned by G. Dumézil (op. cit., p. 174) according to M. Boll, says that the soul, soon after crossing the "Acheron sea," meets a centaur on the way, who is Sagittarius in the zodiac. This corresponds to the exit of the soul through the "gateway of the gods," as I indicate in my next chapter. This gateway of Capricorn is associated with Mount Olympus in sacred geography. (See chap. 6.)

34. M. Delcourt, op. cit., p. 161.

35. Peter Robert Franke, *Die Antiken Münzen von Epirus* (1961). For the coins of Elaea, see p. 43 and Pl. III of Franke's book and p. 131 of mine.

36. See Carapanos, *Dodone et ses ruines* (1878) and the article by Guy Rachet on "Le sanctuaire de Dodone, origine et moyens de divination," B.A.G.B., March 1962.

37. The Selloi interpreted the sound of the wind in the oaks, and cauldrons were then attached to the tree branches. For a description of the oracular practices of Dodona, see G. Lanoë-Villène, vol. cited, article "Chêne," pp. 119ff.

38. Pliny, H.N., II, 106.

39. B.M.C., vol. 7, Pl. XXI. This type is also that of certain coins of Dyrrachium, farther north, on the coast of modern Albania, which is also situated in the sign of Aquarius. (P. Gardner, *The Types of Greek Coins*, 1883, Pl. XVI.)

40. P. Saintyves, op. cit., pp. 158–59.

41. *The Laws*, Book V (745–46), trans. A. E. Taylor, 1934.

42. Ibid., Book V (738).

43. See also ibid., VI (771): "Now our total number [5040] permits of division by twelve, and so likewise does that of the tribe, so each such division must be thought of as a sacred thing, a gift of Heaven corresponding with the months of the year and the revolution of the universe." The number 5040 is indeed divisible by 12, 144, and 360.

44. Ibid., Book V (738).

45. M. Delcourt in her book *L'Oracle de Delphes* wonders, "to what extent Platonic legislation was inspired by authentic Greek customs" (p. 45). The extent was probably very great with regard to twelve-part territorial divisions and the attribution of each region to a sign of the zodiac.

CHAPTER 3

1. The longitudes of Delos and the oasis of Siwa (Ammoneion) are from *Philip's Centenary Mercantile Atlas*, London Geographical Institute, 1935.

Delos: 25 degrees, 15 minutes east of Greenwich.
Siwa: 25 degrees, 20 minutes east of Greenwich.

If, as is probable, this was another alignment established by means of beacon fires (with relays on the north and south coasts of Crete), it is quite remarkable that the discrepancy for the distance Delos-Ammoneion, which is about 900 km, is only 5 minutes of longitude (7 or 8 km at these latitudes).

Between the Peloponnese and Crete, Cythera and Anticythera are relays for alignments and triangulations by means of fire signals. In good weather, the Peloponnesian coast is visible from Akra Spada.

However, this is not the case between the coast of southern Crete and Africa. In fact, between the island of Gaudo and the nearest point as the crow flies on the Libyan coast (Raz-el-tìn), that is, over a distance of 260 km, there are no islands at all. The marking of longitudes could therefore have been made only on the stars, whence, probably, the error we are observing.

According to legend, Apollo wintered on the island of Oesel in the Baltic. The western part of this island is on the meridian of Delphi. The positions are:

Delphi: 22 degrees, 25 minutes east of Greenwich.
Islet of Abro (off the middle of the island of Oesel): 22 degrees, 31 minutes east of Greenwich.

2. Pausanias, III, 23, 3.

3. B.M.C., vol. 23, Pl. XXVII, 9. In regard to the "complementarity of opposing signs," one cannot completely exclude the hypothesis of a complete reversal of the system, which could first have had a south-north orientation, and then the north-south orientation being studied.

4. Pausanias, III, 14, 2.

5. Ibid., II, 30, 4.

6. See W. K. C. Guthrie: *The Greeks and Their Gods*, pp. 105–6.

On the cult of Britomartis-Dictynna, cf. R. Graves, *The Greek Myths*, 89. In Cephallenia, the goddess was named Laphria. The cult of Britomartis was implanted even in Phocis; Pausanias (X, 36, 5) mentions a sanctuary to her at Anticyra.

7. The result of all this is that Dicte-Britomartis has more affinity with the sign of Cancer than with Gemini. The Curetes of Mount Dicte probably represent the Dioscuri associated with this Helen.

8. H. Gallet de Santerre, *Délos primitive et archaïque*, 1958.

9. H. Gallet de Santerre, in the cited work, has summarized the various traditions and opinions concerning the origin of Artemis. On a probable Lycian origin of the Leto-Apollo-Artemis triad, see p. 135. I return to the complex character of Artemis in chap. 5.

10. Seltman, *Greek Coins*, Pl. XII, 14.

11. Leto is identified with a more ancient Lycian goddess, Lada, whose name meant woman in general. See Guthrie, op. cit., pp. 83–84.

12. R. Graves, *The Greek Myths*, 138.

13. Reproductions of the coins of Chios bearing a winged sphinx are found in Seltman, *Greek Coins*, Pl. II, 6 and 7; Pl. XXIX, 12 and 13; Pl. XXX, 1.

14. Coin, probably from Chios, showing a centaur carrying a woman (Babelon, *Traité*, I, Pl. V, 17).

15. C. Seltman, *Greek Coins*, Pl. VI, no. 17. Centaur abducting a nymph. Coin of the Orrheskoi and the Zailioi.

16. Brett, op. cit., Pl. L, nos. 936, 937.

17. Babelon, *Traité*, II, 4, pp. 450–55.

18. C. Seltman, *Greek Coins*, Pl. VI and XXVIII.

19. Ibid., Pl. VIII, 1–2.

20. Ibid., Pl. XI, 4.

21. R. Graves, *The Greek Myths*, vol. 1, 82.

22. Strabo, IX, 2, 7 (Pausanias, IX, 20, 1) saw images of Artemis and Latona in this sanctuary. It seems that the same feasts were celebrated there as at Delos.

23. I was able to complete this chapter thanks to a valuable article by C. Picard, *Le Dèlion de Paros and les Dèlia du Proche-Orient*, R. A., July–Dec. 1964.

CHAPTER 4

1. Response made by the oracle of Delphi to Epimenides of Phaestus, reported by Plutarch, *Oracles*, I, p. 409 F, quoted by M. Delcourt, op. cit., p. 147.

2. M. Delcourt, op. cit., p. 146.

3. Herodotus, I, 6.

4. On this name, which is evidently the same as Manu, see R. Guénon, *Le Roi du Monde*, chap. 2. This is the great lawgiver of a cycle. Manes also seems to be the Lydian name for the lunar god Mên (cf. R. Dussaud, *La Lydie et ses voisins aux hautes époques*, 1930, p. 15, n. 4.

5. At the time of Hadrian and the Antonines, Queen Omphale is represented on coins of Sardis and Maeonia, standing half-clothed, holding a lion's pelt and a club. (B.M.C., vol. XVI, Pl. XXV, 11, and Pl. XIV, 2.)

6. Herodotus, I, 6; Strabo, V, 2 and 3.

7. B.M.C., I, Pl. IV, 20.

8. B.M.C., XVI, Pl. XLII, especially 4.

9. According to Imhoof, the *cista mystica* would have appeared first on coins from Ephesus circa 200 B.C.; it is found on coins of all the cities of the kingdom of Pergamum under the reign of Attalus I. The omphalos figures on coins from Magnesia of Sipylus and Nacrasa; the presence of these images of the center on coins does not always mean that the cities were centers but indicates their attachment to a traditional unity, which here is certainly the one whose main seats were at Ephesus and Sardis.

10. See, for example, Charles Seltman, *Greek Coins*, 1960 ed., chap. 2. Note that the images of zodiacal signs appear on the most ancient Greek coins known, therefore, beginning in the seventh century. Examples hereafter.

11. B.M.C., vol. 13, Pl. VI, 6 (before 387), 10, 11 (between 387 and 300 B.C.).

12. B.M.C., vol. 13, Pl. XXXIV, 21, 23, circa 494 B.C.

This may also correspond to a division into eight or into ten signs, because in this case the sign of Aries covered a greater area.

13. B.M.C., vol. 13, Pl. XXXIV, 6 and 10, 11, 12, 13, 14, 15, from 700 to 494(?) B.C.

The drawing of the zodiacal sign is reproduced in Bouché-Leclerq, *Histoire de l'astrologie grecque*, 1899, p. 133.

14. Museum of Samos, bronze B. 1123, from the Heraion, published by Ernst Buschor, "Samos 1952–1957," in *Neue Deutsche Ausgrabungen in Mittelmeergebiet und im Vorderen Orient*, Berlin, 1959, pp. 208–9, with illustration. I warmly thank Professor Ulf Jantzen of the Archeological Institute of the University of Hamburg, who was so kind as to send the photograph of this bronze reproduced here.

15. Coin in the National Museum of Athens.

16. Hyginus, *Astronomica*, II, 33.

17. See my article "La statue du culte d'Artémis à Éphèse" in *Cahiers astrologiques*, July–Aug., 1968.

18. I shall return to the relationship between Gemini and Poseidon, which establishes a link between Elis and Miletus.

One day Smicros and his adopted brother found a swan and fought with the neighborhood children over who would own it. I will later show that in an ancient zodiac the swan corresponded to Sagittarius, so this story really refers to the opposition-affinity of Gemini and Sagittarius, which sheds lights on the myth of Leda, Sparta also being associated with Gemini in the Delphic system.

It is also probable that the lyre that was figured on the coins of Halicarnassus, Iasus, Calymna, and Cos should be put into relationship with the constellation of Lyra and the Gemini-Sagittarius axis. (B.M.C., vol. 13, Pl. XVIII.)

19. See "Apollo" in the *Dictionnaire des antiquités* of Daremberg and Saglio, by L. de Ronchaud.

20. Seltman, op. cit., Pl. XXX, 7; Brett, op. cit., 2013–17ff., Pl. XCII (from 600 onward).

21. Virgil, *Aeneid*, IV, 143. The coins of Lycia are a real catalogue of symbols of Leo: mask of a lion, Heracles wearing a lion's head, chimaera. One also finds references to the Leo-Aquarius axis (horse and winged horse) and polar symbols (boar, dolphin, goat of Capricorn). See the already old work of C. Fellows, *Coins of Ancient Lycia* (1855).

22. Herodotus, *The Histories*, trans. Aubrey de Sélincourt, 1954.

23. B.M.C., vol. 18, Pl. VII, 11. Brett, coin from Patara, Pl. 96, 2094.

24. Some say that there may have been a verbal assimilation between Apollo *Lykeios* and Apollo *Leukaios* (Apollo of the white island). *Leukos* would have become Apollo *Lukos*, that is, the wolf. I wonder whether the contamination might not have occurred the other way. In a country devoid of lions, a wild animal of equivalent meaning would have been sought, and phonetically, the point of departure would have been *Lykos,* whence Lycia and Lycian Apollo. Also, Wolf is another name for the sign of Capricorn, and Leto-Lada, associated with Cancer, was metamorphosed into a she-wolf. This is another example of an opposition which is at the same time a complementarity.

25. Seltman, op. cit., Pl. XXXI 7, 8; B.M.C., vol. 18, Pl. XXV.
26. B.M.C., vol. 25, Pl. XLII, 6. This coin is from the first century B.C.
27. B.M.C., vol. 16, p. 30.
28. B.M.C., vol. 25, p. 353.
29. A. de Paniagua, *Étymologies divines*, pp. 122–23.
30. See "Lunus," by Adrien Legrand, in *Dictionnaire des antiquités grecques et romaines* of C. Daremberg, vol. 3, 1904, and the photograph of the stele (Pl. 4671 in the *Dictionnaire*) in the B.H.C., 1899, Pl. I. The sign of Libra is traditionally dedicated to Venus, a fact that confirms the concept that Aphrodite had succeeded an ancient lunar deity.
31. B.M.C., vol. 11, see pp. 95ff., Pl. XXI and XXII, many representations of the eagle, most often with a dolphin (480–415 B.C.).
32. B.M.C., vol. 11, Pl. XXXVIII, 4 and 5.
33. G. Dumézil, *Le Problème des centaures* (1929), pp. 247–50.
34. B.M.C., vol. 12, Pl. IX.
35. B.M.C., vol. 12, Pl. XVIII, 3 to 6 (500 B.C.). On the question of whether the symbol was a hippalectryon, see my chap. 14, section 3.
36. Text quoted by V. Magnien, *Les Mystères d'Éleusis*, 1950 ed., pp. 300–301. Notice, in these lines, the probable confusion between Mount Ida of Crete and Mount Ida of the Troad, which led the author, Olympiodorus (*On the Gorgias*), to qualify the myth as "Cretan."
37. Diodorus of Sicily, III, 72.
38. Apollo Aygieus was venerated at Tegea, situated on the solstitial line, Pausanias, VIII, 53, 3. See p. 65 in my book.
39. I am following and summarizing W. K. C. Guthrie, *The Greeks and Their Gods*, pp. 84–86.
40. Pausanias, VII, 2, 6: "The sanctuary of Apollo at Didyma, and his oracle, are earlier than the immigration of the Ionians, while the cult of the Artemis of Ephesus is far more ancient still than their coming." Ibid., VII, 3, 1: "The people of Colophon suppose that the sanctuary at Claros and the oracle were founded in the remotest antiquity." Pausanias goes on to tell the story of Manto, daughter of Tiresias.

CHAPTER 5

1. Note from the translation of Euripides' *Iphigenia in Tauris* by Léon Parmentier and Henri Grégoire, Paris, 1948, p. 91. The whole note is to be read. The references will also be found there.

Several statues found at Brauron portray little "she-bears" offering a hare, symbol of the yearly renewal.

2. P. Chantraine, "Réflexions sur les noms des dieux helléniques," *L'Antiquité classique*, vol. 22, 1953, pp. 65–78, especially pp. 74–78 (on the name θέμις.) The relationship Artemis-Arctos is indicated there.

A. de Paniagua ("Diane," *Étymologies divines*) suggests a derivation for the name Artemis from the Sanskrit *ar, arya,* noble, and *tama*, night. The noble of the night would be the Hyperborean, come from the "empire of the night." This would indirectly indicate a polar significance.

3. Diodorus of Sicily, XVI, 26.

4. P. Grimal, "Arcas," *Dictionnaire de la mythologie grecque et romaine.*

In a note in his *Le Roi du Monde* (chap. 5), R. Guénon wrote: "The name Arthur has a very remarkable meaning which is related to 'polar' symbolism, which I may explain on another occasion." This name is in fact equivalent to Arcturus. (In the Celtic languages "bear" is *Arth.*) King Arthur is thus the Guardian of the Bear, in other words, the depositary of the Hyperborean tradition. And the twelve knights of the Round Table represent the twelve "suns" or twelve Adityas of the Hindu tradition, corresponding to the successive positions of the sun in the zodiacal houses.

In "Le Sanglier et l'ourse" (*Études traditionnelles*, Aug.–Sept. 1936), reprinted in *Symboles fondamentaux de la Science sacrée* (1962), Guénon has established a series of linguistic relationships that support my intuitions. The root *var* of the Nordic languages has given *bor* and boar (or bear), which reappears in the name Brauron. It is preferable to speak of a Borean rather than a "Hyperborean" tradition. Vârâhi (aspect of the Shakti of Vishnu) is Boreas. Varuna is Uranus, from the Sanskrit root *var, vri* which means to cover, to protect, to hide, because "the Heavens cover the earth and represent the upper worlds hidden from the senses." I shall return to these questions in discussing the symbolism of the boar.

5. F. Vian, *Les Origines de Thèbes, Cadmos et les Spartes*, 1963, p. 142. This author establishes the relationship between the names Harmonia and Hermione, by quoting the Homeric words ἀρθμέω (*Iliad*, VII, 302) and ἄρθμιος (*Od.*, XVI, 427), which mean a pact of friendship. It is striking to find once again in these words the root αρθ. So there is also a probable link between Artemis, Hermione, and Harmonia.

6. "Diana was very fond of her, but seeing that Jupiter had seduced her, the goddess transformed her into a bear. Jupiter, however, gave the bear an honor equal to the goddess's by placing her image in the heavens . . . , Aratos calls her Helice" (*Constellations*).

7. P. L. Boyancé, *Le Culte des Muses*, 1937.

8. Let me particularly mention Lycosura, which seems to have been a great sacred site of Arcadia, since it had, besides the sanctuary of the three goddesses, a temple of Zeus and a sanctuary of Apollo. The site is, moreover, on the Hermione-Delos-Didyma line. It may have been related to the constellation of Draco, which formerly contained the Polestar.

9. See F. Courby, *Fouilles de Delphes*, II, "La Terrasse du Temple," fig. from pp. 73 and 76.

10. On the *agrenon,* see Euripides, *Ion*, 224; Strabo, IX, 3, 6.

11. J. Harrison, *Prologomena*, fig. 91, p. 319.

12. M. Delcourt, op. cit., p. 145.

13. R. Guénon, "Le Coeur et l'oeuf du monde," *Études traditionnelles*, Feb. 1938; see also *Le Roi du Monde*, chap. 9.

14. Parke, op. cit., p. 322.

15. Pausanias (XI, 35) describes in detail the cult of Demeter-Chthonia at Hermione.

16. Pausanias, VIII, 37–38. See also the coins of Heraeum (Seltman, Pl. XIII, 7, 8).

17. I should mention that these plane figures aim at suggesting the cube, which represents the earth, as said in the *Timaeus*, 55: "Let us assign the cube to earth; for it is the most immobile of the four bodies and the most retentive of shape, and these are characteristics that must belong to the figure with the most stable faces" (trans. Desmond Lee).

18. Parke, op. cit., p. 101.

19. Parke, op. cit., pp. 7–9.

The common origin of Artemis and Athena may account in part for the role of guardian of the gateways (Pronaia) held by Athena in various sanctuaries of Apollo. F. Vian (*Les Origines de Thèbes*, p. 140, n. 5) gives the examples of Delphi, Ptoon, and the Ismenion of Thebes. Athena played that role, not far from the sacred Gate of Sicyon, and before the sanctuary of Demeter at Buporthmus.

20. Pausanias, II, 34.

21. Strabo, VIII, 6, 12. There is a relationship, emphasized by E. Rhode (*Psyché*, p. 175, n. 1), between the sanctuaries of Demeter and the Plutonia, in particular at Eleusis, Hermione, Pheneus, and Phigalia.

22. *The Geography of Strabo*, trans. J. R. S. Sterrett and H. L. Jones (Harvard and Heinemann), 8 volumes. I have used the index of this edition for this work.

23. Callimachus, *Hymns, Epigrams*, etc., trans. G. R. Mair (Harvard and Heinemann), 1977.

24. In Hubert Gallet de Santerre's book, *Délos primitive et archaïque*, many passages adjoin and confirm what is being observed here. This author notes that Artemis "represents the multiple aspects of nature" (p. 131, n. 3). He points out (pp. 132–33) the affinities of the Delian and the Ephesian Artemis. "The Greek Artemis, daughter of Leto and sister of Apollo, appears to have replaced little by little a deity foreign to the saintly family; she was probably brought over by the first Greek colonists, who found in the site, like in Asia Minor, a cult of the Great Goddess, by which theirs became impregnated" (p. 134).

25. According to Paul Faure, *Fonctions des cavernes crétoises*, 1964, p. 144.

26. On the affinities of the Artemis of Brauron with those of Ephesus and Laconia, see Lilly G. Kahil's study "Autour de l'Artémis antique," *Antike Kunst*, Vol. I, 1965, p. 32.

27. W. K. G. Guthrie, *The Greeks and Their Gods*, p. 107, refers in this context to Cook, *Zeus*, vol. 3, 224.

28. M. Ventris and J. Chadwick, *Documents in Mycenaean Greek*, Cambridge, 1956, pp. 126–27.

29. Strabo, IX, 2, 36, according to the *Iliad*, IV, 8.

Near Alalcomenae may be seen the site of the ancient temple of Athena Itonia (this Phoenician appellation meaning "the imperishable" would, in my opinion, be redundant) on the site of the modern chapel of Saint Athanasius.

30. Pausanias, IX, 34; Callimachus, *On the Bath of Pallas* (60–65).

31. Coins from Tegea, B.M.C., vol. 9, Pl. XXXVII, 11 to 13, head of Pallas; owl on the reverse side of 11 and 13; period 431–370.

Coins from Pergamum, B.M.C., vol. 12, Pl. XXIII, 3 (head of Athena, on the obverse the Palladium); circa 310–283.

Athena and the owl are sometimes replaced by the mask of the Gorgon, ancient guardian of the sign of Virgo. Cf. Seltman, op. cit., Pl. III, 18; Pl. IV, 11, 12 (coins from Athens) and Pl. XV, 10 (coins from Tegea).

32. B.M.C., vol. 9, Pl. 37, 9.

33. The triangle is attributed to Athena.

CHAPTER 6

1. Marie Delcourt, op. cit., p. 146.

2. René Guénon: "La sortie de la caverne," *Études traditionnelles*, April 1938. See also the articles by the same author published in that magazine: "Les Portes solstitiales" (May 1938) and "Le Symbolisme du zodiaque chez les Pythagoriciens," June 1938, which gives an account of certain aspects of the work of J. Carcopino on *La Basilique pythagoricienne de la Porte majeure*. Articles anthologized in *Symboles fondamentaux de la science sacrée* (1962).

3. Bhagavad-Gita, VIII, 24–26:

> (24) Fire, light, daytime, the bright fortnight, the six months of the northern path of the sun—going forth under these signs of light, the knowers of Brahman go to Brahman.
> (25) Smoke, nighttime, the dark fortnight, the six months of the southern path of the sun—going forth under these signs of shadow, the yogi attains the lunar light and returns.
> (26) The bright and the dark, these are thought to be the world's eternal paths; by the bright path one goes, never to return, by the dark, one returns again. (trans. C. Rhone)

4. See various quotations, diagrams, etc., in chap. 5 of Félix Buffière's *Les Mythes d'Homère et la pensée grecque*, 1956, especially pp. 438–53. The solution to the difficulty stemming from the apparent inversion of the north and the south in the distribution of the solstitial gateways is given by R. Guénon in the

third article cited (note 2 above). Sometimes the position of the solstitial gateways in the heavens is being considered, sometimes their position in relation to the annual course of the sun: "The solstitial gateway of winter, or the sign of Capricorn, corresponds to north in the year, but to south in relation to the course of the sun in the sky; similarly, the solstitial gateway of summer, or the sign of Cancer, corresponds to south in the year, and to north in relation to the path of the sun."

5. Pausanias, III, 25, 5.

6. See note 21 below.

7. Christian Zervos, *L'Art des Cyclades*, Paris, 1957, p. 259.

This author refers to the passage in the *Odyssey* (XV, 403ff.) where it is said that Syros was sacred to Apollo and his sister Artemis.

8. F. Cumont wrote (*Syria*, II, p. 41): "Many Greek and Latin witnesses teach us that the star generally called Aphrodite or Venus was, for some, the star of Hera or Juno."

9. M. Delcourt (op. cit., p. 149) perceives a part of this symbolism: "The canal that pierced it served in effect to connect it with the terrestrial matrix."

10. Pausanias, I, 31, 6; II, 19, 8; VIII, 32, 4; and especially for Tegea, VIII, 53, 1, 2, 6.

Apollo Lochios and Artemis Lochia were represented in the form of square pillars surmounted with a head, in the manner of Hermes. Pausanias (VIII, 32, 3) saw such a pillar at Megalopolis.

11. *The Assembly of the Gods*, 15.

12. The seven points or directions are in reality: Delphi, Hyperborea, Crete or Egypt, Delos and the Orient, Leucas and the West, Cape Taenarum, Olympus.

The symbolism of Leucas is double, being closely connected with the idea of death and resurrection; it was associated with both the daily death of the sun and the yearly renewal in spring.

13. By approximation, I find for the longitude of Mount Jumruktchal (ancient Haemus) about 24 degrees, 55 minutes east of Greenwich. Delos is at 25 degrees, 15 minutes (see note 1 of chap. 3 above).

It must have been very difficult to establish an alignment between Delos and the Balkan Mountains, much more so than between Delos and the Libyan coast.

14. H. Gallet de Santerre, op. cit., p. 168.

15. Ibid., pp. 116–19.

16. Ibid., p. 142.

17. *On the E of Delphi* (VIII to XVI).

18. According to Brett, Pl. 79, 1636, obverse.

19. See the texts and references assembled by Michel B. Sakellariou, op. cit., pp. 56–57.

20. Seltman, op. cit., Pl. I, 23, 15.

21. See the series of coins representing the sun in the sign of Leo, or more probably the heliacal rising of Sirius. B.M.C., vol. 13, Pl. XXI.

22. Sakellariou, op. cit., pp. 123–24.

23. *Sylloge Nummorum Graecorum Deutschland*, for example.

Sakellariou, op. cit., pp. 231–32.

24. R. Graves, *The Greek Myths*, 108.

25. Georg Thiele, *Antike Himmelsbilder*, Berlin 1898. See also the work of Franz Boll, *Sphaera*, 1903.

26. R. Graves, *The Greek Myths*, vol. 2, 109.

27. By adding Ursa Minor, Ursa Major, Draco, Cepheus, and Cassiopeia, one obtains the list of the nine circumpolar constellations.

28. Seltman, Pl. XXXVI, 5.

29. B.M.C., vol. 13; coins from Clazomenae, protomes of winged boar, Pl. I, 21; Pl. III, 18; before 500.

30. B.M.C., vol. 21, Pl. XXXV (circa 500–408).

31. B.M.C., vol. 15, Pl. XXXVI, 6, 7.

32. R. Guénon (*Études traditionnelles*, Aug.–Sept. 1936) makes the same parallels. He also points out that Ursa Major is, in the Hindu tradition, the *sapta-riksha*, house of the seven Rishis, and that *riksha*, a word meaning "star" or "light" in general, is related to a root *archis* (from *arch* or *ruch*, which means "to shine, to illuminate"), so between bear and light we have a relationship identical to the one encountered for wolf (see p. 16). Both for the Celts and the Greeks, the wolf was attributed to the solar god Belen or Lycian Apollo.

33. Pausanias, VII, 18, 12.

34. Ibid., III, 18, 19. I will show that the decor of the throne of Amyclae as a whole had a zodiacal character.

35. *Études traditionnelles*, Aug.–Sept. 1936.

36. *Deipnosophistarum*, IX, 13.

37. There is a parallel between Caledonia, the ancient name for Scotland, country of the Kaldes or Celts, and the name of the Chaldaeans to designate a priestly caste. According to R. Guénon, the name of the forest of Calydon is no different from that of the forest of Brocéliande, *bro* or *bar* being the very name of the boar. (Cf. *Brauron*, parallel already mentioned in n. 4 of chap. 5 that does not seem ever to have been made before.)

It will also be seen (chap. 10 and 11 below) that, in a system where the boar corresponds to the winter solstice, the Hesperides are associated with the spring equinox. One could therefore be dealing with the transition from a solstitial symbolism to an equinoctial symbolism.

38. Pausanias, IV, 15, 8.

39. *Iliad*, XIX, 266–68.

40. Pausanias, V, 24, 9–11.

CHAPTER 7

1. *Onomasticon*, VIII, chap. 11, 31.
2. P. Saintyves, *Deux mythes évangéliques*, p. 159.
3. Pausanias, I, 37, 6–7.

4. See Gabriel Welter's article in *Archäologischer Anzeiger*, 1954, pp. 78–83.

5. Pausanias, I, 31–32.

6. R. Graves, *The Greek Myths*, 79.

7. Apollodorus, *The Library*, II, V, 4, cited by G. Dumézil, *Le Problème des Centaures*, pp. 159, 164.

8. Diodorus of Sicily, IV, 14, 3, quoted by G. Dumézil, op. cit., p. 157.

9. The list of the ancient divisions of Attica given by Strabo (IX, 1, 20) is incomplete and corrupt.

10. Julian, *Orations*, "On the Mother of the Gods," 8, based on trans. by E. Talbot, 1863. The "Claws of Scorpio" is the ancient name for the celestial region of Libra.

11. Pausanias, I, 19, 5.

12. Walther Wrede, *Attische Mauern*, 1933, pp. 23–24, figs. 4–5, Pl. 57.

13. While awaiting the publication by M. Petracos, see M. Paraskevaides' article "Un mystérieux monument du IVe siècle" in *Kathemerini* of 17 December 1961 and two photos in the B.C.H. of 1962, p. 659 ("Chronique des fouilles en 1961," by G. Daux).

CHAPTER 8

1. *The Homeric Hymns*, text established and translated by Hugh G. Evelyn-White, Heinemann, 1914. The hymns are quoted according to this translation.

2. Pausanias, VIII, 17, 4.

3. See P. Raingeard, *Hermès psychagogue*, 1935, especially p. 583.

4. P. Raingeard (op. cit.) has indeed perceived the significance of the tortoise. He wrote very pertinently: "The fact is nowhere mentioned that the tortoise, an animal that is doubly chthonian, both by its habitat and its shell, had been able to endow the cithara with power over the world below" (op. cit., p. 425).

The fact that this author nevertheless missed the overall interpretation of the hymn shows that prior knowledge of the zodiacal and planetary diagram was necessary to achieve this. The erect and intertwined serpents of the caduceus symbolize the union of heaven and earth and the awakening of cosmic consciousness in humanity. (Moses' bronze serpent comes to mind.) The symbol is of Sumerian origin (see A. Parrot, *Sumer*, fig. 289, vase from Lagash showing two intertwined serpents). Julius Schwab has already indicated this in *Archetyp und Tierkreis*, Basel, 1951, p. 220.

5. Apollodorus, *The Library*, III, X, 2.

6. Trans. E. V. Rieu, 1946.

7. The simple calculations $50 \times 7 = 350$ (*Odyssey, XII*) and $50 - 2 = 48$ (*Hymn to Hermes*) have the same symbolic meaning. In both cases, starting with

the number 50, this is an attempt to harmonize the lunar/solar year with the planetary spheres (7 × 50) or with the zodiac (12 × 4).

8. Norman O. Brown, *Hermes the Thief, the Evolution of a Myth*, Madison, University of Wisconsin Press, 1947.

9. Religious conservatism may be the reason for the bull sacrifice at Leucas, a probable memory of the time when the yearly renewal was associated with Taurus. One would rather expect the sacrifice of a ram.

10. R. Graves, *The Greek Myths*, 52.

11. Various explanations can be found for this detail. I suggest that it was an inaugural rite. If Hermes demanded part of the sacrifice, in the absence of the other gods, the system as a whole would be forever out of balance in his favor.

12. N. O. Brown, op. cit., pp. 105–6.

13. When the spring equinox had arrived in the sign of Aries, Hermes was portrayed carrying a ram. P. Raingeard has shown the associations of Hermes and Aries; the sacrifice of the ram to Hermes, the god's connection with spring in the festivals relate to the spring equinox, also the fact that he "knew how to find the people of dreams in the neighborhood of the Leucas stone" (op. cit., p. 464). The god often takes on the aspect of a ram-bearer or of a good shepherd (op. cit., pp. 489ff.). It is tempting to relate him to the mysterious god Crios mentioned twice by Hesiod in the *Theogony* (134 and 375).

14. Sacrificing religious facts to the fashion of the purely "sociological" explanation, Norman O. Brown sees in the *Hymn to Hermes* proof of a conflict between the cults of Apollo and Hermes. But, as he emphasizes in one of his notes (op. cit., p. 94), Hermes' lyre is specifically made with a tortoise shell and has seven strings, details which cannot be accounted for by any "sociological" explanation! A dramatic concept of a conflict of cults leads inevitably to the assumption that the end of the hymn is an addition by a different author. Opinions remain divided on this point, but such a hypothesis is pointless in the perspective adopted here; the text is a homogeneous and coherent unit, if one reads it as I suggest.

15. Op. cit., pp. 503–4.

16. Jane Harrison, *Prologomena*, pp. 286–91. Pausanias, IX, 35, 1.

17. See figure 74 of J. Harrison's book, which reproduces a bas-relief of the Museum of Vienna.

18. Homer, *Hymns*, H. G. Evelyn-White ed., vv. 68ff. While coins from Paphos bear symbols of Venus and especially the dove, like those of Cythera, the coins of Amathus represent the lion (B.M.C., vol. 24, Pl. I).

The excavations at Aphrodisias, in the high valley of the Maeander, may shed light on the cult of an Anatolian Aphrodite associated with wild beasts. Aphrodisias is near the Leo-Aquarius axis of the Sardis system and in the sign of Leo. The statue of the Carian Aphrodite in the Museum of Istanbul comes from there.

As will be seen in another volume, the cult of an almost identical Aphrodite spread through the Roman world. The Anatolian or Leonine Aphrodite has, however, been confused until now with a Capricornian Aphrodite worshipped in northern Italy, who naturally succeeded her, taking into account the displacement of the solstitial axis.

The first excavations of Aphrodisias have already delivered a specimen of this Capricornian Aphrodite (see A.J.A., April 1963). Matcheld J. Mellink, "Archeology in Asia Minor," p. 185 and Pl. 40.

19. See the article by J.-E. Dugand, "Aphrodite-Astarté (de l'étymologie du nom d'Aphrodite)" in *Hommage à Pierre Fargues, Annales de la Faculté des Lettres et Sciences humaines de Nice*, no. 21, 1974, pp. 73–98, also cited in my preface.

20. *Hymn to Aphrodite*, vv. 202–6.

21. Coins from Scepsis, fifth century; B.M.C., vol. 15, Pl. XV, circa 460–400.

On the obverse Dionysiac attributes: pine tree and clusters of grapes (the pine is also an image of the world tree).

Vincent Scully (*The Earth, the Temple and the Gods*, pp. 21–22) has had the merit of seeing that Troy was situated on the Mount Ida–Phengari line (summit of Samothrace) and, in mentioning Troy as "Aphrodite's city," of referring to the *Homeric Hymn to Aphrodite*.

22. Herodotus, IV, 33, trans. Aubrey de Sélincourt.

23. Pausanias, I, 31, 2, trans W. H. S. Jones.

24. Coins from Amasia also show Hades and Cerberus. The vision reported by Plutarch is the origin of the invention of the god Serapis.

25. A. de Paniagua, *Étymologies divines*, 1934, p. 149. The author offers this etymology tentatively. It completely agrees with my deductions, although its starting point is entirely different.

26. Marie Delcourt, *Héphaïstos ou la Légende du magicien*, 1957.

27. Ibid., see her map of the cult of Hephaestus, p. 189.

28. *Odyssey*, VIII, 266–366 (probable interpolation). See my commentary on the *Homeric Hymn to Aphrodite* in the preceeding paragraph.

29. Op. cit., pp. 186–87: "Eight solar revolutions correspond almost exactly to 99 lunations of 29½ days. An octaeteride or, to count like the ancients, an enneateride, thus gave the common measure between the year and the month that was so sought after. . . . One may . . . wonder whether, in the Lemnian antiquities, the number 9 has a purely mystical value, or does not have, in addition, an astronomical value. . . . The fine restitution [of the text of Philostratus] by Adolphe Wilhelem has enabled me to state that the procession went every nine years to fetch a new fire at Delos for an island or a god [Hephaestus] . . . a hero [Philocletes], had spent nine years of trials and sufferings."

30. In his study *Le Crime des Lemniennes* (1924), pp. 36–38, G. Dumézil established the relationship between the sudden disappearance of the loss of the

sense of smell and certain feasts of the summer solstice. He concluded: "The loss of the sense of smell disappears because its only purpose is, in fact, to vanish at the time of the 'renewal of the fire.' "

31. *L'Information littéraire*, May–June 1964. Here are the principal journeys that should be studied in relation to zodiacal diagrams: the journey of Apollo (*Pythian Suite*); the journey of Perseus (Pindar, *Xth Pythian*); the flight of the Danaïdes (Aeschylus, *The Suppliants*); the travels of Orestes (*Eumenides*, 238ff.); the wanderings of Io (*Prometheus Bound*, 700–741 and 786–818).

32. Pausanias, VIII, 25, 4; 42, 1.

33. Pausanias, II, 13, 7. See the considerations on Heracles in the Peloponnese in chap. 10.

34. W. K. Guthrie writes: "Poseidon is lord of fresh water as well as salt, and many springs were attributed to a blow from his trident. The most famous is of course that which he struck from the rock of the Akropolis at Athens. Earlier still, in all probability, it was not a blow from the trident, but a stamp of the hoof, which caused them to gush forth. Many springs contain that suggestion in their names—Hippokrene, Aganippe, Hippe. According to tradition, it was the hoof of the winged horse Pegasos that was responsible for Hippokrene, the fount of the Muses on Mount Helikon, but the universality of these "Hippo" names makes it certain that this was not the original story, and we remember that as early as the *Iliad* Poseidon bears the name of Helikonios. Pegasos, whom Homer does not mention although he tells the story of Bellerophon, is in any case said by Hesiod to have been Poseidon's son." (*The Greeks and Their Gods*, 1950, pp. 95–96). Ref. Homer, *Iliad*, XX, 404; VI, 155ff.; See also Hesiod, *Theogony*, 278ff.

The Celtic word μάρχας for ἵππος is mentioned once by Pausanias (X, 19, 11) in speaking of the descent of the Celts on Delphi. I wonder whether there might not be a convincing relationship between the words "mare" and *mare* (Latin, "sea") at an archaic stage of the evolution of the Indo-European languages. The transformation of the god of horses into the god of the Aegean sea would thus be the final result of a homonymy; the spouse of the mare Demeter being changed into a marine god! Let me also mention that in Linear Cretan, horse is read *i-quo* (Lat. *equos*, Sanskrit, *açvah*), a word phonetically close to *aqua*.

The possibility of the alternation *i-e* in the Mycenaean word for horse (*i-quo* > *e-quo*) has been considered by H. Mühlestein, M.H., XII, 1955, p. 125, and C. Gallavotti, *Documenti e struttura del greco nell' età micenea*, 1956, pp. 62, 90, 142 (see A. Yoshida, R.H.R., July–Sept. 1964, p. 25).

35. Pausanias, III, 14, 2, and III, 25, 4.

36. Pausanias, III, 26, 2–3.

37. Strabo, I, 3, 2.

38. See the references assembled by Sakellariou, op. cit., p. 50n., and pp. 72–75.

39. According to P. Grimal, "Poseidon," *Dictionnaire de la mythologie grecque et romaine.*

Pausanias (I, 30, 4) mentions the existence at Athens of a cult of Athena, mare-goddess, associated with Poseidon, horse-god. This is an odd substitution of Athena, guardian of the serpent Erichthonius, for Demeter, and an association of the deities connected with the Mercurial signs of Gemini and Virgo.

40. Strabo, VIII, 6, 14.

41. B.M.C., vol. 1, Pl. VII, 16, Poseidon-Onchestios of the coins of Haliartus, represented nude, armed with the trident; same volume, Pl. XVI, 2; coin from Thebes bearing on one side the shield of Mars, on the other Poseidon's trident. Since the distances between Isthmia-Lycosura and Isthmia-Nicaea are equal, as are the distances between Isthmia-Delphi and Isthmia-Prasiae, it is possible to construct, by taking Isthmia as the center and striking two successive radii, a simple spiral, which from Nicaea (probable seat of the amphictyony of Thermopylae) finishes at Delphi.

CHAPTER 9

1. The cities of the hexarchy were Cnidos, Cos, Halicarnassus, and in the island of Rhodes, Lindos, Camiros and Ialysos.

2. Horodotus, I, 14.

3. Ibid., I, 13.

4. H. W. Parke, op. cit., p. 128.

5. R. Graves, *The Greek Myths*, 8.

6. Ibid., 73. The legend of Perseus establishes the link between Delphi and Ammoneion.

7. Ibid., 60. Triton also plays an important role in the legend of the Argonauts.

8. Ibid., 82.

9. Ibid., 48.

10. Diodorus, III, 67 to 71. The aim of Diodorus's narrative is to exalt the oracle of Ammon (cf. Jeanmaire, *Dionysos*, p. 368).

11. *On Astrology*, 8.

12. Pausanias, IX, 16, 1. This author mentions a *Hymn to Ammon* by Pindar, a lost work.

13. Diodorus, XVII, 50.

14. Guthrie, *The Greeks and Their Gods*, p. 158.

15. A. Parrot, *Sumer*, 1960, fig. 351, p. 285. Four-faced god, one foot on a ram, from Ishchali-Diyala, bronze of the nineteenth century B.C., 17 cm high, in the Museum of the Oriental Institute of Chicago.

On the figurations of Ammon in association with another god, see "Ammon" in Daremberg's *Dictionary*.

16. Pausanias, III, 21, 8. The same author (VIII, 32, 1) mentions a sanctuary of Ammon at Megalopolis. This is, of course, a late foundation.

CHAPTER 10

1. Diodorus of Sicily, IV, 14, 3.
2. Pausanias, II, 13, 3.

At the Heraion of Argos, Pausanias (II, 17, 6) also saw a silver altar decorated with a relief representing the marriage of Heracles and Hebe.

3. *Theogony*, 950–55.
4. Pausanias, II, 13, 3. Coins from Phlius, with their two perpendicular axes, are very good illustrations of the idea of the omphalos; others bear a capital φ which has the same meaning. B.M.C., vol. 9, Pl. VI (map 12, fig. 44). On the other side appears the bull of the New Year.
5. Pausanias, II, 13, 8.
6. Ibid., II, 13, 6.
7. Apollodorus, II, V, 2.
8. Percy Gardner, *The Types of Greek Coins*, 1883, Pl. IX.
9. Apollodorus, II, VII.
10. Diodorus of Sicily, IV, 38, 3; H. W. Parke and D. E. W. Wormell, *The Delphic Oracle*, vol. 2, *The Oracular Responses*, no. 450.

Heracles begins and ends with fire: the very name of Thebes would derive from the Sanskrit *tap*, to burn (A. de Paniagua, *Étymologies divines*, p. 43). The hero's first victory is over the lion, symbol of the devouring fire of the sun. Enfuriated, Heracles throws his children into the fire. Seneca, in his *Hercules at Oeta*, was to write: "Fire itself became one of the labors of Hercules."

11. The island of Thasos is situated on the Sagittarius line and the coin specifically portrays Heracles as an archer (Seltman, op. cit., p. 145, Pl. XXIX, 4, my figure 46, map 12). Thracian coins show the same character. On the Thasian Heracles, see the references given by C. Picard: *Les Religions préhélleniques*, p. 189.
12. *Theogony* starting from 235; Apollodorus, in various places, especially II, IV, and V. The fact that, for example, the eagle that devoured Prometheus's liver is given as a son of Typhon and Echidna, confirms the zodiacal nature of the three monsters.
13. Apollodorus, II, VI, 2; Parke and Wormell, op. cit., vol. 1, p. 341; vol. 2, no. 455.
14. M. Delcourt, *L'Oracle de Delphes*, p. 149.
15. Kerényi, *The Heroes of the Greeks*, p. 192, which refers to the inscriptions of Cos and to Plutarch.
16. Strabo, III, 4, 11.
17. Apollonius of Rhodes, *Argonautica*, I, 1355–56.
18. C. G. Jung, *Psychology and Alchemy*, London, 1955, p. 355, n. 75.

19. R. Graves, *The Greek Myths*, 69. Same rite at the marriage of Cadmus and Harmonia. See the list of vases given by F. Vian (*Les Origines de Thèbes*, p. 120), referring to a study by Schavenburg (*Gymnasium*, 1957, pp. 210–30).

20. Places other than Phlius may have claimed to be the spiritual center of the Peloponnese. This is no doubt why at Lycosura, a city remarkable for its siting and the number of its sanctuaries, boars were sacrificed to Apollo Parrhasios, also called Pythian (Pausanias, VIII, 38, 8).

The principal pediment of the temple of Athena Alea at Tegea, representing Meleagre's hunt, depicted all the other heroes of the various signs of the zodiac, or from the different regions of Greece (which amounts to the same thing) who participated in it (Pausanias, VIII, 4, 6 and 7). Inside the temple, Pausanias also saw a rotten pelt with no bristles which was supposed to be the Calydonian boar's (VIII, 42, 2). See pp. 69–71 for my thoughts on the polar significance of this animal. The result of all this seems to be that the sign of the Boar really characterized the system of symbolic correspondences adopted for the Peloponnese. I shall return in chapter 17 to the connections among Phlius, Calydon, and Tegea.

21. Jane Ellen Harrison, *Themis*, chap. 11.

22. *Trachiniae*, 94–102.

23. Apollodorus, II, V, 11.

24. Diodorus of Sicily, IV, 14, 3.

25. Parke and Wormell, op. cit., vol. 2, nos. 442, 443, 444. Principal texts in Apollodorus, II, IV, 12, and Diodorus of Sicily, IV, 10, 7.

26. Ibid., vol. 1, p. 340; vol. 2, no. 560, according to Arrian, *Anabasis*, IV, 11, 7.

CHAPTER 11

1. Almost all the mythological facts to which I refer and the mention of sources may be found in the *Dictionnaire de la mythologie grecque et romaine* by Pierre Grimal (2nd ed., 1958). Also see the two volumes of *The Greek Myths* by Robert Graves, who has perceived on various occasions the importance of the problems of the calendar for the understanding of Greek mythology. See also C. Kerényi, *The Heroes of the Greeks*.

2. Strabo, X, 2, 14.

3. Ibid., X, 2, 9.

4. The study of F. M. Cornford constitutes chapter 7 of Jane Ellen Harrison's book, *Themis*.

5. Pausanias, VI, 20.

6. Ibid., V, 13, 7. On the Büyük Suret (Great Image) of Sipylus, see Perrot and Chipiez, *Hist. de l'art*, vol. 4, pp. 744 ff.

7. Strabo, XIV, 1, 20.

8. Pausanias, II, 36, 1.
9. Ibid., II, 35, 4.
10. On this meaning of the cuckoo, cf. J. E. Harrison, *Themis*, chap. 6, pp. 177–79, with many references. However, only the most ancient are of interest here, notably Hesiod, *Works and Days*, 486.
11. Strabo, X, 1, 4. See M. Sakellariou: *La Migration grecque en Ionie*, pp. 189–92, a useful summary of the question, especially according to Wehrli.
12. Pausanias, VII, 4, 8–9. He summarizes *The Foundation of Chios*, a lost work of Ion, a native of the island.
13. R. Graves, *The Greek Myths*, 41.
14. Pausanias, IX, 20.
15. Sakellariou, op. cit., p. 237.
16. I am, for the time being, postulating the existence of a system centered on Cumae; I shall demonstrate it in another volume.
17. H. W. Parke and D. E. Wormell, *The Delphic Oracle*, vol. 1, p. 310, mention one version of the oracle that probably comes from Mnaseas, the other from Nonnus. Texts in vol. 2, nos. 142, 374, 501, also with other references.
18. The story of Antiope could be the subject of an individual study. Let me mention only that, when she flees towards Sicyon (south in relation to Thebes), Lykos, who is pursuing her, represents the north and the sign of Capricorn (the Wolf).
19. Pausanias, IX, 5, 7–8. The lyre that Amphion receives from Hermes is, of course, a seven-stringed lyre, which sings the planetary harmony. Pausanias (ibid.) says that Amphion added three strings to the four of the earlier lyre.
20. See my study "Thèbes ou la Lyre d'Amphion" in *Les Cahiers astrologiques*, Nov.–Dec. 1965. This subject will be taken up again and further developed (see preface).
21. Pausanias, IX, 17, 4–5.
22. Pausanias, IV, 35, 9; Strabo, XVI, 2, 28.
23. Pausanias, II, 18, I.
24. Hesiod, *Theogony*, 325.
25. R. Graves, *The Greek Myths*, 75.
26. C. Picard, in his work on *Les Religions préhelléniques* (1948), wrote in regard to Crete: "An Anatolian origin may be attributed to the bull cult" (p. 99).

The bull of Marathon does not seem to have an astrological significance: for once, and quite exceptionally, this story may preserve the memory of a real bull! (Otherwise, a system that would be the reverse of the one reconstituted in chap. 5 would have to be assumed, with a single sign for Aries-Taurus.)

27. The study of coins and place-names suggests that there could have been two successive systems of this type: in one of them, the signs were ordered from east to west, in the other, from west to east. Or should one follow the coast all around the island? I may later devote a special study to this question, important for the origin of astrological beliefs in Greece proper.

There seems to have existed a calendar of plants in Crete.

28. Adoption of an Athenian-type calendar.

29. Plutarch, *Life of Theseus*, 18 and 22.

30. See Ode XVII of Bacchylides ("The Youths"), trans. R. Flacelière, in *Thésée, images et récits*, by C. Dugas and R. Flacelière, 1958.

31. On this point, see *Les Religions préhelléniques* by C. Picard, pp. 187–89. I willingly agree, with Axel W. Persson, that the same goddess of fertility and of the moon was known by the names Ariadne, Europa, Britomartis, Aridda, Dictynna, Eileithyia, Aphaia, Pasiphae, and Helen (*The Religion of Greece in Prehistoric Times*, pp. 135–36, University of California, 1942).

32. In Germanic mythology, the story of Odin hanged from the tree Yggdrasil similarly signifies the cosmic renewal, a death followed by a ressurection: the fruit falls from the tree, takes root, and from it another tree is born.

33. See R. W. Hutchinson, *Prehistoric Crete*, 1962, p. 212.

34. On these various points, see R. Graves, *The White Goddess*.

35. Ibid., p. 298.

36. G. Thomson, "The Greek Calendar," J.H.S., 1943, pp. 52ff.

37. The ferocious female warriors share the characteristics of both Artemis and Athena.

38. Plutarch, *Life of Theseus*, 31.

39. Ibid., 36. Parke, *The Delphic Oracle*, vol. 1, pp. 181–82. Pausanias (III, 3, 7) draws a parallel with the transfer of Orestes' ashes.

40. Many "Melian reliefs" show scenes studied in the present chapter, in particular Perseus and Medusa, or else Eos and Cephalus. See Paul Jacobsthal, *Die Melischen Reliefs*, 1931 (Pl. X, no. 19, British Museum B. 364. Bellerophon and the chimaera; Pl. XXVIII, no. 61, Berlin, Antiquarium 8382, Perseus and Medusa; Pl. XXIX, no. 62, British Museum B. 365, same subject; Pl. XXXVII, no. 75, Eos and Cephalus.) These could be used to illustrate this chapter, as could many paintings of vases showing similar scenes.

CHAPTER 12

1. See notes 16, 17, and 18 of chapter 2 above.

2. Quoted by K. G. Chartophylakidou, Ἱστορίχα ἀνάλεχτα Κέας (*Kea: Historical Selections*), 1962, p. 11.

3. See the article by John L. Caskey, "Excavations in Keos, 1960–1961," *Hesperia*, vol. 31, 1962, pp. 263–283, and the plate facing p. 221.

4. R. Graves, *The Greek Myths*, 52, c.

5. Ibid., 34.

6. Strabo, VIII, 3, 19. Also see Pausanias, V, 5, 5.

7. On the sculpted Attic calendar from the temple of Sarapis and Isis, which is now on the façade of the church of the Small Metropolis in Athens, Artemis and her doe immediately precede the bull.

8. R. Graves, op. cit., 22, 2. Pausanias, furthermore, says that the mere act of entering the cave of the Anigriades nymphs would heal illnesses that whiten the skin, which he calls *alphos* and *leuke* (words that probably designate impetigo and leucodermia).

9. R. Graves, op. cit., 82.

10. See figure 46 in G. Thiele's book, *Antike Himmelsbilder.*

11. P. R. Franke, *Die Antiken Münzen von Epirus* (1961), p. 43, and Pl. III. Reproduced here (map 9, fig. 14) is a coin from Elaea.

12. Strabo, VIII, 15.

13. R. Graves, op. cit., 138.

14. Strabo, I, 3, 21.

15. A French slang expression has a similar meaning: "to swallow one's birth certificate" for "to die."

CHAPTER 13

1. A. Parrot, *Sumer*, 1960, p. 138, fig. 167A.

2. A. Parrot, *Assur*, 1961, p. 159, fig. 200.

3. Ibid., Achaemenidian art, Pierpont Morgan collection, British Museum, p. 201, fig. 250.

4. *Les Religions de Babylonie et d'Assyrie*, by E. Dhorme, *Mana*, vol. 2, 1945, p. 242: "The Akkadians knew a double festival of *akîtu*, one in *Nisan*, the first month of the year, the other in *Tishrît*, the seventh month. The name *Tishrît*, derived from *shurrû*, "to begin, inaugurate," marked the beginning of the autumn year (September–October), while the spring year began in *Nisan* (March–April). The festival of the New Year, the *akîtu*, could thus be celebrated at either the autumn or the spring equinox. Double opportunity for making sacrifice, accomplishing rites, reciting prayers to sanctify the nascent year."

Let me mention, for memory, the work of André Dessenne, *Le Sphinx, étude iconographique*, vol. 1, 1957. In his forthcoming volume 2, the author will undoubtedly address the problem of the meaning of the sphinx, which is left aside in this first volume.

5. Many representations of stags, certainly having a ritual meaning, originate in particular from the excavations of Aladja Höyük.

6. Winged sphinxes with ram's heads (eighth century B.C.) originating from Hadatu (Arslan-Tash), Museum of Aleppo, fig. 326, p. 256, of André Parrot's, *Assur* (1961).

7. Humfry G. Payne, *Protokorinthische Vasenmalerei*, Berlin, 1933, Pl. 19; also see by the same author *Necrocorinthia* (1931), p. 10 and Pl. 3, 1–2.

8. H. G. Payne, ibid., Pl. 19, fig. 2.

9. For comparisons see R. D. Barnett's book *The Nimrud Ivories*, 1935, and the article by the same author, J.H.S., LXVIII, 1948.

10. Corinthian aryballus from the Boston Museum. H. G. Payne, op. cit., Pl. 20, fig. 1; Johansen, *Les Vases Sicyoniens*, Pl. 27; Fairbanks, *Catalogue of the Boston Museum*, 397; Joseph Clark Hoppin, A.J.A. IV, 1900, Pl. 5.

11. This character often appears on Corinthian vases, associated with the lion, the sphinx, the boar, etc. He does not seem to have been identified. He appears on the fragmentary cover of a Corinthian pyxis recently found at Brauron (B.C.H., 1963, "Chronique des fouilles en 1962," by G. Daux, fig. 9, p. 705). Also see the man-eagle placed after a lion, Pl. II, 228, in *Perachora II*, Oxford, 1962, by Thomas J. Dunbabin.

He is frequently portrayed on the Corinthian vases in the Museum of Athens. As previously mentioned (p. 114), it is sometimes difficult to distinguish Orion from Ophion, but the presence of the serpent allows the second character to be identified.

12. Aryballus (Theban according to Johansen), Johansen, op. cit., Pl. 30, 2; Payne, *Necrocorinthia*, Pl. 94, 5; A.J.A., IV, 1900, Pl. 4 with study by J. C. Hoppin. The symbolic image of a hare followed by a dog already appears on Mycenaean vases; for example, on a vase in the Museum of Sparta, from the sanctuary of Zeus-Agamemnon and Alexandra-Cassandra at Amyclae.

13. Johansen, *Les Vases Sicyoniens*, Pl. 29.

14. Ibid., Pl. 34.

One of the warriors has a bull on his shield. The lion is fighting the seagull. The bearded head may be Zeus. The whole seems to commemorate the substitution of a calendar of five seasons by a division of the year into four.

15. H. G. Payne, *Necrocorinthia*, Pl. 17; 2, 3, 10 and Pl. 22; 8.

16. H. G. Payne, *Protokorinthische*, etc., Pl. 31, fig. 2 (Oinochoe of New York), and fig. 5 (Olpe de Caere, Gotha). Very numerous examples in the *Corpus Vasorum Antiquorum*. (See the volumes showing the vases in the Louvre, for example), many specimens in the Museum of Athens.

17. See, for example, the pyxis cover, 1113, Pl. 47 of *Perachora II* of Dunbabin: bull, lion, goose, lioness (or panther).

18. Jane E. Harrison, *Themis*, pp. 280–81. I am reproducing the drawing according to Ernst Pfuhl, *Malerei und Zeichnung der Greichen*, vol. 3, Pl. 77, 288.

It also appears, with regard to the sign of the Eagle, that the Greeks considered the Troad, at least from the symbolic point of view, to be an integral part of their territory. This will be confirmed by a study of the pediments.

(See chap. 17 and map 8.)

19. The indications given here could serve as a commentary on the passage in the *Iliad* (Chant XVII, 313ff.), sometimes considered as an interpolation, in which Zeus enumerates his loves.

CHAPTER 14

1. Anna Roes, *Greek Geometric Art, Its Symbolism and Its Origin*, Oxford, 1933. Various objects described by Roes are on view at the British Museum. This is the case for the Iranian bronze 119445 (seated woman between two horse's heads) and several small Greek bronzes: two goat's heads, 161 and 170; two bull's heads, 168 and 169. Also bronze 4474 from the Museum of Delphi (two ram's heads).

2. On the hippalectryon, see the article by P. Perdrizet, "L'Hippalectryon, contribution à l'étude de l'ionisme," R.E.A., 1904, pp. 7ff., and the one by Dietrich von Bothmer, "The Tawny Hippalektryon," *The Metropolitan Museum of Art Bulletin*, Jan. 1953, pp. 132–35.

3. According to Perdrizet, the Ionian hippalectryon is riderless, while the one from Attica always has a rider. The symbolism is obviously the same. The rider must be identified with the solar hero, Perseus or Bellerophon.

4. R.E.A., 1904, Pl. 1, fig. 1.

5. Perdrizet, op. cit., pp. 26–27. See also the Nicosthenes vase, from Caere, where appear on one side of the neck a helmeted warrior riding a hippalectryon and on the other an *ephebus* riding a hipplectryon, B.C.H., XVII, 1893, p. 437 (Amphora F. 100 in the Louvre). On amphora F. 104 in the Louvre, also signed by Nicothenes, one sees:

A. On the neck Nike or Iris.
B. Same subject, the goddess flying to the right.
C. *Ephebus* on a hippalectryon between two confronted sirens.
D. Same subject.
E. The *thiasus* of Bacchus.

If, as I believe, Victory is in reality a siren (see another example, p. 176), all these figures describe the Leo-Aquarius axis and especially the northwest quarter.

6. Perdrizet, ibid., Pl. I, 5, and fig. 6, p. 26; Hermann Thiersch, *"Tyrrhenische" Amphoren*, 1899, no. 27, p. 157. Also see von Bothmer, op. cit., p. 135.

7. Lamer, "Hippalektryon," *Real Encycl. of Paulys-Wissowa*, col. 1654. According to B.M.C., vol. 12, Pl. XVIII.

8. Examples mentioned in Dietrich von Bothmer's article, p. 134. Also see in the cited book by Thiersch, the description of vase no. 15, in Berlin (Berlin, 1707), on which appear the Calydonian hunt, the panther, the alectryon panther, the alectryon siren. All these symbols describe the northwest region and the solstitial axis.

9. Examples mentioned by Perdrizet, who refers to Furtwängler, *Ant. Gemmen* (Pl. 65, 1), donkey-headed rooster; to Micali, *Storia* (117, 13), lion-headed rooster; and also to Karo, *Strena Helbigiana*, p. 154 (hare-headed bird,

p. 147; bird with head of male goat or dog; bird-griffin with rooster's head). Many more examples could be given.

What I am indicating here can facilitate the study of Greco-Egyptian gems.

10. Bronze from the Louvre, Chantre collection, Inv. A O 9714, drawing in Roes, op. cit., fig. 96. Photo published with the kind permission of M. A. Parrot.

In the exhibition of Iranian art (*Seven Thousand Years of Iranian Art*) at the Palace of the Legion of Honor in San Francisco (Summer 1965), I noticed a similar figure—an eagle perched on the back of a kid—decorating part of a bit from Luristan.

11. A. Parrot, *Sumer*, 1960, p. 133, fig. 162. Bas-relief in the Museum of Baghdad, from Kish, first half of the third millenium.

12. Bibliography in C. Picard, *Les Religions préhélleniques*, p. 280. For the oriental influences on Cretan art, see the work of Pierre Demarque, *La Crête dédalique* (1947).

13. Gordon Loud, *The Megiddo Ivories*, 1939, Pl. I, or the more accessible *The Archeology of Palestine* by W. F. Albright, 1949, ed. of 1954.

14. J. W. Crowfoot and Grace M. Crowfoot, *Early Ivories from Samaria*, London, 1938, Pl. 5, 6, 7 (various sphinxes); 9 (lions); 10 (lion devouring a bull).

It is enough to leaf through R. D. Barnett's work, *The Nimrud Ivories* (1955), to find many interesting examples. Let me mention the decoration of the pyxis on Pl. 34 (two kids and two sphinxes); Pl. 40 (bulls and kids); Pl. 42 (two lions devouring a bull); Pl. 55 (lion and bull); Pl. 65 (four lions and two bulls); Pl. 9 and 37 (griffins); and Pl. 1, 19, 20, 21, 41, 46 (sphinxes).

15. B.C.H., 1878, pp. 185ff., Pl. 17; Pl. 216 in S. Marinatos, *Crete and Mycenae*, London, 1960.

16. For various confrontations of this kind, see the interesting article by Helen J. Kantor, "Ivory Carving in the Mycenaean Period," *Archeology*, spring 1960 (special issue devoted to Mycenaean civilization).

17. See, for example, in the cited book by S. Marinatos, Pl. 119, Minoan seal, lion attacking a stag, prismatic seal—lion and bull; Pl. 208 and 209, seals from Pylos; Pl. 210, seals of Midea and Argolis; Pl. 211, gems from Vaphio, 1500 B.C., goddess with horse, goddess with a ram.

Particularly frequent in Cretan art are griffins (guardians of the pole) and the lion devouring a bull.

18. Andros was attached to Aquarius in the Delian system (see p. 35).

Dr. Jules Desneux, in his work *Les Tétradrachmes d'Akanthos*, Société Royale de Numismatique, Brussels, 1949, has traced the history of the theme of the lion attacking the bull.

On a fifth century coin from Acanthus, the bull is replaced by a boar, which better corresponds to the real position of the city, situated near the Leo-Boar axis in the Delian system. This is an odd association of the two symbols. Coin reproduced by J. Desneux, op. cit., and Babelon, *Traité*, vol. 4, p. 662, and Pl. 318, 21.

19. G. H. Chase, "The Shield Devices of the Greeks," *Harvard Studies in Classical Philology*, XIII, 1902, CVI. For a recent reproduction, see *Corpus Vasorum*, Berlin, Antiquarium (2), Pl. 73, 2 and 4.

20. G. H. Chase, ibid., LV; Ernst Pfuhl, *Malerie und Zeichnung der Griechen*, vol. 3, Pl. 73, 277.

21. In Pryce's catalogue of the British Museum (I, 1), the description of the sculpted blocks is given as follows:

B 292 Satyr to the right
B 293 Boar running to the left
B 294 Leopard to the left, ready to pounce [Panther or lionness, I believe.]
B 295 Lion devouring a stag, to the left
B 296 Panther to the left(?) [Wolf, I believe.]
B 297 Bull to the right
B 298 Satyr to the left.

22. *Xanthos*, II, p. 50, and Pl. 37, 1.

23. The most unusual detail is the presence of a single group (lion devouring a stag) when one would expect at least two sculptures from the category "Dynamic Symbols of Seasonal Variations." Let me nevertheless suggest that this fact may be related to the association of Lycia with the sign of Leo.

CHAPTER 15

1. G. H. Chase, "The Shield Devices of the Greeks,", *Harvard Studies in Classical Philology*, XIII, 1902. Ths study should naturally be revised and updated, taking into account the new framework of classification that I am proposing.

2. See, for example, the photos of this vase in A. Merlin, *Vases grecs de style géométrique au style à figures noires*, especially Pl. 31, or else, *Corpus Vasorum*, Cabinet des Médailles of the Bibliothèque Nationale, Pl. 25.

3. A. Merlin, ibid., Pl. 37.

4. Frank Brommer, *Herakles, die zwölf Taten des Helden in antiker Kunst und Literatur* (Münster, Köln, 1953), Pl. 26, Munich cup.

The design of a second shield showing the octopus of Cancer indicates that Geryon is opposed to all bipartition or quadripartition of the year.

5. *Corpus Vasorum*, Museum of the Villa Giulia, II, III, 1 c., Pl. 15, 3.

6. See, for example, *Corpus Vasorum*, British Museum, I, H, e, Pl. I, fig. 2a, 3a.

The various signs on Athena's shield—dolphin, wheel, bull, tripod, etc.—correspond to the goddess's different roles. G. H. Chase (loc. cit.) has already counted no less than sixty-two! Each motif corresponds to a different function, but several of them have the same meaning.

7. G. H. Chase, loc. cit., LXVII, Harrow vase, J.H.S., 1897, p. 294, and Pl. 6.

8. G. H. Chase, loc. cit., CXXI, Mon. IX, Pl. 6, vase of Naples, 2883.

9. L. D. Caskey, *Attic Vase Paintings in the Museum of Fine Arts*, Boston, 1931, Pl. 35.

10. See the album in the work of Constantin Carapanos, *Dodone et ses ruines*, 1878, Pl. 16.

11. P. Perdrizet, *Fouilles de Delphes*, vol. 5. Decorated monuments, etc., 1908, no. 674, pp. 123–24, and Pl. 21. Claude Rolley, who is now preparing a revised edition of this volume, has kindly contributed new photographs of these plaques, for which I warmly thank him.

12. Perdrizet, op. cit., no. 677, p. 125, and fig. 466.

13. *Iliad*, Chant XV, 256. "Aor" means "light"; it may be compared with Ahura and the root ὁράω>ὁρῶ"to see."

Chrysaor, associated with the solstitial axis, is the father of Geryon and Echidna, guardian monsters of the equinoctial axis (Hesiod, *Theogony*, 287ff.).

14. P. E. Arias and M. Hirmer, *Le Vase grec*, fig. 19.

The large oriental-style amphoras reproduced by E. Pfuhl (*Malerei und Zeichnung* . . . , vol. 3, Pl. 19, 86–89), which include the Nessus amphora, all have coherent zodiacal imagery.

15. Ibid., fig. 29.

16. On a Corinthian plate in Copenhagen, reproduced in Vagn Poulsen's book, *Griechische Vasen und Bauten*, 1963, p. 22, it is indeed the "Mistress of Beasts" who is holding two swans. I shall return to this goddess in chapter 20.

17. P. E. Arias and M. Hirmer, op. cit., fig. 176.

18. D. von Bothmer, *Amazons in Greek Art*, Oxford, 1957, fig. 3.

Fragment of terra-cotta from Attica in the New York Metropolitan Museum. The name Achilles is written on this plaque.

19. Werner Technau, *Exekias*, Leipzig, 1936. Photographs of the vases being studied will be found in this work.

Amphora of the Vatican (from Vulci), fig. 20, 21.
Amphora of Berlin, 1720 (from Vulci), fig. 1.
Amphora B. Museum, B 210, fig. 25.
Amphora B. Museum, B 209, fig. 26.

The Vatican amphora is reproduced in Arias and Hirmer, op. cit., fig. 62 and 63. An amphora in the New York Metropolitan Museum also shows Achilles and Ajax playing (dice?).

20. Quintus of Smyrna, *Posthomerica*, Chant XII.

21. Semni Karouzou, *The Amasis Painter*, Oxford, 1956.

22. Andreas Rumpf, *Sakonides*, 1937.

23. P. E. Arias and M. Hirmer, *Le Vase grec*, fig. 78, XXVII and 79.

24. Ibid., fig. 50.

25. Los Angeles County Museum of Art, William Randolph Hearst Collection; 50-8, 22.

Other similar representations must exist. It is also probable that sirens have often been mistaken for "Victories." (See n. 5 of chap. 14 above.)

26. *Corpus Vasorum*, Louvre, fasc. 12, Corinthian miniaturist style III Ca, Pl. 14, and III Cc, Pl. 11. New photos taken for the present work by M. Chuzeville.

27. In the plaques of Delphi studied in section 3, the lizard is placed on the Pisces-Virgo axis, which gives an angle of 120 degrees in relation to 0 degree Taurus. The angular variation is minimal and the two images are indeed equivalent: in both cases this is an allusion to the former north star Thuban or Alpha in Draco, chronologically associated with Taurus.

CHAPTER 16

1. Emil Kunze, *Archaische Schildbänder*, Berlin, 1950. I warmly thank Professor Kunze who has been kind enough to provide a copy of his fine work and to allow me to reproduce a few illustrations. The present chapter derives entirely from this valuable synthesis.
2. Type I: op. cit., Catalogue, pp. 7–8, Pl. I to VIII.
3. Type IV: op. cit., Catalogue, pp. 10–11, Pl. XII, XVI to XIX; Pl. XIII of the supplement.
4. Op. cit., pp. 213 and 174–75.
5. Type V: op. cit., Catalogue, pp. 11–12, Pl. XX, XXI.
6. Type VII: op. cit. Catalogue, pp. 12–13, Pl. XXII, XXIII.
7. Type VIII: op. cit., Catalogue, pp. 13–14, Pl. XXIV, XXV.
8. Type IX: op. cit., Catalogue, pp. 14–15, Pl. XXVI to XXIX.
9. Type X: op. cit., Catalogue, p. 15, Pl. XXX to XXXII.
10. *Olympia Berichte*, vol. 5, 1956, pp. 36–37 and 50–51.
11. Type XIII: op. cit., Catalogue, pp. 17–18, Pl. XXXVI, XXXVII.
12. See *Olympia Berichte*, vol. 5, 1956, pp. 35ff.
13. A bibliography on this question can be found in Roman Ghirshman's work, *Perse: Proto-Iraniens, Mèdes, Achéménides*, Gallimard, 1963, and two pictures of the quiver covers, ibid., figs. 91 and 423.

CHAPTER 17

1. Étienne Lapalus, *Le Fronton sculpté en Grèce des origines à la fin du IVᵉ siècle*, study on the origins, evolution, technique and themes of tympanal decoration, Paris, E. de Boccard, 1947.
2. I am setting aside, for the time being, the question of the treasuries and minor cult buildings in favor of the pediments for which some rules of interpre-

tation may be composed. Their decoration always refers to the donating city and to the cult of the site where the treasury was erected.

3. E. Lapalus, op. cit., p. 440. See especially G. Rodenwaldt's big book, *Korkyra*, II, 1919.

4. E. Lapalus, op. cit., pp. 89–90.

5. E. Lapalus states: "The Gigantomachy on the right wing is conceived as an isolated motif, a decoration for a metope independent of the rest of the composition" (op. cit., p. 394n.). Also: "The scene of the Iliupersis carved on the left wing of the pediment of Corfu is, like the scene of the Gigantomachy that corresponds to it on the right wing, an independent motif" (ibid., p. 396n.).

6. E. Lapalus, op. cit., p. 431.

7. Ibid., pp. 434–35.

8. Ibid., especially p. 102.

9. E. Lapalus mentions this possibility and then rejects it (op. cit., pp. 102 and 109).

10. E. Lapalus, op. cit., pp. 433–34.

11. Ibid., pp. 436–37.

12. Ibid., p. 453.

13. Ibid., p. 446.

14. Ibid., pp. 445–46.

15. Ibid., p. 430.

16. Ibid., addenda to the beginning of the volume and p. 384.

17. Ibid., p. 390. See also the note on page 394 where the author says: "At Epidaurus, where, it can be said, no theological teaching was dispensed, an Amazonomachy, chosen for its expressive or simply decorative value, would appear on the west tympanum."

18. E. Lapalus, op. cit., p. 87.

19. E. Lapalus, op. cit., p. 404, according to the article by A. Plassart, *R.E.A.*, XLII, 1940, pp. 293–99. From my point of view, what is of real interest in the prologue of the *Eumenides* is its precise evocation of the Delphi-Athens-Delos line.

20. Ibid., p. 148.

21. See the figure established by F. Courby, *B.C.H.*, vol. 38, Pl. VII, 1914 (reproduced by C. Picard, *La Sculpture grecque, période archaïque*, 1935, opposite p. 298) and the revised figure in vol. 4 of *Fouilles de Delphes*, 1931, figs. 7 and 8 (after page 32), reproduced by E. Lapalus, op. cit., opposite p. 142.

The first attempt at reconstructing the east pediment placed Leto and Artemis in the chariot as well, while four characters were distributed in each wing, before the groups of animals.

To establish my zodiacal scheme, I began with the second reconstruction proposed by F. Courby, generally adopted today.

22. Reproductions of these sculptures can be found in vol. 12 of Fouilles de Délos (*Exploration archéologiques de Délos*. The Temples of Apollo, XII, 1931, appendix pp. 237–240).

Also see C. Picard, *La Sculpture grecque, période archaïque*, p. 368.

23. Pausanias, VIII, 45, 3.

24. E. Lapalus, op. cit., pp. 454–55; Pausanias, VIII, 45.

25. E. Lapalus, ibid., pp. 439–40.

26. Pausanias, V, 10, 6.

27. R. Graves, *The Greek Myths*, 109.

28. J. Harrison, *Themis* (chapter on Cornford, especially pp. 218–22).

29. Article by Émile Cahen, *R.A.*, 1937. pp. 1–13.

30. R. Graves, op. cit., 78.

31. These painted metopes are in the Museum of Athens. They are reproduced in Karl Schefold's work, *Frühgrieschische Sagenbilder*, Munich, 1964; Pl. 18 to 21, with the older references.

32. Phyllis Williams Lehmann, *The Pedimental Sculptures of the Hieron in Samothrace* (J. J. Augustin, Glückstadt and Locust Valley, New York, 1962). With an album of plates.

33. Op. cit., pp. 18–19. See figs. 23 and 24 of the album.

34. Jane Ellen Harrison, *Themis*, pp. 514–31.

35. Ibid., p. 517.

36. P. W. Lehmann, op. cit., p. 23, and figs. 39 and 40.

37. There was a victory in each angle of the building (P. W. Lehmann, op. cit., figs. 44 and 51); it is permissible, I believe, to see in this an allusion to the four seasons and the four directions of space. This was also a way of emphasizing the special importance of the Leo-Aquarius axis (Dardanus) and the Gemini-Sagittarius line (the Cabiri) for Samothrace.

It must be remembered that the southern part of the sanctuary did not have a sculpted pediment.

38. This plan may be found in the valuable monograph by Karl Lehmann, *Samothrace, a Guide to the Excavations and the Museum*, 2nd ed., 1960, *in fine*.

It is here reproduced with the addition of the lines described.

CHAPTER 18

1. I have found much useful information in the book by F. Sartiaux, *Les Sculptures et la Restauration du temple d'Assos en Troade*, Paris, 1915; I have gathered my own photographic documentation by writing to the museums where the sculptures in question are located.

2. During the fourth century, the temple of Athena Polias at Pergamum would also be built in the Doric style (F. Sartiaux, op. cit., p. 14).

3. "Eros seated holding a bow," mentioned by Prokesch, is a rather improbable subject. So far as the block with "three horses" described by Hunt is concerned, it was probably the sculpture of three centaurs now in Paris (fig. 117).

4. Frank B. Tarbell published some time ago (A.J.A., XXIV, 1920, pp. 226–31) an article entitled "Centauromachy and Amazonomachy in Greek Art: The Reasons for Their Popularity." The positive part of this article did not contribute anything very interesting because the author concluded that the popularity of these subjects was attributable to the variety of their artistic themes.

The critical considerations, on the other hand, included several arguments that confirm my way of seeing:

1. The scenes in question generally represent undecided battles, where apparently equal forces are in opposition. In general, nothing specifically indicates who will be the winner.
   This is perfectly understandable if, as I believe, these scenes really represent the free play of pairs of cosmic forces.
2. These scenes appear on monuments of all kinds well before the Median wars.
3. Their interpretation as symbolizing the triumph of the Greeks over the barbarian peoples and especially the Persians is excluded by the fact that they appear on Anatolian or Persian monuments, such as the Heroon of Trysa in Lycia, and the Mausoleum of Halicarnassus, where they would be completely out of place if they had this meaning.

5. If one consults the work of R. Demangel, *La Frise ionique*, 1932 (especially the second part, chap. 1, pp. 364–460, "Répertoire des sujets"), one will see the identity of the themes employed on the pediments and the friezes. This identity should not be surprising if, as I believe, the whole of the temple, plan, architecture, and decor constituted an organized and organic unity.

6. Thus there is no difference in nature between the panthers of Corfu and the lions devouring the bulls of Athens; they are symbols of the seasonal variations. Let me nevertheless note that, for the northeast quarter, the dynamic symbol (boar eating a fish) has been very seldom represented; it was quickly supplanted by the panther of Dionysus.

CHAPTER 19

1. Parke, op. cit., pp. 51–52.
2. Ibid., p. 54.
3. Ibid., p. 63, vol. 2, no. 255.
4. Ibid., p. 63, vol. 2, no. 226.
5. Percy Gardner, *The Types of Greek Coins*, 1883, Pl. III, 12.
6. Parke, op. cit., p. 66.
7. Ibid., p. 66.
8. Ibid., pp. 73–77.

9. F. Vian, *Les Origines de Thèbes, Cadmos et les Spartes*, 1963. The references of the following six notes are taken from this work, see especially pp. 78–79.

10. P.W., II, 225–26.

11. Apollodorus, *The Library*, I, IX, 2.

12. F. Vian, op. cit., references p. 79.

There is no reason for surprise in finding the sacrifice of a ram or a bull associated with the founding of cities (Aenea or Ilium for example) that are not in the corresponding signs in the zodiacal diagrams.

This sacrifice is that of the yearly renewal, attested in various places, whose signficance is to be an imitation of the cosmic order. Just as the bull (or later, the ram) began the year, the sacrifice of the animal by the same name would mark the beginning of the city's existence.

This idea of origin would thus often be associated with rites of spring, as would the transparent symbolism of the spring of water, whose discovery helps to determine the selection of a city's site.

In all the rites of foundation, renewal, or purification, the sacrifice of a ram, ewe, bull, or cow, alludes to the spring equinox, that of a goat to the winter solstice.

To give an example, let me mention the offering of a goat to Zeus Ascraios, which is attested at Halicarnassus (F. Vian, op. cit., p. 91). Now, Halicarnassus is on the solstitial axis of the Heraclean system of Sardis (see p. 102 on Eurypylus and Cos).

13. Pausanias, III, 22, 12.

14. F. Vian, op. cit., p. 78.

15. Ibid., p. 102, according to Pars. Damasc., F.H.G., IV, 470, fragment 4.

16. F. Vian, op. cit., p. 78; Libanius, *Orat*. v. 36 (vol. 1, p. 315, Förster); Sakellariou, *La Colonisation grecque en Ionie*, p. 40.

17. The English translation by Arthur S. Way is entitled *The Fall of Troy*.

Hyginus (*Fables*, CVIII) gives a very condensed narrative of the episode of the Trojan Horse.

18. I am not alone in being of this opinion. A. Yoshida in his article, "Survivances de la tripartition fonctionnelle en Grèce", R.H.R., July–Sept. 1964, pp. 21–26, has devoted a few pages to Epeus. He points out the constant association of this hero with animals of the horse family.

Let me add that Epeus is constantly associated with Aquarius. At the funeral games, in honor of Patrocles, his talent as a boxer is worth a mule to Epeus (*Iliad*, XXIII, 653–55).

At Carthaea, in the temple of Apollo, "Epeios" was the name of a water-bearing ass (*Athen*., X, 456ff.).

According to H. Krahe (*Die Sprache der Illyrier*, I, 1955, p. 55), the very name Epeus contains the word for "horse" which, according to P. Kretschmer (*Einleitung*, pp. 247–48; *Glotta*, XXII, 1934, pp. 120–21), the Greeks would have borrowed from the Illyrian.

19. Word for word, this means "replacing the people under a former cult."

20. W. Fröhner, "Troianische Vasenbilder," *Jahrbuch*, VII, 1892, pp. 28–31, and Pl. 2. Illustration reproduced by Karl Schefold in *Frühgriechische Sagenbilder*, 1964, fig. 39.

CHAPTER 20

1. Golden pendants in the British Museum that show a winged goddess holding a wild animal in either hand.

In *The Sanctuary of Artemis Orthia at Sparta*, ed. by R. M. Dawkins, London, 1929, are the inventory and reproductions of many ivory objects depicting animals of zodiacal meaning and winged deities (god and goddess) associated with the bird, the serpent, the sphinx, the lion (Pl. XCIII to XCIX). See, in particular, the goddess with two or four birds (geese or wild swans), which seems to refer to the Gemini-Sagittarius axis related to Sparta.

2. Arias and Hirmer, *Le Vase grec*, Pl. XI.

3. For pictorial reasons (respect of symmetry), the symbols are not drawn in the exact order of the diagram; most important here is their distribution on either side of the goddess.

4. In Georg Karo's work, *Religion des ägäischen Kreises*, Leipzig, 1925, see figs. 66 and 67 that represent two gems where one sees a goddess flanked by a lion and a lioness (well differentiated in both cases). On the first gem, the goddess is surmounted by an image of the celestial vault. (References in Karo, op. cit.)

5. See nevertheless Erika Diehl's work, *Die Hydria, Formgeschichte und Verwendung im Kult des Altertums*, Mayence, 1964.

6. A good bibliography on this bronze and similar handles will be found in *Antike Kunst in der Schweiz*, H. Bloesch, 1943.

7. Herbert Hoffmann, "Two Unknown Greek Bronzes of the Archaic Period," A.J.A., vol. 68, 2, April 1964, pp. 185–88, Pl. 63 and 64.

I here thank Mr. Jerome Vercruysse, who obtained the photo of this bronze, here reproduced with the kind permission of the Royal Museums of Brussels.

8. On these handles, conserved in Ancon and Pesaro, appear horses, which are sometimes accompanied by the Dioscuri.

9. The systems centered on Cumae and Enna (omphalos of Sicily), as well as some Delphic and Delian monuments, have been studied in *Delphes, Délos et Cumes* (1970). I plan to take up and develop in a separate volume my studies of the myth of Geryon ("L'Ombre au triple corps," *Esprit*, April 1971) and "Géographie sacrée de l'île de Chypre," (*L'Astrologue*, 1 Sept. 1979), and also my "Essai de reconstitution du calendrier grec des arbres" (*Atlantis*, May–June 1977).

Index

www.ingramcontent.com/pod-product-compliance
Lightning Source LLC
LaVergne TN
LVHW090803070826
844660LV00022B/1068

* 9 7 8 0 7 9 1 4 2 0 2 4 9 *